THE HANDBOOK OF

CAGE AND AVIARY BIRDS

Revised and Edited by

David Alderton

BLANDFORD

ACKNOWLEDGEMENTS

Most of the colour photographs were taken by Jeremy N. McCabe, by arrangement with the Zoological Gardens, Regent's Park, London; Bleak Hall Bird Farm, Woburn, Bedfordshire; Chessington Zoo, Surrey; Whipsnade Zoological Park, Bedfordshire; Mark Harris, Sydenham, Kent (owner of the lovebirds); Mr Drury, Oakfields, Stapleford Abbotts, Essex; and the late K.A. Norris, former President of the Foreign Birds League.

Other acknowledgements for colour illustrations are as follows: Ardea Photographics 11 and 12; Denis Avon and Tony Tilford (Ardea Photographics) 51, (Wildlife Studies Ltd) 181, 185, 215 and 254; Barnaby's Picture Library 20, 21 and 111; Horst Biefeld 118, 147 and 186; Thomas Brosset 25–28, 42–45, 54–57, 60, 62, 77–80, 89–94, 106, 108, 109 and 189; F. Collet (Ardea Photographics) 141; Colorbank 159, 173, 175, 176, 183 and 184; Rosemary Low 44 and 67; Malcolm McGregor 203; Anthony J. Mobbs 238, 240 and 243; Horst Müller-Schmidz 112, 126, 136, 180, 205, 208, 216 and 221; Plazikowski 138, 148, 190 and 206; P. Ramaekers 139, 161, 164–168, 171, 172, 177, 193 and 244; Phillipa Scott 32 and 34–41.

A BLANDFORD BOOK

First published in the UK 1993 by Blandford, Cassell imprint Villiers House, 41–47 Strand, London WC2N 5JE

Distributed in the United States by Sterling Publishing Co., Inc. 387 Park Avenue South New York, NY 10016–8810

Distributed in Australia by Capricorn Link (Australia) Pty Ltd P.O. Box 665, Lane Cove, NSW 2066

Cataloguing–in–publication data for this title is available from the British Library

ISBN 0–7137–2346–7

Typset by ROM-Data Corporation Ltd, Falmouth, Cornwall Printed and bound in Spain by Cronion S. A., Barcelona

CONTENTS

PREFACE

It was over 25 years ago that I first encountered *The Handbook of Foreign Birds,* when it was initially published as two volumes. There could be only one Christmas present that I wanted then, having seen the set in a pet shop in Lewes which specialised in birds. My long-suffering parents kindly obliged, and I can still remember the joy of unwrapping and opening this present.

From the outset, these books were destined to become avicultural classics. They were the first to offer detailed coverage of those species that are most commonly kept in aviculture. Here was an opportunity for enthusiasts not only to read about the birds and their individual requirements, but also to see them, in the unrivalled selection of colour plates.

At that stage, I could little have foreseen that more than a quarter of a century later I would be undertaking a revision of these volumes. Much has changed since they were first published. It has been a time of rapid advancement in aviculture, and thanks largely to the efforts of individual breeders we now know much more about the birds than was the case then.

I have attempted to incorporate as much new information as possible, which has meant extensive rewriting in some cases, but I hope that this book, which combines what were originally two separate volumes, will still retain the appeal that attracted my attention all those years ago.

Some things, of course, have not altered. In terms of its coverage, this handbook still remains the most definitive guide to foreign birds in aviculture. The requirements of over 400 species can still be found here, and although there have been some changes in this new edition, the balance of species included remains the same.

This book is intended primarily as a specific reference to the birds themselves rather than as a general management guide, but the addition of a bibliography to this new edition will help to direct readers to titles of a more specialist nature that deal in depth with matters such as hand-rearing and colour-breeding.

David Alderton
Brighton
England

INTRODUCTION

People have always found interest and pleasure in domestic pets, and birds have proved a special source of delight for centuries. As long ago as 284BC Kallixenus described in the *Chronicles of Alexandria* how parrots were carried in processions, and Alexander the Great had the distinction of being the first to import Indian Ring-necked Parakeets (*Psittacula krameri manillensis*) into Europe. He saw them in India and took them back to Greece.

This book has been written to cover the broadest range of birds, and it is intended as a reference both for the novice and the more experienced breeder. Because it concentrates on the needs of individual species, it is hoped that it will reduce the risk of problems arising to a minimum. Unnecessary disappointments might well bring to a premature end a 'hobby' that was started with enthusiasm.

The shows that are held annually all over the country not only create interest in the hobby, but also provide an opportunity to study birds and obtain information from fellow enthusiasts regarding the best methods of housing and treatment. Membership of a club will also bring you into contact with aviculturists. The breeding of new colour varieties is another increasingly popular area today, and bird-keepers interested in this subject should join one of the specialist clubs and read the literature on the topic.

As in all hobbies, personal taste plays a large part in the setting up and furnishing of a cage or aviary. It is, of course, possible to employ experts, but a great satisfaction lies in do-it-yourself making of cages and aviaries, and some designs that have proved satisfactory for particular species are outlined.

Nomenclature can be a problem. The scientific names of birds have changed as birds are reclassified, and common names also change over time as well. Throughout this book therefore, both the current scientific name and the English name in common use are given for ease of identification; a number of the more common synonyms are also included. This should help to avoid confusion.

AVIARY ACCOMMODATION

As it is not easy to provide suitable accommodation for a collection of birds indoors, most bird-keepers choose to house their stock in the garden. This is often better for the birds, provided that suitable precautions are taken to protect them from cold winds and a shelter is provided that can, when necessary, be heated in winter and in which artificial lighting can be provided.

There are many possible designs for a garden aviary. It could be built as a lean-to extension to the house or an adjacent wall so that you can see the birds without difficulty from indoors. In addition to permanent aviaries, portable models are also made. Their advantage is that they can be moved to fresh ground when the grass is soiled and no longer suitable. Care must be taken to see that the surface on which the aviary is placed is perfectly level; birds will otherwise escape and vermin may gain access. The structure must also be fixed securely in place.

Some aviaries take up a large area, and it is a glorious sight to watch birds flying in semi-natural surroundings and perhaps nesting in the ivy covering part of a wall or in a shrub growing in an area of lawn. The birds will be perfectly safe, for the mesh attached to the aviary framework will keep out cats and other predators. Flights that take up all the garden are, of course, exceptional, but the sunny side of a small back garden may be turned into an aviary without too much difficulty.

The size and design of the aviary will, of course, depend on the garden, and it may be planned as imaginatively as you wish provided that it is both practical and safe. It is a good plan to build against a south-facing wall, and even if the wall is overgrown, the birds will appreciate the vegetation for nesting purposes.

The shelter should have a door at the back, and it will usually have a connecting door through to the flight. When you want to enter the aviary, the entry point into the flight for the birds should be shut first, so that they are safely retained in the outside flight. Most people prefer the external door to be located in the shelter, and if this is the case it is advisable to add a safety porch made of mesh on a wooden framework around the door opening. This will enable you to enter the aviary with no risk of the birds escaping; you can then close the door of the safety porch before opening that of the aviary.

The birds will enter the shelter only if there is sufficient light, so large windows at the top, front and side are necessary. The inside of the windows should be fitted with a wire-mesh covered frame, which can be fastened in position with bolts. The windows will need to be cleaned on the inside at intervals, so these frames should be readily detachable. The mesh will prevent accidents caused by birds taking fright and flying against the glass, and will also ensure that the birds cannot escape if the glass is broken.

The bolt-hole between the shelter and flight should be fairly large, because some birds will never become accustomed to a small entrance. It is wise to construct the entry point in such a way that it can be operated from outside the flight; it may, for example, be necessary to close it on cold winter nights. The flights themselves can be covered wholly or partially on top by plastic sheeting, which should slope to ensure that rainwater drains off and away from the shelter.

Even in a town it may be possible to construct an outside aviary. Many older houses, for example, have balconies which are no longer used, and these make ideal sites. The shelter will be in the room, and only the flight has to be provided over the balcony. Basements can also be used as shelters, as long as sunlight can be admitted. As a rule, basements are frost-proof and will make suitable birdrooms if they are attached to an outside flight. Another possibility is to convert a loft. This can make very suitable quarters, with a small flight being built out from a dormer window. You must ensure that there is adequate ventilation, because roof spaces can become very hot during the summer.

Wherever you choose to build the aviary, an enclosed shelter at the back of the aviary is essential in winter in temperate areas. There should be a sliding door at the bottom, which will be used by ground birds such as quail, and a higher flap door for other birds. It is wise to have the shelter higher than the outside flight, because birds usually choose the highest place to roost and so will be encouraged to use it.

If different species of birds are to be kept apart for breeding purposes, it is best to build a range of aviaries side by side. The floors of the shelters should be of brick or concrete to keep out rats and other vermin. A solid base to the flight is also recommended. Alternatively, coarse gravel can be used as a floor covering. There are many ways of building a shelter. Often a shed can be converted to serve the purpose, but with a block of aviaries of this type, a service corridor running down the back is to be recommended.

Aviaries entirely covered with wired glass have the advantage that a cat can do little damage, especially if the glass covering projects a short distance all round, which makes it impossible for a cat to climb up on the roof. I like to incorporate a narrow strip that projects from the front of the shelter under which the birds can take cover, while the rest of the aviary is open to all weathers. The birds often enjoy a good shower of rain, and it benefits the shrubs. Many birds actually prefer to go into wet shrubs for a bath instead of into a pan of water, but you will need to discourage them from nesting here, where their nest could become flooded.

Your own cat can probably be trained to become accustomed to the birds; it is the other cats in the neighbourhood that cause most trouble and have to be kept away. They will otherwise upset nervous pairs and cause breeding failure. There are many ways in which the aviary and the birds can be safeguarded from cats, besides using wired glass. It is usually possible to surround a small town garden with ordinary chicken wire of 2in (5cm) mesh, the top part of which can be bent inwards or outwards. This wire can often be fastened to an existing fence. Overhanging branches of a tree, which would allow a cat to climb on to the aviary, should be removed. A double layer of wire-netting may be put around the aviary, leaving a space between the inner and outer layers. This is usually too costly, however, and it will not improve the appearance of the aviary.

The chief enemies that are likely to penetrate into the aviary are, of course, rats, mice and weasels, as well as snakes in some areas. The dimensions of the mesh can help to exclude them, but young mice are small enough to slip through ½in (12mm) wire netting. Not only do they eat and foul the seed, so introducing disease, but they can also cause great damage by disturbing a nest or frightening brooding birds away from the nest at night, which will result in the losses of eggs and chicks.

Never lay poison in the aviary or shelter, not even in places which are difficult for birds to reach; mice have a habit of dragging the poison into the open. Killer traps should never be placed inside the aviary, but you can now purchase traps that should catch these pests alive, with minimum risk to the birds themselves.

If a covered feeding place is made in the outside aviary, the birds will use it most of the time, but you must make sure that the food will be kept dry. It should preferably be close to the door giving access to the flight, so that it can be replenished without entering the aviary and disturbing the birds. The shelter should also have some arrangement for feeding and drinking. Water is less likely to freeze here than in the flight. A choice of feeding sites is especially important in a mixed aviary, because one pair may start to dominate one feeding station, driving off other birds which try to eat here.

In a birdroom, which serves partially as a shelter, it is advisable to have a separate section in which to keep breeding cages and to store food bins, cleaning utensils and so on. The breeding cages should be several feet above the ground, and shelves should be built below on which to keep foodstuffs, medicines and utensils. Partitions made of a wire covered screen will prevent loss of light. In the winter tubular heaters can also be safely placed here, because no birds will be flying loose in this storage area. It also has the advantage that artificial lighting will be available, and this will enable the birds to feed later in the day during the winter months, when the hours of daylight are short.

A net is indispensable, especially when young birds have become independent and need to be placed in other quarters. Troublesome fighting males must also be removed. A large butterfly net, with a deep bag of fine mosquito netting and a well-padded rim, is best. Special trapping cages can also be used. They work well and cause little disturbance. The chasing of birds with a net must always be avoided in an aviary where birds are breeding.

CAGES

For breeding purposes, a box-type cage with a wire front is preferable to the open-mesh cages favoured for pet birds such as tame budgerigars. They offer more privacy. Flight cages can also be of this design. Perches should be fixed firmly in position at various heights. The food and drinking bowls can be put inside through the door and a small rack for green food can also be provided, as well as a clip for a cuttlefish bone.

One or two metal trays, ½–1in (1–2.5cm) deep, should be placed on the floor. Dry bird sand can be sprinkled on these, on top of a layer of newspaper; good clean, sterilised river sand, which is sold specially for this purpose, is recommended. For messy species, including fruit-eaters, the trays should be covered with blotting paper or layers of newspaper, which should be changed regularly. The trays themselves should have handles so that they can be pulled out easily, and the fronts concealed by a hinged wooden flap, which fall into place and prevent any birds from escaping when the trays are pulled out. A plastic plate, 4–6in (10–15cm) high, fitted round the base of the cage will help to contain sand, feathers and seed husks in the cage as the birds fly about.

The minimum measurements of the cage should be 2ft (60cm) long by 16in (40cm) deep by 20in (50cm) high. It is essential to provide adequate space for exercise if small foreign birds are to be kept in perfect health, so smaller sizes should be avoided.

My indoor cages for four or five pairs of waxbills are 4ft (1.2m) long by 2ft (60cm) deep by 40in (1m) high. They are placed one on top of the other. The top one is raised on legs so that the lower cage can be illuminated properly from above. The whole unit is mounted on wheels so that it is easy to clean around the cages with minimum disturbance to the birds. A hanging feeding tray is placed in the top cage, because the birds cannot be seen if they feed on the floor. These cages can be made at home.

Decorative indoor aviaries are now quite widely available. The furnishings are usually very practical – doors at various heights, trays, provision for attaching baths, drinking fountains and even nestboxes.

The cages must, of course, be light and sited where the sun can reach them, although never in direct sunlight, which will be harmful to the birds. A lean-to conservatory, where the temperature does not rise excessively and where shading can be provided or a south-facing bay window would be ideal. The birds must be able to find shade in the cage because they do not always want to be exposed to the sun. It is also important to ensure that they are not exposed to draughts in such surroundings.

Their housing must provide height where the birds can fly if something frightens them. At night, too, they look for the highest spot to roost; this is usually also the warmest spot in the cage. Nesting boxes should be hung high on the back wall so that they cannot be easily interfered with, especially by children.

As the birds must be caught now and again, there should not be too many branches, which also limit the amount of flying space. This particularly applies in indoor flights. In this relatively confined space, the birds are probably best caught by hand.

A cage housing a large bird should not be hung up; its movements will cause the cage to sway, and birds do not like this. They are happiest if their cage is at eye level or a little higher. A tame Budgerigar or Canary, which is allowed to fly freely for a couple of hours a day, does not require elaborate accommodation. Such a bird looks to its owner for companionship, perches on the shoulder or hand and comes to the table for titbits. Birds that are kept singly learn quite rapidly what is expected of them, and it is rarely necessary to catch or chase them. They will return to their cage of their own volition.

THE INDOOR AVIARY

An ideal home for birds can be constructed in a room, a conservatory or a large, south-facing bay window. This is much better for them than cages. The walls must be painted in light, washable paint to make cleaning easy. The windows will need wired frames, so that birds cannot injure themselves by flying directly at the glass, and these must be removable so that the windows can be washed.

The design will depend on the needs of the occupants. Plants in troughs or pots can be put in only if there are no parrots or parakeets flying around. As a rule, foreign finches or small insect-eaters are usually kept in such surroundings, often over the winter period. This saves the expense of providing additional heating and lighting outdoors. A wide choice of plants can be incorporated, because these birds rarely damage vegetation in their quarters, and this will greatly enhance the appearance of the aviary.

Some pairs may even decide to nest in such surroundings. Breeding results are usually much more satisfactory in enclosures of this type than in cages, but there must be harmony among the aviary occupants. It is essential to watch the birds and to segregate any troublemakers.

The room will need a system of thermostatic control to maintain an even temperature, especially if it is not within the house. Lighting shortens the long winter nights, and its use until 8 o'clock in the evening and again at 6 or 7 o'clock in the morning will be sufficient to give even small birds an adequate feeding period. Most birds will still be found at the feeding table in the evening, and a dimmer switch, which will allow you to reduce the light intensity gradually over, say, 15 minutes, is recommended because the birds will be able to go to roost rather than being left stranded in sudden darkness.

PARROTS

Very few of the Australian parakeets should be kept as cage pets; they are active and restless by nature and will not settle well if they are confined in a small space. The large, short-tailed parrots, such as Amazons and the Grey Parrot, and some of the cockatoos, on the other hand, are of a more placid disposition. In a wild state these birds spend more of their time clambering among the branches of forest trees than their smaller, more active relatives. Furthermore, hand-reared chicks of these species will prove naturally tame and confiding companions.

They require a large, all-metal cage with stout, hardwood perches. Such cages are readily obtainable in sectional form, but they are somewhat costly. However, they are to provide a home for a bird that is itself expensive, and once it has been decided to spend a large amount of money on a parrot, no economy should be exercised on its living accommodation. Provided it is well looked after it will probably be a life-long companion and give great pleasure to its owner.

Brass cages, however beautiful or antique, should be avoided because verdigris will form on the metal sooner or later. When the bird climbs round the cage the verdigris is sure to be ingested, and this may prove fatal.

If they are to remain in first-class condition, the birds require more exercise than they are able to obtain in the cage. A climbing pole and cross perch should be kept beside the cage, and the birds should be allowed out daily to clamber on it and stretch their wings. At the same time a shallow pan of water should be available in which they can take a bath if they feel so inclined. If, as is sometimes the case, they refuse to bathe, they should occasionally be sprayed with tepid water, which they will soon grow to enjoy, although they may be nervous at first.

If it does not extend to the ground, the cage should be kept on a firm base, and it should be in good light and away from draughts. It should be partly covered with a cloth at night, as the bird will sleep more comfortably with this added protection from cold and draught.

Large, long-tailed parrots of the macaw family are sometimes kept on T-shaped perches or parrot stands, to which they are secured by a light chain attached to one leg. This is a most unsatisfactory method of keeping any bird, and these birds should really only be kept in a spacious aviary, although they can be allowed to perch freely on a stand once they are very tame.

All members of the parrot family are 'carpenters'. Even Budgerigars and other small grass parakeets will quickly reduce softwood perches to matchwood and damage or destroy all shrubs and growing plants. The larger parakeets, parrots and cockatoos will attack all woodwork in their aviary, and the ordinary light-gauge wire netting is quite inadequate to resist their powerful beaks. It should be at least 16 gauge, which is usually indicated as 16SWG in advertisements and on labels.

Enclosures for the larger species should ideally be constructed of heavy gauge chain link wire on a frame of metal tubes or angle iron. This form of construction is, of course, expensive, and because the aviaries must be large, the total cost will be considerable. If several pairs are to be kept for breeding purposes it is preferable, and in most cases essential, to house each pair separately, and it may then be found more convenient to construct a range of uniform aviaries, with blockwork shelters and a service corridor. Food and water can then be supplied with a minimum of disturbance to the birds and if a feeding hatch is provided it will not be necessary to enter each enclosure directly. This can be particularly useful during the breeding season, when some larger parrots can become rather aggressive in the vicinity of their nestboxes.

As long as there is sufficient room for the birds to obtain plenty of exercise by flying from end to end, it is not necessary for the enclosures to be very large. As a guide, a width of 3ft (1m) and a height of 6ft (1.8m) will be sufficient for a pair of the smallest parakeets, with the flights being not be less than 8–10ft (2.4–3m) long. In addition, simple shelters, about 3 × 4ft (90 × 120cm) and of the same height as the flights, should be provided, with windows at the back to provide plenty of light.

The front of the shelter should be entirely enclosed apart from an entrance for the birds, which should be placed near the top and be about 12in (30cm) wide and 18in (46cm) high. A sliding door, which can be used to shut in the birds when required, is necessary. The wooden frame of this entrance hole should be carefully protected with sheet metal to prevent the birds from gnawing it away. Food and water should always be given in the shelters, not only as a convenience to the bird-keeper but also to encourage the birds to enter freely of their own accord.

It will not, of course, be possible to shut the birds in the shelter if they are nesting, as breeding operations are usually more successful when the nestboxes are positioned under cover in the open flight. Some birds, especially hanging parrots, have a tendency to roost hanging on the wire-netting, and this must be discouraged, because they may be injured by owls or prowling cats during the night. They could also lose their toes through frost-bite on a cold winter's night.

The cocks of many species become aggressive during the nesting season and will often attempt to fight their neighbours through the mesh dividing the enclosures and attack young birds that happen to alight on the wire. Serious injuries to toes and beaks may result, and it is therefore essential that the partitions are made of double wire with at least 1in (2.5cm) space between each side. Mesh should be applied on both faces of the framework. Any woodwork should be covered to protect it from the parrots' beaks as far as possible. This, will of course, add to the initial cost of the aviaries, but these measures will help to safeguard the welfare of your birds in the long run.

There is little point in planting shrubs in the flights, as these will almost certainly be destroyed by the birds. However, turf may be laid, and seed plants, such as canary grass, sunflower and rape, can be grown to provide a useful addition to the diet. Such plants will be greatly appreciated, especially when young birds are being reared.

Shallow baths can be provided in the flights, although some species will seldom enter water, often preferring to climb on wet mesh after a shower of rain. During a prolonged period of drought, the birds greatly enjoy an occasional spraying from a hose. Any grass that is growing in the flights should be kept well watered so that it can provide a source of food when the birds are breeding.

Natural branches make the best perches, but you must be prepared to renew these at frequent intervals, because the birds will strip off all foliage and bark and will eventually destroy the wood. Many parrots are particularly fond of fresh elder or sycamore branches, and there is no doubt that the constant gnawing helps to sharpen the birds' beaks and prevent them from becoming overgrown.

PHEASANTS

Pheasants should not be kept indoors. These birds should be acquired only if spacious outdoor accommodation is available, preferably in some corner of an orchard or woodland where large aviaries can be constructed for them. Many pheasants can be seen in country districts. In addition to well-known species such as the Reeves's, Silver, Golden and Lady Amherst's Pheasants, a number of other rarer species such as Swinhoe's and Elliott's are now being bred regularly, and aviculture is helping to safeguard their futures.

Pheasants can often be safely associated with other species, since they spend most of the time on the ground and seldom interfere with perching birds, which usually seek out the highest available perches. Although the perching birds will descend to the ground occasionally during the day, this is not usually a source of problems.

In a well-planted flight populated by small finches, a trio of Golden Pheasants or Lady Amherst's Pheasants could be included without any interference with the breeding operations. However, the large Silver Pheasants and the Blue-eared Pheasants are better kept in the company of a few of the larger parakeets. On several occasions I have missed some Zebra Finch fledglings and other young foreign finches, which had just tried their wings, only to have discovered that they had been eaten by the Silver Pheasants. Ordinary Budgerigars, on the other hand, are quite able to look after themselves and are safe in the flight with the pheasants.

Most pheasants are polygamous, and two or three hens can usually run with one cock. The Common Pheasant will take as many as seven hens, and the eggs will all be fertile in the spring. Some species, however, are monogamous; both the Scintillating Copper Pheasant and the Peacock Pheasant, for example, will accept one hen only. Cock pheasants themselves are highly aggressive and must be kept apart.

Several books have been written especially for the pheasant enthusiast, and here we shall discuss only some of the more popular species and give general directions for their housing, care and breeding.

Although an ordinary flight of at least 12 × 18ft (3.7 × 5.5m) would comfortably house a few pheasants together with other birds, it would be more advisable – provided always that room and the necessary funds are available – to have special aviaries for the pheasants. These should be at least 30–45ft (9–13.7m) long and 10–12ft (3–3.7m) wide, with a height of 8ft (2.4m). Most of the species of pheasants described here are quite hardy, and the shelters need not be fitted with doors.

If you are seriously contemplating keeping pheasants, do not begin on too small a scale. You should consider making at least four runs next to each other, building them in such a way that the range can be extended at any time. In most cases, additions will eventually be required as the collection grows and new species are acquired. There should be a passage running behind the shelter from which food and drink can be supplied. This passage need be divided from the shelters only by wire-covered frame partitions.

The roof should slope down towards the back. It is important that the back is not directly on the boundary of your property; otherwise neighbours may complain. The roof should be covered with adequate rainproofing material. The shelters can be made of wood and are best set on concrete flooring, while the floor of the flight must be well-drained, so that the birds' plumage will not become saturated with mud during wet weather.

The partitions between the various runs should be made of the smallest mesh wire available. This is because the cocks tend to fight, and to obviate this as much as possible the partitions should be of boarding or covered with rush matting to a height of 2ft (60cm) from the ground. Alternatively, a brick or concrete wall of similar height should be constructed. Such a wall could, with advantage, be built all around the outer perimeter of the four runs to give the pheasants much more seclusion.

If roosting perches – preferably thick ones – are provided in the flights, the pheasants will always be found sleeping outside at night. It is usually desirable, at least during the winter, that the birds roost under cover, so perches should be placed in the shelter only, otherwise the pheasants will almost always choose those that are in the open, even in frost and snow, and will roost in a shelter only if they are compelled to do so by lack of perches elsewhere. The perches should be arranged in such a way that the birds cannot damage their long tails when they are roosting or flying. The distance from the back wall should be at least 4ft 6in (1.4m), but the perches need not be more than 3–4ft (90–120cm) from the ground.

Communicating doors should be made between the aviaries. The wire netting should be buried into the soil all round the outside of the aviaries to a depth of at least 20in (50cm) to guard against mice and other intruders. If small perching birds are also to be kept in the aviaries and enclosed shelters are provided, an entrance for use by the pheasants should be made at ground level with another entrance, high up, for the smaller birds.

Special attention must be given to the ground of the aviary. If a good, porous, sandy soil is not available, ample drainage must be provided by artificial means. The soil should be dug to a depth of 3ft (90cm) and a layer of rubble or ashes put in. A layer of gravel should be placed over this, and there should be a final covering of good soil, mixed with peat and sharp sand. A 4in (10cm) layer of sharp sand should be included under the shelter roof at the rear of the aviary where it will not get wet, because pheasants are very partial to sand baths.

Pheasants have a habit of walking round and round the boundaries of their enclosures, and it is as well to provide a dry path, which can be of gravel or concrete on which coarse gravel has been scattered while the cement is still wet to give a roughened surface and look more attractive. This path will prevent the ground from becoming a mud bath during wet weather. The corners of the aviary should, if possible, be rounded and all angles eliminated, because the pheasants' long tails are easily damaged when the birds continually pace round and round the boundary. Alternatively, some shrubs or small pine trees can be planted in the corners quite close to the wire netting. Elder trees and rhododendrons are ideal for this purpose, but yews must be avoided, because they have poisonous berries.

There are many ways in which a pheasant aviary can be made more attractive. A narrow ornamental pond, with reeds or bamboo planted along the borders, can be constructed to run through all four flights. Small bridges or old tree trunks will beautify the interior. Parrots should not be kept in an aviary thus ornamented because they will quickly destroy all plants, but many birds, such as various softbills, will cause little damage. Turf is greatly appreciated as flooring by all birds, both large and small, but care needs to be taken because it can harbour parasites in the form of worm eggs.

A thick layer of hay or straw may be placed in the shelter during spells of severe weather. This will be appreciated by the pheasants, and, if the perches are then removed, they will be compelled to remain on the bed of straw at night and will not suffer from frost-bite. The straw also keeps their underparts warm when they are sleeping at night. If the floor of the shelter is made of cement or concrete, it should be covered with a layer of peat or sharp sand during the summer.

Nylon netting, which is now often used as a top covering for pheasant aviaries, is a most successful means of preventing the birds from damaging their heads when they fly upwards, as they are always apt to do if frightened. If this material is used it must be so fixed that it is quite flexible, with plenty of 'give'. It should be under a solid mesh roof to protect the birds from predators.

It is advisable to cover part of the flight with plastic sheeting, extending 4–5ft (1.2–1.5m) from the shelter. On rainy days this will permit the birds to be in the open without being exposed to the rain.

Most species of pheasants are accustomed to cold and, in fact, seem to like it. They must not, therefore, be exposed to excessive heat of the sun. If the aviary is situated among trees or in an orchard, useful shade will be provided, otherwise you should plant dense growing shrubs in the flights to give the birds the necessary protection from the sun. Rhododendrons are very suitable for this purpose.

During the mating season the cocks are apt to persecute the hens, which must be able to find some retreat or they will soon become exhausted and may be badly scalped. The shrubs will afford them some cover, but it may occasionally be necessary to remove the cock for a while to give the hens a little peace. Bad-tempered cocks are best kept in a separate pen and allowed to run with the hens only for a short time for mating.

ORNAMENTAL WATERFOWL

A whole book could be written on this subject, but I intend to refer only to the well-known species that I have kept in my own flights for many years.

A pond will be the first essential for this special hobby. It can be quickly dug as it need only be relatively small in area. One or two pairs of ducks can easily be kept on a small area of land, and the cost of constructing a pond and of providing the necessary wire fencing need not be ruinous. A pair of ornamental ducks will not cost an excessive amount, and in any case, some of the most colourful and easily accommodated species are also the least expensive to purchase in the first instance.

If land alongside a brook is available or if there is a natural tarn or fen, the possibilities are endless. Large numbers of ducks can then be kept, for they will obtain their food mostly from the water, so that their keep costs little. The collection can consist of many species, even swans and geese, although these may well need to be separated.

The borders of the pond can be left to grow naturally, but care must be taken to keep down natural enemies such as rats and other vermin. Many a paradise for fish and ducks has been created on small areas of private property, although it may take four to eight years to become established. More and more plants, brought from far and near by birds visiting the newly created ponds, will add to the existing flora.

Breeding baskets can be placed close to the water in the spring, while a floating feeding-table may be made, supported by a couple of empty oil drums and moored to the bank by a chain. Thick-growing shrubs around the pond will give any visiting wild ducks a sense of security.

If a brook or river runs along or through the property, quite different opportunities are offered. A fenced-off pool adjoining the border can be constructed and fed from the stream. Duck ponds can be made in the same way from wide ditches, with no current, and if the water is renewed regularly, very good accommodation for ducks can be provided. A number of such ponds or basins can be built next to each other to accommodate collections of several different species.

Care must be taken to see that the edges of the pond slope gradually and easily to the water, otherwise the ducks cannot land in comfort, and little ducklings may die if they cannot climb to firm soil easily.

As island can be created in a small pond without much trouble, or you can provide a floating island on which a breeding box can be placed, away from most potential predators. Given the necessary planting, this soon becomes quite effective and tasteful. A plank can be used to connect it to dry land when necessary.

All kinds of ideas can be gathered from visits to zoos and aviaries in parks. There are also magazines and periodicals wholly or partly devoted to waterfowl, and these will give further insight into constructing suitable habitats.

Making an artificial pond presents some difficulties but here, too, success can be achieved without the help of craftsmen. Butyl rubber can be used as a liner, and it has proved sufficiently durable to last for years. The pond must have smooth and gradually sloping sides, and this is easily achieved by digging out the correct profile and simply inserting the liner.

Many people, however, prefer to use a more permanent material, such as concrete, and a mixture of one part cement to three parts fine gravel and sharp sand gives good results. After the excavating has been completed, the soil must be firmed down and a layer of ash or rubble stamped in. It is essential that some system of draining the pond is incorporated. A drain-pipe should be placed so that the opening is in the exact centre of the pond and at its deepest point. The exposed end should be covered by a tin to prevent it from becoming blocked when the cement is being laid. The pipe must terminate somewhere in a drain or ditch, and it must be set in concrete, consisting of one part of cement to one of sand, otherwise there will be every chance of leakage. It should be closed with a tight-fitting rubber plug, attached to a chain (like a bath stop).

The diameter of the pond should be at least 8–9ft (2.4–2.7m). This will be enough for two or three ducks. The pond need not be deeper that 16–20in (40–50cm) in the centre, and the slope should be gradual. The edge should be 1in (2.5cm) above the surrounding ground and at least 10in (25cm) wide. A fairly wide walk of flagstones, tiles or concrete should be laid around the pond so that the ducks do not continually carry earth into the water and thus muddy it unduly.

Round ponds are most easily fashioned from concrete. Rectangular ones can be made quite well with butyl rubber, and even large pre-formed pools can be used, although these are relatively expensive and do not usually have drainage. If concrete is used, it need not be thicker than 4in (10cm). It looks very simple and easy on paper, but it requires skill and, above all, patience to obtain a smooth surface and a level top edge. It is quite pretty and effective to make the pond on a level slightly higher than the surrounding ground and drainage will be much simpler.

Many different species of ducks can be kept without an elaborate shelter. The birds can stay out, summer and winter, provided they can find adequate cover under thick shrubbery. A simple pen is, however, useful, because some species prefer extra seclusion, especially when they are laying, and it will also provide good protection for the ducklings. If the ducks are allowed to roam about an open lawn or meadow, it must be fenced off with wire netting about 2ft (60cm) high, assuming they are pinioned and so cannot fly off.

WINTER ACCOMMODATION

Many people think that tropical birds can be kept only in a well-warmed room. Some refuse to believe that our summers, which as a rule do not excel in sunshine and warmth, offer suitable living conditions for these birds. Nothing could be further from the truth.

Experience has shown that many foreign birds, especially parrots, can thrive without additional heat in northern European climates throughout the year, once they are properly acclimatised. Most birds will actually reach their normal lifespan, and often live much longer, in aviaries. In their natural surroundings, which are full of dangers, birds frequently do not reach the ages they attain in captivity, where, even though they become a little less active, they do not have to contend with natural enemies and shortages of food.

Small foreign finches and other more delicate birds must be brought indoors during the winter and put in a room or other accommodation that can be heated when necessary. This is when a well-insulated birdroom, where heating and lighting are available, can be so valuable. Thermostatically controlled electric tubular heaters are the safest and most reliable means of heating, and lighting can be controlled by a timer and dimmer switch. Any heating equipment and all electrical wiring must be kept out of reach of the birds.

If they have been kept outside through the summer and autumn and are in good feather condition, most parrots and larger softbills may well be able to winter outdoors without additional heat. Watch them closely in cold weather, however, and if they are not comfortable, they soon show it by perching with their feathers ruffled and seeming to shiver. Any such birds must be transferred to heated accommodation without delay, and they will show a rapid improvement the moment the temperature is raised. They will need to be kept in the new accommodation until the following spring, and only allowed back into their aviary when the weather is warm again.

A single bird, if unwell, can be placed in a separate cage in a warm room, under an infrared lamp which emits heat rather than light. As the bird recovers, so the temperature of its surroundings can be gradually reduced, but again, if it falls ill during the winter, it will need to be kept inside until spring. Birds that start moulting badly in the colder months of the year should be watched closely, as they are most likely to be prone to illness.

As a rule, temperatures a few degrees above freezing are better than significantly higher temperatures. The latter are really necessary only for sick birds or recently imported ones. It is advisable to have some cages on hand so that if the need should suddenly arise the birds can be kept indoors.

If just a shelter and outside aviary are available, new birds should not be acquired during the winter unless they come from similar accommodation. In summer, recently imported birds can be placed straight into an outside aviary, but this is generally advisable only if the weather is set fair. A particularly close watch must be kept on them at this stage.

The aviary should be designed in such a way that by the time the nights become cold and wet, the birds have grown used to roosting in the shelter at night. A start can be made by keeping their food there, and in the winter, when the lights go on in the evening, the birds will come in naturally. It is advisable to adopt a routine when shutting the trap doors between the aviary shelter and flight, and it is much better to close the birds in every night. A sliding track, with a length of stout wire extending through the aviary mesh will make it possible to cover the opening from the outside so that it is not necessary to enter the aviary for this purpose. The birds will soon become accustomed to this routine and it will soon be found that at 'closing time' none remain outside. They can then be let out in the morning with minimum disturbance.

AVIARY FURNISHINGS

Birds should always be provided with natural living conditions as far as possible, and branches are always to be preferred for perching purposes. An outside aviary with a shelter needs an adequate number of perches of varying thicknesses. These should be positioned across rather than lengthways in the aviary, and those in the shelter should be fixed at a higher point than those in the flight, so that the birds are attracted to roost here.

In a cage, fresh branches are better than rounded dowel perches. The birds' claws must be in contact with the sides of the perch, and if only very thin branches are used, the birds' claws will grow too long. The birds keep their claws trimmed by rubbing along the length of some thick perches. Even destructive birds, such as parrots, should never be given metal perches. Although they are more hygienic because they will not harbour lice or mites and are easy to keep clean, they are absolutely unsuitable, because they deprive the bird of an opportunity to use its beak, which may also become overgrown.

Branches with the bark on are best. These retain their natural resilience for a long time and help to keep the birds' legs in good condition. Soiled perches must be changed regularly. Branches under the birds' chosen sleeping perches are likely to become very soiled, and they must be removed, except during breeding period, when the aviary or cage should not be disturbed.

In a small cage, perches should be positioned so that as much uninterrupted flying space as possible remains. Too many branches will obstruct the flight. Birds with long tails require perches that are arranged so that their tails can hang down freely, and they must also be sufficiently far away from the mesh to permit freedom of movement without causing damage to the tail feathers.

In small cages particularly, perches should be attached to the bars at various heights by means of hooks or clamps at one end only. They will then be springy and more closely resemble natural branches and twigs. They must, however, be firmly positioned, or the birds may have difficulty in mating successfully.

NESTING FACILITIES

Although many birds prefer to nest in shrubs, small finches like to use nestboxes filled with dried grasses, hemp teasings and feathers. Such boxes should be supplied at breeding time and hung at varying heights. Some birds prefer hidden spots; these can be provided by tying up bundles of heather and hanging them close together with nestboxes in between. Pine branches, bundles of reeds and branches of broom can also be used to provide seclusion. Part of the wall may be covered with tree bark, and if any of the pieces stand away from the wall, the space behind may be filled with dried grass to create suitable nesting cavities, which some birds prefer.

The well-known silver birch and poplar log nests can be obtained in all sizes, but small finches should be provided with a choice of breeding sites and nestboxes. A small hole should be drilled in the side wall of nestboxes to improve the ventilation, because the parent birds may sit for hours in the opening so that very little fresh air may reach the youngsters.

Coconuts provide the handyman with a means of making more natural-looking nests. Only a small amount of drilling and sawing is necessary. The size of the entrance hole should be made to suit the size of the bird, and the lids can be removed for inspection of the nest and for cleaning purposes.

Much more ingenious are nesting baskets, which are easy to make for those who have learnt basket-making or which can be purchased from most garden centres or pet shops. Birds are sure to prefer such natural material. It will be necessary to keep these free from parasites, such as red mite, by the use of one of the special sprays now available for this purpose, which are not dangerous to the birds.

Foreign finches may need a relatively large amount of nesting material, for they often build large nests, especially if these are not in nestboxes or baskets. As well as straw and woollen threads, they may use strips of paper, bits of material, horse hair, coconut fibres and assorted feathers. A large quantity of this sort of material should be available during the breeding period.

Some birds prefer dark material, others stick to dried and fresh blades of grass, and moss is also well liked. The nestboxes are sometimes packed tight, the nest itself being at the top. Some birds take over old nests, especially those of weavers, which hang from various places around an aviary, often from branches, and which are well built. They are frequently lined with different kinds of soft materials, and they have a side entrance. If it is necessary, they can be carefully transferred to other flights without breaking up.

FOOD UTENSILS

Automatic seed hoppers can be put on the ground or on a shelf or suspended in the aviary, depending on their design. The larger hoppers have the advantage of not needing to be replenished daily, but they must function perfectly, because if there is any blockage, the birds will be left without food. Seed hoppers of this type must, therefore, be placed where they can be inspected at a glance twice every day. They will keep the seed clean, and have the further advantage that little seed is wasted. The birds cannot spill it and the husks fall into a tray beneath. A separate hopper is normally used for each kind of seed, making it possible to see which seed is most popular.

All hoppers or food pots must be fixed in such a way that they keep dry, and the feeding table should be sited where it is always both 'mouse-proof' and will not be soiled by birds on perches above it. Suspended tables will be out of the reach of the mice and other vermin.

If there are insufficient growing plants in the flight, including grass and weeds, green food may have to be supplied daily and hung in a rack. Any remains must be removed at the end of the day. These racks can also be used to hold nesting materials.

Special holders for cuttlefish bone are available, and these should be provided for all parrots and seedeaters throughout the year, since the bone serves as a valuable source of calcium and other minerals. However, cuttlefish bone can also be hung up on a loop of wire. Oystershell grit can be provided in a pot, and traditionally, a little powdered charcoal is added to it to reduce the likelihood of gastric trouble.

Special sealed drinkers should be used for both drinking water and nectar. These will not be easily soiled, unlike open pots. These drinkers usually have hooks so that they can be attached to the side of the cage or aviary. Drinking bottles with stainless steel spouts are favoured for parrots, whose powerful bills can crush plastic containers, and water fountains are usually given to pheasants and quail, which should be fed and watered on the floor of their quarters.

BATHS

Bathing facilities must be provided in order to keep birds in good condition. Flat stones can be put on the floor of the birdroom close to the wire and a shallow dish of water placed on them so that it can easily be filled from outside.

For the cage or inside aviary it is better to use plastic-enclosed baths, which hang on the front of the cage so that water is not splashed on the floor. These baths must have ribbed bottoms to help the bird maintain its grip here. If flat stones are placed in the dishes, they must be cleaned regularly. Deep bowls, in which young birds might drown, must be avoided at all costs.

Flower-pot saucers make excellent baths, but larger shallow dishes or shallow cemented ponds are more suitable for an aviary, and if water is supplied direct from the mains it is possible to have a small fountain playing. Bath water should be changed at least twice daily, reducing the risk that the birds will drink dirty water.

SUITABLE PLANTS FOR AN OUTSIDE FLIGHT

The following is a list of plants that are popular for growing in aviary surroundings. They give cover, attract insects and in some cases provide fruit or berries for the birds to enjoy. Aviaries for most parrots cannot be planted successfully, however, because the birds are liable to destroy any vegetation. Plants can usually be purchased in containers from garden centres, but if kept in containers, they are likely to require watering through the summer and rarely grow as vigorously as when they are actually set in the ground.

Berberis hortorum
This shrub will reach a height of nearly 5ft (1.5m). It flowers in April and May with bunches of yellow blooms and in autumn bears numberless blue berries, of which the birds are very fond. The leaves remain on during the winter and colour beautifully. It will grow on any soil, in either sunshine or shade, and is also very suitable as underplanting.

Buxus sempervirens (common box)
The box is a most useful shrub, especially for small nesting waxbills. The trimmed bushes are the best for nesting, but the untrimmed and un-trammelled growth is extremely suitable for shelter. This evergreen will do well in sun or shade and on practically any kind of soil. It grows slowly and is, consequently, relatively expensive to purchase.

Carpinus betulus (common hornbeam)
The hornbeam makes a close hedge. During the autumn, the leaves will turn a beautiful yellow and brown. It flowers in April and May with smallish catkins. It may be trimmed and will grow in any soil.

Ceanothus americanus
This grows to 20–36in (50–90cm) high. It blooms from June to September, with bunches of white flowers. It loses its leaves in winter and must be pruned in spring. It requires sandy soil and a sunny, sheltered spot.

Ceanothus thyrsiflorus
Flowers in May and June, and is evergreen. However it may grow to 20ft (6m) in the right conditions.

Cotoneaster horizontalis (wall spray)
Prostrate habit and may spread to 5ft (1.5m). Bears pinkish-white flowers

in May and June. Very useful against a low wall. Red berries in autumn and winter. The foliage, which stays on all winter, becomes a beautiful dark red and brown colour.

Cotoneaster rotundifolia
Similar to previous species but with more upright habit and has larger flowers and berries. Both require a sunny spot. Autumn colouring not so attractive. It usually retains its foliage throughout the winter.

Crataegus monogyna (common hawthorn)
This shrub or tree grows quite high and dense and is very suitable for nesting. It bears scented umbels of pinkish-red flowers in May and June. The red berries are popular with several species of birds. It can also be used as a hedge. Hawthorn will thrive in any soil, but likes a sunny spot best.

Deutzia gracilis (deutzia)
This shrub will grow to 2–3ft (60–90cm) high and blooms in May and June with bunches of white flowers. It is deciduous. It requires a sunny spot and nourishing garden soil.

Deutzia × *magnifica*
Will grow to more than 9ft (2.7m) high and flowers in June with double white blossoms in bunches. It requires a sunny spot and nourishing, not too dry soil.

Hedera helix (ivy)
Very useful for covering the fence or wall of an aviary. In places that get little or no sun, ivy maintains its evergreen colour both winter and summer. The insignificant flowers appear in September, and the black berries are eaten by many birds. The large-leaved variety 'Hibernica' is the most useful.

Ilex aquifolium (holly)
If male and female bushes are placed alternatively there will be a rich harvest of bright red berries. It demands a sunny spot and not too dry a soil. The variety 'Pyramidalis' lends itself well to hedges and offers suitable nesting sites. Fruits abundantly.

Juniperus spp. (juniper)
These evergreen shrubs grow best on dry sandy soil and often assume most decorative shapes. When purchasing from a nursery, choose the most

freakish growths for the aviary; these are generally unsuitable for gardens and parks, but most attractive to the birds.

Ligustrum vulgare (privet)

One of the most common and useful of hedge shrubs, privet sheds its leaves only in very severe winters, although they generally turn a little darker in winter. Privet grows very quickly and can be trimmed into any shape. It is remarkably good for nesting purposes. Small foreign finches find privet a paradise for nesting and roosting accommodation. Any soil is suitable. Privet will tolerate sun or will grow in shade.

Mahonia aquifolium (Oregon grape)

An evergreen shrub of spreading habit. Bright yellow flowers are borne in clusters in February to May, followed by black berries heavily powdered with violet bloom. It has a creeping rootstock. The leaves turn purple or red during the winter. The dewy blue berries are greatly appreciated by many birds.

Philadelphus coronarius (mock orange)

A strong growing shrub which may reach a height of 15ft (4.6m). Flowers in June, with delightfully scented blooms.

Picea spp. (spruce)

Various species are available. They grow mainly in sandy soil and do very well in suitable surroundings. The choice of species will be governed by the space available.

Prunus serotina (black cherry)

Strong-growing shrub; bears bunches of white flowers in May and June; the black fruit is appreciated by birds.

Prunus virginiana (Virginian bird cherry)

Bears bunches of large white blooms in May and June. It can be cut down to a low hedge and is then suitable for nesting.

Rhododendron ponticum

Although a very robust grower, it can be used as underplanting, but will then flower less prolifically. It needs a peaty mixture and dislikes lime. It retains its dark green leaves in the winter. It is likely to be poisonous to Budgerigars and all other parrots, but is quite safe with other birds which do not destroy vegetation.

Rosa multiflora (wild rose)

There are many species of wild rose that can be grown to cover fences and wiring. They also form a thick hedge in which the birds can build their nests. They like a sunny spot and damp soil, and flower in June and July.

Rubus fruticosus (blackberry)

A strong-growing variety from the Himalayas. Bears large fruits, which are greatly appreciated by the birds. Will grow in almost any soil, but likes a damp and shady spot. It propagates itself by rootstock and multiplies quickly.

Sambucus nigra (elderberry)

An easy and rapidly growing shrub, which will thrive in any soil, provided there is a good layer of humus, which retains moisture. It likes sunshine, however, as well as damp conditions. Blooms May to June with numberless white flowers set in umbels. The elderberries, which become blackish as they ripen, are much liked by the birds. Insects attracted to the elderberry provide valuable variety to the diets of insect-eating birds.

Symphoricarpus albus (snowberry)

This shrub will grow to 5ft (1.5m) and has pink blossom in June and July. The large white berries, which appear in autumn and stay on until the winter, are especially appreciated by quails.

Vibernum opulus (Guelder rose)

May grow to more than 12ft (3.7m). Blooms from May to June with creamy white flowerets. Later bears red berries, which are well liked by the birds.

Vibernum opulus 'Flore Pleno'

Ball-shaped flower umbels, borne in May and June. The red berries are well liked by the birds.

For small seedeaters, ground cover is also important, especially during the breeding season. Their flight must be well planted with various grasses and weeds. These will then attract a host of invertebrates, which the birds will hunt avidly once their chicks have hatched.

FOOD AND DIET

The birds described in this book can be divided into four groups. This is not an arbitrary division; it is based on their feeding requirements. By far the largest group is that containing small seed-eating birds. Second come the parrots and parrot-like species, which in most cases require a different and rather specialised diet. The third group contains insect- and fruit-eaters and the nectar-feeders, known collectively as softbills. Then there is the fourth group, which consists of pigeons, doves, quail, pheasants and waterfowl, which will eat grain, although in reality, as in other cases, a more varied diet needs to be provided for them.

SMALL SEED-EATING BIRDS

The basis of a seed mixture suitable for all small seed-eating birds in this group is best-quality panicum millet and other varieties, mixed with plain canary seed. The proportion in which the seeds should be mixed will vary according to the individual tastes of the species, and for this reason some bird-keepers prefer to supply each kind of seed in separate dishes or automatic feeding hoppers.

Yellow millet is also used extensively for feeding small foreign finches, and although it is a much harder seed, some of the smallest finches prefer it. In addition, small quantities of other seeds may be given to avoid monotonous feeding, and rape, niger, linseed, hemp and teasel are all useful for providing variety. The actual proportions required differ somewhat according to the species concerned, as explained in the second section of this book.

Seeding weeds and grasses are always acceptable, and spray millet is a valuable addition to the diet and is greatly enjoyed by nearly all species.

Excellent mixtures, in which various seeds have been added to the basic canary and millets, can be purchased, and many bird-keepers prefer to select one of these as a basic diet for their stock. If, however, the mixing is to be done at home, much experiment will be necessary. An aviary containing several species of finches should be supplied with three food pots in which canary, white and yellow millet may be given separately, with about 2oz (60g) in each pot. The husks should be blown away carefully and the contents of the pots weighed daily. After a week the proportion of each seed eaten will be known. The seed can then be mixed in that proportion.

This method, of course, is not entirely reliable. Weather conditions influence the birds' choice of food. The amount of carbohydrate, protein, water, minerals, fat, calcium and phosphorus contained in the seeds varies, and during the winter more fats will usually be needed. In a heated winter aviary, for example, less canary seed will be eaten than in a frost-proof but colder aviary. It will also be possible to determine whether seeds rich in minerals are preferred during the moult.

The following is an analysis of the percentage of ingredients of various seeds. It will be seen that the composition of canary seed, white and yellow millet varies very little:

| | Percentage of | | | |
	Fats	Carbohydrates	Proteins	Minerals
Canary (white seed)	6	55	14	2
White millet	4	60	11	3
Yellow millet	4	63	11	3
Oats	5	56	11	2
Hemp	32	18	19	2
Sunflower	22	21	16	3
Maw	40	12	17	6
Niger	32	15	17	7
Rape	40	10	19	4
Linseed	34	24	21	6
Vetch (tares)	2	50	23	3
Wheat	2	70	11	2
Barley	2	70	10	2
Maize	7	65	10	2

To compare the food value of these seeds, it is necessary to investigate the effect of fats, carbohydrates, proteins and minerals on the birds. The percentage may vary slightly with the quality of the seed, but the essential proportion of the constituent parts is not greatly affected.

Fats provide warmth and energy in a concentrated form. Carbo-hydrates also supply energy and heat for the body. Proteins build up the body and are used for healing processes and growth; the protein requirement typically increases during the moult. Minerals have a variety of functions; they are indispensable for healthy bone formation, for example, and for individual cellular functions.

When the seeds are given unmixed, it will soon be evident which seeds are preferred and this can be followed. If, however, some birds react unfavourably to a certain kind of seed and get out of condition – by growing too fat, for example – the seed menu must be changed to provide fewer fattening elements. Cage birds especially should not be given seeds that are too fattening because they already have a tendency to obesity as a result of insufficient exercise.

Tests have shown that birds thrive better on canary seed, mixed or unmixed with millet, than on oats. Oats stimulate copulation and can be given with advantage before the breeding season. As soon as sitting has commenced, the feeding of oats should be discontinued, as a male's advances might result in the chicks being neglected.

A more fatty mixture does no harm during the winter. It guards against cold and in the spring the birds soon lose any excess fat, provided that sufficient exercise is possible. If the fatty food is continued too long into the spring, egg production may cease, for fat birds are bad layers.

Keeping in mind the low percentage of fat in the three basic kinds, it can be readily understood why the addition of maw seed (fat content 40 per cent), rape-seed (40 per cent), linseed (40 per cent) and hemp seed (32 per cent) may sometimes be necessary. These seeds also have a high mineral and a low carbohydrate percentage.

Although some Canary fanciers believe that the birds should be forced to eat all the various seeds included in the mixture and therefore give only small quantities so that the birds will eat everything because they are famished, I have never found that the health of the birds has been impaired when they have had the opportunity to choose their own menu. I place a number of jars in a row, each filled with a different kind of seed, and in this way I have discovered which the birds eat most. Sprays of millet are supplied regularly as extras.

The following table shows the exact proportion of seed mixtures I have found to be preferred by small finches:

	Tiger Finch	Zebra Finch	Bronze Mannikin	Bengalese Finch	Nun	Cuban Finch
Canary seed	5	3	7	7	24	10
White millet	4	40	17	50	48	10
Yellow millet	91	57	76	43	28	80

It will be seen from this that it is not unnatural to house these six species together in an aviary. It would be possible to add the Sharp-tailed Finch, Bicheno's Finch and others that show a definite preference for the yellow millet (65 per cent and 75 per cent respectively). Starting with the six pairs of birds quoted, the following proportion is reached: canary seed 10 per cent; white millet 35 per cent; yellow millet 55 per cent.

If some Bicheno's Finches were added to this collection a theoretical shortage of yellow millet would occur. On the other hand, should a pair of Rice Birds (Java Sparrows), which eat 30 per cent canary seed, 45 per cent white millet and 25 per cent yellow millet, be added, the result would be quite different. It would be possible to give numerous examples of small foreign finches that show a special preference for certain seeds and thus to prove that the supply of a standard mixture is practically impossible.

One simple way of calculating how much of each is necessary for a particular collection of birds, is to separate each species of bird into a not too small aviary for a fortnight and to note the quantity of the three kinds of seed, supplied in separate containers, eaten each day. Care should be taken to gather up the shelled seeds that have been scattered and return them to the container.

If, say, six species have been tested in this way, it should not be difficult to determine the proportions of each seed eaten. If more than one specimen of any kind of bird is kept, the result is simply multiplied by the number of such birds. Now, all the weights of the canary seed used must be added; then all the weights of the white millet; and finally those of the yellow millet. In order to calculate the percentages, all three figures must be added and this result set over a hundred. It is then not difficult to see the percentages.

Many bird-keepers change their collections from time to time, as some birds go and others take their places, but for general purposes, the following mixture is suggested as suitable for most of the small seed-eaters: 25 per cent each of canary seed, white millet, yellow millet and Senegal millet.

Although the birds can be kept in good health for many years on this mixture and they may remain in excellent condition, it will be found that it is the 'little extra' that will make all the difference, and as more experience is gained, the proportions may be varied and other seeds added to provide variety or to suit the special requirements of individual birds.

The quality of the seed is of the utmost importance and apparently attractive 'special offers' of cheap seed should be carefully investigated before purchase. Such offers often consist of inferior seed, which should have been ground in a cattle fodder mixture but which it has been found more profitable to sell as bird seed. This cheap seed can usually no longer be germinated and it lacks essential qualities. It is the living element in the seed or grain that is of paramount importance.

It matters little whether seeds for mixing are bought in packets or by bulk. The most important thing is to buy top quality, well-cleaned, shiny seeds. It may happen that in some areas after wet summers, ergot or spurred rye may get mixed with the seed. These large, violet-black seeds are very poisonous and may lead to paralysis should the birds eat them. They are still more deadly when germinated. When canary seed is soaked, therefore, great care should be taken to see that no violet-black seeds are mixed with it.

Powdered yeast is often added as an extra. It should not be given as a regular ingredient, however, and only occasionally and in small quantities. An easy way of giving it, for the birds will most certainly not take it from a pot, is to add it to seed that has been made sticky by a few drops of cod-liver oil. It attaches itself to the seed and the yeast is taken in the minute quantities required, serving as a valuable source of B vitamins.

Most seed-eaters also appreciate a little animal food, and one of the softbill mixtures now available, together with a few live insects, should be offered daily. This is particularly important if young are being reared, as many species of granivorous birds feed their young entirely on insects during the early stages, and breeding failure will result if insufficient live food is on offer.

It is remarkable that nearly all species of small seedeaters will take the special food that I provide for my Zosterops. It is made from one part clear honey dissolved in three parts of water, along with part of a fresh orange. Zebra Finches especially are very fond of the oranges. A food that should never be overlooked, especially during the breeding season, is soaked seed, because when seed is partially germinated, the vitamin content is higher than normal. Seeds must be soaked, initially in warm water, for a day. The water should be poured off, and the seed rinsed thoroughly and carefully with tepid water. It may be useful to add a special powder, which will inhibit the development of moulds, as these could otherwise harm the birds. Only a small quantity should be prepared at any time for this reason, but in most cases, it is readily consumed, with the birds eating it in preference to their usual dry seed. There is no better food for young birds, and millet sprays prepared in this way are especially popular. Any remaining uneaten seed must be removed at the end of the day.

The vitamins in the foodstuffs are indispensable to the well-being of the birds. Fresh green food, given daily, contains most of the essential vitamins. The two most important, A and D3, can be provided by means of a special food supplement, which can be sprinkled over the cut surfaces of fruit or damp green food.

Of the green food, chickweed (*Stellaria media*), is the most important. All birds love it, and it is rich in vitamin E. Spinach and dandelion leaves are also always appreciated. All greenstuff must be collected from safe sites, where herbicides have not been used. Frozen green food is not to be recommended. Lettuce can be given, but it has relatively little nutritional value compared with other green foods. It must always be carefully washed and preferably fresh-cut. A head of lettuce should be given in preference to loose leaves, and it will usually be picked clean. Any uneaten green food should be removed, as it can cause digestive upsets.

All kinds of grasses, especially those with ripening seedheads, are taken readily by most finches, and they should always be supplied regularly when there are young in the nest. Plantain (*Plantago lanceolata*), dandelion (*Taraxacum vulgare*), groundsel (*Senecio vulgaris*), shepherd's purse (*Capsella bursa pastoris*), clover (*Trifolium pratenis*) and all manner of other herbs and weeds provide seeds that are very much liked. The various thistles, *Carduus* and *Cirsium*, make a greatly appreciated delicacy. There is ample scope for experimenting in feeding, provided these wild plants can be collected from uncontaminated surroundings.

Grit should be scattered about or placed in a bowl in a corner of the cage, but not beneath the perches where it would be fouled. It should be finely graded and should consist of ground oystershell with which some minerals have been mixed. During the breeding season especially the birds need pieces of cuttlefish bone. These are vital sources of calcium, an essential ingredient of sound egg-shells, and they can be hung or fixed in the birds' quarters with special clips.

A Norwegian bird-keeper has found that dried and finely ground seaweed is beneficial to all his birds and makes their plumage extra glossy. This is not strange, since sea water contains many minerals, notably iodine, that may be temporarily lacking in the birds' diet. Seaweed powder is available on the market, and experiments can be carried out with herb mixtures as well.

Every effort must be made to vary the food that is offered. Far too little is still known about foreign birds and their food requirements, but it is certain that in the wild they will not only pick up many entirely different foodstuffs from those that the bird-keeper provides in the aviary but also that their diet will vary through the year.

If quantities of insects are eaten during the mating season and breeding period, the birds will often confine themselves to seed during the winter. If they are to be kept in the best possible condition they should not be deprived of this natural cycle. A rich menu followed by a period when less rich food is offered will give the best results.

Cultivation of canary seed and millet

Even a small plot, if sunny, is enough for seed cultivation. This does not mean competing with seed merchants, but birds are passionately fond of half-ripe seeds, which are especially rich in vitamins, particularly when they are rearing their young.

To produce good millet sprays, seeds should be sown about 4in (10cm) apart, leaving 6in (15cm) between the rows. Plants will quickly grow to a height of 3ft (90cm) in well-manured soil. Sowing should not be started until night frost is past; the beginning of May at the earliest in northern climates. Thin the seedlings as necessary so they are not too close together. Only when the plant has plenty of room and can absorb all the sun available will it grow large and heavy. The yellowing of the stalks shows that the sprays are ripe and the harvest may be gathered. It is now that the birds may be given the sprays regularly, but you may need to cover the seed with netting to deter wild birds from feeding on it.

Canary seed needs less attention and can be sown more closely. Unlike spray millet, the stalks have round seed heads, full of pointed husks. Song birds enjoy these greatly, and the birds will often peck the seeds if a bunch is hung up at an accessible point in their quarters.

PARROTS AND PARAKEETS

With the exception of the nectar-feeding parrots, which include the lories and lorikeets, all members of the parrot family feed largely on seeds, and suitable mixtures are available from most seed merchants.

The basis of all mixtures for Budgerigars, Australian parakeets and lovebirds, and the Cockatiel should be good quality white millet and bold canary seed. Other forms of millet may also be used, to give a mixture consisting of, say, a quarter part each of bold canary seed, and white, yellow and panicum millet.

As a change, the proportion of panicum millet may be halved and the balance replaced with groats (dehulled oats), but groats are more fattening and should not be given too often when Budgerigars are in breeding cages.

The following mixture is suitable for the larger parakeets: a quarter part each of canary seed, mixed white and yellow millet, and an eighth part each of groats, sunflower, hemp and fresh peanuts.

Although most species will remain in good condition on these mixtures for many years, variety is again important. Buckwheat, pine nuts, wheat and maize may all be used occasionally to vary the mixture supplied to the larger species, and all birds enjoy millet sprays. Parrot pellets, which are suitable for a range of species, are now available, and Brazil nuts and walnuts are especially appreciated by the large macaws. In addition, fresh green food such as chickweed, dandelion, lettuce and spinach should always be available for parrots, and raw carrot, sweet apple and other sound fruit should be offered each day.

As already mentioned, the birds will also benefit from a supply of fresh twigs and branches from which they can strip the buds and bark, and for this purpose all forms of fruit trees, prunus and hawthorn are suitable, provided that they have not been recently sprayed with chemicals. Never use laurel, yew or laburnum, which are poisonous.

It will be found that the consumption of green food and fruit will greatly increase when the birds are feeding their young, and at this time it is advisable also to offer rearing foods, such as a little bread and milk made with stale brown bread and fresh milk sweetened with sugar or honey. Care must be taken, however, to ensure that all such foods are removed before they become tainted or sour.

Some species also consume a quantity of insects, and a few mealworms may be offered daily and also fresh ant pupae when available. A clean, sharp grit containing minerals and charcoal, as well as cuttlefish bone should always be provided.

One word of warning: a pet parrot should not be given all kinds of scraps from the table. Sweet biscuits or small pieces of plain cake may be offered occasionally as a treat, but parrots should not have butter or other forms of fat nor salted nuts, which are likely to prove harmful.

If you wish to hand-rear young parrots or parakeets, specially formulated, commercially prepared foods are now available. In an emergency, the following mixture may be used: mix rusks, crushed and moistened with sufficient water to make the crumbs soft but not pappy, with an equal quantity of finely ground millet and canary seed from which the husks have been blown away, and add a few drops of cod-liver oil or vitamins C and D in liquid form.

Suitable foods for lories and lorikeets are mentioned in the entries dealing specially with these birds. Again, the advent of formulated pastes and powders has done much to remove the uncertainty of caring for these birds, and contributed to a great improvement in breeding results with them. Fruit must also be supplied for them every day, as well as green food. Special feeding requirements are discussed under the descriptions of individual species.

SOFTBILLS

The feeding of the insect- and fruit-eaters and the nectar-feeders presents rather more difficulty. Generally speaking, the former group is the hardest to cater for, because in the wild they may consume enormous numbers of many different kinds of insects each day. Such live insects as are available should be given regularly as a supplement, and in time, some birds may become sufficiently tame that they will feed from the hand. While it is possible to purchase supplies of certain kinds of live insects, it is not practicable to keep the birds on these alone since not only would such a diet not provide sufficient variety but it would be costly.

It is, therefore, necessary to use a food that is more readily obtainable and that contains all the elements essential to maintain the birds in good health and provide them with a properly balanced diet. Various proprietary brands of softbill foods are available, either in bulk or in smaller packets, and these are usually supplied in two or more different grades, modified to suit the special needs of the type of birds to be fed. For insectivorous birds, the best kinds contain a percentage of dried insects among their ingredients.

Some of these foods may be supplied to the birds without further preparation. Others need to be moistened, either with water or, occasionally, with carrot juice or finely grated raw carrot. The carrot is itself an excellent food, has a good vitamin content and greatly assists in maintaining the natural coloration of a bird's plumage.

For the sake of convenience, the fine-grade softbill foods that should be used for all small and more delicate species are often referred to as 'nightingale' food, and the coarser grade, which is suitable for the larger species such as the thrushes and starlings, as 'universal' food. Although some bird-keepers still prepare their own softbill foods, the vast majority now rely on prepared formulations. Recently imported birds or newly fledged young may not take readily to this type of diet, but sprinkling mealworms or other live foods on top should encourage them. In addition, more frugivorous birds will benefit from having softbill food sprinkled over their fruit. Otherwise, they may simply consume fruit and so receive an imbalanced diet.

Some softbills, notably the hummingbirds, sunbirds and sugarbirds, subsist mainly on pollen and nectar, which they extract from flowers, and on minute insects, although sugarbirds may also take a little fruit. Special nectar mixes are available for this group of birds, and fruit flies can be cultured as live food. Most of the insect- and fruit-eaters are also passionately fond of honey, and their needs may be supplied by the following mixture: one tablespoon honey; one tablespoon condensed milk; one tablespoon baby food. Six to eight tablespoonfuls of hot water should be added, and the mixture allowed to cool before being fed to the birds. It needs to be given in special sealed drinkers so that the birds are not tempted to bathe in the solution. These drinkers should be hung in the cage or aviary within easy reach of a perch, and care must be taken to ensure that the mixture is always fresh. Even in the winter the supply should be changed at least once during the day, and in warm weather it must be replaced more frequently.

This food is inclined to be rather fattening, and some bird-keepers prefer to replace the evening feed with a solution of pure honey made in the proportion of one spoonful of honey to three or four spoonfuls of water. The solution has the added advantage that it does not turn sour and will remain sufficiently fresh during the night for the birds to drink it with safety in the early hours of the following morning. Two or three times a week a little meat extract and a few drops of vitamins A and D should be added.

One special word of warning must be given: all food dishes and tubes used for feeding insectivorous foods and nectar must be kept scrupulously clean, and tubes should be scalded before every use. If the containers are allowed to become tainted with stale food, they will be a source of serious danger to the health of the birds. Another very important point is that all food and drinking water, whether on the ground or hung high up, should be placed in the shade. It will deteriorate much more rapidly if exposed to the sun.

Most bird–keepers will already have some knowledge of the essential part vitamins play in promoting healthy growth and maintaining good condition. More detailed information about their use is easily obtainable, and there are many special avian preparations available that contain various combinations of the most important vitamins. Only glass, plastic or china containers should be used as containers for vitamin solutions however; the chemicals may otherwise interact with metal of any kind.

Live food

The most difficult aspect of the diet to provide is live food, in the form of insects and other invertebrates. Mealworms are the least troublesome to obtain but, unfortunately, the hard chitin body casing of these larvae is not easily digested by all birds. In addition, they are so well liked that unless they are strictly rationed, the birds may well take too many and fall ill. As a guide, a bird should not have more than eight to ten at a time, and the small finches should never have more than one or two a day.

During the breeding season, mealworms should be cut up. Alternatively, they can be thrown into boiling water and used whole, because the water will have softened the chitin. Very young mealworms or those that are still white after casting their skin can be given as they are. These insects can be used at all stages of development, but the very young larvae are probably the best.

If mealworms are to be bred at home, prepare a box 2ft (60cm) by 20in (50cm) wide by 1ft (30cm) deep. Drill holes 1½in (4cm) in diameter along the sides and about 1in (2.5cm) from the bottom, and cover these on the inside with fine mesh mosquito gauze. This will admit air into the box when it has been filled up. At the bottom place a layer of chopped straw, adding sufficient to come just above the air holes. Place an old piece of woollen material on the straw and cover it with chicken meal to a depth of 1in (2.5cm). Lay another piece of woollen material over this, and another layer of food on top of that. Continue until there are four layers, then cover the whole surface with material. Place a piece of greased paper with cut apple to supply moisture on top.

If live meal beetles can be obtained, place as many as possible in the prepared box. The beetles lay eggs, which are invisible to the human eye, on the woollen material, and from these eggs come the worms that provide the food for the birds. These larvae develop into inert whitish, comma-shaped pupae and in time, change into dark beetles. The box must not be damp nor too cool, and the temperature should be kept even to speed up the growth process. The lid must fit well and be covered with mosquito netting. Nailing a piece of zinc around the top inside edge of the box will stop the beetles and worms from escaping between box and lid. Do not remove the worms every day, as this disturbs the brood. Take a large enough quantity once a week and change the apple at the same time.

Crickets are another excellent live food, and they are available in a variety of sizes from specialist suppliers. Tiny hatchlings are ideal for small finches, and special dusting powder is available to improve their nutritional value. Larger birds can be offered hoppers and adult locusts, while soft-bodied tebos and waxmoth larvae are very popular with many softbills.

The growth of suppliers of such invertebrates has meant that blowfly maggots are now rarely used for bird food. Although they were popular in the past, these maggots are potentially very hazardous, because they feed on putrid meat and can cause botulism in birds. This applies even if they are left to eat only bran for several days with the aim of removing any harmful toxins from their guts. In some cases, this does not prove effective, and the results can be devastating. Birds affected by botulism suffer paralysis and are likely to die.

Enchytraea, thin, white worms up to 1½in (4cm) long, are found in decaying wood and leaves. These are an ideal live food for small finches and are a very valuable rearing food. They can be cultured quite easily to ensure a regular supply. Whiteworms will multiply quickly if they are kept in a dark box with some leaf mould dampened with old leaves. They should be given a little oatmeal as food.

There has been much controversy about the advisability of feeding birds on earthworms. Large birds like them, but some bird-keepers refuse to use them. Earthworms that have been specially cultured and sold by specialist live food suppliers are to be recommended. Those that are dug up in the garden could infect the birds with parasitic worms such as gapeworm. The same applies to snails.

Daphnia are invaluable during the raising of the young. Avadavats and small foreign finches are very fond of them. Also known as water fleas, they can readily be caught in ponds, as can mosquito larvae. In fact, during the summer an enormous quantity of insects can be found in the country-side, and many are suitable for the birds.

All insect-eating birds are fond of aphids, which are found on plants such as elderberry and rose trees, bean plants, mock orange and nasturtium. Both the green and black species are eaten greedily. If branches covered with greenfly are hung in the cage or aviary, the birds will soon be seen carefully picking off all the insects. Never provide flies, mosquitoes or other insects that have been killed by chemicals.

Ants' cocoons, misnamed ants' eggs in the trade, are probably the most valuable form of live food obtainable, and they are especially useful for rearing young during the early stages, and all birds, both seed-eaters and insectivorous species, will take them readily, especially when fresh. They can be collected from ants' nests, preferably on warm, sunny days, when the ants will have moved the cocoons near to the top of the nest. Nests may frequently be found in old tree stumps, and quantities of cocoons will be concealed behind the bark on the sunny side of the stump. After removing the bark, the cocoons can easily be scraped into a tin. They may also be found underneath flat stones and other damp places. The hills made by the small meadow ants may be shovelled into a large biscuit tin, covered with a close-fitting lid and carried home to be tipped into the aviary where the birds will quickly sort out the cocoons.

The best supply will be obtained from the large nests constructed by wood ants. These ants are very beneficial to the woods in which they live and they should not be disturbed more than is absolutely necessary, nor should the whole nest be removed. It should be carefully opened, the required quantity of cocoons removed and then covered up again.

One of the best ways of collecting the cocoons is as follows. Spread a white sheet on the ground in the sun and place upsidedown flower-pots round the edge, slightly raising a side of the pots with a stone or piece of wood. Gather a pailful of the cocoons, ants and nest material and tip it in the centre of the sheet. The ants will immediately start to collect the exposed cocoons and carry them to the edge of the sheet, placing them in the shade under the flower-pots, leaving the debris from the nest in the centre of the sheet. When they have completed their task, the pots can be lifted and the cocoons scooped into a tin. The debris can then be returned to the nest. During the whole process, it is advisable to wear leather gloves because these ants bite viciously.

If the 'eggs' cannot be collected fresh each day, they may be kept for about a week if spread out on newspaper in a cool place. They are, however, only fit for use while they are a good white colour. Once they become blue or show signs of mildew they are no longer suitable as food for the birds. If you want to keep them a little longer, they can be sterilised by placing a layer about 1½in (4cm) thick in a saucepan, which should then be stood in a pan of boiling water and covered with a lid so that the steam can reach the cocoons. When the water has cooled, the cocoons should be spread out on card until they are thoroughly dry, and they will then keep for about a fortnight.

During the winter, it is impossible to obtain fresh ants' eggs, and the dried variety will have to suffice. It may happen that the birds will refuse to change from the fresh to the dried eggs or from the dried to the fresh ones, and so it is best to give dried eggs at all times, adding fresh eggs in the summer months.

It is possible to lay in a stock for the winter, and this is cheaper than buying. To do this, gather the cocoons, pick out the leaves, pine needles and so on and spread them out in a spot where there is no wind. When they have dried for a day in the open, fill some small preserving jars right up to the top, shaking down the cocoons. Do not add water. Place a rubber ring round the top and screw down the lid. Sterilise in the ordinary way, but maintain the temperature at 212°F (100°C) for a full hour. Allow to cool slowly.

When these eggs are used during the winter, the whole contents of the jar must be finished quickly, and kept in a refrigerator once the jar is open because when the air has got to the cocoons they soon deteriorate. If dried ants' cocoons are used in winter, they should be soaked in milk for a little while before being given to the birds; they will swell and can be mixed with the other food.

Fruit

A good variety of fruit should be included as part of the diet of many birds – not just softbills, but also parrots. One of the most widely used fruits is dessert apple, which can be supplied cut into chunks or diced into smaller pieces. Orange may be useful as well, if it is not too acidic. The fruit should be cut across, so that the birds can suck the juice and pick out the pith as well. An orange can be useful in helping to accustom the birds to insectivorous food. A section should be cut away from the fruity part and replaced with insectivorous food. The bird will suck the juice and the food will disappear quite readily. Ants' eggs and mealworms may also be placed on the orange.

Grapes are excellent for most birds, and ripe, sweet pears are usually greatly appreciated. Bananas cut up and, if desired, mixed with cubes of other fruit, can be served readily, but they should be given sparingly as they tend to fatten the birds. Canned fruit is also useful, as are dried fruits, such as sultanas, which should be soaked in water overnight and then rinsed thoroughly. Some birds like berries, which can be added to their regular food when available. All fruit should be washed thoroughly before it is given to the birds.

QUAIL, PIGEONS, DOVES, PHEASANTS AND WATERFOWL

Small doves and quail require a seed mixture containing 25 per cent canary seed; 25 per cent large white millet or yellow millet; 25 per cent Senegal millet and 10 per cent hemp, to which may be added 15 per cent groats or 5 per cent groats and 10 per cent dari. Whole or broken wheat, red and white dari and buckwheat in equal proportions should be added to the above mixture for larger species.

All quail are partly insectivorous, and in addition to the seed mixture, some live food such as mealworms, beetles, tebos and ants' cocoons must be provided. Some of the doves may also take a little live food from time to time. Pheasants will also eat a combination of seeds, invertebrates and greenstuff. During the early months of the year, extra hemp and groats can be provided, with additional maize when the weather is cold. All kinds of green food will be eaten, such as chickweed, Scotch kale and dandelions. Earthworms are eaten avidly.

Weed seeds and grated raw carrot are also beneficial, and because these birds do not shell the seed they must always have access to a supply of good sharp grit to help them grind and digest their food. Some species of pigeons live predominantly on fruits rather than seeds, however, and suitable diets for these are mentioned under the individual entries.

Wheat, coarse bran, maize meal and fish meal form the main ingredients of a good duck feed, and it should be offered in the proportion of 55 per cent, 15 per cent, and 15 per cent. Some bird-keepers add stale bread and scraps from the table. This mixture should be given well moistened, because ducks will have difficulty in picking up and eating dry food.

If the birds are fed in the open, the wheat may be given separately in a trough of water, which will prevent sparrows from stealing it. It is a great advantage if the ducks can have access to meadowland, where they will forage for slugs, snails, worms and insects of all kinds, as well as eating quantities of fresh, tender grass.

For those who prefer to buy ready-mixed foods, good proprietary pheasant and duck foods are available, and these offer a well-balanced diet. These mixes and pellets can be obtained from most corn merchants.

STARTING WITH STOCK

Birds that are established and have been kept by another bird-keeper and youngsters obtained from a breeder will be easier to manage than recently imported stock. If you are looking for a pet bird, it is important that you start out with a genuine young bird; and if you want a parrot, you should preferably find one that has been hand reared. Contact with breeders can be made through the various avicultural magazines, in which stock is usually advertised for sale. If you are starting out, try to buy locally. You may find that you have a specialist pet shop or even a bird farm in your area.

The best seasons for buying are spring and summer. Watch out for the following when you are selecting birds, especially recently imported ones. They should not sit with their feathers puffed up and their eyes closed; there should be no soiling on the plumage around the vent; there should be no damage to the legs; their eyes should be bright and clear; the bird should appear lively. The condition of the plumage is not of such importance, but birds which have completed the moult are preferable to those which are still moulting.

There is little difference in the appearance of the sexes of many species, and it often happens that two birds bought as a pair are really of one sex. Differences in the birds' behaviour should be apparent after they have settled down, and it should be a condition of purchase that one bird can be exchanged if they do not prove a true pair. It may sometimes be wise to take an extra pair and to change the surplus birds later on. Alternatively, the birds on offer may have been sexed surgically or chromosomally, so there should be no doubt about their gender. This applies mainly to larger birds such as parrots.

When the birds have been brought home safely, it is advisable to keep them in separate cages for the first few days. Try not to vary their diet from the one they are used to more than necessary. It is often a good idea to use a probiotic to minimise the stress of their move. Assuming that the birds remain in good condition, they can be transferred to their permanent home, after being treated with a suitable spray against lice and other external parasites. Deworming is also recommended.

If they are to be housed in an outside aviary, the season and the weather must be taken into account. In northern temperate climates most birds can safely be housed in the open between June and September; in the remaining cold months, they may need to be transferred indoors again. If they have come from an outside aviary, however, they can be placed in a similar enclosure without undue risk.

New arrivals should be placed inside the aviary shelter and left there for a day. Then they should be given freedom to fly about the shelter and investigate it, and after another few days the door to the outside aviary can be opened. They will by now be used to the feeding places and not come to any harm.

MIXED COLLECTIONS

It is impossible to state exactly which species of birds can be kept together in an aviary; there are too many species and too many possible combinations.

In addition, the size of the aviary has an important bearing on the selection of species that may be safely associated with each other. Birds are always less tolerant in a small aviary than in a large flight. Those that always quarrel in a small aviary may live in perfect peace and harmony in a large space because they are then able to secure their own territory without interference from other aviary occupants.

Usually the following rules may be applied:

- Birds with which it is intended to breed are best kept in breeding pens or in separate aviaries on their own.
- Pairs of birds of similar species usually do not tolerate one another unless they are colony breeders, and even then there may be quarrelling unless the aviary is very large. Hens or cocks of related species will live in peace together, but as soon as a bird of the opposite sex appears there is likely to be a disturbance and even fighting.
- Birds of similar size and habits may be kept together; for instance, a collection of seed-eaters or a number of insect-eaters, as long as they are of different species, can probably be kept together.
- Insect-eating and large omnivorous birds can be kept together only if they are of similar size and temperament.

It must always be remembered that the characters of individual birds frequently differ, and therefore, when you are building up an aviary collection, much will depend on observation. The introduction of a new bird into an existing community can lead to great difficulties and trouble because the established 'pecking order' of the birds may be instantly disturbed by a single 'intruder'. A less dominant species should be introduced into the aviary first, so that it can explore every nook and cranny and find where it can hide safely.

The bird-keeper can also do much to prevent subsequent disruptions in a mixed aviary. The feeding place can be a source of discord, and if several feeding sites are provided, this cause of trouble may be removed. A shortage of nesting and roosting sites can also cause unrest and fighting. The provision of plenty of perches and nestboxes will help to prevent bickering. The nestboxes should not be close together but well distributed about the aviary. Remember, too, that aggression is always most likely at the start of the breeding season.

Below are several lists of species that may, as a rule, be safely kept together. Obviously the number to be kept will depend on the size of the cage or aviary available. The fewer pairs that are together, the greater will be the chance of successful breeding:

- Cordon Bleu; Tiger Finch; Firefinch; Red-eared Waxbill; Lavender Finch; Golden-breasted Waxbill; African Silverbill; Indian Silverbill; Common Spice Finch; Three-coloured Mannikin; Bengalese; Zebra Finch; Green Avadavat; Green Singing Finch; Indian White Eye; Blue-breasted Quail.
- Bronze Mannikin; Long-tailed Grassfinch; Cherry Finch; Red-headed Finch; Diamond Sparrow; Zebra Finch; Bengalese; Lavender Finch; Olive Finch; Grey Singing Finch; Diamond Dove.
- Gouldian Finch; Rufous-tailed Grassfinch; Parson Finch; Long-tailed Grassfinch; Zebra Finch; Bengalese; Blue-breasted Quail.
- Budgerigars; Bourke's Parakeet; Cockatiel; Californian Quail; Weavers; Zebra Finch.
- Whydahs; Weavers; Cut-throats; Cardinals; Java Sparrow; Diamond Dove; Californian Quail.
- Indigo Bunting; Rainbow Bunting; Pileated and Red-crested Finches; Common Saffron Finch; Golden Sparrow; Canaries; Java Sparrow; Weavers; Pekin Robin.
- Pekin Robin; Bourke's Parakeet; Cockatiel; Shama; Glossy Starling; Tanagers; Green Cardinal; Whydahs; Bulbuls; Golden-fronted Fruit-suckers; Mynahs (not Hill Mynahs); Virginian Cardinal; Common Hangnest.
- Weavers; Whydahs; Senegal Combassou; Cut-throats; Long-tailed Grassfinch; Masked Grassfinch.

BREEDING IN AVICULTURE

In the descriptions of the individual species, detailed information is given about specific breeding habits. This chapter is concerned with some more general observations on breeding.

Most beginners often start with an aviary primarily designed to accommodate a mixed collection of brightly coloured or singing birds. If this is the case, males only will normally be kept, since they are more peaceful and sing better when no females are present, provided that not more than one of a kind is included in the collection. Sooner or later, however, most bird-keepers want to try their hand at breeding, and although difficulties will most certainly arise, success is now more likely to be achieved than at any time in the past. Some kinds of birds will nest very readily if pairs are obtained, and both Bengalese and Zebra Finches are recommended for this purpose, as are Cockatiels and Budgerigars.

Bengalese Finches will also be of value as foster parents, if more foreign finches are kept. Once the beginner has become accustomed to the treatment of the Bengalese and Zebra Finches and has succeeded in getting them to breed and to raise their young, these birds can be given eggs from other species to hatch. Another suitable species is the Silverbill, but this is not so easy to handle as the Bengalese. Nor should the Canary be forgotten; if simple rules are observed, this bird is not difficult to breed.

One pair of birds will breed undisturbed in a cage or aviary, but as soon as more pairs of the same species are housed together they may quarrel about nesting material and nestboxes. Even so, it is possible to house a number of finches in breeding groups, and success may even be more likely under these surroundings than if they are housed in individual pairs.

Most of the birds from which it is best to start breeding belong to species that are effectively domesticated – many of the Australian finches, for example – yet still retain a strong natural instinct to select secluded spots for their nests. The Canary is probably the one exception to this rule: wherever the nestpan is placed, there the Canary will lay and hatch her eggs.

It should be remembered that in their natural state most birds choose well-concealed nesting sites, and the instinct to do so will persist however tame they may have become and no matter how long they have been kept in a cage or aviary. No birds can breed successfully if they are in an all-wire cage set in the centre of a room through which people are continually passing. As has already been emphasised, breeding in a box-type cage is preferable because the birds can always find seclusion there.

A first essential is that the birds have a quiet corner where they will feel secure. The open aviary, therefore, needs planting. Nesting boxes should be hung at varying heights along the back wall, which should preferably be enclosed, and, if possible the boxes should be partly concealed with bunches of heather or fir branches. If the shelter is sufficiently light, nestboxes may be hung there as well, and many birds prefer that situation. There must, however, be a lean-to or some sort of cover above the nesting boxes so that rain cannot cause damage. As a general rule, each pair of birds should have the choice of two nests. This prevents quarrels.

During the breeding season, no change in the arrangement of the aviary can be made. Branches and twigs that cover the nests should be left undisturbed; even when they fade and die, no new ones must be added as they would cause the birds to abandon the nest even if it contained eggs or a brood.

The outside aviary should not be raked over every weekend to show a 'tidy' birds' home to admiring friends. What is needed is not an immaculate garden but a home entirely dedicated to the wants of the birds. It is much better to let the spilled seed germinate and grow and to let weeds flourish. The birds are fond of weeds, and all kinds of insects will be attracted to them and they are, in turn, good for the birds. A little grass and weed seed might even be sown in a corner of the aviary where the rain could reach it, this should be allowed to grow and seed as much as the birds will permit. Experience has shown that if chickweed and other weeds are growing in an aviary shrubs will stand a good chance of remaining undamaged.

In a birdroom, a breeding cage should not be too small. Special types are available for Canaries. When the young are fully grown and independent, they should, of course, be removed to other accommodation. In general, do not breed from birds younger than eight months. If this rule is not observed the results will prove disappointing; the hens are more likely to succumb to egg-binding, while infertility is a problem associated with young cock birds.

Birds cannot be forced to pair, and a cock and hen selected by the fancier may not always prove to be a suitable choice of mates. If no inclination to mating is observed, a change of male may sometimes have the desired effect, and this applies particularly with the larger parrots. Although two birds may appear to be happily mated, the pair may simply show no desire to nest.

Appearances are no guide to physical defects, and until a good pair has been selected by trial and error the results may be disappointing. Many species show no obvious differences between the sexes, and both may sometimes seem to be laying. They will often sit close together, behave as a true pair and yet eventually prove to be of the same sex. The only clear indication may be the behaviour of the male towards the female. If the 'male' does not display himself, dance or hop about with straws or grasses in his beak, it is doubtful whether a pair has been found. Sometimes the song of the male (as in the case of the Bengalese) will be a pointer, but the use of surgical sexing, carried out by a veterinarian, will confirm the gender of larger birds. Chromosomal sexing, which can be carried out in a laboratory from a feather sample, is now being used increasingly as an alternative, but it is rather too expensive for use with smaller birds, and you will be better off purchasing several birds with a view to obtaining at least one pair.

FEEDING

It is obvious that the food given to the parent birds while they are rearing their brood is vitally important to the young in the nest. The chicks grow very rapidly, with some fledging when only 12 days old. Inappropriate feeding may also be responsible for the failure of pairs to nest in the first instance, and the later death of an embryo can often be traced to an incomplete diet of the parent birds.

Most finches, which, for the sake of simplicity, are known as seed-eaters, live for a great part of the year almost exclusively on seeds. During the breeding season, however, they need a far more varied and nutritious diet. In the wild they satisfy this need by changing their feeding habits and becoming largely insectivorous. In the early stages, their young are also fed mainly on insects, and if the supply is inadequate, the chicks will not be reared successfully. The least the bird-keeper can do is to supply both small nutritious live foods, such as whiteworm, and a rearing food. The rearing food sold in packets for Canaries is suitable for many species of foreign birds, and if there is plenty of undergrowth in the aviary, the birds will find further small insects and larvae.

Germinated sprays of millet and other soaked seeds have a higher protein and vitamin value, as well as being more easily digestible by young birds. Ideal, too, are the many grasses that are just seeding and can readily be gathered by the wayside. Seed can be sown easily and grown in flower-pots, and when it starts to grow, it can be placed, pot and all, in the aviary. In a short time the birds will have fed wisely and well on it, as will be shown by their improved condition.

If nestlings have to be placed with foster parents because their own parents refuse to feed them or abandon them after a few days, the foster birds should be chosen from species that rear their own young with similar rearing food. They should also have young at a similar stage of development, because they may otherwise ignore the youngsters.

Hand-rearing parrots and other chicks is very demanding, because the young birds will generally need regular feeding around the clock, with perhaps a four hour gap between 2 o'clock and 6 o'clock in the morning. Special diets that are mixed with water can be obtained, which makes the task a little easier. The chicks themselves will need to be kept warm in a brooder, starting at a temperature close to 99°F (37.2°C). This can gradually be reduced as they grow older and feather up. Detailed information on hand-rearing parrots and other birds can be found in titles listed in the bibliography at the end of this book.

PHEASANTS

Young pheasants, quail and waterfowl do not require hand-rearing because they hatch in a relatively advanced state of development. Even so, they do need parental care if they are to thrive, and chilling is a major potential cause of mortality among young birds.

Most pheasants will commence laying towards the end of April and sometimes continue until the end of July in the northern hemisphere. Various methods of hatching and rearing can be adopted. Some species hatch and rear their own young very well – for instance, many Golden and the Lady Amherst's Pheasants do very well – and this is obviously preferable. However, the use of bantams, especially Wyandottes and Silkies, as foster parents is widespread, and the results in such cases are usually excellent. Where there is doubt about a pheasant's parenting skills, the first batch of eggs is often hatched under a bantam, while the second clutch may be left to the pheasant hen herself to hatch and rear. When she starts to incubate, other hens should be removed to another run as also should the cock if he tries to disturb the sitting hen.

When a bantam hen is used, she should be set by herself with 10 eggs in a box without an artificial floor. A hollow should be made in the sand and lined with straw, which should be sprinkled with insect powder, and the eggs placed in this artificial nest. The bantam should not have feathered legs because the feathers tend to get under the eggs or small chicks and lift them from the nest when she moves. As long as the bantam leaves the nest regularly to eat and perform her natural functions and returns without undue delay, all should be well. The run should be covered with sand and some sieved ashes so that she can take her daily dustbath.

Hatching in an incubator is quite a different matter. Several efficient and inexpensive machines, in which 50–60 eggs can be hatched in one batch, are available, and smaller machines, which have found favour with parrot-breeders in recent years, can also be bought. Many quail, partridges and pheasants are hatched annually in incubators. Several points require special attention, the chief of which is maintaining the correct relative humidity (58 per cent) and a temperature of 102°F (39°C). A great deal depends on the care of the eggs; they need to be turned at least twice a day, preferably by means of an automatic turning device incorporated into the incubator. The eggs should be set in the machine with the thick end upwards. After about a fortnight the embryo chick will turn itself lengthways so that its head is to the air chamber at the highest point.

It is advisable to place only evenly sized, clean eggs in the incubator. Even if the eggs have been incubated by a bantam hen, it may be just as well to take them away from her the day before they are due to hatch and set them in the incubator, because some bantams are apt to lead the first two or three chicks to hatch away from the nest and the remaining eggs become chilled before the young birds can emerge. The young can be returned to the hen the day after they have left the eggs. Prior to this the relative humidity in the incubator should be raised significantly to help the chicks break out of the eggs.

After the chicks have appeared, extra care is necessary for a while. The bantam should have an enclosed run, which should be moved on to fresh grass every day and entirely covered by plastic during bad weather. Young pheasants cannot stand damp. If possible, it is still better to have a run of two compartments divided by a sliding door, and with one compartment permanently covered with some waterproof material which nevertheless admits full light. During wet weather, the chicks can be confined to the covered compartment and on fine days allowed the freedom of the whole run.

If the young have been hatched in an incubator and no bantams are available to act as foster mothers, a brooder will be needed. The young must remain inside for the first few weeks, and allowed to go into an open run during the day if the weather is fine and sunny. An infrared lamp will be valuable at this stage to keep them warm, and a reflector attachment will direct the warmth down to the chicks.

A good quality commercial pheasant- or turkey-rearing food should be used, together with ants' eggs, mealworms, canary seed and possibly even a canary-rearing food. Chick crumbs, in which all the necessary foodstuffs have been incorporated, are the easiest to use. Do not forget to provide charcoal and fine grit along with a shallow, enclosed drinker of water. After a few days, finely chopped chickweed and other green food should be added to the rearing food.

With a little care, rearing under the foster mother presents few problems. If the young pheasants run about freely with the bantam, their wings must be clipped or they will start to roost high up in the trees at an early age and may be completely lost. When they reach the stage of wanting to roost on their own, they must be caught and put in the aviary.

WATERFOWL

Most species of waterfowl will breed in confinement. Boxes covered with branches of trees or bunches of twigs and heather should be placed on the ground, and a layer of straw should be put inside each box. The ducks will soon find the boxes. When laying commences, a daily check should be made and the eggs collected and replaced by nest eggs until the whole clutch is complete.

When the duck starts covering the eggs with down, good results may be anticipated, and the eggs can be replaced in the nest so that the duck can start incubating. When the ducklings have hatched, the mother and her young should be placed in a small run with a little pond. Boiled and mashed potatoes, bran, maize meal and some barley meal make excellent duck food, and they should be supplemented with charcoal, grit and lime. The addition of some fish meal is also often recommended.

Ornamental waterfowl are traditionally pinioned at this early stage by clipping off the tip of one wing with sharp scissors, to prevent them flying away when they are older. Carried out soon after hatching, this procedure causes no obvious distress to the duckling, but you must always seek veterinary advice or the help of an experienced breeder if you have not pinioned a duckling before. Newly bought ducks must be inspected carefully before they are let loose to see if they are healthy and have been pinioned. This is particularly important if they are to swim about in a large pond where it will not be easy to retrieve them. It is, however, advisable to set a trap cage, in which the ducks should be regularly fed, and catching will then present no difficulty. All that is needed is to scatter the food and wait quietly until they have entered the cage.

Apart from allowing the duck to hatch her own eggs, there are various alternative methods of rearing the young. The eggs can be hatched by a broody bantam. If this method is employed, the one problem is ensuring that the ducklings have enough oil on their down to make it waterproof, because a hen cannot cover them with enough natural oil before they enter the water, whereas a duck will carefully grease her young before going on to the water with them.

The hen should be housed in a roomy run with the ducklings, in such a way that the chicks can get into a second compartment where their rearing food is placed. This second compartment should be separated from the first by a wide meshed partition; the ducklings can easily slip through this but the hen cannot follow and eat their special food. The run should be movable and placed on a fresh piece of turf every day.

BIRD HEALTH

Birds, like other pets, are liable to sickness, but their treatment is much more difficult. It is not usually easy to diagnose the ailment, and even an experienced veterinarian is likely to rely to some extent on laboratory testing for this purpose.

A sick bird can usually be noticed without difficulty; it will fluff out its feathers and appear rather depressed. It may show laboured breathing or droop its wings, and it frequently sleeps with both feet on the perch, which a healthy bird rarely does.

The first consideration with a sick bird is to move it to a warmer environment, which will improve its chances of recovery. Hospital cages can be used for smaller species; alternatively, a dull-emitter infrared lamp suspended over a cage will be equally beneficial. This emits heat without light and so will be less disturbing than an ordinary light bulb, which switches itself on and off to maintain the required level of warmth. Seek veterinary advice without delay, because the sooner that treatment begins, the greater will be the likelihood of recovery, which may often be assisted by the judicious use of antibiotics.

Parasitic problems can also be a cause of concern for bird-keepers, and it is often advisable to treat all new stock as appropriate. Some parasites are easier to detect than others, with perhaps the most widespread but elusive being red mite. These mites, which are almost invisible to the naked eye, are difficult to identify because they do not actually live on the bird but in its environment. They emerge from crevices after dark to feed on the bird's blood, which gives them their characteristic coloration.

Second-hand cages can represent a particular danger of introducing these parasites to a bird room. They must be washed thoroughly in a special mite-killing preparation produced for use with birds. As an added precaution, the bird room should be stripped down and washed out at the end of the breeding season. These mites are very resilient and can overwinter in cages without feeding. Under favourable conditions they can reproduce very quickly. Because of their feeding habits, red mites may cause anaemia and even the death of young chicks, as well as triggering feather-plucking in older birds by the irritation they cause.

All new purchases should be sprayed with a special aerosol intended for use on birds that kill mites and also lice, which can cause problems too. These particular parasites spend their entire life-cycle on the bird, and so are much easier to control than red mite by this means. Lice may also cause feather irritation, and some actually eat the feathers, creating a rough appearance.

A more obvious parasitic problem is scaly-leg, which is caused by *Cnemidocoptes* mites. This can be a particular problem in Budgerigars, and the mites are spread by direct contact. In time, they result in coral-like growths on the head, around and on the beak, as well as sometimes affecting the legs. A proprietary remedy available from a pet shop will resolve this problem without difficulty. If a beak is badly affected, however, permanent distortion may result and regular clipping back may be required for the rest of the bird's life.

Internal parasites usually present more of a problem because they are less conspicuous. Air-sac mites, which are typically encountered in Gouldian Finches, can result in respiratory difficulties. Affected birds may wheeze badly after a period of exercise. The new group of drugs to combat parasitic infections, known as ivermectins, will prove valuable in such cases, and because they are absorbed through the skin, they are easy to administer.

Parasitic roundworms are particularly associated with Australian parakeets and lovebirds. The parasitic worm eggs are passed out in their droppings, and after a short period in the environment will become infectious. Literally thousands of the microscopic eggs can accumulate in the aviary over a period of time and will remain viable for years. In addition to treating the birds, therefore, the aviary itself must also be thoroughly cleaned to minimise the risk of the birds becoming re-infected.

Tapeworms are perhaps less of a hazard because they cannot be spread directly. Their life-cycle depends on an intermediate host, which is usually an invertebrate such as a beetle. Only when a bird eats the invertebrate is the risk of a tapeworm infection realised. Some birds are, for dietary reasons, much more vulnerable to tapeworms than others.

Advice on dealing with such problems can be obtained from a veterinarian. Testing the droppings by means of a faecal sample to ascertain whether a bird is infected with parasitic worms is possible. Some birds are more vulnerable to particular types of worm than others. Gapeworm (*Syngamus*), for example, is most often encountered in pheasants and starlings. Effective treatment can usually be given, provided that the problem is recognised at an early stage and the stress of handling is kept to a minimum.

Protozoal parasites are also a particular problem associated with gallinaceous birds, such as pheasants. Weight loss and blood in the faeces, often coupled with widespread mortality, are typical signs affecting young birds, although older individuals may develop some immunity. Sulpha-based drugs are typically used for treatment and preventative purposes against coccidosis and diseases of this type.

Newly acquired or moulting birds are probably most vulnerable to illness. Once they are established in their quarters, the vast majority of birds will remain in good health for many years. A regular daily check should be made on the birds to ensure that they all appear healthy. Recognising the signs of illness at an early stage will dramatically increase the likelihood of a successful cure, as treatment can begin at an early stage.

On occasions birds may need to be caught if their claws become overgrown. This applies especially to weavers and mannikins, which are prone to this problem. Clipping must be carried out in a good light. The overgrown tip should be cut off with a sharp pair of scissors, without touching the blood vessel, which will be visible as a thick pinkish-red streak, extending from the base of the nail. Otherwise, bleeding will result.

SPECIES DESCRIPTIONS

The most popular and widely kept foreign birds are described in the following pages, and detailed discussions of over 400 species are given here.

The accompanying measurements all refer to the birds' approximate length; where only one size is shown, this is the typical size for both cock and hen. Descriptions of their coloration are also indicated, together with the means of distinguishing between the sexes on the basis of differences in their plumage and other characteristics where appropriate. But it is not always easy to describe the colouring and markings of a bird's plumage accurately, especially as in some cases there may be regional variations between individuals, and this needs to be borne in mind.

The diagram below is included as a visual guide to the parts of a bird's body. In the descriptions of the individual species, a clear indication of the area of plumage referred to – the rump or nape, for example – can then be obtained here if in doubt. The wings present a particular difficulty because they can be inspected either spread or when folded, which may obscure the coloration of certain feathers. As a result, this diagram shows the areas

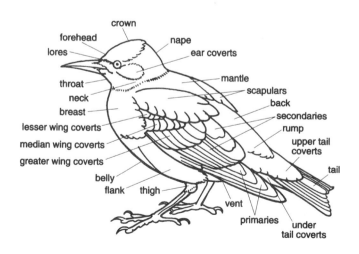

covered by the various types of wing feathers, and how they appear when the wing is folded.

The wings of different species of birds may differ in shape, but the distribution of feathers is always the same. A description of wing markings and their coloration, including those on the various coverts, will be simplified by this illustration. It also indicates the areas of feather tracts elsewhere on the body, with their appropriate names.

QUAIL, PARTRIDGES AND PHEASANTS

Scaled Quail (Blue Quail) *Callipepla squamata*

Origin: *Mexico and southwestern USA*

Cock: *10in (25cm) Forehead and sides of head grey; ear coverts brown; elongated crown feathers brown with white tips; chin and throat yellow; neck, mantle, breast and sides light grey with black margins to the feathers, creating an impression of scales. Towards the breast the ground colour becomes beige; markings on underparts are brown and angular. Upperparts and wings grey-brown. Tail grey with narrow white margins along the outermost feathers. Iris brownish-black; beak horn-coloured; legs and feet horn-coloured.*

Hen: *Recognisable by buff-coloured crest and darker feathering in the vicinity of the throat.*

These quail spend much of the day perching among the branches in their quarters, but at night they may prefer to seek a roosting spot on the aviary floor under thick cover. Once they are established in their quarters they settle down and will spend more time on the ground, searching for seeds and insects, dust-bathing and sometimes even lying in the sun. Keep a close watch for external parasites on these and other quail. Feather lice may damage the plumage, creating a ragged appearance, while mites are likely to cause feather irritation, resulting in excessive preening. Provided they are kept in clean surroundings that have not previously been occupied by poultry, the risk of such problems is dramatically reduced.

The aviary should be well planted with thick, low-growing shrubs to provide suitable nesting conditions. There should also be a patch of dry, sandy soil where the quail can dust-bathe.

Oats, hemp, millet, canary seed and maw should be provided as a basic diet. This can be supplemented with soaked seed, softbill food, mealworms, egg food and chopped green food to provide additional variety in the diet; do not forget to provide grit and cuttlefish bone.

Their general care is similar to that outlined for the Californian Quail. Hens typically lay a clutch of 10–12 eggs, usually in a slight hollow scratched in the ground under a shrub or concealed in thick grass. On occasions both parents will share the incubation duties, with the cock also brooding the young chicks. The hatching quail must be kept dry as they are very susceptible to chilling in damp conditions, possibly because the species originates from a rather arid part of the world.

The eggs may also be successfully hatched in an incubator, and a foster mother can then be used to rear the chicks or they can be reared on their own. Invertebrates with soft bodies, such as white, moulting mealworms, and egg food are particularly valuable at this stage. A shallow saucer of water should also be provided. It is advisable to place a layer of small, clean pebbles in the bottom of the dish to give the young birds a footing so that they cannot become saturated and drown.

Californian Quail *Callipepla californica (Lophortyx californica)*

Origin: *west coast of USA from Oregon to southern California*

Cock: 10in (25cm) Forehead buff-white; crown black, fading to chestnut; nape and mantle grey, marked with white and the feathers edged with black; eyebrow stripe white; throat, ear coverts and foreneck black outlined with white. Long, forward-pointing curved black crest of club-like feathers. Back brown. Tail coverts olive-brown; tail dull brown. Breast slate grey, remainder of underparts buff, toning to chestnut in the centre, each feather distinctly outlined with black. Iris hazel; beak black; legs and feet blackish.

Hen: Has a short brown crest and lacks the black and white pattern on the head, which is dull grey-brown.

These pugnacious birds can be safely associated only with large birds; they should not be housed with other quails. Cocks will also be highly aggressive towards each other. A large, well-planted aviary with low-growing shrubs is recommended. They will usually choose a roosting place high among the branches under the covered part of the flight. Housed in this way, they can remain in the aviary both summer and winter as they are quite hardy, although they should not be encouraged to roost without cover for fear of frost-bite. Dry roosting quarters are also important, because these quails can be sensitive to damp.

They are generally undemanding. A mixture of seeds, including some crushed maize and groats, as well as canary seed and millet, will suit them well. They will also take various invertebrates, including mealworms, as well as soft food and green food, such as chickweed.

Breeding in aviary surroundings is likely to be successful only if the birds are not disturbed. Housed in a flight planted with grass, clumps of heather and low-growing shrubs, with dry, sandy areas hidden here, the hen is likely to make a shallow scrape in the ground, where she may lay as many as 14 eggs. She will sit alone, with the incubation period lasting about three weeks. If the hen shows no interest in sitting on her eggs, it is possible to hatch them successfully in an incubator.

An ideal rearing mixture can be made up using soft food, including hard-boiled egg. Greenstuff and small, easily digestible invertebrates should also be available, along with soaked millet sprays. Sand, grit and cuttlefish bone must always be available and within reach of the birds on the ground. It is a good idea to remove chicks once the hen starts to lose interest in them because they may be attacked if the adults decide to breed again. They can rear two broods in a season.

Bobwhite Quail

(Virginian Quail, Common Bobwhite) *Colinus virginianus*

Origin: *USA and Mexico*

Cock: 9in (23cm) Forehead black; primaries black spotted with brown. Neck feathers white with black and brown spots. A black band runs from the eyes to the ear coverts; throat white as is the remainder of the head. Back brown, with black cross bands; remainder of upperparts olive-grey with rust coloured spots. Red-brown breast, merging into white on the belly with black markings. Feathers of undertail coverts have a black spot on a light brown ground. Iris brown; beak dark horn-coloured; legs and feet blue-grey.

Hen: Has smaller markings on the head and the spots, which are white on the head of the cock, are browny-white in the case of hens.

The Bobwhite is a very popular species in aviculture, and many are bred each year; as a result stocks are readily obtainable. They are quite hardy and can be kept outdoors in an aviary throughout the year. A spacious aviary is recommended, partly because in a relatively small area they can be disruptive to other aviary occupants as they will readily perch, especially if frightened.

In addition to various seeds, which form the basis of their diet, Bobwhite Quail will also eat berries, green food and invertebrates.

Breeding can start early in the year. The hen makes a scrape in the sand and lines this with grass and leaves. A typical clutch of 12–16 eggs will hatch after a period of 23 days, with both parents sharing in the care and rearing of the resulting chicks. Suitable rearing foods as suggested for the Californian Quail should be available. These are reasonably long-lived birds in aviary surroundings, with a possible lifespan of eight years or more.

1 Chinese Painted Quail (Blue-breasted Quail, King Quail)

Excalfactoria chinensis (Coturnix chinensis)

Origin: *Indian subcontinent, Indonesia, north Australia and the Philippines*

Cock: 5in (13cm) Upperparts brown mottled with black, and with a blackish forehead. Cheeks white, outlined by a black line extending from the beak, below the eyes and joining the black throat. Broad white crescent below black throat, extending backwards to base of the ear coverts, bordered with black. Chest and flanks blue-grey; breast and belly deep chestnut. Iris hazel; beak blackish; legs and feet yellow; claws black.

Hen: Lacks the black and white markings of the head and upper breast, and also the blue-grey of the chest and flanks and the chestnut breast. Dull brown overall, mottled on the upperparts and paler on the breast.

The smallest of the quail, these birds are very popular because, unlike their larger relatives, they will nearly always remain on the floor of their quarters and so will not prove a disturbance in an aviary. In fact, they are ideal companions for finches, as they will eat millet and other small seeds spilt on the floor. Even so, they must be provided with their own food supply, preferably in a special quail feeder, which should prevent them from scattering the seed widely in search of favoured items in a mixture.

When housed in a flight, these quail should be given adequate cover, which will also encourage breeding. In spite of their small size, male Chinese Painted Quail can prove very aggressive and should be kept apart from each other. Unfortunately, a cock can also prove difficult in the company of a hen, persecuting her relentlessly. He may peck at her, pulling out feathers and even cause bleeding, typically on the back. For breeding purposes, therefore, it is better to keep these quails in groups of three, composed of a cock and two hens, since this will deflect the interests of the cock from just a single partner. In severe cases, you may need to separate the pair, reintroducing the cock at a later date.

In most cases today, the hen simply lays her eggs and then ignores them, so they will need to be hatched artificially. It is thought that incubator hatching over many generations has led to a loss of the birds' parenting instincts, but it may also be because they feel insecure in their quarters. A densely planted flight can be helpful for this reason.

If the hen does decide to incubate the eggs, she sits alone, with the cock remaining in the vicinity of the nest but taking no part in this process. After 16 days the young quail should hatch and will follow their mother around almost immediately. They are tiny at this stage – barely larger than a bumble bee – and can slip through the smallest gap, so you will need to check the base of the aviary to see there are no holes here. Soft foods, aphids, soaked millet sprays and starter crumbs can all be offered at this stage. A very shallow saucer of water, lined with clean pebbles to prevent the birds from becoming saturated, should also be provided.

The cock bird may be somewhat resentful of his family, and should he show signs of aggression at this stage, he is best removed from the aviary. The chicks should be fully independent by the time they are four weeks old, and they must be separated from their parents, who may then nest again. In recent years, various colour mutations of this species have been developed, with the silver form being most common at present. Cocks retain their reddish markings, although these are paler than in the normal form, so that sexing these birds is equally straightforward.

Chinese Painted Quail can be kept in an outdoor aviary throughout the year, but they must have access to a dry shelter, and adequate cover must also be provided in the flight. A bolthole, sited at ground level, will enable them to move back and forth without difficulty. If the weather turns particularly bad, it is sensible to confine the quail indoors for a period, especially if the floor becomes very wet and muddy.

Common Quail *Coturnix coturnix*

Origin: *Europe, Asia, parts of Africa*

Cock: 7in (18cm) Head warm buff with two dark brown lines running from beak to the nape and with prominent whitish eyebrow stripes, plus short, dark moustache marks; cheeks warm brown and throat pale buff, both outlined with dark brown stripe from ear coverts, meeting under the chin where it forms a black patch. Upperparts dark brown striated with buff and faintly mottled with black; breast and flanks reddish-brown flecked with black and striated on the flanks with prominent whitish markings; belly white or very pale buff. Tail brown, very short and almost completely concealed by the hairlike feathers of the rump. Iris brown; beak yellow; legs and feet pale yellow.

Hen: Slightly larger than cock; less distinctly marked and lacking the dark band and patch on the throat.

Although they are not especially popular in aviculture because of their rather nervous natures, these quail are quite easy to maintain. Their aviary roof should, however, have a false roof, made of nylon netting to prevent them from injuring their heads. They are inclined to fly straight upwards and may suffer a fatal injury if they collide with the unprotected mesh. Common Quail may also be active after dark, and this can prove upsetting for other types of bird sharing their accommodation.

If there is plenty of cover in their aviary, a pair will usually attempt to nest, with a simple scrape concealed in a tussock of grass often providing the basis of the nest. Around 10 eggs may be laid, and they should hatch after an incubation period of 18 days. A typical diet as recommended for other quail suits them well, and, again, they should be fed on the ground under cover.

A close relative of the Common Quail, the Japanese Quail (*Coturnix japonica*) is likely to prove much steadier in aviary surroundings. This species has been domesticated in Japan for centuries, and it is now valued both as a table bird and for laying purposes. They are known under a variety of general names, including Pharaoh Quail and Coturnix Laying Quail, while specific strains also have their own names, such as the Tuxedo, which is a pied variant with white underparts.

Rain Quail (Black-breasted Quail) *Corturnix coromandelica*

Origin: *Indian subcontinent*

Cock: 6in (15cm) Resembles Common Quail but has more distinctive black markings on the throat and neck. There is a large black spot in the centre of the breast, while the sides of the head are black with white margins. Wings brown. Iris brown; beak horn-coloured; legs and feet flesh-coloured.

Hen: Lacks spot on breast and the black markings on the throat, which is otherwise white.

This species used to be available in the past and was occasionally imported, but it has now become quite scarce. The birds are only slightly larger than the Chinese Painted Quail and require similar care. Rain Quail will live quite happily in the company of other birds, with pairs being housed on their own. At first they may be nervous when transferred to new surroundings, but they will soon settle and in time can become quite tame. Hens in particular may, with patience, be persuaded to take mealworms from the hand, but, as with partridges, cock birds tend to remain more aloof.

They will eat a wide range of seeds, such as various kinds of millet, maw, canary seed and rape, and they can sometimes be persuaded to sample softbill food as well. Green food, particularly chickweed, is often eaten with relish, and they will also forage for all sorts of invertebrates, such as spiders and aphids. The cock will often catch items of this type, and give them to his mate.

Breeding results are most likely to be obtained in a small outside aviary, the floor of which should largely be covered with a thick layer of river sand. There should also be a dense area of undergrowth, preferably under cover, which offers a secluded nesting site. Here the hen will lay 6–10 eggs in a small hollow, lined with fine grasses, incubating them alone for 17 days until they hatch.

If the cock bird starts pecking at the youngsters, which may sometimes happen when his mating instinct becomes too strong, he will need to be removed from the aviary. Normally, everything goes quite well, and both adult birds will be seen with the chicks searching for food, which should be left on the ground and in food bowls to encourage the young quail to eat by themselves.

Cleanliness is very important at this stage, because stale soft food may trigger enteritis. Fresh food is required twice daily while the chicks are young, and a feeding tray of some sort may be useful, because this can simply be removed and washed. A little maw seed sprinkled on the soft food will encourage them to acquire a taste for seed. Avoid feeding mealworms, which are too large for the chicks to swallow without difficulty and which are also likely to be relatively indigestible because of their chitinous body casing.

If necessary, the eggs of Rain Quail can be hatched quite successfully in an incubator. This is a better option than using a bantam, which is really too large for these tiny chicks and may tread on them, with fatal results. Although relatively hardy, these quail should have access to a dry shelter, and they will benefit from being kept in frost-proof accommodation over the winter, where there will be no risk of them suffering from frost-bite.

Harlequin Quail *Coturnix delegorguei*

Origin: *southern Arabian Peninsula and parts of Africa*

Cock: 6in (15cm) Crown black-brown, with a lighter centre stripe. A black stripe runs through the eye, extending behind the ear coverts and a white stripe runs above the eye to the nape. Cheeks and throat white, with a black band across the cheeks, which continues down the front and encircles the throat. The breast is black in the centre, with red-brown stripes running lengthways to the sides. Belly and undertail coverts brown-red. Upperparts blackish-brown with small lighter cross stripes and with long yellow stripes over the scapulars and back. Iris light brown; beak light horn in colour; legs and feet light yellow-brown.

Hen: Black as well as white markings on the head and throat entirely absent or very faint. Throat pale whitish-buff, with the remainder of the underparts being brown with light margins and paler black markings.

The management of this species should be exactly the same as recommended for the Chinese Painted Quail. Harlequin Quail are ideal companions for smaller, non-aggressive birds such as Zebra Finches, since they spend their time on the ground and do not regularly fly up and perch. Nevertheless, although they will eat spilt seed, they must be provided with their own food and water supply.

For breeding purposes, these quail must be housed in individual pairs. Although they might live without serious dispute for a period, aggression becomes almost inevitable as the breeding season approaches and cock birds assume a murderous mood.

Hens lay in a slight hollow on the ground, and may produce two clutches in a season, each containing up to 10 eggs. Incubation lasts 17 days, and, if necessary, the eggs can be hatched quite easily in an incubator, with the temperature maintained at 99.5°F (37.5°C) and a relative humidity reading of 60 per cent, which will need to be raised when hatching is imminent. The chicks can then be reared in a brooder. By the time they are four weeks old, they will resemble adults and can be sexed without difficulty.

Little Button Quail (Andalusian Hemipode) *Turnix sylvatica*

Origin: *Iberian Peninsula, Africa, Asia and northwest Australia*

Cock: 5in (13cm) *A little smaller in size than the hen, with upperparts yellow-brown with light margins to the feathering of the mantle. Crown of the head alternately barred with pale yellow and dark brown. Back and sides spotted with black. Chin and throat duller in colour, with fewer markings as well. Iris yellow; beak grey-blue; legs and feet flesh-coloured.*

Hen: 6in (15cm) *Larger than the cock. Upperparts rusty-brown, with a reddish-yellow stripe over the crown and a similar stripe running above the eyes. Sides of the head brownish. Feathers of the mantle and the scapulars show black cross banding and yellow margins. Throat and chin white with a transverse stripe of rust-colour running across the crop and breast. Sides are brown-yellow with black, drop-like markings; underparts whitish.*

In spite of the alternative name of Button Quail, which sometimes gives rise to confusion, these are not true quail, although they resemble these birds in appearance. They are not widely kept, but although they may not be especially colourful, their habits are fascinating and well worth study. Unlike quail and other members of the Phasianidae family, the hemipodes lack a crop and a hind toe on each foot. They walk in a rather distinctive way, lifting their feet high at each step.

Hens play the leading role in their family life. An individual hen may display and mate with several cocks in succession, leaving them to hatch the eggs and rear the resulting chicks, although this is not true in all instances. In some cases a more lasting pair bond is formed, and both adults help to care for the young birds.

The strongest call note, resembling a deep, powerful grumble, is produced by the hen. When housing hemipodes together, it is important to bear in mind that she will be dominant and may peck at the male, especially in the vicinity of the back of the head. Although they do not need a large aviary, it must be densely planted, so that the cock can retreat for safety. If this persecution continues, the birds will need to be separated, because serious injury could otherwise follow. In contrast, several hens can usually be housed together in relative harmony.

It is the cock bird who seeks out a nesting site and scratches a hole in the ground, where, ultimately, the hen will lay her eggs. Nesting material is gathered from nearby. This usually consists of fine grasses, which are used to line the hollow. The hen will lay three or four eggs in a clutch, and these take about 13 days to hatch. The cock bird may pull grasses over himself while he is incubating, to conceal his presence at the nest site as far as possible.

The chicks are tiny when they hatch, and boarding may be required around the sides of the aviary to prevent them from slipping through the mesh, which should ideally be ½in (12mm) square. Once the chicks have hatched, small invertebrates such as aphids, spiders and hatchling crickets are important in the early stages. A suitable rearing food, sprinkled with maw seed, should also be offered fresh twice daily.

The young are fed at first by the cock, and by the hen as well if she is involved in their care. They should have grown sufficiently to take chick starter crumbs (as sold for poultry) and seed by the time they are six days old. The cock is largely responsible for brooding the chicks until they are about two weeks old.

Young hemipodes of all species grow very quickly, and resemble adults just six weeks after hatching. They also mature rapidly, with hens often laying by the time that they are three months old.

These birds need to be kept relatively warm in the winter in temperate parts of the world, and they will benefit from a heated birdroom. Here, housed in flights with suitable cover, they can be let out when the weather is mild. Hemipodes may often sunbathe in an outdoor aviary and also appreciate the opportunity to dust-bathe. They may be nervous at first in new surroundings, and clipping one wing should be sufficient to prevent a shy individual from flying up and colliding with the roof of its quarters when the birds are first introduced here. Fitting a false roof is another option which can be considered.

2 Chukar Partridge *Alectoris chukar*

Origin: *Greece eastwards via India and the Himalayas to northern China*

Cock: 14in (36cm) Larger and stockier than the hen, with a fiery red bill. Beige-grey in colour, with a yellowish-white throat and foreneck, surrounded by a black band. On the sides of the body there are black bars on a brown-yellow ground. Orbital ring encircling the eye is red. Iris reddish-brown; beak red; spurred legs and feet red.

Hen: Distinctly smaller than the cock, and usually lacks spurs, although some older hens occasionally develop small spurs.

One of the main essentials when keeping these partridges is to provide them with a spacious aviary in which a rockery can be constructed, for these active birds feel most at home on rocky ground. They generally tame readily, particularly the hen, and it may even be possible to allow her out into the garden for periods if her wing is clipped. Only one hen can be kept in the company of a cock, because others are likely to be attacked and even killed by him.

A well-planted aviary is essential during the breeding season so that the hen can escape from the constant and sometimes aggressive attentions of her mate. She is likely to lay a clutch of 8–12 eggs in a shallow depression usually hidden behind stones during the early summer.

59

Should she appear unwilling to incubate them, the eggs can be transferred to an incubator or put under a broody bantam. Removing the eggs each day will encourage further egg-laying, and the hen may produce as many as 40 in a season as a result. She must have free access to grit and cuttlefish bone if the eggshells are to remain firm, because egg-laying makes considerable demands of her body's stores of calcium and other minerals.

Hatching takes 24 days, and the young partridges require a diet of a suitable softfood, diced green food and maw seed. Later, soaked millet sprays and millet seeds can be added to the diet, along with chick starter crumbs.

It will take about three months for the young birds to assume full adult plumage. The beak, which is black at first, then begins to turn red. The cocks are usually distinguishable at first by their large size, and it is only after eight months that their spurs become visible.

These partridges may be kept outside in both summer and winter as they are quite hardy, although young birds, especially those reared in a brooder, must be carefully acclimatised to outdoor life. Green food appears to be an important part of the diet of this species and should be freely available every day. Poultry or pheasant food is also required, and they will also take invertebrates such as mealworms.

2 Red-legged Partridge *Alectoris rufa*

Origin: *central and southern Europe; introduced to Britain in 1770 and now well established*

Cock: 14in (36cm) *Grey forecrown, with rufous crown and hindneck; broad whitish eyebrow streak extending on to the nape; chin and throat white bordered with black, the black running through the eyes, lores and over the beak. Upper breast warm buff flecked with black; breast blue-grey; abdomen cinnamon; flanks grey broadly barred with white, black and chestnut. Whole of upperparts olive-brown. Iris red-brown, orbital ring red; beak red; legs and feet red, with spurs evident on the legs.*

Hen: *Slightly smaller and duller, lacking the spur-like knobs present on the legs of adult cocks.*

When housed in a large aviary, which is planted with plenty of tall, rough grass and low shrubs, and fed on a diet of various grains, green food and a few invertebrates such as mealworms each day, these partridges will do well. They are not social birds, however, and only one pair should be kept in an aviary. They are completely hardy and will live outside in both summer and winter without needing artificial heat, although shelter from the worst of the weather should be provided.

The cocks will seek a raised area or even a tree stump in their aviary on which to stand and call to their mates. A slovenly nest of grass is prepared in a shallow scrape, usually well concealed by vegetation. The hen will lay 12–18 brownish-yellow eggs, which are spotted and blotched with brown and purple markings. Incubation lasts 24 days and the young can be reared as recommended for the Chukar Partridge.

17 Golden Pheasant *Chrysolophus pictus*

Origin: *central China; there is a small feral population in Britain*

Cock: 40–44in (102–112cm) *On the crown of the head is a crest of elongated, silky, bright yellow feathers. Ear band is a brownish-grey, with the rest of the face, as well as the chin, throat and neck brownish-red. The tippet or ruff is formed of broad, rectangular feathers, the visible parts of which are light orange in colour. Every feather in the tippet has two dark blue bars across the tip. Upperpart of back is deep green, and every feather is margined with velvet black. Lower part of the back and rump are deep, golden-yellow colour. Tail feathers mottled and predominantly brown and black. Wings have dark red on the tips, deep blue tertiaries, black and brown bands on primary and secondary quills. Entire underparts scarlet, merging into a light chestnut in the middle of the abdomen and thighs. Undertail coverts red. Iris and the naked skin round the eye light yellow; beak yellowish; legs and feet horn-yellow.*

Hen: 26–27in (66–69cm) *Significantly smaller and with much plainer plumage. The colours are mainly light, medium and very dark brown, with an occasional pale yellow feather. The feathers show a black mottled or barred patterning, although the actual depth of coloration varies somewhat among individuals. The iris is also brown.*

The Golden ranks as one of the most attractive of all pheasants, and it is very widely kept and bred. Several different colour variants have emerged in captive stock, of which a pale yellow form with a lemon-yellow rather than red body is most widely seen at present. A salmon-coloured strain is also known.

These pheasants should be kept in groups of one cock and at least two hens. Once mating has taken place, the cock bird can be transferred to another female, which should restrict his aggressive tendencies. In the wild they are naturally polygamous, pairing with more than one female. Up to 12 eggs may be laid, and they should hatch after about 23 days. Suitable rearing foods, including starter crumbs, should be supplied for the young pheasants. It will take two years for cock birds to acquire their magnificent breeding plumage.

16 Lady Amherst's Pheasant *Chrysolophus amherstiae*

Origin: *Tibet, Burma and China; there is also a small feral population in Britain*

Cock: 52–68in (132–172cm) *Crown covered with short, metallic green feathers; narrow crest of stiff, elongated crimson feathers; ruff of rounded feathers, white with a blue and black border; mantle and scapulars of scale-like feathers, metallic bluish-green with a black border edged with scintillant green. Feathers of back broad and square, black with a green bar and a wide buff-yellow fringe; those of the rump have a contrasting vermilion fringe. Tail coverts mottled black and white with long orange-vermilion tips; central rectrices irregularly lined black and white with black cross bars; other rectrices similar on the narrow inner web, silver-grey passing to brown on the outer webs, with curved black bars. Wings dark metallic blue with black borders, the primaries only blackish-brown sparsely barred with buff. Face and throat black, with metallic green spots, breast-like mantle, borders of feathers wider and brighter; rest of underparts pure white, the base of the feathers grey, except the lower flanks and vent which are barred with black and brown. Undertail coverts black and dark green more or less barred with white. Iris pale yellow; bare facial skin and lappet bluish or greenish-white; beak greyish; legs and feet bluish-grey.*

Hen: 26–27in (66–69cm) *Similar to Golden Pheasant hen, but larger, the dark barring blacker, with a green sheen; sides of head, neck, mantle, lower throat and upper breast strongly washed with reddish-chestnut; upper throat and abdomen pale, sometimes white; lores, cheeks and ear coverts silvery-grey spotted with black. Back strongly vermiculated; tail feathers rounded, not pointed at the tip as in the Golden Pheasant, and much more strongly marked with broad irregular bars of black, buff and pale grey vermiculated with black. Iris brown, sometimes pale yellow or greyish in older birds; orbital skin slaty-blue.*

This pheasant has been known in Britain since 1928, and slightly earlier in mainland Europe. Unfortunately, as a result of a shortage of hens in these early days, male Lady Amherst's Pheasants were often crossed with Golden Pheasant hens. The hybrid youngsters which were produced proved fertile, and the purity of strains of Lady Amherst's Pheasants suffered accordingly. Breeders soon realised the potential problem, and have since concentrated in recent years on producing pure stock. Any signs of red feathers intermixed with white on the breast of a mature cock Lady Amherst's is indicative of a hybrid ancestry. It is harder to recognise hybrid hens, but these usually have yellowish legs, resembling those of the Golden Pheasant, whereas pure Lady Amherst's hens have bluish-grey legs.

Like their near relative, the Lady Amherst's Pheasant has adapted well to aviculture. They can be kept outside in both summer and winter, but it is important to encourage them to roost under cover, in a snug shelter, to protect them from frost-bite.

If given an opportunity, some still seem to prefer to roost in the outer part of the flight, even when snow falls. They can be prevented from so doing by removing the perches, restricting the pheasants to a platform with a thick layer of straw in the shelter. The pheasants should then roost here, with their legs and toes well protected in the straw.

Two or three hens may be run alongside one cock bird. As a rule, hens will sit well and rear their brood without problems, producing as many as 10 chicks or more. Some breeders prefer to remove the first clutch of eggs soon after laying, transferring them to a broody bantam or an incubator, and then let the hen hatch and raise a second clutch. This usually encourages her to lay more rapidly and, particularly if the weather turns inclement, it may increase the number of chicks that is reared successfully.

The display of the cock bird during the breeding period is most interesting to watch. The collar is spread and drawn to one side, allowing the gorgeous colours of the mantle to be revealed in all their beauty. Again, it will take two years for young cocks to reach full adult plumage, but they may mate successfully from the end of their first year onwards.

Elliot's Pheasant *Syrmaticus ellioti*

Origin: *southeast Asia*

Cock: 32in (81cm) Bright red orbital patch; crown and sides of the head light grey with dark brown shading. White eyebrow stripe; a row of small white feathers with black tips under the eye. Back and breast bright copper with black markings and a metallic sheen. Wings chestnut-brown and blue-black with white bands. Tail grey and brown, margined with black. Iris brown; beak greenish; legs and feet greenish-grey.

Hen: 20in (51cm) Beige-red head with a red-brown crown; pale grey feathers under the eyes. Neck grey to black with white margins to the small feathers. White belly; brown-grey tail with narrow dark barring and black and white spots.

This species, with its exquisite coloration, is always in demand, but Elliot's Pheasants require a large, densely planted aviary, which incorporates suitable high roosting perches, with those in the shelter being the furthest off the ground to encourage the birds to roost there on cold winter nights.

Although a cock can be housed with two hens, it is often better to design the aviary so that he is accommodated separately in the centre, with hens in adjoining aviaries. Male Elliot's Pheasants often prove very aggressive, and keeping the birds apart should prevent the hens from being persecuted and even seriously injured as a result of the cock's persistent attention.

It is possible to place Golden or Common Pheasant hens with a cock Elliot's for company, and they are likely to be ignored. This may help to provide aviary space elsewhere, but the pheasants should be watched closely for any signs of aggression.

During the breeding season a shield of matting, approximately 3ft (1m) high, should be fixed between the aviaries. The cock can then be placed with one hen on one day, and another hen on the next day, alternating them in this fashion. This will prevent the hens from being persecuted excessively, and at the same time should ensure that they are together with the cock for sufficiently long to mate successfully.

An Elliot's hen will usually start to lay in March, producing one egg every day. She will lay about 20 eggs in the course of a season, so they must be collected regularly and placed in an incubator or under a broody bantam. A bantam has the added advantage that she will look after the youngsters when they hatch, dispensing with the need for a brooder.

While young pheasant hens may prove unreliable parents at first, this does not mean that they will not sit properly later on. A three-year-old hen can usually be relied on to hatch and rear her own chicks, although it is probably best to restrict her to just eight eggs.

Incubation takes 25 days. The method of rearing young Elliot's Pheasants is similar to that for other pheasants. Softfoods for this purpose can later be augmented with starter chick crumbs, while chopped green food such as chickweed can also be beneficial, along with small live foods. Drinking water should be supplied, but in shallow dishes to prevent the youngsters from drowning.

It is only after 10 weeks, when the adult plumage begins to show, that the young cocks can be recognised by their greyish-yellow tail quills. They will attain full colouring in the same year, which is a great advantage to a breeder who wishes to dispose of surplus stock, because they will usually be more attractive to prospective purchasers at this stage.

You do not need to purchase birds when starting out with these or similar species. Breeders may sell fertile eggs, which can be incubated at home and which should give rise to chicks. Choose only clean eggs and check their fertility if possible. Carefully transfer them back to the incubator or broody hen with the minimum of delay, and handle them no more than is strictly necessary, always with clean hands.

15 Hume's Bar-tailed Pheasant

(Mrs Hume's Pheasant) *Syrmaticus humiae*

Origin: *Burma and Yunnan, China*

Cock: 32in (81cm) Crown brown; neck, upper mantle, chin and throat metallic steel-blue; mantle fiery red; lower back and rump blue-green with narrow white fringe. Wings fiery bronze-red with small, subterminal black spots. Shoulder stripe and two bars on the secondaries white. Breast chestnut with bluish gloss and fiery margins; belly and sides chestnut; middle tail feathers greyish-white with narrow bars of chestnut and black; outer feathers mainly black with grey bars. Bare facial patch crimson. Iris brown; beak horn-coloured; legs and feet black.

Hen: 20in (51cm) Very similar to Elliot's Pheasant hen, but lacks the black on the throat and foreneck.

This pheasant resembles Elliot's Pheasant, to which it is closely related. It is quite rare in collections, but its treatment should be as suggested for other pheasants, and its maintenance should present no particular problems.

However, when they first hatch the chicks are very small and do require special care during the early stages of rearing. For the first few days they will not readily accept any food that is not moving, and they should, therefore, be supplied with a range of small invertebrates. Avoid offering large mealworms, which will be relatively indigestible. Once they have passed this stage, they will usually progress without further difficulty if treated in the same way as other pheasant chicks.

4 Mikado Pheasant *Syrmaticus mikado*

Origin: *Taiwan*

Cock: 35in (89cm) Predominantly black, with feathers of the head, back and lower breast laced with steel-blue, while those on the throat, neck and upper breast have a violent-purple lustre. Coverts and flight feathers are black, with triangular white marks on the former. Tail black, central feathers most elongated and all barred with white. Facial patch bright crimson. Iris brown; beak black; legs and feet greyish.

Hen: 21in (53cm) Dark brown, heavily mottled, lighter on the throat and upper breast. Tail shorter than in the case of the male, central feathers bright chestnut with buff and black transverse bars. Facial patch smaller and paler.

The feeding and care of the Mikado Pheasant is as for Elliot's Pheasant, but they require larger quantities of green food, which should be provided as part of their regular diet every day. They are hardy but dislike damp, foggy winter weather, and, if applicable, they should be kept on a very well-drained soil. The Mikado Pheasant is not a particularly common species in collections at present.

3 Reeves's Pheasant *Syrmaticus reevesii*

Origin: *northern and central China*

Cock: 84in (213cm) Head, chin, throat and nape white margined below with a black collar and with a broad black line from the beak passing through the eye and meeting behind the head. Mantle, back and rump golden-buff; wing coverts white all margined with black. Breast and sides of body white barred and margined with chestnut. Flanks white margined with buff; remainder of underparts black. Tail up to 5ft (1.5m) long, the two central feathers silvery, barred with chestnut and black, and the remainder cinnamon barred with black. Iris brown; beak greyish-horn; legs and feet greyish.

Hen: 30in (76cm) Head brown with yellowish-buff on the sides of the face; ear coverts and nuchal band blackish. Mantle chestnut tipped with grey and mottled with black. Body and wing coverts are mainly greyish-brown with white, buff and black markings. Long tail is pointed and greyish-brown barred with buff and black, and with black and white tips to the feathers. Breast and abdomen is lighter in tone, shading from chestnut to buff, lightly mottled.

The beauty of these pheasants can be fully appreciated only if they are housed in a very large aviary. Particular consideration needs to be given to their long tail feathers. The perches must be placed high up and sufficiently far away from the sides of the enclosure so that the tail cannot be damaged when the pheasants are perching.

Reeves's Pheasants are one of the hardiest species and may be kept outside in both summer and winter without artificial heat. It is, however, recommended that the perches are moved from the open, uncovered part of the flight during the colder months of the year, which should encourage the pheasants to roost under cover, where they will be far less susceptible to frost-bite. Some breeders have recently attached special strip heaters to the undersides of perches to keep them warm on freezing nights, so that their stock will not be afflicted by frost-bite. These strips, which emit a gentle heat, are used in the chemical industry to prevent the contents of pipes from freezing.

The care of these pheasants is similar to that required by other species. They will need either a commercial pheasant or poultry diet, which should be supplemented with regular supplies of green food and invertebrates, as well as grit and cuttlefish bone.

This is one of the most widely kept species at present, but cock birds can become exceedingly aggressive during the breeding season, which can make successful pairings difficult. Each cock requires two or three hens, and they need to be watched carefully to ensure that they are not being unduly harassed. If this happens, he must be kept in a separate pen, with the hens being introduced here for short periods only so that they are less likely to be harmed.

After mating the hens can be kept on their own. They usually sit well, but often their first clutch may need to be hatched artificially, in an incubator or under a broody bantam. Clutch size varies from 7 to 15 eggs, and, if fertile, these hatch after about 25 days.

The rearing of the young should be similar to that of other pheasants. Offer a good supply of green food and invertebrates and make sure that the chicks are kept dry. They should grow quite rapidly and should then be transferred to more spacious accommodation. Young cock birds may be aggressive towards each other even at this early stage and need separating accordingly.

9 **Black-breasted Kalij** (Kalij Pheasant, Horsfield's Kalij)

Lophura leucomelana

Origin: *Bhutan, the Himalayas, Nepal, Burma and Thailand*

Cock: 23in (58cm) Entire plumage black, glossed with purple, the feathers of the lower back, rump and uppertail coverts margined with white. Crest long and the feathers hair-like. Facial wattles deep scarlet. Iris brown; beak bluish-black; legs and feet bluish-black.

Hen: 20in (51cm) Olive-brown, chin and throat whitish; wings and central feathers tipped with buff. Central tail feathers shorter than those of the male and of a deep ferruginous tone.

Although not as brightly coloured as some pheasants, the Black-breasted Kalij is not a difficult species to maintain, but, perhaps unsurprisingly, it is often less freely available. A well-planted aviary suits them well, and they should be housed in groups of a cock and two hens. Incubation of the dozen or so eggs laid by each hen lasts approximately 25 days. Rearing presents no particular problems, but in aviary surroundings especially the chicks are very shy, retreating and remaining hidden at the slightest hint of danger. They gain their adult plumage by the end of the first year.

0 **Silver Pheasant** *Lophura nycthemera*

Origin: *China, Burma, Indo-China and southeastern Asia*

Cock: 49in (124cm) The size and depth of white coloration may vary somewhat, depending on the individual subspecies. Upper body has a chalk-white colour with three to four narrow black lines running across each feather in a wavy pattern. Underparts, the chin, throat and the long crest are a magnificent, glossy deep bluish-black. The rectrices are very striking because of their great length. The central pair is pure white and the remainder are decorated on the outer web by a few narrow broken black lines. Iris brown; beak yellowish; legs and feet red.

The cock assumes adult plumage only in his second year, being considerably duller in coloration up to this point. Immature cocks lack the pure white under-body, with this area being a finely vermiculated white, reddish-yellow and black. The tail has not yet attained its full length, resembling that of the hen, although longer and more coarsely vermiculated. V-shaped white lines run across the underparts, which are otherwise black, like the crest.

Hen: 28in (71cm) May vary quite considerably in her markings, but generally olive-brown overall, with relatively inconspicuous black vermiculation. Chin and throat are spotted with grey; the crest is tipped with black.

This pheasant is a closer relative of domestic poultry than the other species already described and has even been kept with chickens as companions. Silver Pheasants are quieter, however, although cocks can become very savage during the breeding period when hens are laying, and nest inspections should be carried out discreetly, otherwise, the cock may strike out with his sharp spurs, inflicting a painful cut on the hand.

The clutch size may be quite small, especially in the case of young hens laying for the first time, who may produce as few as six eggs. The hen usually sits alone, but may be joined occasionally by her mate, who may also brood the chicks once they hatch. Incubation lasts about 25 days. Again, as these pheasants prove polygamous, a cock should be housed with at least a pair of hens, in a good size, well-planted aviary, to reduce the likelihood of displays of aggression.

Imperial Pheasant *Lophura imperialis*

Origin: *northern and central Indo-China*

Cock: 30in (76cm) *The entire body is a dark, steel-blue. Body feathers black with a broad blue fringe. Those of the lower back and rump, wing and tail coverts deep black with bright metallic blue borders. The pure black crest is rather short and pointed. The long, broad and slightly arched central rectrices are also pointed and have brown spots, as well as the back and wings. Skin of face or wattle scarlet. Iris reddish-orange; beak pale yellowish-green and blackish at its base; legs and feet reddish.*

Hen: 24in (61cm) *Feathers of the crown relatively elongated and often raised, but do not form a full crest. Head light greyish-brown; cheeks, chin and throat paler. Upperparts chestnut, with inconspicuous black spots. Underparts light greyish-brown and sometimes slightly mottled.*

First discovered in Annam, Vietnam, in 1923, this appears to be a very rare species in the wild and is not common in collections, although its care presents no particular problems. Attempts were made in the 1960s to ensure its survival by a series of matings involving Silver Pheasants, and this resulted in the production of many hybrid offspring. Refinement was then carried out to select those progeny that showed greatest similarity to the Imperial Pheasant, and breeding concentrated with these, in the hope of effectively recreating a population of birds identical in appearance to the species. Young cocks assume adult plumage at 18 months old.

11 Edwards's Pheasant *Lophura edwardsii*

Origin: *central Vietnam*

Cock: 25in (64cm) *Tail relatively short, compared with the rest of the body. It is quite straight, apart from the two central rectrices, which are somewhat rounded and blunt-ended. The crest is generally white, lightly flecked with black, and quite*

S

hort. *Overall body dark blue with broad metallic blue edges to the feathers. On the lower back, tail coverts and rump these edges are preceded by a deep velvet-black border. The outer fringe of the wing coverts has a more greenish tone. Forewattles are scarlet and can be distended into two large, scarlet lobes. Iris reddish-brown; beak greenish-white; legs and feet crimson.*

Hen: 16in (41cm) As with most other pheasant hens, the hen Edwards's is mainly brown, although in this case, the brown tends towards a shade of chestnut. This colour is richest on the mantle and dullest – almost brown-grey – on the head and neck. There is hardly any crest. Entire plumage is covered by almost invisible black vermiculations. The six central rectrices are dark brown, with the remainder being black. The same division of coloration can be seen on the primaries. Facial area scarlet; beak honey-brown; legs and feet scarlet.

This species may no longer survive in the wild, as a consequence of the Vietnam War, which was fought across its habitat. Trapping for food and the use of chemical defoliants are considered to be prime reasons for its decline. A small captive population still exists, however, and this offers hope for its long-term survival.

In the past, Edwards's Pheasant proved adaptable and prolific in collections, although its relative lack of colour meant that it never assumed the widespread popularity of some other related species.

2 Swinhoe's Pheasant *Lophura swinhoiei*

Origin: *mountain forests of Taiwan*

Cock: 31in (79cm) A whitish crest, mixed with bluish-black feathering is present on the head. There is an irregularly shaped white patch on the back, with the remainder of head and neck, the back and underparts being glossy blue. The pattern of cross barring seen in Edwards's Pheasant is present on the feathers of the rump, lower back and tail coverts, except that Swinhoe's patterning differs in that the black subterminal bar is narrower and the blue border is wider. Wing coverts black with green borders; scapulars red, and, together with the white patch on the back, they are the identifying characteristics of the Swinhoe's Pheasant. Tail dark blue, apart from the two greatly elongated central rectrices, which are entirely white and pointed. Facial wattles scarlet. Irish reddish-brown; beak horn-yellow; legs and feet crimson.

Hen: 21in (53cm) Face and throat are dull white to pale grey. Body feathers mainly chestnut, vermiculated black. On the breast, the black vermiculation is in a V-shaped pattern, fading into the abdomen.

These hardy pheasants can live outside in a suitable aviary throughout the year, provided that their run is well drained and affords them some cover. In addition, a shelter must, of course, be available. A typical pheasant diet suits them well. They can prove very prolific when breeding. The first pair brought to Europe produced 80 chicks for their owner, Baron Rothschild, between 1866 and 1869. The display of the cock bird involves inflating the scarlet skin on the sides of the face and erecting the crest feathers.

Care must be taken to ensure that the hens do not become injured by the cock's advances. Assuming all goes well, they should each lay around a dozen eggs, with the incubation period lasting 25 days. Young cocks will obtain their adult plumage in their second year. An unusual cinnamon mutation has been recorded in this species, first from France and then Italy, but it has disappeared, although this colour variant could well re-emerge again in the future.

8 Red Junglefowl *Gallus gallus*

Origin: *Himalayas and India, Burma, Indo-China, southeast Asia, Sumatra and Java, and elsewhere in the Far East where it has been introduced and become naturalised*

Cock: *24in (61cm) Head, neck and hackles reddish golden-brown, becoming straw-coloured on the longer hackles; mantle and coverts metallic green and purple; median coverts, scapulars and mantle dark maroon; rump orange-red. Flights cinnamon. Tail metallic green. Underparts velvety-black. Face, tall serrated comb and throat wattles crimson, with a white wattle below the ear. Iris reddish-brown; beak blackish; legs and feet blackish, with long and exceedingly sharp spurs on the legs.*

Hen: *20in (51cm) Head rusty-red, neck and mantle orange, shading to pale yellow mottled with black; remainder of upperparts dull brown finely mottled with black. Throat, foreneck chestnut; remainder of underparts pale, light red. Very small comb, face and small throat wattles as cock.*

Four species of junglefowl are known, widely distributed across southern parts of Asia. They live in forests and thickets, usually venturing into the open to feed, often on roadsides or into cultivated fields near villages, in the early morning and evening. Their food consists of seeds, berries and insects, and in captivity a basic diet similar to that provided for poultry suits them well.

The Red Junglefowl has proved to be the hardiest of the four species, and it is also the ancestor of all today's many breeds of domestic poultry. Stock is usually available, but unfortunately, crossings with bantams have occurred, and some birds have hybrid origins, often reflected in their yellow rather than blackish legs.

Adult junglefowl are powerful fliers compared with domestic chickens, and it is not safe to keep them at liberty in a garden unless they are pinioned or have their flight feathers clipped. Cocks must be kept apart in any event, because they are extremely aggressive towards each other. Fighting is almost inevitable when two cocks come into contact and is likely to have a fatal outcome.

They are delightful birds to keep in rural areas, where there are no close neighbours. Chicks can soon be tamed sufficiently to feed from the hand. Unfortunately, the voice of the cock is shrill and loud, and they will crow at the break of dawn, and often at intervals through the night. It is not advisable to keep them in a built-up area, where they are likely to provoke complaints.

7 Sonnerat's Junglefowl (Grey Junglefowl) *Gallus sonnerati*

Origin: *west and south India*

Cock: 30in (76cm) *Hackles and mantle pencilled with grey, white and black, the tips of the feathers having the barbs united, forming yellowish-white spots, which look like sealing-wax. Wing coverts orange-red, with the same unusual appearance. Back, lesser coverts and underparts dark brown or blackish, the feathers having a fringe and a central stripe of grey. Rump and tail coverts purplish; tail feathers metallic green. Serrated comb and wattles crimson. Iris brownish; beak yellow; legs and feet yellowish, slightly tinged with red.*

Hen: 15in (38cm) *Mantle rusty-brown with broad buff shaft marks; upperparts brown mottled with black and with light shaft marks. Underparts mainly white, fringed and lightly mottled with black and with a wash of brown on the abdomen.*

This species is reasonably hardy but should be provided with a frost-proof shelter in winter. Some kind of artificial heating, either in the form of a tubular heater or an infrared lamp, should be provided in very cold weather.

Like other junglefowl, Sonnerat's is polygamous, and each cock should be provided with two or more hens. They usually prove to be reliable and quite prolific when breeding, and if they are in a good sized enclosure, with plenty of natural cover, the hens will incubate and rear their own chicks. A broody bantam can be used if required.

Incubation takes 18-21 days, and the chicks sometimes prove rather delicate when first hatched. They should, therefore, be kept away from damp and cold until they are well grown. Chick starter crumbs can usefully be provided for them in the early stages, while care needs to be taken to ensure that they cannot become saturated in their drinking water.

Crested Fireback Pheasant *Lophura ignita*

Origin: *southeast Asia, Sumatra and Borneo*

Cock: 26in (66cm) *General colour black, with rich purple-blue sheen. Back, rump, belly and sides fiery bronze-red. Central tail feathers rich buff. Long, bare-shafted crest. Bare facial skin blue. Iris orangish; beak greyish; legs and feet greyish.*

Hen: 22in (56cm) *Upperparts predominantly rich chestnut lightly mottled with black; neck pale chestnut, chin and throat white; breast chestnut, remainder of underparts dark brown, all feathers edged with white.*

The firebacks, which are named after the bright red patch of feathering on their lower back and rump, are divided into two groups, depending whether or not they are crested. Those without crests are exceedingly rare in aviculture and very little has been written about them. Much more is known about the Crested Firebacks, which were first documented in aviculture during the last century. They are characterised by their short, thick crest of crowded, stiff feathers. In hens, the crest is always much less developed than in cocks.

These pheasants are less hardy than other species, disliking both cold and prolonged periods of damp, foggy weather. They need adequate protection during the winter months, as they are particularly susceptible to frost-bite. Hens may lay relatively late in the year, and the chicks will need special care through the winter months in temperate areas, although they usually grow rapidly. Clean surroundings are essential, because they are prone to enteric diseases. They will moult into adult plumage by the time they are a year old, but they are unlikely to breed until the following year. Cocks tend to be less aggressive towards their partners than other species.

Siamese Fireback *Lophura diardi*

Origin: *southeast Asia and China*

Cock: 32in (81cm) Head and throat black; long tufted crest steel-blue. Neck, mantle, breast and wings grey, finely vermiculated with black. Wing coverts with white edges and a black band near the tips. Upper back shining gold; lower back and rump bronzy-red. Underparts and tail black with a steel-blue gloss. Face scarlet. Iris orangish-brown; beak greenish-grey; legs and feet reddish.

Hen: 24in (61cm) Head and neck brown; mantle, outer tail feathers and underparts chestnut; lower breast and belly margined with white. Wings, central tail feathers, lower back and rump black mottled and banded with white. Face scarlet, as with the cock.

Siamese Firebacks are generally considered to be the easiest of the crested firebacks to maintain in aviary surroundings. They are usually less susceptible to cold and frost, and when properly acclimatised they are hardy, even in northern parts of Europe. These pheasants clearly dislike very damp or snowy weather, however, and it is better to confine them to their aviary shelter when the weather is bad. Because they are relatively hardy, a heated shelter is not essential, but they should be encouraged to roost on a platform of straw, which will help to keep their feet warm.

A diet as recommended for other pheasants suits them well. Siamese Firebacks are monogamous, but care should be taken during the breeding season, because the cock can become rather too persistent in his advances. Adult cocks have long, sharp spurs, and they can then inflict serious injury on hens at this stage.

Hens typically lay a clutch of from six to eight eggs in a scrape under a low bush, with incubation lasting for 24 days. The chicks are relatively insectivorous in the early stages and require suitable live food. Although they usually acquire adult plumage by a year old, hens may not lay for a further two years.

5 Japanese Green Pheasant (Southern Green Pheasant)

Phasianus versicolor

Origin: *Japan*

Cock: 26in (66cm) *Crown, mantle, throat, breast and belly dark metallic green; neck rich purple; scapulars coppery-red with mantle feathers black centred, with fine buff margins; wing coverts bluish-grey; rump and uppertail coverts greenish-grey; tail greenish-grey barred with black and fringed with purple. Bare facial patches crimson; short ear tufts metallic green. Iris brownish; beak horn-yellow; legs and feet blackish.*

Hen: 22in (56cm) *Predominantly sandy-buff marked and barred with dark brown and black. Neck and mantle with a pinkish tone, and the centre of the latter black, feathers tipped with metallic green; lores, chin and throat clear buff and with a patch below the eye white; tail pinkish-buff barred with black and pale buff.*

These birds share the restless and wary nature of all game pheasants, and they are usually less tame in aviary surroundings than ornamental species. If disturbed suddenly, they are inclined to fly straight up and may seriously injure their heads by colliding with the mesh. It is therefore essential to provide a large, thickly-planted aviary where they can feel secure, with shrubs to provide cover.

In addition to the usual grain mixture, which forms the basis of most pheasant diets, the Japanese Green Pheasant also appreciates quantities of fresh green food and invertebrates. Hens typically lay 7–14 eggs in a well-concealed scrape under vegetation. These should hatch about 24 days later. The hen usually proves a reliable parent, but dislikes disturbance both during the incubation period and subsequently, when the chicks have hatched.

6 Himalayan Monal (Impeyan Pheasant)

Lophophorus impeyanus

Origin: *Himalayas from Afghanistan to Bhutan*

Cock: 29in (74cm) *Head, throat and high, racket-shaped crest metallic green. Nape and sides of the neck reddish-copper; mantle golden-green. Wings purple and blue. Lower back pure white; rump and uppertail coverts shining blue; underparts dull black, tail chestnut. Iris brownish; beak blackish; legs and feet dark brown.*

Hen: Just slightly smaller than the cock. Upperparts mostly brown streaked and mottled with buff; rump brown with distinct buff bar. Underparts paler brown with prominent white shaft stripes. Throat and half-collar white, tail dark brown with reddish-brown bars. Small, blue naked eye patches are present in both the cock and hen.

The three species of monal are all true mountain birds. Their colours are overwhelmingly beautiful, and these birds are considered perhaps the most magnificent representatives of the entire pheasant family. The only birds to equal the multi-coloured, metallic reflections, in shades of blue, purple, green and red, present in their plumage are hummingbirds and birds of paradise.

The display of the cock monal serves to show his wealth of colour to the fullest advantage. It is interesting to note that at all times during the display ritual, the cock keeps one wing lowered, hiding his legs and feet from the hen.

Monals are best kept on a coarse, well-drained sandy soil. They need a roomy pen, and as a guide, an area of 150 sq ft (14 sq m) will be required to ensure satisfactory breeding results. It is also essential to provide dense cover in the aviary, partly to ensure that the hen can escape from an over-arduous partner, and partly to ensure that she can nest without disturbance under a bush. She will lay approximately six eggs in a clutch, but if these are removed, a further clutch should be laid soon afterwards. Incubation lasts about 27 days. The young monals will not acquire adult plumage until their second year, but evidence of black feathering in the vicinity of the throat indicates an immature cock bird.

Although relatively hardy, monals require a shelter, which should be 6ft (1.8m) square and equipped with perches, although the birds may prefer to roost on a broad board. Introducing young stock will offer the best likelihood of compatibility. Never try to introduce a hen to a cock, because he is very likely to persecute her relentlessly under these circumstances. A meeting on neutral ground is more likely to pass without signs of aggression.

White-eared Pheasant   *Crossoptilon crossoptilon*

Origin: *the mountains of northwestern Yunnan and central Szechuan, China, and southeastern Tibet*

Cock: 37in (94cm) Crown, short curled feathers black. Elongated ear coverts, entire body plumage pure white, greyish on wing and tail coverts, flights brownish. Tail similar to that of other Eared Pheasants, having 20 feathers, which are dark brown, glossed with green and with purple at the tips. Wattles crimson. Iris brownish; beak horn-coloured; legs and feet red, with short spurs.

Hen: Fractionally smaller and lacks the cock's spurs.

Unfortunately, this attractive pheasant has become very rare, and it is not commonly seen in collections. It originates at high altitude, ranging close to the snowline and so is quite hardy.

Hens lay around 16 greenish eggs, spotted with brown markings, which should hatch after 24 days. Although young birds may appear aggressive at first, this phase usually passes, and, in fact, the White-eared Pheasant has a reputation for being relatively docile, even during the breeding season. The chicks are brown at first, before moulting into bluish plumage, and then finally attaining their snow white coloration. They require the same food and care as other related pheasants.

Brown-eared Pheasant (Hoki) *Crossoptilon mantchuricum*

Origin: *northeast China*

Cock: 40in (102cm) Crown black, the feathers here being short and curled; elongated ear coverts white; neck black shading into brown on the mantle. Lower back and rump dull greyish-white; breast blackish-brown, with remaining underparts being lighter. Tail resembles that of the Blue-eared Pheasant but has 22 feathers, mainly whitish, with just the tips being brown, glossed with purple and blue. Wattles crimson. Iris brownish; beak pale horn-colour; legs and feet red with short spurs.

Hen: Slightly smaller and lacks the cock's spurs.

Almost from its introduction into aviculture, which took place in 1864, the original bloodline has been maintained. Apart from the initial cock and two hens, today's stock has apparently been augmented only by two additional cocks, which were received by London Zoo in 1866. This may account for the fact that cocks today have a reputation for infertility, which is doubtless the results of constant inbreeding for more than a century. If you find that the eggs are persistently clear, artificial insemination can help to overcome this difficulty. Typical clutch size averages between five and eight eggs, which should hatch after an incubation period of about 26 days. The youngsters will attain full colouring at around the age of five months.

If you have a secure garden it is possible to keep them in a state of semi-liberty, with the flight feathers on one wing clipped as necessary, or, alternatively, if the pheasant has been pinioned by a vet. Brown-eared Pheasants usually become very tame and are quite hardy, although protection against frost-bite is necessary. Nevertheless, they seem to prefer cold weather to the heat of a summer's day.

Brown-eared Pheasants are tolerant of other pheasants and domestic poultry. They are normally kept in pairs, requiring a large aviary if they are not to become bored and resort to feather-plucking. When kept at semi-liberty, these birds do sometimes dig, using their beaks for this purpose, which can result in damage to plants and may even ruin a small area of lawn.

Blue-eared Pheasant *Crossoptilon auritum*

Origin: *mountainous areas of western China*

Cock: 38in (97cm) *General colour slate-blue, with the short, curled feathers of the crown being black. Ear coverts white and greatly elongated, giving the appearance of long, tufted ears. Chin and throat white. The tail has 24 long and wide feathers, arched and fringed, black glossed with purple, with the outer pairs having the basal three-quarters white. Wattles crimson. Iris brown; beak long, stout and curved, horn in colour; legs and feet red, with spurs on the legs.*

Hen: Similar, but slightly smaller and lacks the spurs of the cock.

These pheasants can be easily maintained on a diet of various seeds, supplied with greenstuff and live food. In an aviary with a grass floor, they will search for roots and grubs in the soil, using their strong, curved beaks for this purpose. Unlike domestic poultry, they do not scratch the ground with their feet to locate items of food.

Blue-eared Pheasants were first bred in captivity in 1932. They are monogamous, but in the wild they certainly associate in larger groups outside the breeding season. Having lined her scrape with grass or similar material, the hen will lay as many as 15 eggs in the clutch. She sits alone throughout the incubation period, which lasts for about 27 days. The youngsters will be fully developed by a month old, and are then brownish in colour, with darker striations present on their plumage, with their tail feathers being a striking shade of steel-blue.

3 Satyr Tragopan *Tragopan satyra*

Origin: *central and eastern parts of the Himalayas*

Cock: 28in (71cm) *Forehead and crown black, with a flattened crest evident, with tufts of fiery orange behind. Ear coverts orange-red and black. The top of the back and the corresponding part of the breast are deep red. Abdomen and undertail coverts red, with the entire underparts being spangled with white spots outlined with black and increasing in size towards the abdomen. Remainder of the back, wings and the short, rounded tail brown, marked with small spots, which are red, olive-green, black and white in colour. Deep purple-blue skin around the eyes, with the throat wattle also being blue, darkest at the centre, with four triangular red spots present on each side. Fleshy horns on the head are blue. Iris brown; beak black; legs and feet pink.*

Hen: 23in (58cm) *Duller, with reddish-brown upperparts, broken by buff and black markings; chin and throat yellowish-brown also with black markings. The lower part of the body is a paler shade, with the lower abdomen being greyish-white. The bare skin surrounding the eye is blue, with the legs and feet also greyish-white.*

Five species of tragopan are recognised. The pattern of their plumage is so elaborate and the colouring so varied that it is almost impossible to convey an accurate description of the various species by words alone, especially to anyone unfamiliar with the general appearance of these pheasants.

While the coloured bib-like throat wattles or lappets may be almost invisible when these pheasants are resting, they will be inflated with air during their display. The lappets may then reach a width of 2–3in (5–7.5cm), and measure up to 6in (15cm) long. The horns will also exceed 2in (5cm) at this time. These are quite unique to the tragopans, and have given rise to the alternative name of 'horned pheasants' for this group.

The area of distribution of tragopans extends from Kashmir in the west across the Himalayas and Burma into central China. Through their range, they are most likely to be encountered at altitudes of between 3,000 and 12,000ft (900–3,600m). Their food consists of leaves, berries, seed and insects.

4 Temminck's Tragopan *Tragopan temminckii*

Origin: *mountains of the extreme southeast of Tibet and northeastern Assam, east to central China*

Cock: 27in (69cm) Forehead, sides of the neck, ear coverts and the area surrounding the throat wattle black, as is the centre of the breast, with the underlying feathers here being reddish-orange. The horns are greenish-blue, with the bare skin around the eyes being a combination of violet-blue and green. The throat wattle is red with blue edges, and marked with shades of blue at the centre. Tail feathers dark brown, with the plumage here being barred and fretted with light buff-brown at the base. The remainder of the body plumage is deep red to orangish-red, with the individual feathers of the upperparts being marked individually with a pearl-grey spot, highlighted with a black surround, and on the underparts with a large buff-grey mark. Iris brown; beak black; legs and feet pink.

Hen: Predominantly reddish-grey-brown in coloration, with the feathers being spangled with black, and showing arrow-like markings of yellowish-white and grey. Bare skin around the eye is bluish. The plumage on the throat is whitish with black stripes, while the abdomen is light brown overall, offset with large, pearl-grey spots, highlighted by yellowish-buff.

Compared with other pheasants, tragopans are strong fliers, and they consequently tend to spend less time on the ground. They will often feed in trees and adopt old nests made by crows and other large birds. If, however, there is no readily available nest, hen tragopans will build a well-constructed nest of branches and twigs, often at quite a considerable height off the ground. In the aviary therefore, it is advisable to construct an artificial nest or nesting platform in a tall shrub or on suspended branches. A shallow fruit box or large wicker tray is useful for this purpose and will give good support. Providing the tragopans with an artificial nest of this type may well encourage them to breed.

These pheasants are perfectly hardy and are, in fact, more likely to require protection from the summer sun rather than from the winter cold. They need plenty of natural shade in their quarters, which must also be spacious. This species was first bred at London Zoo over 100 years ago, when the hen laid a clutch of seven eggs and hatching occurred 28 days later, and there have been many successes since then. Their food should consist of the same mixture of seeds and grains provided for other pheasants, but a supply of fresh green food (although not cabbage) and some fruit should ideally be provided every day. Invertebrates are also appreciated, particularly when chicks are being reared, as they will feed almost exclusively on live food at first.

Great Argus Pheasant (Malay Argus Pheasant)

Argusianus argus

Origin: *southeast Asia, Sumatra and central Borneo*

Cock: *68–80in (173–203cm) Head and neck bare and blue in colour, apart from short black feathers on top of the head and nape. General colour above is black, mottled and dotted with buff, and with white on the mantle and coverts. Neck and upper breast rusty-red with lighter shaft marks. Secondaries and flights grey-brown with narrow wavy lines of black and dark brown, with the former feathers having become greatly elongated. Their outer webs are decorated with a row of large ocelli, yellowish-white and reddish in colour, each enclosed by a narrow margin of black. Central tail feathers very long and broad, tapering to narrow points, greyish-brown on inner webs and rufus on outer, finely vermiculated with black and buff. When fully grown, these tail feathers may reach a length of 4ft (1.2m). Underparts rufous, finely mottled and barred with dark brown and black. Iris brown; beak yellowish-horn; legs and feet red.*

Hen: *30in (76cm) Resembles the cock in appearance, although lacking the long wings and tail.*

Argus Pheasants are only very occasionally seen in private collections, because they are rarely obtainable and need very spacious surroundings. There are actually three species distributed through the Malay Peninsula, Borneo and Sumatra, where they are found at low and moderate altitudes. The Bornean form (Plate 18) is quite distinctive in its appearance.

Only when displaying does the cock reveal the marvellous splendour of his plumage. At rest he appears to be a rather drab bird. In the wild, these pheasants do not appear to be especially rare, but they are very wary and so are seldom seen. They prefer dry, rocky country, at heights ranging from sea level to about 4,265ft (1,300m).

The hens fly strongly, but the cocks are rather awkward in flight because of the abnormal development of their secondary feathers into a long train.

The sexes live apart throughout the year. Only during the breeding season do hens seek out a cock, probably associating with him only briefly during the mating phase.

Argus cocks will prove dangerous towards their chicks, so it is advisable to remove them from the aviary as soon as it is certain that mating has taken place. The aviaries for these pheasants must, of course, be very spacious because of the enormous length of the cock's tail and wings. A typical pheasant diet suits them well.

The hen will lay just three or four eggs, which should take about 25 days to hatch. She is usually a very reliable parent and can be allowed to rear her own chicks. This will restrict her to laying a single clutch in a season, but it is preferable to have two live chicks rather than any number of failures. Argus chicks grow slowly and have to be given a great deal of care during the first year. They require heating over the winter period and will be fully mature only in their third year. Even so, their wing and tail feathers will continue to grow over successive moults for another three or four years, before reaching their full length.

Even fully grown Argus Pheasants never really become accustomed to the damp winters of temperate areas, so adequate protection, particularly at night, is essential. This species may be reasonably peaceable, often not resenting the company of other species of pheasant, but it is not advisable to attempt to keep more than one cock Argus Pheasant in the same enclosure, however large this may be, because they will inevitably fight.

Indian Peafowl (Blue Peafowl) *Pavo cristatus*

Origin: *India, Sri Lanka*

Cock: 78–92in (198–234cm) Head, throat and breast are a royal metallic blue, with the tall spatulate crest being greenish-blue. Bare white areas are present above and below the eyes. Feathers on the back resemble scales, lustrous bronze-green in colour, shading into the blue of the mantle, with each edged with black. Secondaries bluish-black; flights chestnut. There may be as many as 150 feathers in the magnificent train of mature cocks, with those on the extreme outsides being fringed heavily on the outer webs, which are curved and shining green in colour. The other feathers here are graduated, with the central ones being longest, and terminating in ends that resemble fish tails. Webbing here is not apparent, while they are metallic green in colour, with shades of bronze and gold. The characteristic 'eyes' or ocelli are deep purple at the centre, with royal blue superimposed on fiery bronze, along with rings of mauve, purple and mauvish-white. The graduated tail is of only moderate length in comparison, being completely concealed by the train it helps to support. The plumage here is chestnut. Below the base, three dense cushions of downy feathers are present, the central one of which is white, surrounded by two black ones. Thighs clear buff, with the rest of the abdomen being greenish-black to velvety black. Iris brown; beak horn-coloured; feet and legs greyish-brown, with spurs present on the legs.

Hen: *35–39in (89–99cm) Has a rufous head and hindneck; green mantle. Back is brown with buff mottling; wing coverts are heavily mottled with a combination of buff, brown and black. Foreneck and throat are whitish, with the breast being brownish-black edged with green, while the rest of the underparts are buff.*

Unmistakable in appearance and widely kept throughout the world, peafowl have been bred for so long in captivity that a number of colour variants is now well established. Loss of pigmentation has occurred, and today as a result an entirely white variety is often seen (Plate 19). Provided that the plumage remains clean, this is a very beautiful form. As a consequence of the peculiar structure of the feathers, the ocelli, with faint colouring and the iridescence of mother-of-pearl, can be clearly seen.

Pied peafowl have also been bred from crosses between the white and normal forms, and these are frequently available. They have patches of white of varying size, indiscriminately mixed with normal coloration. Compared with the pure forms, such birds are not particularly attractive.

A further variety, known as the black-winged, is darker in coloration than the normal, with the wings of cocks being almost entirely black. In contrast, the hens are much lighter overall than the true species and are, in fact, often pied.

Their large size and the magnificent train of peacocks gives these birds an imposing appearance. Their feeding is very simple, with their basic diet being composed of grain and green food, although they will also eat invertebrates readily, and indeed, a certain amount of live food is essential for young chicks. When kept at liberty, in a large garden or park, they will forage for much of their food.

Peafowl are polygamous in the wild, and usually live in small groups of a cock accompanied by as many as five hens. They nest on the ground, usually in tall, thick grass or among dense shrubs. A typical clutch will have four to eight eggs, with incubation lasting about 28 days. Peahens usually prove reliable parents, and their chicks are quite easy to rear, although they do not grow rapidly.

Young peafowl chicks show no visible markings when in down plumage. Instead, the underparts of the body are reddish-brown, becoming brownish-yellow on the abdomen. Their backs are light brown in colour, with darker moulting apparent here, with their beaks and feet also being brownish in colour.

As they grow, young cocks moult into mottled plumage in their first year, with a dull blue head and throat. The neck and breast are a combination of grey, green and black, as are the upperparts, with the abdomen itself being buff. They resemble the adult cock more closely by the end of the second year, but their train will not become apparent until the end of the third year, and continues to develop over successive moults.

Green Peafowl   (Burmese Peafowl)   *Pavo muticus*

Origin: *southeastern Assam, Burma, southeast Asia, Java and Indo-China*

Cock: 78–92in (198–234cm) Crown covered with small, iridescent green, scale-like feathers, with the remainder of the head, throat and upper part of the neck having short, bluish-green metallic feathers. Bare face, which is a combination of blue and yellow in colour, apart from a thin line of bluish-black feathers extending from the eyes to the beak. The upright, pointed crest is dark green. The plumage of the mantle, breast and neck is green, with deep blue centres, reminiscent of scales and edged with golden-bronze. The remainder of the upperparts are a stunning metallic green and copper-bronze. The small wing coverts are green and blue, with the greater wing coverts and flights being clear chestnut. The tail is brownish-buff with darker markings, with the train itself resembling that of the Blue Peafowl but having a more golden gloss. Lower part of the body is dark green, becoming grey towards the vent. Iris, beak, legs and feet are all blackish, with the legs themselves being equipped with powerful spurs.

Hen: 35–39in (89–99cm) Similar to the cock, but lacks the brilliant green gloss on the upperparts, which are mottled with buff. The uppertail coverts are considerably lengthened, almost extending to the end of the tail, although there is no train. An unusual feature is that hens also have spurs on their tarsi, at the back of the legs, which, in virtually all other species of gallinaceous birds, is a characteristic of cocks only.

These peafowl are generally considered to be even more beautiful than their Indian relative. Unfortunately, the two species will interbreed readily, and their offspring are fertile. This has meant that it can be difficult to obtain pure Green Peafowl stock, especially as they are less widely available than the Indian.

In terms of habits and care, they are similar, but usually prove rather more nervous and wary. Green Peafowl do well at liberty in a park, but they are less hardy than the Indian species and require some protection during the winter. They breed readily, but the chicks are also not so easily reared and must be protected from frost, especially at night when they are best shut in a closed pen. Provided that the shelter is well insulated, it should not be necessary to have artificial heating installed.

If kept in an enclosure on a permanent basis, they must have plenty of space to ensure that their plumage remains in good condition. They can usually be associated quite safely with other birds, even with pheasants. Cocks, unfortunately are exceedingly aggressive, and it is not possible to keep them together, even at liberty in a park, without the risk of serious fighting, which is liable to prove fatal.

It should be added that all peafowl are strong fliers, and, given their active natures, it is very difficult to confine them in a garden or park if they decide to stray. Even with one wing clipped, they will easily leap to the top of a 6ft (1.8m) fence or into the branches of a tree. They prefer to roost well off the ground at night, and a hen will lead her chicks on to a high branch as dusk falls once they are able to fly. Their ghostly, raucous calls may often be heard after dark and are liable to lead to complaints from near neighbours in urban areas.

PIGEONS AND DOVES

Waalia Fruit Pigeon (Yellow-bellied Green Pigeon, Bruce's Green Pigeon) *Treron waalia*

Origin: *north Africa, eastwards to southwest Arabian Peninsula*

Cock: 12in (30cm) *Neck, uppertail coverts and flanks grey-green; remainder of the upperparts dark yellow-green. Breast and belly yellow. Undertail coverts grey-green and brown-red with white margins. Wings purplish wine-red and dark yellow-green. Iris bluish with yellow and wine-red rims; beak blue-grey with a reddish, wax-like base; legs and feet yellow.*

Hen: *Almost identical but may be smaller and slightly duller in coloration.*

There are 25 species of Green Pigeon, forming the genus *Treron*, and although the majority are essentially unknown in aviculture, this is perhaps the most commonly available African species. Others species from Asia that are sometimes seen include the Thick-billed (*Treron curvirostra*), Pompadour (*Treron pompadora*) and the Pink-necked (*Treron vernans*), all of which have the advantage that they can be sexed easily, because the cocks are more brightly coloured than the hens, which are predominantly green.

A variety of fruit, sprinkled with softbill food, should be provided fresh each day, together with either softbill or parrot pellets. These can be offered in a separate container, and, provided that they do not become wet, need not be discarded at the end of the day if they are uneaten.

A planted aviary may encourage these pigeons to breed, especially if wicker baskets can be provided in various localities under cover in a secluded part of the flight. At first, pairs may be nervous and abandon their eggs, but in time they should sit properly and incubate them. The typical clutch has two eggs, with the incubation period lasting 14 days.

The chicks fledge relatively early, often before they can fly properly, and they must be checked to ensure that they do not become saturated and chilled in heavy rain. These pigeons are relatively hardy once they are established in their quarters, but they should always be encouraged to roost under cover, particularly on cold nights.

Lilac-crowned Fruit Dove (Lilac-capped Fruit Dove) *Ptilinopus coronulatus*

Origin: *New Guinea and the Aru Islands*

Cock: 8in (20cm) *Crown rose-lilac, becoming purple towards the nape and surrounded by a thin yellow line. The face is grey, suffused with green, apart from the chin, which is yellowish. Nape, neck, breast and entire upperparts bright green. Abdomen, undertail coverts yellow, with a central reddish-purple area here; flanks barred in green. The wing feathers have yellow edges, and the tips of the tail are yellow. Iris yellow; beak pale olive-green; legs and feet dark red.*

Hen: *Resembles the cock but may have paler yellow markings.*

Fruit pigeons in general are not popular aviary birds, which is surprising because members of this genus in particular are every bit as colourful as many parrots, and, given suitable conditions, they will often attempt to breed. They do need careful attention when first imported, because their feathering may be in poor condition. However, they will not thrive in cages, and an indoor flight will suit them best under these circumstances, although once they are properly acclimatised they can live outdoors throughout the year without artificial heat, provided that they have a suitable shelter. Regular daily spraying is essential to keep their plumage in good condition if they are kept indoors.

An open-fronted nestbox or a wicker basket lined with twigs and feathers may be used as a nesting site. A single egg is laid, and this is incubated in turn by both parents for about 14 days, and the chick will fledge after a similar interval. As soon as it is independent, which will be at about five weeks, the youngster should be removed from the aviary, and the adults are then likely to nest again soon afterwards.

A diet as recommended for the Waalia Fruit Pigeon suits these birds well. Pairs must be housed individually, otherwise fighting may occur, but they can be kept in the company of other softbills, which will not harm them, although breeding is perhaps less likely under these circumstances. Recognising pairs in the case of this and related species can be difficult, since there may be no means of distinguishing the sexes by their plumage, but surgical or chromosomal sexing can be used for this purpose. Hens are often slightly smaller in size if these options are not available.

Green Imperial Pigeon *Ducula aenea*

Origin: *India eastwards across southeast Asia and Indo-China; also present on Sri Lanka, the Andamans, Indonesian islands and the Philippines*

Cock: *18in (46cm) Head, neck, breast and abdomen pale grey, often with a vinaceous tone, with the area at the base of the beak, the plumage around the eyes and on the chin tending to be white. Mantle, back and wings glossy green, sometimes with a coppery-bronze hue in some lights. Undertail coverts dark chestnut. Iris dark reddish-brown; beak greyish; legs and feet carmine red.*

Hen: *Resembles the cock.*

Because it occurs over such a wide area, it is perhaps not surprising that there are local variations in the appearance of these pigeons, with some of the most distinctive forms being present on various islands in the Philippines and Indonesia. The Philippino race *D.a. nuchalis*, for example, has a purplish-maroon patch evident on the nape of the neck.

In avicultural terms this is the best known of the 36 species in this genus. All are relatively large and tend to lack the bright colours associated with the Fruit Doves belonging to the genus *Ptilinopus*, although they require identical care. Compatibility is an important factor in the successful breeding of these pigeons. Some cocks can prove very aggressive towards their intended mates, and they must be separated before they cause serious injury. Birds that perch close together, reflecting a pair bond, should be selected as far as possible if a group is available. It is also a good idea to treat them against tapeworm, using pigeon medication for this purpose. Imported fruit pigeons appear to have a quite heavy burden of these parasites, and this can lead to loss of condition. Routine prophylaxis against *Trichomonas*, a crop parasite frequently associated with pigeons, is also to be recommended prior to the breeding season.

A single egg, laid on a suitable platform nest, is incubated by both parents in turn, with the cock tending to sit for much of the day. This lasts for 28 days, and the chick is covered in dark reddish-brown down, until it starts to sprout its proper feathers. It will leave the nest barely able to fly and with its tail feathers barely developed, and it is fed by the cock until it is eating independently. The most easily identifiable indicator of young birds, aside from their small size, is the coloration of their legs and feet, which are grey at first. It takes two years for this to change to the bright carmine red colour seen in adults.

Triangular-spotted Pigeon (Speckled Pigeon, Guinea Pigeon) *Columba guinea*

Origin: *much of Africa south of the Sahara, in open country, extending down to South Africa*

Cock: 12in (30cm) Head grey, neck feathers reddish-brown with grey tips and a green lustre. Back is a rich shade of red-brown. Underparts as well as the rump and secondaries are grey. Wings red-brown, with numerous triangular white spots and some grey ones as well. Tail grey with a broad white band across the tip. Iris reddish-brown, complete with a broad red, naked orbital ring; beak black; legs and feet red.

Hen: Similar but may be slightly smaller, with less prominent spotting on the wings.

This is one of the smaller pigeons represented in aviculture, and it is very easy to maintain, being quite hardy once acclimatised. Its diet should consist of various kinds of seeds, including millets, groats, kibbled maize and canary seed. Green food such as chickweed may also be taken, and cuttlefish bone and grit should always be provided.

Pairs tend to nest quite readily, sometimes preferring to breed on the ground in a well-planted aviary rather than using a large pigeon pan on a suitable shelf. The cock bows to the hen, but rarely proves aggressive. Indeed, these pigeons are naturally quite social, and in suitably spacious surroundings, more than one pair may be housed together.

Two white eggs form the usual clutch, hatching after an incubation period lasting 15 days. The chicks should fledge around three weeks later. Soaked millet sprays make a good rearing food. The young should then be removed from the aviary, because they are otherwise likely to be attacked by the adult cock once the hen is ready to nest again. Two or three broods during the course of a season can be anticipated.

23 White-crowned Pigeon *Columba leucocephala*

Origin: *West Indies and southern Florida, USA*

Cock: 13in (33cm) *Crown white, with a conspicuous red-brown spot on the nape. Neck feathers scale-like with a metallic gloss. Remainder dark grey, becoming lighter towards the belly. Iris light brown; cere reddish with the beak itself being greenish-white with a reddish, waxy overlay; legs and feet red.*

Hen: *Crown brownish-white, and the slate-grey of the upperparts shows olive-brown suffusion.*

This species is now rarely seen in collections, although it was first kept at London Zoo in 1865 and bred there soon afterwards. A diet of mixed seeds and grain will suit them well, and this can be augmented with chickweed and other green food.

In view of their large size and relatively nervous nature, White-crowned Pigeons must be kept in a large aviary. Here, a pair may well attempt to breed, although they should be encouraged to use a support in the form of a nesting pan for this purpose. Otherwise, their loosely constructed platform of twigs is likely to collapse, resulting in the loss of eggs and chicks. One or two eggs form the typical clutch, with incubation lasting around 17 days.

It may be possible to keep these pigeons in a group in a suitably sized enclosure, because they are social in the wild, but care should be taken to ensure that fighting does not occur in these surroundings. They are quite hardy once they are properly acclimatised.

Mourning Dove (Carolina Dove) *Zenaida macroura*

Origin: *North America, south into Central America and the Caribbean*

Cock: 12in (30cm) *Forehead and sides of the head light brown; neck and crown grey, with a black spot below the ear coverts; throat yellow-brown; breast vinaceous with a metallic violet spot on each side of the neck. Underparts yellowish-white, upperparts greyish-brown, wings brown with black spots and grey with white tips. Iris brown, with narrow patch of bluish bare skin encircling the eyes; beak red at base and black along the rest of its length; legs and feet dull red.*

Hen: *Paler and duller in coloration, lacking the pinkish tone on the breast of cocks, and with less iridescence on the neck.*

These doves, whose common name originates from their rather mournful call, are a common sight in parks and gardens throughout their range. They are easy to care for in aviary surroundings, with millets, canary seed and other similar seeds forming the basis for their diet. Mourning Doves are particularly fond of peas, and they will also take green food and invertebrates.

Pairs can be easily induced to breed. Often they build a nest just a short distance off the ground, in a dense bush or shrub, and they have even been recorded breeding in a hole in the ground. It is, however, better to persuade them to nest in more substantial surroundings, provided by an open-fronted nestbox or wicker basket sited in a secluded part of the aviary. Here, the hen will lay the usual clutch of two eggs, which should hatch after a period of two weeks, with both parents sharing the incubation duties. The young should fledge after a similar interval, and they should be removed from the aviary once they are feeding independently. As many as three broods may be raised in one season, with nesting often beginning as early as March, in the northern hemisphere. These doves are quite hardy, and can be kept outside throughout the year without artificial heat, once they are properly acclimatised.

The White-winged Dove (*Zenaida asiatica*) (Plate 28) is another member of this genus that is often kept, and it requires similar management in aviary surroundings. There are two distinctive populations of these doves in the wild—one occurs through much of Central America, while the other is present on the western side of South America, ranging from southwest Ecuador to Peru and north Chile. The skin around the eyes is bluish in both sexes, although hens are duller in coloration, being brownish rather than vinous-pink in the vicinity of the neck and upper breast. This distinction is most obvious when the birds are viewed in a good light outdoors.

Cape Dove (Namaqua Dove, Masked Dove, Long-tailed Dove)

Oena capensis

Origin: *Senegal east to Arabian Peninsula and south to Cape Province and Madagascar*

Cock: *9in (23cm) Whole front is black, sharply defined against soft grey, becoming whitish towards the vent. Back and wings are brownish-grey. Rump striped black and white, undertail coverts black. Iris brownish; beak red at the base, becoming yellow; legs and feet pinkish.*

Hen: *Soft brown-grey overall, lighter on the abdomen.*

These doves can be recommended for housing with small foreign finches, as they are peaceable and soon become tame. They also need similar care, feeding mainly on a diet of mixed millets and plain canary seed, augmented with green stuff, such as chickweed and seeding grasses, and small invertebrates. Cape Doves are not particularly hardy and need careful acclimatisation. They should be overwintered indoors in temperate areas, particularly as they may often decide to nest at this stage.

A canary nest pan or small wicker basket should be provided, on which the doves can build their flimsy, untidy nest. Without such support, it is liable to disintegrate, causing eggs and young to be lost.

When displaying, the cock will perform a kind of dance as he gracefully trips around the hen. These doves spend much of their time on the ground, typically among grass and shrubs, where they search avidly for seeds and insects. As the breeding season approaches in late summer, the cock calls with a melodious 'coorrooroo', often holding his tail high and fanning it, while he bows to his mate. The typical clutch has two eggs, which hatch after an incubation period of a fortnight. The young fledge after a similar period, and two or three broods may be produced in succession. Pairs are often slower than other small doves to start breeding when they are first acquired, and it may be two or three years before they commence nesting.

Laughing Dove (Senegal Dove, Palm Dove)

Streptopelia senegalensis

Origin: *widely distributed in Africa and east to India*

Cock: *10in (25cm) Throat, head and chest reddish-brown. Collar black with each feather having a reddish-brown tip. Upperparts red-brown, merging into grey. Abdomen and chin white. Iris brown, with red eyelids; beak black; legs and feet red.*

Hen: *Paler and duller in coloration, with greyer rather than reddish-brown upperparts.*

There may be some variation in the coloration of these doves, with a number of distinctive races occurring through their range. They are easy to maintain and make suitable companions for cockatiels, although their larger size may be disturbing in an aviary housing smaller finches. A diet based on millets and other small cereal seeds suits them well.

In a planted flight, Laughing Doves will soon build a slovenly nest out of twigs, straw and feathers. This will need to be reinforced with a wicker basket of the kind sold in many garden centres for flower-arranging purposes.

At this stage, the cock may feed the hen, and, once the two eggs are laid, they share the task of incubation. The eggs should hatch after about 13 days, and the young fly after a further 12 days or so. They will soon become independent, when they must be removed from the aviary, as their parents will soon nest again, and the cock in particular will resent the presence of his older chicks. With any luck they may have as many as five broods during a season, with the chicks almost invariably turning out to be a cock and a hen.

Laughing Doves can become quite tame, and they also tend to be livelier than many other doves.

22 Chinese Necklaced Dove (Spotted Dove,
Chinese Spotted Turtle Dove) *Streptopelia chinensis*

Origin: *India east to southeast Asia, Borneo, Sumatra, Taiwan and China*

Cock: 13in (33cm) Head grey, lighter on the forehead; nape pale vinaceous. A wide, black necklace with white spots is evident on the back and sides of the neck. Light brown upperparts; grey undertail coverts; remainder of the underparts vinaceous, lighter on the chin and belly. Wings dark grey with lighter margins and brown; some feathers have white tips. Iris orange, with mauvish-red orbital ring; beak black; legs and feet red.

Hen: Virtually identical but may be lighter in coloration.

Chinese Necklaced Doves are pretty and make attractive aviary occupants. There are several races of this dove which is, in spite of its name, widely distributed in Asia. They are all similar in appearance, and their care is exactly the same. Those from India can be recognised by their white rather than grey undertail coverts.

These doves require a diet of various millets, plain canary seed, groats and a little hemp. Green food and live food are less important, as is soft food, although this may be eaten in larger quantities when there are chicks in the nest. They will spend much of their time searching for seeds on the ground.

In typical pigeon fashion, they will build their nest on a suitable shelf or in a wicker basket in their quarters. This consists largely of small twigs and feathers assembled in an untidy fashion. They will sit only if they are not disturbed, and they are likely to be particularly nervous when they first start breeding. At the least noise, they will probably leave the nest, and they may even desert their eggs if disturbed frequently. Breeding details are similar to those of the Laughing Dove.

Red Turtle Dove (Dwarf Turtle Dove) *Streptopelia tranquebarica*

Origin: *northwest India, east to Burma, southeast Asia extending to the Philippines*

Cock: 9in (23cm) An attractive shade of vinaceous red, of a paler shade on the underparts. The head and neck are grey, and there is a broad black half-collar on the hindneck. Head, lower back and rump are bluish-grey, with black primaries.

Iris brown, with the bare area of surrounding skin greyish; beak blackish; legs and feet purplish-red.

Hen: *Easily distinguished by brown rather than vinaceous red plumage; brownish-grey rather than bluish-grey elsewhere as well.*

These hardy, attractive doves are easy to maintain in aviary surroundings, and they can be kept alongside cockatiels, although they can be rather disturbing to smaller birds because of their size. Pairs require a diet based on millets, kibbled maize, groats and other similar cereal seeds. They will also eat some green food. Cuttlefish bone and grit are essential, as for all seed-eating species.

They will build a typically loosely assembled nest of twigs, dried grasses, moss and feathers and can usually be persuaded to adopt a nesting basket for this purpose, which will provide additional support. Two eggs form the usual clutch, and both parents share the task of incubation. Breeding details are similar to those of other *Streptopelia* species.

Unfortunately, as in other cases, a pair may not prove entirely reliable when rearing their chicks, and they sometimes neglect their youngest offspring. Supplementary hand-feeding may be required under these circumstances, with the distinction in the growth rate of the chicks becoming apparent as they start to feather up.

If necessary, it is also possible to foster either eggs or chicks to Barbary Doves, which are a domesticated variety of the African Collared Dove (*Streptopelia roseogrisea*). They can be housed quite satisfactorily in breeding cages, being very tame and steady by nature. Most specialist breeders of pigeons and doves will keep a pair of Barbary Doves to assist in an emergency. Male Barbary Doves tend to be noticeably paler than hens.

27 Zebra Dove (Barred Ground Dove, Peaceful Dove)

Geopelia striata

Origin: *India, east to Indonesia and parts of Australia*

Cock: *9in (23cm) Forehead and throat grey. Nape pink; breast, neck and side of the head covered with black and white horizontal stripes. Breast fawn; abdomen white. Wings brown with black stripes. Tail dusky with white spots. Beak and iris brownish-grey; legs and feet red.*

Hen: *Very similar but often slightly smaller and duller in coloration than the cock.*

The care of Zebra Doves is identical to that required for other small doves. They can be kept in an aviary in the company of small finches, and they will become quite steady in these surroundings. They may spend much of their time on the ground, foraging for seeds such as millet and plain canary seed, which should form the basis of their diet. Even so, food should be provided only in the aviary shelter, where it will remain dry and is less likely to attract rodents.

An open-sided nestbox or wicker basket in the aviary will encourage breeding activity. It is difficult to select a true pair, as the cock can largely only be distinguished by his display and behaviour. Some people consider these doves rather dull, as they seem to sit still for much of their time on their nest site, often flying only when they are disturbed. In fact, however, they can be most fascinating occupants of the aviary, particularly when they start breeding.

It is important to avoid sudden movements in their vicinity, as they are inclined to take flight and fly around the aviary in a panic, even injuring themselves if they collide with the mesh.

Once established, pairs will breed throughout the summer, with the incubation period lasting just 12 days. When winter comes, they must be brought indoors into a moderately heated room, having the same requirements at this stage as small foreign finches. They are less hardy than the Diamond Dove.

5 Diamond Dove *Geopelia cuneata*

Origin: *Australia*

Cock: 8in (20cm) Head, neck and breast pale silvery-grey; nape and back pale brown. Wing coverts dark grey, each feather having a round white spot near the end. Central tail feathers dark grey and blackish towards the tips, outer feathers tipped with white; abdomen and undertail coverts white. Iris orange-red, surrounded by a bright coral-red ring; beak dark olive-brown; legs and feet flesh pink.

Hen: Upperparts tend to be more brownish in tone and iris paler. In addition, the spotting on the wings is normally less pronounced.

These birds are one of the smallest of all doves, with their tail accounting for more than half their total body length. They are ideal companions for small finches, particularly in a large flight where they will spend much of their time rummaging around on the ground, foraging for spilt seed. They will soon begin to breed if a true pair has been obtained. The cock will be clearly evident, as he bows and fans his tail feathers in front of his mate. Another difference, which becomes apparent during the breeding period, is that the deep red orbital ring becomes significantly larger in the cock.

They can be persuaded to use either a canary nest pan or an open-fronted nestbox, which will provide support for their untidy nest. Small twigs, coarse, dried grass and moss may all be used in its construction. Two eggs are usually laid, with incubation duties being shared by both parents until they hatch about 13 days later.

The chicks will leave the nest after a similar period, but they will not be able to fly very effectively at this stage, and care must be taken to ensure they do not become saturated in a shower of rain, which could be fatal. Young Diamond Doves are considerably duller in coloration than their parents at first, with the orbital skin being grey rather than red.

As soon as they are independent, they will need to be transferred to another aviary, as their parents are likely to be nesting again and may persecute them. From a normal clutch of two eggs, the youngsters will usually prove to be a cock and a hen. It is recommended that they should not be paired together, though, because possible weaknesses may arise from inbreeding.

Diamond Doves are so prolific that they may nest throughout the year, but certainly in an outdoor aviary in the northern hemisphere the best breeding time will be from May through to August. It is usually possible to prevent the birds from breeding simply by removing the nest pan, but otherwise you will need to separate them. In any event, more than one pair cannot be kept safely together, and even an odd bird, if left in the company of a pair, will be ruthlessly persecuted, especially if it is a cock.

Small seeds should form the basis of the diet for these doves, with various millets, canary seed, a little rape and maw seed being ideal. They may also eat a little chickweed, as well as soft food and even a softbill food, particularly when they have chicks in the nest. Soaked millet sprays are also valuable, particularly during the breeding season as a rearing food. Grit and cuttlefish bone are essential.

Diamond Doves can be allowed to overwinter in an outdoor aviary, provided that they have a snug shelter attached to their flight. Alternatively, they can be brought indoors, and, unlike most doves, they will breed quite happily in such surroundings if housed in a double-budgerigar breeding cage.

A number of colour variants have occurred during recent years, beginning with the silver, which is still best known. As its name suggests, this form is lighter than the normal, being a pure silvery colour. Other, newer mutations include the white-rumped, plus yellow and red forms, although these are not pure colours, but variants of the normal, displaying a yellower or redder tone. They appear to have originated in South Africa, from where stock has been exported to Europe and North America.

Bar-shouldered Dove *Geopelia humeralis*

Origin: *south New Guinea and Australia*

Cock: 11in (28cm) Head, throat and sides of the neck grey; neck itself golden-brown, with the back being a duller shade of brown, all feathers having black margins. Underparts pale vinaceous; belly white. Wings brown; tail grey-brown and chestnut-brown. Iris yellow, with bluish-grey orbital skin and beak; legs and feet red.

Hen: Similar to the cock, but may be duller in overall coloration, with a greyer breast.

Unlike some of their relatives, these doves tend to be very active and will run about busily on the ground, searching for seeds and other food. They require similar care to the Diamond Dove, feeding mainly on seed and barely touching green food, although they may eat some live food.

Bar-shouldered Doves need space and will not settle well in the confines of a cage, but they can live quite satisfactorily alongside small finches and softbills. Pairs must not be housed in the company of other doves however, because the cock in particular will become very aggressive as the breeding season approaches. A pair may nest rather late in the summer, with both birds taking turns at incubation. Their nest needs support, and if wire mesh is used for this purpose, it should be sufficiently fine to ensure that there is no risk of eggs or young chicks being lost through the strands of mesh. Breeding details are similar to those of the Diamond Dove.

Plain-breasted Ground Dove (Grey Ground Dove)

Columbina minuta

Origin: *from Mexico southwards as far as Brazil and Paraguay, although the distribution is patchy, not continuous*

Cock: 6in (15cm) Crown, neck and uppertail coverts grey. Nape brownish; forehead with a vinaceous sheen; back grey-brown. Neck and breast vinaceous blending into grey-white on the belly. Wings brown, black and grey; tail grey and brown with white towards the tip. Iris yellowish-orange; beak brownish; legs and feet pinkish.

Hen: Duller than the cock, lacking the vinaceous tones of the cock. Upperparts are lighter; throat and belly whitish, with the breast being greyish-brown.

The seven species of *Columbina* Ground Dove are often not well identified in aviculture, but in all cases it is possible to sex them on the basis that hens are of duller coloration than cocks, although an examination for this purpose may need to be carried out in good light. One of the most distinctive and common forms is the Gold-billed Ground Dove (*Columbina cruziana*), which, as its name suggests, has a golden base to its bill.

Sometimes known also as Pygmy Doves because of their size, the needs of these doves are all very similar. They can be associated quite safely with small foreign finches and will breed in these surroundings. They are quiet by nature, but cocks are likely to prove aggressive if they are housed together. A diet based on small seeds, such as various millets and plain canary seed, supplemented occasionally with green food, softbill food and small invertebrates, suits them well.

Having built their nest in an open-fronted nestbox or canary nest pan, both cock and hen share the task of incubation. The two eggs should hatch about two weeks later, and the young should fledge after a similar interval. Pairs usually breed repeatedly, having perhaps four broods or more in a season. It is usually recommended to overwinter them indoors, or at least in a heated aviary, because they dislike damp, wet conditions.

These doves can even settle quite well in a spacious box cage in the house, and their soft cooing is never irritating. They can become relatively tame but must always be carefully accustomed to new surroundings. At first, they will be shy and inclined to fly upwards when approached. Like other doves, these birds may be quite long-lived, with a life expectancy of 10 years or more in aviary surroundings.

Blue-spotted Wood Dove (Sapphire-spotted Dove)

Turtur afer

Origin: *Senegal east to Ethiopia and south to southern Africa*

Cock: 8in (20cm) Forehead white; crown grey; cheeks vinaceous with the remainder of the head being grey. Neck and back brownish-grey, with two black cross bars on the rump and a brown band across the middle. Breast vinaceous, belly white. Wings brown-grey, with iridescent wing spots, which are typically dark blue; flights brown, with dark margins. Iris brown; beak pale red, yellowish at the tip and of a purple tone towards the base; legs and feet red.

Hen: Similar in appearance.

There is sometimes confusion about the wood doves, because of the similarity between this species, the Black-billed (*Turtur abyssinicus*) and the Green-spotted Wood Dove (*Turtur chalcospilos*). Beak coloration serves to distinguish the Blue-spotted and Black-billed Wood Doves, while the coloration of the wing spots can be used to distinguish them from the Green-spotted Wood Dove, where the spots are entirely green, with no hint of blue. All species require identical care.

None is difficult to cater for, although they are more insectivorous than the doves discussed previously. In addition to seeds, therefore, they should be offered both softbill food and live food on a regular basis, along with green food. Cuttlefish bone is also important, not only as a source of calcium, but also to prevent their beaks from becoming overgrown. Pecking at its powdery surface keeps the tips of the beak sharp.

Although a pair may not nest immediately when transferred to new surroundings, they can subsequently prove quite prolific and may breed through much of the year. They will build a loose nest for their eggs on a suitable nesting platform, placed in a secluded part of a well-planted aviary.

The cock will display to his mate by flicking his wings, with the metallic wing spots being particularly conspicuous at this stage. Two eggs are likely to be laid, with the incubation and fledging periods both lasting about 13 days. The chicks will be feeding themselves after a further week or so, and they can then be transferred to separate quarters.

The voice of these doves is soft and may frequently be heard at night during the summer months when they are nesting. Nesting facilities and material should be withdrawn at the end of September in northern temperate climates, to prevent them breeding, as the nights are becoming longer and colder, which reduce the likelihood of success. If properly acclimatised however, wood doves may be kept outdoors through the winter, provided their accommodation is well-sheltered.

Green-winged Dove (Emerald Dove) *Chalcophaps indica*

Origin: *India east to the Philippines, extending to Indonesia, New Guinea and Australia.*

Cock: 10in (25cm) Forehead and eyebrow stripe white; head and neck grey; sides of head, hindneck and breast deep vinaceous. Underparts grey. Mantle grey with a golden-green sheen; lower parts of the back black-grey with light grey cross bars and a bronze sheen. Wings iridescent golden-green, flights red-brown. Tail black. Iris dark brown; beak red; legs and feet red.

Hen: Distinguishable by dull grey forehead and narrower eye stripe; crown, nape and upper back brown; underside reddish-brown lightly speckled with grey; brown shoulder. Four central tail feathers brownish-black, while the two on each side have a chestnut tinge towards the base and the outer feathers are grey with a black band towards the tip.

Various different races of this widely distributed dove are likely to be encountered, so it is advisable to purchase a group at the outset for a serious breeding project. This should obviate the need to interbreed different races at a later stage. Pairs are not social, however, particularly in breeding condition, and they need to be housed on their own, rather than with their own kind. They will not interfere with other birds sharing their quarters, however, spending much of their time running busily on the ground in search of seeds and insects. They will also eat green food, as well as berries and even a little fruit.

At other times, these doves will remain quietly perched on a branch, although they are likely to fly about wildly if disturbed, certainly until they are well settled in their quarters. Plenty of cover, in the form of plants, will give them a sense of security and will also encourage breeding activity. The hen may choose to nest on the ground, although a site in a shrub is more often preferred. They can be persuaded to adopt mesh platforms, or wicker baskets, which can be wired in place on a stout stem.

Green-winged Doves build relatively bulky nests and will continue adding material to them over successive clutches. Two eggs form the usual clutch, with incubation lasting a fortnight. The chicks fledge when they are around 13 days old and should be feeding independently by three weeks of age. Two or even three broods may be reared during the course of a season.

Provided they are properly acclimatised, these doves can live outside throughout the year, but their aviary must be equipped with a well-insulated shelter. Since they spend much of their time on the ground, a substantial part of the flight should also be enclosed, to keep this area dry for them. Adequate drainage here is also very important.

29 Common Bronze-winged Pigeon *Phaps chalcoptera*

Origin: *Australia, including Tasmania*

Cock: 14in (36cm) *Buff-white forehead; crown and nape brown with a purple gloss on the side of the head; lores black; cheeks, ear coverts and neck grey, with a pale buff stripe running above and below the eye. Throat white, upperparts brown-grey, the feathers margined with buff; underparts wine red merging into grey. Wings brown-grey with metallic bronze and green spots. Iris red-brown; beak purplish-black; legs and feet pinkish-red.*

Hen: *Paler in coloration, with a greyish forehead, with rusty-brown head coloration and lacking the reddish tinge present on the breast of cocks. Spots on the wings tend to be golden-green, although these may sometimes resemble those of the male.*

First kept outside Australia in 1844, these pigeons have since proved to be quite free-breeding, and stock is well established in many countries. A pair should be housed in a large aviary and not in the company of other pigeons or doves, since cocks are likely to become very aggressive in the breeding season. They should always be watched at this stage to ensure that they do not harass their partners unduly. If this appears to be the case, you may need to separate the pair, or clip one of the cock's wings, so that the hen can escape his attentions more easily with less risk of being hurt.

Bronze-winged Pigeons are easy to keep on a diet of small cereal seeds, even kibbled maize, supplemented with live food and greenstuff. They will build a fairly loose nest, sometimes on the ground, or in a low bush. The hen may be persuaded to use a shelf or open-sided nestbox, which will help to prevent the nest from collapsing, with the loss of eggs or chicks. Incubation lasts around 16 days, with the young flying by the time they are about three weeks of age. Breeding details are identical to those of the closely related Crested Bronze-winged Pigeon.

31 Crested Bronze-winged Pigeon (Australian Crested Pigeon)
Ocyphaps lophotes

Origin: *central Australia*

Cock: 13in (33cm) *Head, breast and abdomen grey; high, pointed crest black. Upperparts olivaceous grey. Uppertail coverts tipped with white. Sides of neck and breast with pink flush. Wing coverts sandy-grey to pure grey, each feather with a black subterminal band; greater coverts metallic green with white borders; primaries dull brownish-black; secondaries with metallic purple and blue broadly edged with white. Tail blackish-brown faintly washed with purple, blue and green on the outer webs. Iris orange surrounded by reddish naked skin; beak blackish; legs and feet crimson.*

Hen: Similar, but may be slightly smaller.

Although not widely available, a few of these pigeons are represented in collections outside Australia, particularly in mainland Europe, and they make interesting and hardy aviary occupants. Their care is similar to that required by the Common Bronze-winged Pigeon, and they are likely to prove equally hardy, provided that their quarters are well screened through the winter months.

Pairs may be housed quite satisfactorily with non-aggressive birds, although, because of their size, in a reasonably small enclosure they may well prove disruptive when kept alongside finches. Crested Bronze-winged Pigeons were first bred in 1865, and true pairs usually prove reliable parents. The cock is most easily identified by his display at this stage. He will bow to a hen, keeping his tail erect while revealing the blue and reddish wing markings to full effect.

Suitable platforms around the aviary, preferably under cover, will encourage breeding. These pigeons like to make a rather untidy nest, which may be in an open-sided nestbox or on a shallow tray, in a secluded part of their quarters, preferably screened with heather or fir branches.

They share incubation duties, with the cock tending to sit mainly during the afternoon. Two white eggs form the typical clutch, and these should hatch after a period of about 15 days. The crests of the chicks soon start to become apparent, but it will be six months before they moult into adult plumage for the first time, gaining the full iridescence on their wings and tail. These pigeons dust-bathe and can be provided with a tray of fine sand for this purpose on the floor of their quarters.

White-bellied Ground Dove (Jamaican Ground Dove)

Leptotila jamaicensis

Origin: *north Yucatan peninsula, Mexico and neighbouring Caribbean islands, including Jamaica and Grand Cayman*

Cock: 12in (30cm) Forehead white; crown ash-grey; back and sides of neck metallic pink with gold and green iridescence. Back and wings olive-brown. Cheeks, throat, and whole of the underparts white. Two central tail feathers olive, remainder grey-brown with white tips. Iris white, surrounded by a bare area of dull purple orbital skin; beak greyish-black, becoming greyer at the base; legs and feet red.

Hen: Usually duller in coloration, with less iridescence on the neck. Forehead greyish, with the white parts being less pure, having a greyish or buff tone.

This species usually has a particular gentle and peaceful nature, spending much of its time on the ground, which means that it is a very suitable subject for a mixed collection. It is reasonably hardy once acclimatised, but it dislikes damp surroundings and must be provided with a dry, frost-proof shelter during the winter months.

Mixed seeds, including various millets, dari, small wheat and groats, form a suitable staple diet, and for a change, fruit pips such as apple and orange, as well as broken peanuts are also appreciated. Some green food will also be eaten, along with a small quantity of live food.

The nest, which is usually a flimsy platform of twigs and leaves, is located in a shrub close to the ground, and a suitable support should be provided for this purpose. Incubation of the two white eggs takes 16 days, with the chicks leaving the nest for the first time after a further 16 days. In addition to the seed mixture and greenstuff, a canary-rearing food and a softbill food should be offered when the young are being reared.

Although they are not especially common, these doves will breed fairly readily in collections, and the first recorded breeding occurred in England in 1903. It is advisable to restrict their breeding activities to the spring and summer months. Four nests of chicks may be produced during this period, and cuttlefish bone must always be provided to ensure that the hen does not suffer from a calcium deficiency. Once independent, the young should be transferred to separate accommodation so that the adult birds can nest again, unmolested by their previous offspring.

30 Luzon Bleeding-heart Pigeon *Gallicolumba luzonica*

Origin: *islands of Luzon and Polillo in the Philippines*

Cock: 10in (25cm) Forehead and crown pale grey, merging into dark grey towards the back and tail; a green and reddish sheen is apparent over the feathers. Cheeks, breast and throat white, with a characteristic blood red spot in the centre of the breast. Belly yellow-white to white. Wings grey with brown and a black cross band just in front of the tips. Iris blue with orbital skin being grey; beak blackish, becoming greyish at its base; legs and feet purple-red.

Hen: Similar, but may be distinguished by purplish coloration of the iris. It has also been suggested that the underparts are more buff, and the red on the breast is smaller.

These pigeons have a relatively restricted range in the wild, and they are thought to be declining here because of widespread deforestation. Four similar species are found on neighbouring islands, but these are even rarer in aviculture, or, in the case of the Tawi-Tawi Bleeding-heart Dove (*Gallicolumba menagei*), completely unknown.

Bleeding-heart Doves are active birds, and spend much of their time walking and running on the ground of their enclosure, as indicated by their relatively long legs. They will generally not molest other birds, except of their own kind, and pairs should be housed individually. With the reliable sexing methods now available, identifying a pair of these birds is now quite straightforward.

A mixed diet, of various small seeds, grated carrot, softbill food and suitable live food, suits them well. Breeding is most likely to occur in a densely planted flight, although pairs are often slower to commence nesting than other pigeons and doves. Nesting baskets should be concealed securely in suitable shrubs, with dried grass, moss and other items being left nearby. They prefer a site quite close to the ground.

The cock usually collects the material and carries it to the hen at their chosen nest site, but the ultimate result is a rather loose structure, which may well collapse without support. Once the two eggs have been laid, the cock incubates for much of the day, and may then feed his mate on the nest. It will take approximately two weeks for the eggs to hatch, and the chicks will leave the nest for the first time about 10 days later.

They are very timid at first, and may be hard to spot in the flight, being well-concealed by their dull brown nest feathering. By six weeks old however, the distinctive red spot on the breast becomes visible, and in another 10 weeks there is no noticeable difference in appearance between the youngsters and the adult birds.

Unfortunately, these pigeons are not always fertile, which may be a reflection of past inbreeding, since available stock is now likely to be entirely captive-bred. As a precautionary measure, it is worth obtaining birds from different sources at the outset to minimise the chances of their being closely related, and also to purchase only immature birds. These will obviously be from fertile stock, and the young cocks should themselves prove fertile in due course.

It is advisable to overwinter them inside, although they can be housed in an outside flight during the warmer months of the year. The roof covering should be fairly extensive however, so that the floor of their quarters does not become flooded during periods of heavy rain. This could prove fatal for young chicks.

WATERFOWL

32 White-faced Tree Duck (White-faced Whistling Duck)

Dendrocygna viduata

Origin: *tropical South America and southern Africa*

Drake: 20in (51cm) Crown, forehead, face, chin and throat pure white; nape and back of neck black. Remainder of plumage warm brown, the feathers of the back being lanceolated and streaked with buff. Sides of breast and flanks finely barred with buff and black; belly very dark brown to blackish. Iris dark brown; beak black; legs and feet dark grey.

Duck: Similar in appearance but often smaller.

The distribution of this species is extremely unusual, since it occurs naturally in both Africa and South America. There are eight different species of tree duck, all of which display the characteristic upright gait, which is emphasised by their relatively long legs. They may roost in trees on occasions, and even nest there, but in the wild they are more likely to be encountered in reedbeds, where they occur in small groups.

The White-faced Tree Duck is one of the most widely kept members of the group and usually becomes extremely tame. It makes a delightful addition to any collection of waterfowl and once it is used to its surroundings will seldom stray, even when fully winged. Even so, you may prefer to restrict the flying abilities of these waterfowl by clipping the flight feathers on one wing, as it will then be easier to round them up during the winter.

Tree ducks are generally rather sensitive to severe cold, and they are best kept in an enclosed pen during the winter, particularly in the case of ducklings. Here they will graze on grass and other greenstuff, as well as eating grain and a duck food mixture, which can often be obtained from agricultural merchants or specialist seed suppliers.

34 Red-billed Whistling Tree Duck (Red-billed Whistling Duck,
35 Black-bellied Tree Duck) *Dendrocygna autumnalis*

Origin: *Texas, USA, southwards through Central America to Ecuador and northern Argentina*

Drake: 20in (51cm) Forehead greyish, with the crown and a line running down the back of the neck varying from dark brown to black; remainder of the head, throat and upper neck grey; lower neck and chest dark, warm brown, with the remainder of the underparts being black. Back and wings dark brown, with a prominent white patch on the wings; tail black. Iris brown; beak red; legs and feet pink.

Duck: Similar in appearance but may be slightly smaller.

The alternative name of 'whistling duck' for this group of waterfowl comes from their unusual whistling call, which sounds like a high-pitched 'breereereeree'. Unlike the White-faced Tree Duck, these ducks will lay on the ground, often under a bush, or in thick vegetation, although they may occasionally be persuaded to use a specially constructed nestbox, like a small dog kennel in appearance, with a wooden platform leading up to it.

Breeding in the northern hemisphere usually occurs during May, with a typical clutch of 12–16 eggs. Incubation, which may be shared, lasts about 27 days, although not all pairs will sit readily. If this happens, the eggs may need to be transferred to an incubator or placed under a broody bantam.

If they are hatched outside, it is vital to protect the young ducklings from damp, as they are delicate, especially in the first few days after hatching, and prone to chilling. They should be confined to a hen house or dry shed during rainy weather.

Egg food, finely-chopped green food and similar foods will be suitable for the young ducklings at first. As they grow, they will eat grain, berries and possibly live food as well. This species may be less hardy than the White-faced Tree Duck, and in periods of frosty or snowy weather the ducks should be encouraged into a barn or shed. Like other tree ducks, they usually become very friendly and will live alongside other ducks without proving troublesome.

36 Common Pintail (Northern Pintail) *Anas acuta*

37 Origin: *Europe, northern Asia and North America, being migratory through this range and heading south at the start of winter*

Drake: 23in (58cm) Whole of head and throat warm brown; a broad line of blackish-brown runs down the back of the neck from the nape to the shoulder; white line on the sides of the neck joins the pure white breast and abdomen. Back and flanks vermiculated grey; ventral feathers yellowish-buff; upper- and undertail coverts black; mantle feathers elongated, white with broad, blue-black shaft stripes; reddish speculum on the wings. Tail black; central feathers greatly elongated. Iris hazel-brown; beak dark grey, legs and feet blackish. When in eclipse plumage outside the breeding season, the drake closely resembles the duck, but has a bolder appearance, which should serve to distinguish the sexes.

Duck: General colour fawn, mottled and streaked with various shades of brown; the line running down the neck is less well defined and the central tail feathers are not as long as those of the drake.

The name of this group of waterfowl derives from the appearance of their narrow tail feathers, giving rise to the description of 'pintail'. Given their migratory habits, stock should be pinioned or the flight feathers of one wing of older birds must be clipped to restrict their flying abilities. Otherwise, they are likely to disappear. They are quite hardy and can be allowed to remain outside throughout the year, although additional food may well be required during the winter months, particularly if the surface of their pond is frozen.

Common Pintails can be accommodated quite satisfactorily on a relatively small area of water, but they do need adequate cover for breeding purposes, and clearly, potential predators such as foxes should be excluded if at all possible. It may be possible to persuade a pair to adopt a nestbox, although thick tussocks of grass, hidden by shrubs, are more likely to be preferred as a nesting site.

A typical clutch contains about eight buff-coloured eggs, with the incubation period lasting 24 days. Pintail ducklings are quite easy to rear, and they develop rapidly. Any which are hatched in the confines of an incubator or under a bantam will, of course, lack the natural water-proofing oil that is normally transferred to the plumage of ducklings by their parents. They must not, therefore, be allowed free access to a pond until they develop their own water-proofing oil, which is produced by the preen gland at the base of the back. Otherwise, they are likely to drown.

38 Common Shelduck *Tadorna tadorna*

Origin: *from the coasts of west Europe to the shores of the Mediterranean; also present in Asia, where it occurs on salt lakes in some areas; migratory, heading south in the winter to north Africa and more southerly parts of Asia*

Drake: 24in (61cm) *Head and neck black with a rich, dark green sheen, as also are a band across the shoulders, the tips of the wings and the tail. There is a green and reddish wing speculum, and a broad chestnut band encircles the back and chest. Undertail coverts dark brown, with the remainder of the plumage pure white. Iris brown; beak bright red with a swollen caruncle, which is lost during the eclipse period; legs and feet pink.*

Duck: *Resembles the drake, but slightly smaller in size and lacks the caruncle. Outside the breeding period the feathers of the face turn light grey, so that sexing is straightforward throughout the year.*

In the wild, the Common Shelduck is found in coastal areas, where there is salt water, feeding mainly on small molluscs and crustaceans. They adapt readily to freshwater surroundings however, and a pair can be kept quite satisfactorily on a pond in a garden. If they are being kept at liberty, they must either be pinioned or have the flight feathers on one wing trimmed after the moult to prevent straying.

Common Shelducks nest in holes in the ground, and so should be provided with artificial burrows. These can be in the form of large wooden boxes buried in the ground; tunnel entrances can be made with concrete drainpipes of a suitable diameter. Glazed pipes should not be used, however, because the slippery surfaces will discourage the ducks from entering.

Various nesting material, such as leaves and moss, will be used to line the nest site, and the duck will line this with down feathers, plucked from her breast. A typical clutch has about eight eggs, which should hatch after being incubated by the duck alone for a period of about 28 days. A regular supply of suitable live food is particularly important at this stage.

Common Shelducks are hardy, and are not, as a rule, dangerous in a mixed collection, although they may show a tendency to bully other, less robust species. The young, which will be fully feathered by about two months old, should start to nest during their second year.

53 **Muscovy Duck** *Cairina moschata*

Origin: *from Mexico south to Uruguay and Peru*

Drake: 32in (81cm) Natural coloration dark brown, with a beautiful green and purple sheen; wing coverts white. Iris yellowish-brown; beak black and rose-coloured, with a prominent red boss on the upper beak in front of the nostrils; legs and feet black. In the rather less attractive domesticated form, however, the ducks appear somewhat coarse, and the wattles are considerably enlarged. The natural coloration has been replaced or broken by white or black coloration, with a black and white pied form being common.

Duck: 24in (61cm) Similar but significantly smaller, lacking the red boss on the beak.

This is one of the most remarkable of all ducks. Indeed, it looks more like a goose than a duck and may weigh up to 10lb (4.5kg). As a rule, drakes of most species can be recognised by their curled tail feathers, but not so in the case of the Muscovy. The drake is distinguished from a distance by his larger size.

Today's Muscovys are partly the result of hybridisation in waterfowl collections, as they have bred repeatedly with various other species of waterfowl, such as shelducks and even geese, although not all such crosses result in fertile offspring. The name derives from a gland in the neck, which emits a strong odour of musk. The peculiar fleshy warts on the head are also involved in this process, which means that this part of the body must be removed as soon as the bird is dead, if it is to be eaten, otherwise, the musky secretions render the carcass inedible.

If it is intended to keep Muscovys in the company of other ducks, they must be kept in pairs, because drakes on their own are invariably a nuisance. They are mute, however, and do not require a large stretch of water, which makes them suitable for ponds in urban areas, although they will prove arboreal. Their sharp claws enable them to climb, and these ducks often favour perching in the open on relatively horizontal tree trunks. They feed mainly on grass, but will also take various grains.

Muscovy Ducks are always good parents. The duck herself lays readily, often adopting a suitable nestbox for this purpose. The eggs have a relatively long incubation period, of about 36 days. The ducklings themselves mature slowly, and will not be fully feathered in less than 16 weeks, unlike most other species of duck, which have their full plumage about three months after hatching.

Female Muscovy Ducks have a reputation for long and patient sitting, and they can prove valuable as foster parents for other, less reliable or less prolific species. Eggs that are on the point of hatching, for example, may be removed from the nest to an incubator, and replaced by fresh eggs, which the duck will continue to incubate until these are also ready to hatch.

Although Muscovy Ducks tame easily and a drake can be kept with up to eight ducks, it is important to separate drakes before they mature. Otherwise, fighting is almost inevitable. Like other waterfowl, Muscovy Ducks have a relatively long lifespan, which can be in excess of 20 years, and they are also quite hardy.

40 **Mandarin Duck** *Aix galericulata*

Origin: *northeast Asia, including Korea, east China, Taiwan and Japan*

Drake: 18in (46cm) In breeding plumage, the crown is greenish-black at the front, fading to bright chestnut and then terminating again in greenish-black feathering, which incorporates the long, sweeping crest. Sides of the head white, extending back to the tip of the crest, with warm chestnut staining in front of the eyes; cheeks and sides of the neck have elongated feathers, which form a mane of rich chestnut, striated with fine, white lines. Hindneck and mantle rich metallic dark green. Back, tail coverts and tail dark brown; chest rich purplish-brown, divided from whitish breast by a broad band of white with triple greenish-black bars each side. Sides and flanks darker brown, finely pencilled with black and terminated by a broad white and black band, which has metallic green reflections. Standing above the sides are two greatly developed fans of bright chestnut feathers, having the appearance of sails, a form of ornamentation that is unique to Mandarin drakes. Iris dark brown; beak orange-red; legs and feet yellow. In eclipse plumage, the drake resembles the duck, but has a paler face and retains the reddish beak.

Duck: Head and depressed crest dark brown, but with pronounced white eyebrow stripe which makes identification quite easy. Throat whitish; neck, breast and underparts dull brown mottled with greyish-white. Wing coverts warm brown; flights blackish-brown with white margins. Beak blackish with almost white tip; legs and feet blackish.

This species is probably the most beautiful of all waterfowl. They are easy to care for, since they can even be housed quite satisfactorily in a garden aviary with a pond. In the wild, these ducks spend much of their time in trees, and an enclosure for them should be designed accordingly. This may be a better option than keeping them at semi-liberty, unless they are pinioned, because otherwise they will almost inevitably stray.

For breeding purposes, Mandarin Ducks require a nestbox, which should be at least 10in (25cm) square, lined with a covering of dried grass and dead leaves. This should be placed on a pole, about 2–3 ft (60–90cm) off the ground, with a tree trunk or small ladder enabling the duck to reach the entrance.

Here the ducks will lay 6–12 eggs on a nest bed made by plucking her own down feathering. Incubation lasts 28 days. When the ducklings hatch, their mother will oil their down thoroughly, using oil from her preen gland, and then she will coax them out of the nest and down to the ground. In spite of tumbling some distance to the ground, they seldom suffer any injury.

If the eggs have been hatched under a hen or in an incubator, it is important to remember that the ducklings will not have received a protective coating of oil on their feathers. They must therefore be kept out of water, for the first few days after hatching, until their own preen glands begin to function, otherwise they will become waterlogged and are likely to drown.

Young Mandarin ducklings grow rapidly, often foraging for duckweed on the water's surface. Alternatively, chopped green food, such as chickweed, and egg food can be provided, and later both shrimp meal and maize meal can be offered. They are also particularly fond of earthworms, which can be purchased in quantity from a specialist live-food supplier and kept in a container of damp soil until required, when the ducklings are several weeks old. Alternatively, even during a dry spell, you may be able to attract earthworms to the soil surface regularly, by watering an area of garden daily, and keeping this patch covered with hessian sacking to retain the moisture. Loosely forking the surface should then reveal the worms.

▮1 Carolina Duck (Wood Duck) *Aix sponsa*

Origin: *North America, from British Columbia to California on the west and from the Great Lakes south on the east*

Drake: 18in (46cm) In breeding plumage the crown feathers extend into a long crest lying flat over the nape, showing metallic dark green with purple reflections; narrow white lines extend from the nostrils to the nape, and from behind the ears. Ear coverts and cheeks violet, divided by a white line curving down from below the eye and joining the chin, throat and collar, which are all white. The wings are rich, shining green and purple; breast rich purple-brown spangled with small white spots and outlined with white. Back and uppertail coverts metallic green and violet; tail blackish; undertail coverts are chestnut, belly greyish-brown fading to white. Sides warm brown divided from ventral feathers by broad white and black bands, and with black and white crescents on the upper border. Iris dark brown surrounded with a ring of bare scarlet skin; beak dark brown, becoming orange-scarlet at the base of the upper mandible; legs and feet yellow. In eclipse plumage the drake is similar to the duck but more colourful, particularly on the crown and back.

Duck: *Mainly brown, dark on the crown and nape, dull greyish-brown on the cheeks, warm on the back and wings with a slight green and purplish sheen; chin and throat greyish-white; underparts dull brown with pale whitish spots on the sides, beak dull black; legs and feet dull brownish-black.*

Very similar in habits to the Mandarin Duck, the Carolina Duck is equally hardy and will move about on the ground quite readily, even after a snowfall. These ducks will roost under any low conifers or thick bushes, but must be protected from foxes. They require a small pond, because they actually mate on the water. The behaviour and display of the drake is very interesting at this stage, as he bobs around after his intended mate.

Breeding may commence as early as April in the northern hemisphere, and, as with the Mandarin, a suitable barrel or nestbox should be provided on a platform raised off the ground, with a sloping board up which the duck can scramble. Pairs can prove quite prolific, sometimes nesting twice during the course of a season, with the hen incubating alone for 28 days.

Carolina Ducks like to eat berries, insects, snails and worms, as well as acorns and beech masts. Grain and green food normally form the basis of their diet however, although they will obviously find their own food to some extent if kept under conditions of semi-liberty. The ducklings can be sexed by the time they have acquired their adult plumage, at around eight weeks of age. Carolina Ducks are quite social by nature and can be kept together in a group; indeed, this will then reduce the likelihood of hybridisation, which can occur if an odd individual is kept in the company of other ducks.

39 Red-crested Pochard *Netta rufina*

Origin: *from Spain east across parts of Europe as far as central Asia; migrates south during the winter*

Drake: *22in (56cm) Head and throat a mass of soft, bright chestnut feathers; back of the neck, chest and breast, as well as the vent, upper- and undertail coverts plus the short tail velvety-black with a greenish sheen. Mantle dull brown; shoulders and flanks white. Iris, beak, legs and feet red. In eclipse plumage, however, the drake is similar to the duck.*

Duck: *Entirely dull brown, with the cheeks, upper breast and flanks being pale greyish-brown; beak, legs and feet blackish.*

These attractive ducks need a reasonable area of water, partly because they tend to spend much of their time swimming. In addition, they will dive under the water to obtain aquatic vegetation and other food such as molluscs. They will also feed on land, grazing on grass.

When nesting, Red-crested Pochard build a relatively bulky nest, using twigs, and often concealing this in a bed of reeds. They start to nest quite early in the year, but usually produce only one group of ducklings. Up to 14 eggs may be laid, with incubation typically lasting for as long as 27 days. The brighter beaks of the young drakes will soon become apparent.

This species is quite hardy and adaptable in its feeding habits, although duckweed is often favoured. This can easily be grown on a pond however, simply by introducing some from elsewhere as it spreads rapidly. Green food should always figure prominently in the diet of these ducks.

PARROTS

52 **Ornate Lorikeet** *Trichoglossus ornatus*

Origin: *Sulawesi (formerly Celebes) and neighbouring Indonesian islands*

Cock: 10in (25cm) Crown and ear coverts purplish-blue; a band of red with transverse blue-black lines on the occiput and a yellow line running down the sides of the neck. Nape, back, tail, wings and abdomen bright green, the latter lightly barred with blue-black. Flights blackish-green. Throat, cheeks and breast bright red, the breast lightly barred with bluish-black; flanks barred with light green and yellow. Iris hazel-brown; beak orange; legs and feet grey.

Hen: Similar in appearance.

Careful acclimatisation is necessary with these and other lorikeets, particularly if they are in poor feather condition. They will probably need to be brought inside for their first winter, before they can be considered fully acclimatised in the following year.

The diet should be based on fruit and nectar and must be altered only gradually in the case of newly acquired birds, otherwise they may suffer serious digestive disturbances. The nectar solution must be made up fresh every day, and cleanliness is vital with these and other nectar-feeding parrots. The pots must be cleaned thoroughly between feeds.

Ornate Lorikeets are less commonly seen these days than in the past, but they are still represented in a number of collections. Pairs will nest quite readily, with the earliest breeding record dating back to 1883. Surgical sexing has removed the uncertainty of identifying pairs, and two rounds of chicks may be reared during a season.

Two or three eggs form the typical clutch, and they hatch after a period of 26 days. Young birds are unusual in having more yellow feathering on the abdomen than adults. Like most lorikeets, they have playful natures, and youngsters can become very tame, although their rather fluid diet means they are likely to be messy in the home.

50 **Swainson's Lorikeet** (Rainbow Lorikeet,
Blue Mountain Lorikeet) *Trichoglossus haematodus moluccanus*

Origin: *east Australia and Tasmania*

Cock: 12in (30cm) Head and throat purplish-blue; back, wings and tail green with a yellowish band on the nape; breast and underwing coverts vermilion; belly bright blue. Undertail coverts yellow tipped with green. A yellow band is also present on the undersurface of the wings. Iris reddish-brown; beak orange-red with a paler tip; legs and feet dark grey.

Hen: Similar in appearance.

In their natural habitat great flocks of these lorikeets visit eucalyptus trees to feed on the blossoms, and, with their arrow-like flight, they flash through the air like sparkling jewels. They have a shrill screech, which may be heard when they are in flight. Their diet is largely composed of nectar, flowers, fruit seeds and, occasionally, insects.

These lorikeets have sticky, fluid droppings, which reflect their diet. This should consist of nectar, apple and other fruit, a little seed, plus green food and vegetables such as grated carrot. It is not advisable to keep them on a diet mainly of seed, although they may subsist on this for a period without obvious problems.

In recent years nectar mixes that can be fed dry, either in a dish or sprinkled over fruit, have become more popular for these birds, but it is usually advisable to augment such foods with a fluid nectar as well. Fresh drinking water must always be offered to lories and lorikeets, whatever their diet.

In large aviaries these lorikeets have been kept and bred successfully in groups, but in general, breeding results are much better if they are housed in individual pairs. They require a solid nestbox, with an entrance hole of about 3in (7.5cm) in diameter, and soft wooden chips, which they can whittle away to form an absorbent nest lining.

Two eggs form the typical clutch, with the hen incubating alone, although her mate will feed her while she is sitting. The chicks should hatch after about 26 days, and they remain in the nest for about two months. There may be two or even three broods in a season. Although the first breeding results appear to have been obtained in Britain in 1907, these lorikeets have since become scarce here, although they are widely bred in Australian collections.

Red-collared Lorikeet *Trichoglossus haematodus rubitorquis*

Origin: *from the Kimberley area of Western Australia east to the Gulf of Carpentaria, Queensland, in the north*

Cock: 12in (30cm) Head and throat blue, distinctive orange-red neck band, extending around the nape, bordered by a broad blue band below. Breast orange-red, as is the band around the neck. All the upperparts are green, with the belly being blackish-green. Flanks yellow, flecked with red and green; wings and tail green. Iris red; beak reddish; legs and feet grey.

Hen: Similar in appearance.

Over 20 distinctive forms of this species are recognised by most taxonomists, and only comparatively recently have breeders started to appreciate the need to prevent haphazard crossings between these various races, which range north from Australia to Indonesia. A number are localised to small individual groups of islands, and with deforestation occurring on a fairly widespread scale in this part of the world, there is a real need to develop secure captive populations.

The nominate form, known as the Green-naped (*T.h. haematodus*), is probably most widely kept and bred at present. It originates from New Guinea and neighbouring Indonesian islands, with imported stock having been quite readily available during recent years. The neck band in this case is greenish, as the name implies.

There is also often a distinction in terms of the coloration of the plumage on the breast. In the case of the attractive Edward's Lorikeet (*T.h. capistratus*), which occurs only on the island of Timor, Indonesia, the breast feathering is entirely yellow. The very similar Wetar Lorikeet (*T.h. flavotectus*) has green instead of orange coloration on the underwing coverts.

One of the more northerly races is Massena's Lorikeet (*T.h. massena*), sometimes also known as the Coconut Lorikeet, which is found in the Bismarck Archipelago of New Guinea, extending to the Solomon Islands and the New Hebrides. Its head coloration is dark blue, becoming blackish on the cheeks. Dark brown feathering is present in the vicinity of the nape, while the plumage of the breast is red with black edging. The absence of this black barring is a feature of Forsten's Lorikeet (*T.h. forsteni*), from the Indonesian island of Sumbawa, and this is also one of the smaller races, averaging 9in (23cm) in length.

Irrespective of their origins, all these lorikeets need similar care, as recommended for Swainson's Lorikeet, and breeding details are identical. In common with other nectar-feeding parrots, newly imported individuals may suffer from tapeworm infections. This may be because they eat the invertebrates responsible for spreading these parasites when feeding on the flowers, although they will take live foods only very rarely in aviary surroundings. Loss of condition may be indicative of infection, and veterinary advice should be sought under these circumstances.

Goldie's Lorikeet *Trichoglossus goldiei*

Origin: *New Guinea, extending from the southeast Papua to the Weyland Mountains near Geelvink Bay*

Cock: 7in (18cm) Scarlet forehead and crown, surrounded by an area of mauve, which becomes bluish-pink in the vicinity of the ear coverts, cheeks and lores. Upperparts dark green, with the underparts being of a lighter shade, broken by darker streaks of green. This streaking often becomes more prominent at the sides of the neck, and also occurs on the undertail coverts. Iris dark brown; beak black; legs and feet dark grey.

Hen: Similar, but may be less heavily streaked.

These attractive small lorikeets were largely unknown in aviculture until 1977, but since then they have proved prolific and become very popular. They are ideal occupants for an aviary in a relatively small suburban garden, being significantly quieter than some of the bigger species and having a call which is unlikely to cause offence to near neighbours. Young birds can also become delightfully tame, although their fluid, sticky droppings mean that particular attention must be paid to cleanliness if they are kept in a cage at home.

A diet based on a nectar solution, provided fresh each day, along with dry nectar, fruit and a little seed, such as spray millet, will suit these lorikeets well.

Their display can help to identify the cock bird, as he swirls his head in front of his mate. Two eggs form the typical clutch, with incubation lasting around 24 days. Generally the hen sits alone, but she may on occasions be joined by her mate in the nestbox. In some cases, he may actually play a more active part in the incubation process. The youngsters should fledge at about two months old, and more than one brood may be reared during the course of a season.

Purple-capped Lory (Purple-naped Lory) *Lorius domicella*

Origin: *Seram and Ambon islands, Indonesia; also introduced to Buru*

Cock: 12in (30cm) Crown of the head black at the front, blending into deep purple. Orange band across the upper breast, with the remainder of the body being a deep velvety red, being darker on the back; wings green and the webs of the flight feathers yellow. There is a small patch of pale blue on the bend of the wings, and the thighs are rich cobalt. Tail red, with a purple-coloured band just above the tip. Iris brown; beak orange; legs blackish.

Hen: Similar in appearance.

Members of this genus can be rather noisy, but they are strikingly colourful aviary occupants and are able to live outdoors throughout the year once they are fully acclimatised. They do not require artificial heat, but their accommodation should be well-insulated against the elements. They must also have a nestbox or hollow log available for roosting purposes throughout the year.

Nectar, fruit, greenstuff and a little seed will again make a suitable diet for these lories. Although perhaps less commonly seen in aviculture today than in the past, pairs can usually be persuaded to nest without difficulty. Their normal clutch has two eggs, which should hatch after being incubated by the hen for about 25 days.

The chicks are covered in white down at first, which is replaced by a denser grey down by the time they are three weeks old. The young lories will leave the nestbox for the first time when they are about 10 weeks old.

Surprisingly at this stage, they will be more colourful than their parents, with a more prominent area of yellow on the chest. The beak also serves to distinguish recently fledged Purple-capped Lories, since it is black at this stage. The first recorded breeding of this species took place in Belgium as long ago as 1916.

Chattering Lory (Scarlet Lory) *Lorius garrulus*

Origin: *Indonesian islands, centred on the Moluccas*

Cock: 12in (30cm) Predominantly deep scarlet, with green wings, except for the bends of the wings, which are yellow. Top part of the tail is red, with the lower part being purple tinged with green. Base of the primaries red; underwing coverts yellow. Iris orange; beak orangish-red; legs and feet dusky grey.

Hen: Similar in appearance.

The length and shape of the tail serve to distinguish the lories from the lorikeets. Lories as a group have shorter, square tail feathers, whereas those of lorikeets are longer and pointed. The Chattering Lory itself has long been an avicultural favourite, although it is often the Yellow-backed race (*L.g. flavopalliatus*) (Plate 53) that is most commonly available. Birds of this form can be easily distinguished from the nominate race by the large yellow patch on the mantle, at the top of the back.

Unfortunately, the main drawback of this species is its rather loud and harsh voice, which may be audible even after dark. It requires the same treatment as the Purple-capped Lory. Once they are properly acclimatised, these lories are sufficiently hardy to overwinter in an outdoor aviary equipped with an adequate shelter, and pairs have nested in collections around the world. Incubation lasts about 26 days, with the chicks fledging about 10 weeks later. Hand-reared youngsters are invariably very tame and may even learn a few words.

Dusky Lory (White-backed Lory) *Pseudeos fuscata*

Origin: *most of New Guinea, apart from the central region, and extends to the western Papuan islands and Japen Island, Geelvink Bay*

Cock: 10in (25cm) Plumage coloration tends to be highly individual in all cases. A distinctly bright, fiery orange form, and a relatively dull yellow version are recognised, with this coloration being most markedly apparent on the breast in the vicinity of the neck, and lower down, above the abdomen. The forehead is black, becoming golden-bronze on the crown, with the ear coverts also being black. Upperparts brownish-black; secondary coverts brown; underwing coverts orange with orange spot also present on the primaries. Rump varies from silvery to yellowish-white. Upper surface of tail bronze and blue, sometimes with orange visible on the inner webs, with lower surface being bronze and undertail coverts a dark blue. Iris orange-red; bare orange skin encircles the lower part of the beak, which is also orange; iris orange-red; legs and feet dark grey.

Hen: *Similar in appearance.*

Although these lories were another avicultural rarity until the 1970s, they have since become well established, being bred in large numbers in many countries each year. They are also quite hardy once established, and are long lived, with a life expectancy of perhaps 20 years or more.

Up to four eggs may be laid, with incubation lasting about 24 days. The chicks should fledge about 10 weeks later, and more than one clutch of eggs may be laid during the warmer months of the year in temperate areas.

Unfortunately, as with other species of lories and lorikeets, some pairs will pluck their young before they fledge. A particular watch needs to be kept on these chicks, as they may become chilled, especially if the weather is cold and wet. However, the plumage will regrow over the course of several weeks, depending on the severity of the problem. It would seem that this behaviour may, at least initially, reflect a desire on the part of the adult birds to persuade their chicks to leave the nest, but it then becomes habitual. There is little that can be done once the feathers have been pulled out, but with a known pair of feather-plucking birds, you may be able to overcome the problem by sprinkling a little powdered aloes on the necks of the chicks just as they start to feather up. The bitter taste of the aloes should deter the parents from pulling their feathering, because they are most vulnerable before the feathers have unfurled.

Chicks should also be watched to ensure that one of the youngsters is not favoured over another. If this occurs, supplementary feeding may be required. Usually, it is the youngest chick which is most likely to need attention.

It seems that while yellow-phase Dusky Lories may produce youngsters of either colour form, only those of the deeper orange coloration have similarly coloured offspring.

Greater Sulphur-crested Cockatoo

(Sulphur Crested Cockatoo) *Cacatua galerita*

Origin: *Australia, New Guinea and Indonesia*

Cock: *20in (51cm) Body plumage entirely white, with only a yellow suffusion on the ear coverts and the tail coverts. The crest is yellow, with the exception of frontal feathers, which are white. Iris black, surrounded by bare orbital skin, which is whitish (blue in some races); beak black; legs and feet greyish.*

Hen: *Similar in appearance but can be distinguished by brownish-red irises.*

The Australian form is relatively scarce in overseas collections, where the race known as the Medium Sulphur-crested Cockatoo (*C.g. eleonora*) from the Aru Islands of Indonesia is best known. It is smaller in size. Other subspecies which may be seen occasionally are the Triton Cockatoo (*C.g. triton*), which is distinguishable by its blue orbital skin and broader crest feathers, and the Blue-eyed Cockatoo (*C.g. ophthalmica*), which has even darker blue coloration here and an exceedingly wide crest, which is more like that of the Umbrella Cockatoo than that of the Greater Sulphur-crested Cockatoo.

These active birds are best housed in a well-built outside aviary. Although they can become tame, especially when obtained as hand-reared chicks, they will often screech and yell in a most unpleasant fashion. This characteristic makes then an unsuitable choice for suburban aviaries, where their screeching will almost certainly lead to complaints from near neighbours.

Greater Sulphur-crested Cockatoos may live to a great age, sometimes for 70 years or more. They are quite hardy when acclimatised, and pairs should nest quite readily, if they are provided with a suitable stout nestbox or barrel. Breeding results were first reported from Algiers back in 1879, and subsequently from Germany and Britain, in 1883 and 1915 respectively. The birds should be watched during the initial stages, however, because the cock may become very aggressive towards his mate at this stage.

Both parents share the incubation process, which lasts about a month. Their offspring should fledge after a further two months, although the younger of the two chicks may be neglected, in preference to the elder one. You will either have to provide regular supplementary feeding or remove it for hand-rearing, because the growth of this chick will otherwise suffer and it may die before fledging. Inspections should be carried out with care, however, because these cockatoos are liable to prove aggressive when their nestbox is approached during the breeding period.

A varied diet is likely to encourage the parents to rear both their chicks successfully. This should include not only a staple parrot mix, but other items, including greenstuff, fruit and parrot pellets.

55 Lesser Sulphur-crested Cockatoo *Cacatua sulphurea*

Origin: *Sulawesi (formerly Celebes) and other neighbouring Indonesian islands*

Cock: 14in (36cm) Predominantly white, with a yellowish tinge on some parts of the body; cheek patches yellow; long, curved crest, which is raised when the bird is alarmed or excited, yellow. Undersurface of wings and tail yellow. Iris black; beak black; legs and feet blackish-grey.

Hen: Similar in appearance but usually has reddish-brown irises.

One of the most popular of the cockatoos, this species has long been a popular pet. Young birds are readily tamed and become very affectionate, although their talking skills are relatively limited. As they mature, however, they are likely to become more noisy and sometimes bite with little provocation.

Acclimatised pairs can be housed in a suitably robust aviary throughout the year, without the need for artificial heat, although they need a well-insulated shelter to which they can retreat when the weather is at its worst. Like other cockatoos, however, the calls of the Lesser Sulphur-crested are raucous and can be repeated frequently, especially when the birds are in breeding condition. This means that they are likely to cause a disturbance when kept outside in urban areas.

Compatible pairs will nest quite readily, but again, cocks can be savage towards their mates. Tame and hand-reared birds tend to be the worst in this regard, because they have little, if any, fear. A close watch must, therefore, be kept on pairs which have not nested together before, although even established pairs may sometimes be affected as well. If the cock does become aggressive, he must have his wings clipped or be removed from the aviary, because the hen may even be killed.

Two, or occasionally three, eggs will be laid in a stoutly constructed nestbox or a suitably robust hollow log. The nesting site should be positioned in such a way that access is reasonably straightforward, so that a watch can be kept on the chicks' development. Incubation lasts about 28 days, with the young birds fledging at around 10 weeks old. The first breeding result with this species was obtained in Britain in 1922.

On occasions, other races of the Lesser Sulphur-crested Cockatoo (sometimes referred to as LSC, distinguishing it from the Greater, GSC, and Medium Sulphur-crested, MSC, forms) are available. The best known and most distinctive of these is the Citron-crested (*C.s. citrinocristata*), which is found only on the Indonesian island of Sumba. In this case, the yellow of the Lesser Sulphur-crested is replaced by bright orange. The Timor Cockatoo (*C.s. parvula*), from the island of that name, is also sometimes available. It more closely resembles the Lesser Sulphur-crested, but may be distinguished by its smaller size; it averages about 12in (30cm) in length.

Umbrella Cockatoo (Great White Cockatoo,

White-crested Cockatoo) *Cacatua alba*

Origin: *north and central Moluccas, Indonesia*

Cock: 19in (48cm) Entirely white, apart from a sulphur yellow tinge at the base of the inner webs of the flight and tail feathers. Crest large, white and rounded in shape. Naked orbital skin bluish. Iris black; beak black; legs and feet also black.

Hen: Similar in appearance but with warm brown irises.

These large cockatoos are relatively easy to maintain, although in view of their size, they should always be housed in flights or aviaries rather than in cages. Should they become bored, they are likely to resort to feather-plucking, to which cockatoos as a group appear quite susceptible.

When purchasing stock, particular attention should be paid to the birds' plumage, as these and other cockatoos are also prone to the viral infection now referred to as Psittacine Beak and Feather Disease (PBFD), for which there is at present no cure. Scruffy, dirty brown feathering, and overgrown, soft beak and claws are features of this ailment. In time, almost all the body feathering is likely to be lost, with the cockatoo usually succumbing to a bacterial or fungal infection, which overwhelms its impaired body defences.

The best means of keeping Umbrella Cockatoos is in a large robust aviary, where they have adequate opportunity to bathe. This helps to keep their feathering in good condition. They should be encouraged to eat a varied diet as well, which can consist of sunflower, maize, oats, pine nuts, peanuts and larger nuts, such as Brazils, as well as carrot, fruits and greenstuff.

When breeding, the adult birds share the incubation duties, as in the other *Cacatua* species. Two eggs again form the normal clutch, and should hatch after a period of about 30 days. Fledging takes place about 10 weeks later, although it may be four or five years before the young birds themselves start to breed for the first time.

54 Moluccan Cockatoo (Salmon-crested Cockatoo, Pink-crested Cockatoo, Rose-crested Cockatoo)

Cacatua moluccensis

Origin: *south Moluccas, Indonesia*

Cock: 20in (51cm) Whitish, with a variable depth of salmon-pink suffusion, most evident in the vicinity of the breast. Broad crest, which is long, with the central feathers being salmon-red and the remainder white. Deep salmon suffusion is apparent on the underside of the flight feathers, with those of the tail being more orangish on their lower surface. Bare area of skin encircling the eyes whitish, with a variable blue tinge. Iris black, as are the beak, legs and feet.

Hen: Similar in appearance, but usually discernible by dark brown irises, although surgical sexing has now confirmed this is not entirely reliable as a means of distinguishing the sexes in every case.

These cockatoos have declined dramatically in the wild in recent years and are now fully protected in their homeland, although whether deforestation of their native islands will continue to affect the remaining populations is unclear. Recent survey work suggests that they are not yet facing imminent extinction, however, whereas previously their precise status was unclear.

Moluccan Cockatoos have been kept in many collections around the world, but it was not until 1951 that the species was first bred; this occurred at the San Diego Zoo, California. Since then, many other public collections and private aviculturists have reported breeding successes, and in some countries, stud books have been set up to assist in the conservation of the species.

Unfortunately, the loud screeching of these cockatoos means that breeders in suburban areas are likely to receive complaints from neighbours. Moluccan Cockatoos also require a very stout aviary because of their powerful beaks. They destroy woodwork without difficulty, although regular provision of a plentiful supply of fresh branches should serve to attract them away from destroying their nestbox.

The coloration of individual Moluccan Cockatoos can differ quite markedly. Some birds are so pale that they are almost indistinguishable from the Umbrella Cockatoo except by the coloration of the crest feathers. In other cases, the pink suffusion can be widespread, extending over most of the body. This does not appear to be related to the bird's gender, and the actual depth of coloration does not appear to vary through its life.

Feeding and breeding details for the Moluccan Cockatoo are identical to those of the Umbrella Cockatoo. Although young birds can become very tame and develop into lively companions, it may, in view of the status of this species, be better to keep them for breeding purposes only. Controls may apply to the sale of young, since the Moluccan Cockatoo is classed as an endangered species under the international CITES agreement. Advice on the current position can be sought from the government department concerned with wildlife and CITES matters.

Bare-eyed Cockatoo (Little Corella, Short-billed Corella)

Cacatua sanguinea

Origin: *Australia and southern New Guinea*

Cock: 15in (38cm) General colour white; feathers of the lores and head rose-red at the base. Relatively inconspicuous crest. Inner webs of the primaries and of all but the central pair of tail feathers sulphur yellow. Bare skin encircling the eyes is dark bluish-grey. Iris blackish-brown; beak greyish-brown; legs and feet grey.

Hen: Similar in appearance.

This species is very common in Australia, and flocks of many thousands are sometimes seen. It normally feeds on the ground, chiefly on the seeds of various grasses and on plants, roots and bulbs. The site chosen for nesting is often a hole in a large gum tree, close to water, with the clutch usually consisting of three pure white eggs.

Best known as an aviary bird in its homeland, Bare-eyed Cockatoos are sometimes seen in collections elsewhere. They have a reputation for being pugnacious although hardy birds, capable of overwintering in an outside aviary, which includes a well-insulated shelter. A nestbox or hollow tree trunk should be available throughout the year, because these cockatoos often prefer to roost here even outside the breeding period, rather than remaining on the perches in the aviary.

Their food should consist of a good quality parrot food mixture, augmented with cereal seeds such as millet sprays, plain canary seed and groats. Pine nuts are also often favoured. Raw vegetables, such as peas in their pods and diced carrot, should also be supplied, along with fruit such as sweet apple, together with greenstuff. If these cockatoos are kept in an aviary with a solid floor, such as concrete, a fresh turf can be provided regularly, as it will give them an opportunity to dig with their beaks.

Bare-eyed Cockatoos first nested successfully at London Zoo in 1907. Their incubation period lasts 27 days, with the chicks fledging about nine weeks later. A similar species, the Long-billed Corella (*C. tenuirostris*), which has a longer upper bill, is sometimes seen in Australian collections. It requires identical care, but is at present almost unknown in collections elsewhere.

59 Leadbeater's Cockatoo (Major Mitchell's Cockatoo)

Cacatua leadbeateri

Origin: *western and interior areas of Australia*

Cock: 16in (41cm) *White flushed with pink on the sides of the head, neck, breast and abdomen; the coloration is most evident beneath the wings and at the base of the tail. The feathers of the forehead are also rosy-pink at their bases, and this is particularly noticeable when the crest is raised. The deep orange-vermilion crest is long and pointed with a central band of yellow, and the tips of the feathers are white. Iris blackish; beak pale yellowish; legs and feet blackish-grey.*

Hen: Similar in appearance but irises are warm brown.

These beautiful cockatoos are relatively scarce in aviculture, and this is not helped by the aggression of cock birds, which can make pairing a difficult process. It is best to start with young birds, which have been sexed to ensure they are a pair, as compatibility is more likely if a pair bond can be established before they attain sexual maturity.

Youngsters of both sexes have blackish irises, and so they cannot be distinguished visually at this stage. The colour change occurs slowly, and it can be over a year before the eyes of hens have changed to their characteristic brownish shade. It will take about four years before they are fully mature and likely to start breeding.

In the wild, Leadbeater's Cockatoos feed mainly on the ground, hunting for grass seeds and other foods. Their diet should consist of sunflower seed, groundnuts, pine nuts, canary seed, millets, groats and maize, along with plenty of green food, carrot, fruit and similar items.

Leadbeater's Cockatoos were first bred in Britain in 1901. The clutch consists of three or four eggs, and the cock bird incubates for much of the day, with the hen taking over at dusk and sitting through the night. The chicks should hatch after 28 days and leave the nestbox when they are about two months old. They are usually reared largely on green food and fruit, as well as regurgitated seed. Soaked millet sprays are often eaten readily by the adults when they have chicks in the nest.

8 Roseate Cockatoo (Galah, Rose-breasted Cockatoo)
Eolophus roseicapillus

Origin: *throughout most of Australia*

Cock: 14in (36cm) General colour above silvery-grey, lighter on the rump. Outer webs of the wing coverts and secondaries, crown, hindneck and feathers below the eye rose tinted with white. Throat, cheeks, breast, abdomen and underwing coverts deep rose red. Flanks and undertail coverts light grey. Naked skin around the eyes dull red. Iris dark brown; beak whitish-cream; legs and feet dark grey.

Hen: Similar in appearance but with lighter coloured irises.

Variation is often apparent in the coloration of these cockatoos. Some have much lighter grey coloration over the back and wings, bordering on white in some cases, although the rose-coloured body markings remain unaffected. This colour is sometimes described as an 'albino' form, but this is not actually the case, because only the melanin colour pigment, responsible for the grey plumage, is absent. The red pigment is unaffected; in a true albino no colour pigment whatsoever would be present.

Huge flocks of these cockatoos cause widespread damage to ripening crops and represent an agricultural menace in Australia. Although well represented in aviculture here, they are less common in other countries overseas. Yet they have much in their favour, being somewhat quieter and less destructive than their *Cacatua* relatives. Even so, they require a stout aviary.

Compatibility when breeding also tends to be less of a problem with Roseate Cockatoos than other species. In addition, they can prove quite prolific, rearing two rounds of chicks during a season, with hens laying as many as five eggs in a clutch. Incubation lasts for 25 days, and the young cockatoos leave the nest when they are about seven weeks old.

Feeding is an important consideration with the Roseate Cockatoo, however, because they are susceptible to tumours, known as lipomas. These are generally benign (non-cancerous) but can develop to a sufficiently large size to handicap the bird's flight and compromise its ability to mate successfully. The only method of treatment available is surgery, which may not always be practicable, depending on the site and the size of the tumour. The areas most often affected are close to the breastbone and in the vicinity of the vent.

The diet of these cockatoos should therefore be based on cereal seeds, such as canary seed, millet and kibbled maize, rather than on sunflower or other oil seeds, which have a relatively high fat content. An iodine nibble is also essential, because this trace element is used by the thyroid glands in the neck to produce hormones that regulate the body's metabolism. A deficiency of iodine in the diet, by affecting the correct functioning of the thyroid glands, is in turn likely to predispose to obesity.

Finally, providing Roseate Cockatoos with plenty of space to exercise is also recommended. This can be best achieved in an aviary, where acclimatised pairs can be housed all year without artificial heat, as long as suitable shelter is available for them.

60 Cockatiel *Nymphicus hollandicus*

62 **Origin:** *Australia, especially the interior*

Cock: 12in (30cm) General colour greyish, being silvery-grey on the rump and uppertail coverts. Wings often a dark shade of grey, becoming blackish towards the tips; primary coverts almost black. An oblong white patch extends down the centre of the wing. Central pair of tail feathers grey, with the remainder blackish-brown; pale grey evident on the outer webs. Crown, the long, pointed crest and sides of head lemon-yellow, with circular orange ear coverts. Iris dark brown; beak dark grey; legs and feet blackish-grey.

Hen: Significantly duller in coloration, with the head and crest being brownish-grey, with little yellow evident here. The ear coverts are dull orange. Narrow yellowish transverse bars on the grey of the rump and uppertail coverts. Central pair of tail feathers are greyish-brown speckled with white, while the two outermost pairs are lemon-yellow mottled and barred with dark brown. Lower abdomen and undertail coverts barred with yellow.

Although it is quite easy to distinguish the sexes of adult birds, this is much harder in the case of immature birds, when both sexes resemble the adult hen. Young cocks tend to start singing before they acquire mature plumage, and this will prove the most reliable means of identifying them. In addition, when they first leave the nest, their ceres are pinkish, rather than grey.

Since becoming known in Europe around the same time as the Budgerigar in the 1840s, the Cockatiel has become one of the best known of all parrots. There are few birds more suitable for a back garden aviary or as pets. The voice of the Cockatiel is pleasant, never harsh, and cocks have an attractive warbling song. In the home, a young bird, obtained when it is around eight weeks old, will tame very quickly and should soon learn to whistle simple tunes. It can even be taught to say a few words.

Cockatiels also have very tolerant natures and can be housed alongside other smaller birds, such as Diamond Doves or even Zebra Finches, in a mixed aviary, where they will breed without molesting their companions. Cockatiels are also quite hardy and can be housed outdoors throughout the year, provided a well-covered shelter is available. Even in these surroundings, they are likely to become quite tame, and their graceful flight will be readily appreciated.

These birds are easy to maintain on a diet consisting mainly of millets, canary seed, groats, some sunflower and a little hemp, augmented with plenty of green food, such as chickweed and seeding grasses, as well as carrot and sweet apple.

Breeding is usually quite straightforward, and a nesting box should be provided only during the warmer months of the year, because Cockatiels may nest at any stage. The results are likely to be disappointing during the winter months, however, and hens are more likely to be afflicted with egg-binding at this time of year. Thin pieces of wood should be provided on the floor of the nestbox, which the birds can whittle away to form a nest lining. This is a better option than peat, which is usually scraped out of the box by the birds, leaving no bed for the eggs to rest on, and increasing the risk of their becoming chilled during the incubation period.

Cockatiels are prolific breeders, and hens may lay seven or more eggs in a single clutch. These are incubated by both adults in turn, with cocks sitting for most of the day. The chicks, which have a reasonably thick covering of yellow down, start to hatch after 19 days. Unfortunately, with a large clutch there may be up to a week's difference in the ages of the chicks, and the youngest do not always survive through the critical early days.

Nest inspection should be carried out carefully, with the sitting bird being drawn off the nest by the provision of green food, for example. Avoid direct disturbance when one of the adults is within the nest, because this is likely to lead to eggs being scattered and damaged or chicks being injured as the parent bird flies out. As they grow older, the young Cockatiels will sit upright, and rock to-and-fro continually, making a rather menacing hissing noise when anyone peeps at them.

They leave the nest when they are around five weeks old, and once they are known to be feeding themselves they should be removed from the aviary without delay, otherwise they are likely to disturb the adults, which by this time are likely to be nesting again. Be sure to maintain a constant supply of cuttlefish bone, especially during the breeding period, to avoid the problem of soft-shelled eggs. Adult pairs should be restricted to having two or perhaps three rounds of chicks during a season. The youngsters themselves should not be encouraged to nest until they are a year old and fully mature.

The first breeding results with Cockatiels were reported from France in 1850. Since then, countless generations have been reared successfully in aviaries, and not surprisingly, as with the Budgerigar, a range of colour mutations has occurred, although this was a relatively slow process in the case of the Cockatiel.

The earliest colour mutation was the pied, which arose in California in 1949. The normal coloration of these Cockatiels is broken by variable patches of yellowish-white plumage. Shortly afterwards, what has since become the most popular of the Cockatiel colours, the Lutino, was recorded from Florida, also in the USA. These birds are pale lemon in colour, but the orange cheek patches are still present. The Lutino is actually quite variable in its depth of coloration, however, with some individuals being a much deeper shade of lemon than others. These birds display no grey coloration, but the orange cheek patches are retained. It is possible to sex them by the appearance of their tail feathers, with those of hens being barred, although this distinction is less evident from a distance than with the normal grey form.

The cinnamon mutation has resulted in Cockatiels with warm brown rather than grey plumage. This, like the Lutino, is a sex-linked mutation. An unusual mutation, which affects the individual feathers, is the pearl, which first appeared in Germany during 1967. In this case, the centres of the feathers are lighter, with the yellowish plumage here contrasting with a grey border.

The white-faced form of the Cockatiel occurred about 1969 in the Netherlands. These Cockatiels have pure white heads, lacking even the orange ear coverts, and no hint of yellow elsewhere on their bodies, with these areas also being white. The sexes can again be distinguished easily on the basis of their tail coloration.

Various colour forms have since been bred using these mutations, with the white-faced being used in combination with the Lutino to produce pure, snow white albino Cockatiels. Devoid of all colour pigment, these cannot be sexed visually. There are also multiple combinations such as pearl-pied, white-faced cinnamons now being bred, and in some countries judging standards are established for such varieties. New mutations are also still emerging. One of the most recent has been the dominant silver, which, as its name suggests, has a distinctly silvery-grey tone, with the rest of its coloration being unaffected.

42 Hyacinthine Macaw *Anodorhynchus hyacinthinus*

Origin: *south-central parts of Brazil; also recorded from Bolivia and Paraguay*

Cock: 36in (91cm) Entirely cobalt blue, with darker and lighter shades, the wings and back tending to be of more intense, glossy colour than the remainder of the plumage. There is a prominent area of yellow skin encircling the eyes, and also extending around the base of the lower mandible. Tongue has prominent yellow area and a black tip. Iris dark brown; beak, legs and feet black.

Hen: Similar in appearance.

The Hyacinthine Macaw is the largest and most spectacular member of the entire parrot family, and although these birds can become tame and affectionate, their huge size and powerful beaks mean that they must be housed in a large, very strong, steel aviary. While the numbers of these macaws are thought to have fallen quite dramatically in the wild, breeding results with captive stock are becoming increasingly common, in spite of their demanding housing requirements.

The first successful breeding was recorded at Posnan Zoo in Poland. Since then, chicks have been reared in many other countries, particularly in North America and South Africa. It was not until 1983 that Hyacinthine Macaws first nested successfully in Britain, however. They were housed in a flight 40ft (12m) long. Two eggs form the usual clutch, with incubation taking about 29 days. The young develop quite slowly, although they are nearly fully feathered by six weeks of age, but their tails are still considerably shorter than those of adult birds. Fledging is unlikely before they are 11 weeks old.

Feeding these macaws presents no particular problems, as a diet of mixed nuts, sunflower, maize and similar foods suits them well. Parrot pellets can also be provided, along with items such as corn on the cob and assorted fruit. Like many of the larger parrots, they are potentially long lived and will breed over the course of decades.

Lear's Macaw *Anodorhynchus leari*

Origin: *northeast Bahia, Brazil*

Cock: 30in (76cm) *Dull cobalt blue, with the back and wing coverts having pale edges to the feathers. Head, neck and underparts are greenish-blue, with the plumage of the abdomen having bluer edges. Undersurface of the tail feathers black, as are the inner webs of the primaries. Bare yellowish skin encircles the eyes, and a more prominent area is present at the base of the lower bill than is the case with the Hyacinthine Macaw. Iris dark brown; beak, legs and feet black.*

Hen: *Similar in appearance.*

This species closely resembles the Hyacinthine Macaw in its overall appearance, but it is a little smaller and the blue coloration of its plumage is less intense. Very little is known about it – indeed its area of distribution was not discovered until 1978. The total number of Lear's Macaws in the wild may consist of fewer than a hundred individuals, making it one of the most endangered of the world's parrots. It is extremely rare in aviculture, although a pair was kept for a number of years at Birdland, Bourton-on-the-Water in Gloucestershire, England, during the 1970s.

Blue and Gold Macaw (Blue and Yellow Macaw) *Ara ararauna*

Origin: *east Panama south as far as Paraguay and south Brazil*

Cock: 34in (86cm) *Upperparts blue, with the feathering of the forehead, crown and rump having a greenish tone. Flights and tail purplish-indigo, being yellowish on the underside. The underparts are a deep shade of golden yellow, with the undertail coverts being greenish-blue. There is a broad, naked greyish-white facial patch transversed by rows of tiny black feathers, and a broad black band extending from the ear coverts around the throat. Iris pale yellow; beak black; legs and feet dark grey.*

Hen: *Similar in appearance.*

These attractive macaws have long been popular in avicultural circles, with breeding reports dating back to 1818, when a pair nested successfully in France. During recent years the advent of reliable sexing methods has done much to facilitate breeding successes, although not all pairs prove to be successful parents. Young birds in particular may lose chicks when they are nesting for the first time, apparently because they encounter initial difficulties in feeding their offspring. Once this stage has passed however, few parrots have a longer reproductive life, with pairs nesting annually for perhaps 30 years or more.

In view of their large size, these and the other multi-coloured macaws need fairly spacious surroundings, although breeding results in what can be described as little more than cages are often achieved. A strong aviary is needed for them, and prospective owners should be aware of the vocal capabilities of these parrots. They tend to become particularly noisy at the start of the breeding period.

It is always best to start with a compatible pair of macaws, rather than attempting to pair up individuals, which can be a fraught process. The birds must always be introduced on neutral territory, to minimise the risk of fighting, and they must always be closely supervised at first as well, in case they do have a disagreement.

A large, solid nestbox is required for a breeding pair, with wooden offcuts provided at the base, which the birds can use to form their nest lining. Two, sometimes three, eggs will be laid, and the hen incubates alone for 28 days until they hatch, although her mate may join her in the box for periods. The chicks will leave the nest about 13 weeks later. Corn on the cob and plenty of green food will usually be eaten readily when the youngsters are being reared.

43 Red and Gold Macaw (Red and Yellow Macaw, Scarlet Macaw) *Ara macao*

Origin: *south Mexico through Central America to Bolivia and central Brazil*

Cock: *34in (86cm) Predominantly scarlet red in coloration, with the wing coverts golden-yellow, tipped with green. Flights blue; rump, upper- and undertail coverts also blue. Two central tail feathers scarlet, tipped with blue; with blue predominating on the other tail feathers, so that the outer ones are almost entirely blue. The broad area of skin on the cheeks is flesh-coloured and feathering here is very* *indistinct. Iris yellowish-white; the upper mandible of the beak whitish tipped with black, while the lower mandible is entirely black; legs and feet blackish.*

Hen: *Similar in appearance.*

Concern over populations of this macaw in Central America has led to it being listed as an endangered species, but in reality it has one of the widest distributions of all parrots in the Americas. Unfortunately, however, the listing decision has meant that breeders are likely to require permits before they may sell even home-bred youngsters. Contact your government department which deals with conservation and specifically CITES matters to ascertain the current position.

The Red and Gold Macaw has very similar requirements to the Blue and Gold Macaw. A diet based on a good quality parrot mix, augmented with nuts such as walnuts and Brazils, will keep these birds in good condition, but they must also have a good selection of fruit, vegetables, such as peas in the pod or corn on the cob, and greenstuff, preferably provided on a daily basis.

Pomegranates are a particular favourite, and these macaws delight in pulling out the seeds. Although Red and Gold Macaws, like many other parrots, will hold food with their feet, pomegranates should be cut into quarters with a sharp knife for them, so that the pieces can be held more easily.

Good hygiene is important, and the floor of the birds' quarters should be cleaned thoroughly each day, so that discarded fresh food cannot turn mouldy. Using paper to cover the floor is ideal, as the sheets can be simply folded up, so that unwanted food and seed husks can be easily removed.

The macaws will also need an opportunity to exercise their powerful beaks, and a good supply of perches must be available for them. Although these will have to be replaced regularly as they are gnawed away, they will prevent the macaws' beaks from becoming overgrown and should also serve to distract their attention from the framework of their quarters.

Red and Gold Macaws have been mated with Blue and Gold Macaws, giving rise to hybrid offspring described as Catalina Macaws. Such hybrids will make suitable pets (assuming their potential owner can offer them sufficient space in the home and is prepared to tolerate their piercing calls), but they should not themselves be used for breeding purposes. In any event, they may be infertile, but breeders should be striving to build up pure strains of captive-bred parrots, without resorting to unwarranted hybridisation.

Green-winged Macaw (Red and Blue Macaw) *Ara chloroptera*

Origin: *from Panama south as far as north Argentina*

Cock: *35in (89cm) a deep shade of crimson overall, with rump, upper- and undertail coverts pale blue; the wings and lesser coverts also crimson, with the* *median coverts here being dark green; greater coverts blue; flights blue. Two long central tail feathers deep red tipped with blue, with the next two pairs being blue with red edges towards the base. The remainder are almost entirely blue, with the underside of the feathers being of a golden hue. Naked skin on the face flesh-coloured, lined with tiny red feathers, which may be maroon in young birds. Iris yellow; upper mandible horn-white, black at the base, lower mandible black; legs and feet greyish-black.*

Hen: Similar in appearance.

This species may be easily distinguished from the Red and Gold Macaw because there is no yellow coloration over the wings. It is also a darker shade of red, with more prominent feathering on the face. In spite of its powerful beak, the Green-winged Macaw can be very gentle, but its large size and loud calls tend to make it unsuitable for the domestic environment. If they are kept indoors, these birds should always be housed in flights rather than cages so that they have more space for exercise. As with other macaws, the Green-winged is not an especially talented mimic but can learn a few words if obtained as a youngster. At this age, the iris is dark rather than straw-yellow, and their overall coloration is duller, as is the case with most young parrots.

Consistent breeding results have been recorded, especially in recent years now that reliable sexing methods are available to distinguish pairs. A stout nestbox or barrel will be required, and the birds must have easy access by means of a wire ladder fixed securely in the box, beneath the entrance hole.

The hen sits alone, with incubation and fledging details being as for the Blue and Gold Macaw. Although normally producing only one round of chicks, these parrots can be double-clutched quite successfully. This entails removing the first round of eggs soon after laying, which should then encourage the hen to lay again shortly afterwards, effectively doubling their reproductive potential over the course of the year. Obviously, the eggs that are removed will need to be hatched in an incubator, however, and the subsequent chicks reared by hand, which is a time-consuming task.

Military Macaw (Great Green Macaw) *Ara militaris*

Origin: *limited areas of Mexico, northwestern South America, Bolivia and north Argentina*

Cock: 26in (66cm) Red forehead; green crown; olive-green back; blue uppertail coverts and rump. Blue and red tail; olive-green underparts with blue undertail coverts; flights green and blue. Bare cheek patches flesh-coloured, with rows of small black feathers. Iris yellowish; beak black; legs and feet greyish.

Hen: Similar in appearance.

The Military Macaw and its larger relative, Buffon's Macaw (*Ara ambigua*), have never been especially popular in aviculture, although more are now being bred. This is another species listed on CITES Appendix I, and it is believed to be endangered in the wild, so that these macaws should be kept only for breeding purposes and not as pets.

Their care is similar to that of other large macaws, and again, with compatible pairs, consistent results can be anticipated. In Zimbabwe, for example, a breeder has reared 15 chicks from a single pair over a period of six years. Three or four eggs form the usual clutch and hatch after a period of about 28 days. The young should fledge about three months later, and they are again distinguishable by their darker irises.

Although these macaws can make an atrocious noise when they are excited, they fortunately do not call very often, although they certainly become noisier at the start of the breeding period. Plenty of fresh branches should be provided as perching, so that the birds can whittle these away and keep their beaks in trim. This should also serve to attract their attention away from the aviary structure, which nevertheless must be robust, with no accessible lengths of timber within the macaws' reach.

46 Severe Macaw (Chestnut-fronted Macaw) *Ara severa*

Origin: *from Panama southwards as far as Brazil*

Cock: 20in (51cm) Almost entirely green, with a bluish tinge on the head. A brown band and red spot run across the forehead, chin and cheeks. Cheeks bare and whitish, with some dark feathers extending across this part of the face. Wings blue and green; tail green with a blue tip. Iris yellow; beak black; legs and feet brownish-black.

Hen: Similar in appearance.

These dwarf macaws are not well represented in aviculture, although they are quite easy to maintain, being less demanding than their larger, multi-coloured relatives. Even so, they require a robust aviary, covered with mesh which should be 16SWG (standard wire gauge) in thickness. Woodwork in their quarters must also be protected from their powerful beaks.

A stout nestbox or hollow log in a quiet corner of their shelter will need to be provided. Here the birds will roost at night and, hopefully, should breed as well. The most likely indicator of imminent breeding is that the hen will spend time in the nest during the day. Blocks of softwood must be provided, which the birds can whittle away to form a nest lining. This will provide a good base for the eggs.

The incubation period lasts about 28 days, with two or three eggs forming the typical clutch. The youngsters should leave the nest around 10 weeks later. At this stage, they resemble their parents, but can be distinguished by their dark irises. The first breeding success with this species was obtained in Copenhagen in 1954.

If obtained at an early age, a single bird soon becomes tame, and can learn to repeat a few words, although these parrots are not talented talkers.

Red-bellied Macaw *Ara manilata*

Origin: *much of northern South America, from Colombia east of the Andes via Venezuela, Guyana and Guyane to Mato Grosso and Bahia, Brazil; also found in Peru and Ecuador, as well as Trinidad*

Cock: 19in (48cm) Predominantly green, darker on the wings, with a maroon area centred on the lower abdomen and extending to the vent. The coloration of the underparts is otherwise a yellowish-green, extending to the undersides of the tail feathers. The crown is bluish, with the throat and upper breast also showing traces of blue coloration. The bare area of facial skin is distinctly yellowish rather than white, unlike other dwarf macaws. Iris dark brown; beak black; legs and feet greyish-black.

Hen: Similar in appearance.

This species may be distinguished quite easily from the rare Illiger's Macaw (*Ara maracana*) (Plate 45) by the coloration of the facial skin, which is yellow rather than white, although both have areas of red plumage on the belly. Red-bellied Macaws used to be quite scarce in aviculture until the 1980s, although not in the wild. Since then, it has become one of the most commonly seen dwarf macaws, although its care is more demanding than that of other species. Red-bellied Macaws appear to be susceptible to obesity, and they must be provided with a varied diet, which includes plenty of cereal seeds, such as millet and plain canary seed, with rather less sunflower seed than is often fed to larger parrots. Greenstuff and fruit should also figure prominently in their diet.

These macaws are less hardy than other *Ara* species, and acclimatisation must be carried out carefully. Indeed, they may well be better housed in indoor surroundings over the winter. In any event, they must always have a nestbox available for roosting purposes. Red-bellied Macaws can be rather nervous by nature, although they are not especially noisy. Their quarters should be designed to provide them with adequate privacy.

During recent years, breeding results have started to be recorded with this species. The earliest success occurred in Florida in 1982, and since then, these macaws have been bred in various countries, with the first British breeding being recorded as recently as 1986. As many as four eggs may be laid in a clutch, with incubation lasting about 27 days. In common with other dwarf macaws, these birds usually prove to be very diligent parents. Youngsters fledge at about 11 weeks of age, and have paler facial skin at this stage and a pale stripe running down the centre of the upper bill.

Yellow-collared Macaw (Yellow-naped Macaw,

Cassin's Macaw, Golden-collared Macaw,

Golden-naped Macaw) *Ara auricollis*

Origin: *south South America, from Mato Grosso, Brazil, Bolivia and Paraguay to northwest Argentina*

Cock: 16in (41cm) Predominantly green, with the forehead, crown and lower cheeks being brownish-black. The leading edge of the wing, the primary coverts and the primaries themselves are blue. The tail feathers are blue on their upper surface, becoming reddish towards the base, and olive-yellow on the undersides. The most distinctive feature of this species is the yellow collar, which is present on the hindneck. Bare facial skin whitish, with very small dark feathers. Iris dark maroon; beak blackish, with a lighter streak on the centre of the upper bill; legs and feet pink.

Hen: Similar in appearance.

These macaws are now well established in aviculture, having become available for a period beginning in the late 1970s. Pairs have subsequently proved to be quite prolific, nesting reliably over a number of years. Compatibility is an important consideration in the breeding of all macaws, and ideally, it is best to start with a proven pair. Alternatively, if space and funds permit, these macaws may be housed in a group until they start pairing off, and then the pairs can be transferred to separate breeding accommodation.

Two, sometimes three, eggs form the typical clutch, and they are incubated by the hen alone. They should hatch after a period of about 26 days. The chicks will leave the nest approximately 10 weeks later and will resemble their parents in terms of their plumage coloration. However, they can be distinguished quite easily by their feet and legs, which are greyish rather than pink.

Red-shouldered Macaw (Hahn's Macaw) *Ara nobilis*

Origin: *Guyana, Venezuela, Surinam, parts of Guyane and northeast Brazil*

Cock: 12in (30cm) Predominantly green, more yellowish below. Forehead and stripe above the eyes bluish. Outer webs of flights blue; bend of wings scarlet; underside of wing golden-olive and scarlet. Underside of tail golden-olive. Naked facial skin whitish. Iris yellow; beak dark grey; legs and feet pinkish-grey.

Hen: Similar in appearance.

This is the smallest of the macaws, and young birds will develop into good pets, having tame and gentle natures. Their sizes makes them much easier to accommodate than their larger relatives, and their calls are less raucous. Even so, when excited or alarmed, they can blush in a similar fashion, with the bare facial skin becoming redder, as the result of the increased blood flow.

This race is now much more common in aviculture than the Noble Macaw (*A.n. cumanensis*) (Plate 49), which originates south of the Amazon in Brazil. Although identical in terms of plumage, this form can be distinguished by the coloration of its beak. The upper mandible of the Noble Macaw is pale horn, with just the tip being black.

These dwarf macaws have been bred successfully on the colony system in a large aviary, but results may be better when pairs are housed individually. They tend to be quite prolific, laying three or four eggs in a clutch, and sometimes breeding twice during a season.

A nestbox measuring 18in (46cm) deep and 9in (23cm) square will suffice. It should be lined with soft wood blocks, which can be whittled away to form the nest lining. Incubation lasts around 25 days, with the chicks remaining in the box for just under eight weeks.

64 Red-headed Conure (Red-masked Conure)

Aratinga erythrogenys

Origin: *southwest Ecuador and northwest Peru*

Cock: 13in (33cm) The red coloration on the head is more pronounced than in related species, extending from the forehead to the centre of the crown, as well as the face, lores, chin, underwing coverts, edges of the wings and the thighs. Remainder of plumage entirely green. Iris yellow; beak pale horn; legs and feet brownish.

Hen: Similar in appearance.

Conures are simply parakeets that belong to certain genera originating in the New World. Within the *Aratinga* genus are a number of species that are predominantly green with red markings on the head, and it can be difficult to distinguish among them. In the case of the Red-headed Conure, the entire head is red, whereas red plumage is restricted just to the crown and forehead in Wagler's Conure (*A. wagleri*). Mitred Conures (*A. mitrata*) have more widely distributed red markings, extending in some cases over much of the face, but this patterning may be speckled, particularly on the cheeks, rather than solid. A bare area of whitish skin encircles the eyes in all cases.

Breeding results with the Red-headed Conure and other members of the genus are now becoming more frequent, largely as a result of the development of reliable sexing methods. Three or four eggs form the typical clutch, and they should hatch after a period of about 26 days. The chicks will fledge when they are between eight and nine weeks of age. At this stage they lack the characteristic red coloration on the head, which starts to appear by the time the young conures are about six months old, initially as flecking, before becoming solid. For a period, the youngsters may then resemble Mitred Conures, but the orbital skin is distinctly yellowish rather than white.

White-eyed Conure *Aratinga leucophthalmus*

Origin: *much of north South America, although absent from the west of the continent, from east Colombia through Venezuela and Guyana and Guyane south as far as north Paraguay and north Argentina*

Cock: 13in (33cm) Predominantly green, although yellow coloration is apparent on the outermost greater wing coverts. There is also red feathering on the leading edge of the wing, plus scattered red feathers on the head and neck. A narrow circle of bare white skin encircles the eyes. Iris deep orangish; beak horn-coloured; legs and feet greyish-black.

Hen: Similar in appearance.

The marking of these conures are highly individual, with a very random scattering of red plumage in the vicinity of the head and neck. They have never been especially popular in avicultural circles but are not difficult to look after, and pairs usually prove to be reliable parents. In addition, they may be double-brooded, rearing two rounds of chicks during the course of a season.

The earliest breeding was recorded in the USA during 1934, but in Britain the first success was obtained only in 1975. The pair concerned laid in a nestbox measuring 18in (45cm) deep and 12in (30cm) square. Four eggs form the typical clutch, and they are incubated by the hen alone for approximately 26 days. Fledging takes place about nine weeks later. Young White-eyed Conures are duller than their parents, with the red markings replaced by green.

Jendaya Conure (Yellow-headed Conure) *Aratinga jandaya*

Origin: *northeast Brazil*

Cock: 12in (30cm) Head and neck bright yellow suffused with orange-red on the forehead, throat and round the eyes. Back green; lower back orange-red. Wing coverts green, remainder blue, the base of flights green on outer webs; tail above blue merging into olive-green at the base, black below. Underparts orange-yellow. Iris greyish-brown; beak black; legs and feet greyish.

Hen: Similar in appearance.

The Jendaya ranks among one of the most colourful of all conures although, as with the Dusky Lory, there appear to be two distinctive forms, one of which is more brightly coloured than the other, which has more yellowish rather than orange underparts. Young birds are also duller than their parents, having a greenish edging to their plumage.

This species has a long avicultural history, having been first bred at Hastings in England in 1891. Jendaya Conures tend to be quite peaceable, even with others of the same species, and it may be possible to keep them

131

together in a group without fighting if they are introduced into the aviary at the same time.

They will gnaw branches provided as perches, but are not especially destructive by nature. Their calls can be rather harsh, however, although they are nowhere near as loud as those of the larger parrots, and this should be considered if you are living in fairly urban surroundings.

Like other conures, the Jendaya is quite hardy once it is established in its quarters, but it must always be provided with a snug nestbox for roosting purposes, preferably in the aviary shelter, during the winter months.

Sun Conure (Yellow Conure) *Aratinga solstitialis*

Origin: *southwest Venezuela, Guyana, Guyane and northeast Brazil*

Cock: 12in (30cm) Shades of yellow and orange, becoming a more fiery shade of orange over some parts of the body. Secondaries yellow and green; primaries dark blue. Tail olive-green, being bluish near the tip of the upper surface and dusky olive beneath; undertail coverts green with yellowish tinge. Naked circle of skin around the eyes whitish; iris greyish-brown; beak black; legs and feet greyish.

Hen: Similar in appearance.

Although bred during the 1880s, this species was exceedingly rare in aviculture throughout much of the present century until 1971. Its stunning coloration and readiness to breed in aviary surroundings have since ensured that it is now widely available. As in the case of the Jendaya Conure, the appearance of individual birds can differ considerably, with some being much more colourful than others. Young birds also tend to show more green plumage, notably on the wings, although this coloration may extend more widely, and in some instances cover much of the body.

Sun Conures can be quite strident, particularly at the outset of the breeding period. They may also display a greater tendency to pluck their chicks than other species of conure, although this may be linked to a desire on the part of the parent birds to be nesting again. They can be very prolific. A pair in Zimbabwe, for example, is on record as laying four clutches, which yielded 17 chicks over a period of 18 months.

The incubation period lasts 26 days, with fledging taking place about nine weeks later. Soaked millet sprays and plenty of green food and fruit are usually taken readily by the adults, especially when there are chicks in the nest. A mixture of seeds should form the basis of their diet, and grit and cuttlefish bone should be provided.

66 **Brown-throated Conure** (St Thomas Conure) *Aratinga pertinax*

Origin: *central and much of north South America, including offshore islands such as Curaçao*

Cock: 10in (25cm) Green on the upperparts, with a slight bluish tinge on the crown of the head. Forehead, cheeks, ear coverts and throat brown; breast, abdomen and undertail coverts greenish-yellow with orange-yellow feathering in the middle of the abdomen. Flights blue; tail green with blue at the tips of the central feathers. Narrow bare orbital skin encircling the eyes is greyish-yellow. Iris orange-yellow; beak, legs and feet greyish.

Hen: Similar in appearance.

With about 14 different races of this conure, all differing to a greater or lesser extent in their coloration, plumage variations should not be relied upon when selecting a pair. In addition, as with most conures, two birds housed together will always act as though they were a true pair, irrespective of their sex.

They are somewhat quieter than Sun Conures, but they require similar care. These conures can be housed outside throughout the year, once they are acclimatised, provided that they have a nestbox where they can roost. This should be located in the shelter. It is usually possible to keep them together in groups outside the breeding period, but pairs are best kept on their own.

Brown-throated Conures require a diet composed of millets, plain canary seed, groats, some sunflower and small pine nuts, as well as plenty of green food, such as chickweed, fruit, including pomegranate and sweet apple, as well as carrot. Fresh branches should also be provided so that they can keep their beaks in trim.

Four eggs form the typical clutch, and they are incubated by the hen alone, although the cock is likely to join her in the nestbox for periods during the day and at night. The eggs should hatch after about 26 days, and the chicks leave the nest just six weeks or so later. As with other conures, bread and milk is often a favoured rearing food, but care must be taken to ensure that it does not turn sour in hot weather. If it is provided in the morning, it will need to be removed that same evening.

Young Brown-throated Conures soon become tame and will readily accept food such as sunflower seeds from the hand. They may well learn to say a few words, and although their calls can be disturbing at close quarters, they are far less likely to screech once they are used to their surroundings. As in the case of other conures, they may live for 20 years or so.

61 Cactus Conure *Aratinga cactorum*

Origin: *northeast Brazil*

Cock: 10in (25cm) *Green above; forehead grey-brown; crown blue-grey. Side of head and throat grey-brown. Breast and abdomen orange-yellow. Narrow area of bare skin encircling the eyes is white. Iris orangish; beak horn-coloured; legs and feet greyish.*

Hen: Similar in appearance.

These conures are now relatively rare in collections, although not in the wild. Unfortunately, stocks were limited when Brazil banned the export of native species in 1967, and at this time breeding results with *Aratinga* species in general were far less common than they are today. Their care presents no particular problems, however, with the first breeding results being recorded from France as long ago as 1883. Cactus Conures may prove quite prolific, with hens often laying clutches of six eggs. Their young are mature by a year old.

Golden-crowned Conure (Peach-fronted Conure)
Aratinga aurea

Origin: *Brazil, Bolivia and Argentina*

Cock: 11in (28cm) *Large orange-yellow area extending from the forehead to the centre of the head, with blue evident on the crown; lores blue; orbital skin greyish, surrounded by a variable orange area of plumage. Upperparts green, with the cheeks, neck and breast being olive-green. Underparts yellow-green. Wings green and blue, with dark tips. Tail green, with a bluish tip. Iris orangish; beak black; legs and feet greyish.*

Hen: Similar in appearance.

While the amount of orange feathering around the eyes may be thought to indicate a difference in the sex of these conures, this is not a reliable means of distinction. Some hens may be more colourful than cocks, and vice versa. They are attractive aviary occupants, with pairs being quite devoted to each other and usually ready to nest.

A nestbox measuring about 12in (30cm) deep and 10in (25cm) square will suffice. It should be lined with soft wooden offcuts, which the conures will gnaw away to form a base for their eggs. The box should be located in a quiet, preferably darkened, corner of their aviary, even in the shelter if necessary. Three or four eggs may be laid here, with incubation lasting 26 days. The young will fledge when they are around seven weeks old, by which time they will have a reduced area of orange feathering on the head with the remainder being yellow. Their bill is also paler than that of adults.

The first breeding results were reported from Germany in 1880. On occasions, pairs may prove to be double-brooded. Golden-crowned Conures are quite hardy, and their calls are less piercing than those of other conures, although they have a fairly harsh call when alarmed.

Black-headed Conure (Nanday Conure) *Aratinga nenday*

Origin: *Bolivia, Paraguay and Argentina*

Cock: 12in (30cm) Upperparts grass-green; forehead, crown and front of the cheeks are black, back of head being dark brown. Ear coverts, rump and abdomen yellowish-green; throat and upper breast greyish blue-green. Flights, secondaries and primary coverts blue, with the latter being edged with yellowish-green. Tail olive-green tipped with blue; thighs red. Iris dark brown; beak blackish; legs and feet dark grey.

Hen: Similar in appearance.

This species has become somewhat scarcer in aviculture during recent years, having obtained a reputation for being rather noisy. Nevertheless, Black-headed Conures are lively birds and make attractive aviary occupants. They also prove quite hardy when acclimatised. They can then be kept outside quite safely throughout the winter, provided a draught-proof shelter is available, along with a nestbox where they will roost at night.

A variety of seeds, including various millets, plain canary seed, sunflower, small pine nuts, peanuts and groats, will provide a basic diet. This can be supplemented with parrot pellets, which are valuable for all species. Green food, fruit and vegetables, such as carrot and peas in the pod, should also be offered on a regular basis.

The first breeding reports again originate from France, where the species bred in 1881. Some pairs prove more nervous than others when nesting, so disturbances should always be kept to a minimum. The hen will lay four or five eggs in a clutch and incubate on her own, although the cock may enter the box at times. The chicks should hatch about 26 days later, and fledge about two months after that. At this stage, they are almost indistinguishable from adults, except that their tail feathers are still shorter.

Maroon-bellied Conure (Red-bellied Conure) *Pyrrhura frontalis*

Origin: *Brazil, Paraguay, Uruguay and Argentina*

Cock: 11in (28cm) Upperparts deep grass-green, with a reddish-maroon band across forehead, immediately adjacent to the cere. Ear coverts brownish. Wings green, with the flights being bluish. The breast is olive, scalloped with a lighter shade, creating the typical 'scaly-breasted' markings associated with this group of

135

conures. There is also a prominent maroon patch at the centre of the abdomen. Iris brownish; beak black; legs and feet greyish.

Hen: *Similar in appearance.*

For many years the best known member of this appealing genus of conures in aviculture, the Maroon-bellied is an ideal occupant of a garden aviary, becoming very tame in these surroundings, even to the point of taking favoured items such as a piece of carrot from the hand. Their calls are quiet and generally undisturbing, although the presence of a cat on, or close to, their aviary will evoke a more noisy response.

Pairs also prove prolific. They have an interesting display, with cocks stalking up and down the perch, with their head feathers raised in a very deliberate fashion. Hens may lay five or six eggs in a clutch, with incubation again lasting about 26 days. They bred for the first time in Britain in 1924.

A typical diet as recommended for other conures suits the Maroon-bellied well, and again, they must have a nestbox available for roosting purposes throughout the year. Young birds will become very tame, and can develop into delightful companions, although they are unlikely to prove talented talkers.

65 White-eared Conure *Pyrrhura leucotis*

Origin: *north Venezuela and east Brazil*

Cock: *8in (20cm) Green upperparts, with a reddish-brown rump. Head dark brown; ear coverts greyish-white; forehead and cheek stripes reddish-brown; nape and throat blue. Breast greenish, also showing black and white horizontal stripes. Abdomen green, with a reddish-maroon area in the centre. Wings green. Tail reddish-brown, becoming greenish at the base. Iris brown; beak black; legs and feet greyish.*

Hen: *Similar in appearance.*

The two populations of the White-eared Conure have a widely separated distribution, with the races found in Venezuela being identifiable by their bluish forecrown. The subspecies known as Emma's Conure (*P.l. emma*) used to be most common, but it has now become scarce in aviculture. Even so, compatible pairs can prove prolific. Those in the Palmitos Park collection in Grand Canaria have nested repeatedly in recent years, laying up to seven eggs in a clutch. The first breeding of this species apparently took place in Austria in 1880.

Other *Pyrrhura* conures which may be seen in collections on occasions include the Green-cheeked or Molina's Conure (*P. molinae*), which was virtually unknown in aviculture until the late 1970s. Today, it is widely bred and may be easily distinguished from the Maroon-bellied Conure by the maroon upper surface to its tail.

The brownish beak coloration of the Black-tailed Conure (*P. melanura*) is an identifying feature of this species, while the more colourful Painted Conure (*P. picta*) is also sometimes available. None of these conures is sexually dimorphic, so you will need to have them sexed in order to be certain of obtaining a true breeding pair.

Quaker Parakeet (Monk Parakeet) *Myiopsitta monarchus*

Origin: *Argentina, Paraguay, Uruguay and Bolivia*

Cock: 12in (30cm) Predominantly green, becoming yellower on the underparts. Wings green with blue secondaries and flights. Forehead, face, throat and breast grey, with most of these feathers having very pale margins, which convey the impression of scales. Iris brown, beak horn-coloured; legs and feet greyish.

Hen: Similar in appearance.

These birds are among the most interesting of all parrots, simply because they do not nest in hollow trees, but build enormous nests of branches and twigs. In aviary surroundings, they are lively and active, and will start to build a nest almost immediately if they are provided with a good supply of twiggy branches. They will break off twigs with their beaks and form a pile on a suitable platform, which gradually evolves into a domed nest as these are woven together. The more room that is available, the larger will be the nest itself. Quaker Parakeets usually incorporate two compartments – one for breeding while the other may be used for roosting purposes. The vaulted entrance serves as a look-out post.

Social by nature, these parakeets live well in groups, and will breed as a colony. Unfortunately, they do have rather a harsh screech, which can be a problem in areas where there are close neighbours.

A wide variety of seeds, such as groats, sunflower seed, hemp, corn on the cob, millets and canary seed, will be eaten. Fruit, greenstuff and fresh twigs with buds must also be included in their diet. During the nesting period, bread and milk should be provided fresh every day, and egg food may be eaten as a rearing food when there are chicks in the nest. There is a well-recognised blue mutation, which apparently arose in the Netherlands, as well as an even rarer yellow form of this parakeet.

Lineolated Parakeet (Barred Parakeet) *Bolborhynchus lineola*

Origin: *Mexico to Panama; also occurs in northwest South America*

Cock: 7in (18cm) Head and neck yellowish-green, with the remainder of the upperparts being entirely green, while all feathers have narrow black margins. Wings are a combination of green and black. Tail green with darker quill stripes. Iris yellowish-brown; beak light horn; legs and feet pink.

Hen: Similar in appearance.

These small parakeets are highly desirable aviary occupants. Their soft chattering is not disturbing, and they are tolerant by nature. Unfortunately, the extent of their barring is not an entirely reliable means of distinguishing their gender, although many hens tend to be less heavily barred. Even so, it is probably better to keep them in a group and allow them to pair off. If you provide a range of nestboxes all at the same height, this should ensure that there is no dispute among pairs. They will also breed inside quite readily in a budgerigar-type cage and attached nestbox.

The clutch size can vary from three to six eggs, with the incubation period lasting 18 days. The chicks will fledge about five weeks later. At this stage they can be recognised by the more prominent blue coloration on their foreheads.

There has been increasing interest in keeping and breeding these parakeets during recent years, and colour mutations are now starting to be established. The blue form is currently most popular, although an olive variant is also known.

A range of millets and plain canary seed, as well as smaller amounts of groats should form the basis of their diet. They also take green food, such as chickweed, readily and nibble branches with buds, such as hawthorn, when these are available. Lineolated Parakeets are reasonably hardy once acclimatised, but they should be encouraged to roost in the aviary shelter when the weather is cold.

Green-rumped Parrotlet (Guyana Parrotlet) *Forpus passerinus*

Origin: *Colombia, Venezuela, Guyana, Guyane and Brazil.*

Cock: 5in (13cm)   ich green with yellowish tone on the face and underparts, and emerald feathering around the eyes. Lower back, secondaries and wing coverts deep blue. Iris brown; beak whitish; legs and feet greyish.

Hen: Plumage entirely green in colour.

These birds are best kept in pairs, often proving affectionate towards each other under these circumstances. They should not be housed in groups, when they are likely to fight viciously. They are not noisy by nature, and their call is like the soft 'chirrup' of a sparrow.

The largest part of their seed mix should be canary seed and millets, to which a small quantity of groats, hemp and sunflower seed can be added. Seeding grasses and other greenstuff, as well as fruit, such as sweet apple, should be offered regularly. These parrotlets are reasonably hardy once acclimatised, but adequate winter protection, in the form of a snug, dry shelter, is essential. If you have a birdroom it may be better to transfer them to an indoor flight during the cold months.

Keeping pairs in adjoining flights is not to be recommended, because cocks in particular may bicker through the mesh and so be distracted from breeding activities. In any event, flights of this type must always be double-wired, on both sides of the framework, so that the parrotlets' toes cannot reach each other.

Mutations of this species are becoming quite well established, with blues again being most common at present, but there is also a Lutino form in Brazil, which opens up the way for the development of an albino variety, and a cinnamon mutation as well.

Celestial Parrotlet (Pacific Parrotlet) *Forpus coelestis*

Origin: *Ecuador and Peru*

Cock: 5in (13cm) Shades of green, which are especially bright on the crown and cheeks, while blue markings are evident behind the eyes. Lower back and rump cobalt blue, as are the wing coverts and underwing coverts. Iris brown; beak horn; legs and feet pinkish.

Hen: Predominantly green, with a slight trace of blue behind the eyes and bluish suffusion on the rump.

Probably the best known of the parrotlets in aviculture, the Celestial has been bred on countless occasions, both in cage and aviary surroundings, although when bred in cages, chicks need to be removed as soon as they are feeding on their own or even before then if there are signs of aggression from the cock. Otherwise, they may be severely attacked, with young cock birds being most at risk. This usually reflects a desire on the part of the adult cock to nest again, and is an attempt to drive his earlier youngsters away.

For nesting purposes, parrotlets will use either a nestbox or a hollow log. The hen lays between four and nine eggs, which she incubates on her own for about 23 days. Soaked millet sprays are a popular rearing food, and the chicks will leave the nest when they are about four weeks old. Two or even three clutches of eggs may be laid during the breeding season, but with parrotlets in particular, banding the young birds can be a hazardous procedure. The adult birds may resent the presence of the rings, and mutilate the legs of their chicks in a bid to remove them.

Yellow-faced Parrotlet *Forpus xanthops*

Origin: *the upper Marañon Valley, north Peru*

Cock: 6in (15cm) Similar in appearance to the Celestial Parrotlet, but easily distinguishable by its facial coloration, which is bright yellow. Underparts yellowish-green; upperparts greyish-green. Lower back and rump cobalt blue, as are the uppertail coverts and wing coverts. Iris brownish; beak brown centre and tip, with the remainder being horn-coloured; legs and feet pinkish.

Hen: *Duller in coloration with light blue rather than cobalt rump.*

Unknown in aviculture until the late 1970s, these parrotlets have a very limited area of distribution in the wild. Trade occurred for only a short period, but a fairly secure captive population has been established from this stock. These parrotlets appear to be no more difficult to maintain than other members of the genus and to be equally ready to reproduce. They have been bred successfully in a colony, but it is always safer to house pairs individually.

Between three and six eggs appear to form the usual clutch, and incubation lasts up to 23 days. The chicks can be sexed while they are still in the nest. Rearing foods should be provided for the parent birds, along with plenty of fruit and green food. The young parrotlets leave the nest when they are about six weeks old, and at this stage, the yellow coloration on their heads is less extensive than in adults.

70 White-winged Parakeet *Brotogeris versicolurus versicolurus*

Origin: *east Ecuador into north Brazil*

Cock: *9in (23cm) Deep grass green upperparts, becoming more yellowish-green below. Forehead, lores and upper part of the cheeks bluish-grey. Outer flight feathers black with outer web and tip blue, with the adjoining three flights being blue with a green outer edge, while the remaining flights and secondaries are white, with the latter having a slight yellowish tone; greater wing coverts yellow. Iris brown; beak horn-coloured; legs and feet pinkish.*

Hen: *Similar in appearance.*

Generally less well known than the Canary-winged Parakeet, these parakeets require identical care. They are surprisingly destructive for their size and need an ample supply of perches to keep their bills in trim. This may also discourage them from attacking the woodwork of their aviary flight.

Once properly acclimatised, White-winged Parakeets are quite hardy, but they should always be encouraged to roost under cover at night. They will often use a nestbox for this purpose. A diet based on a mixture of smaller cereal seeds, such as millet, and larger items, such as sunflower and small pine nuts, will be suitable, but this needs to be augmented with regular supplies of fruit. These parakeets are often less enthusiastic about green food.

Canary-winged Parakeet *Brotogeris versicolurus chiriri*

Origin: *Bolivia, Brazil and Argentina*

Cock: 9in (23cm) Entirely green, being a lighter shade than the White-winged Parakeet, becoming yellowish on the underparts. The primary coverts are a distinctive shade of canary yellow, apparent even when the wing is closed. Tail blue on its lower surface. Iris brown; beak horn-coloured; legs and feet flesh-coloured.

Hen: Similar in appearance.

Although the voice of these parakeets as a group can be rather loud and screeching, they make interesting aviary subjects. It is possible to house them in a colony, and breeding results are usually better if more than one pair are at least kept within sight and sound of each other. Even so, as a group in a large aviary, a distinct pecking order evolves, and there will almost inevitably be a dominant pair. Should any bird need to be removed from the group, it will be very difficult to reintroduce it successfully at a later date, as its place in the flock will have been lost, and the bird is likely to end up being mobbed by its former companions.

While adult *Brotogeris* parakeets tend to be rather shy, young hand-reared chicks can become exceedingly tame and devoted to their owners. They may also learn to say a few words, but you will need to take care that they do not become jealous of other pets, such as dogs, which may lead to an outbreak of screeching.

Tovi Parakeet (Orange-chinned Parakeet) *Brotogeris jugularis*

Origin: *Mexico south to Colombia and Venezuela*

Cock: 8in (20cm) Predominantly green, with a distinctive orange spot on the chin. The wings are green and brown, with blue evident on the primary coverts. Iris brown; beak horn-coloured; legs and feet pinkish.

Hen: Similar in appearance.

When first imported, these birds need careful management, and they should not be placed in an outdoor flight until all risk of frost has passed. They may then need to be brought in and overwintered in unheated accommodation for their first winter, before being released back into their aviary during the following spring, by which time they should be fully acclimatised and able to remain outdoors for successive winters.

Although they will eat seed readily, plenty of fruit should be offered, ideally on a daily basis. The presence of an area of bare skin around the lower bill in this and other *Brotogeris* species is an indication that they normally feed extensively on various fruits in the wild. Any feathering here would simply become saturated with juice and so would be a handicap.

141

Breeding successes with *Brotogeris* parakeets are not numerous. This may be due to their diet, but is more likely to be a reflection of their accommodation. It is preferable to keep them within sight and sound of others of their kind, although pairs can be housed individually. A nestbox should also be provided in a secluded part of the aviary, possibly within the shelter itself.

It may be worth providing a choice of nesting sites in the first instance, to see which the birds prefer. A number of wood offcuts in the base will soon be whittled away as the birds start using the nestbox, even if it is only for roosting purposes at first. The Tovi was first bred in Germany in 1873. Breeding details are similar to those of other members of the genus.

Golden-winged Parakeet *Brotogeris chrysopterus*

Origin: *Venezuela, Guyana, Guyane and Brazil*

Cock: 7in (18cm) Predominantly green, lighter on the underparts, with the head bluish. Narrow stripe of golden-yellow on the forehead and a brownish-orange chin spot. Wing coverts orange; primaries violet with green margins and tips, with the undersides of the flight feathers being bluish-green. Iris dark brown; beak horn-coloured; legs and feet pinkish.

Hen: Similar in appearance.

Various races of this parakeet are recognised, but the form from Guyana is best known in aviculture. They require similar care to that recommended for other *Brotogeris* species. Unfortunately, such is the social nature of these parakeets that two birds will usually behave as a pair and engage in mutual preening even if they are of the same sex.

For breeding purposes, they will need to be sexed, although if this is not possible at the time of purchase, watch the members of a group carefully. You may then be able to detect a true pair, although keeping track of them while you catch them can be exceedingly difficult. It may be possible to identify cocks by their bolder heads, while young birds may be distinguished easily, since they have green rather than orange wing coverts.

Golden-winged Parakeets are quite hardy once they are acclimatised. They should be provided with plenty of fresh perches, so that they can keep their beaks in trim. The upper mandible in particular may show a tendency to become overgrown if the bird cannot use its bill effectively. Provided that the parakeet can eat without difficulty it may be better to allow it to gnaw, so that the beak is trimmed back naturally, rather than clipping it, which is more traumatic. These parakeets have a fairly fast and direct flight, but will also climb around their quarters. Here they may gnaw any exposed areas of woodwork that are accessible to them, even through the mesh, and a watch should be kept to ensure that they do not loosen any netting staples as a result.

9 **Tui Parakeet** *Brotogeris sanctithomae*

Origin: *occurs throughout the Amazon basin in Colombia, Venezuela, Brazil, Peru and Ecuador*

Cock: 7in (18cm) Predominantly green, with rump and underparts being a lighter shade. Distinctive yellow forehead and yellow stripe behind the eye, with blue evident in the wings. Iris orangish; beak brownish-horn; legs and feet pinkish.

Hen: Similar in appearance.

Although it extends over a wide area in the wild, this is not a widely kept species in aviculture. Like other members of the genus, it may nest in termite mounds but will accept a standard nestbox quite readily. Breeding details do not differ significantly from those of other *Brotogeris* species. Their voice is sharp, but not especially disturbing.

A diet that includes generous quantities of fruit should be provided for them. Pollen granules, sprinkled over the fruit, may also be eaten and will add useful variety to their diet. Cuttlefish bone must always be available, although is more likely to be consumed when the hen is coming into breeding condition.

As with other *Brotogeris* parakeets, it is likely to take Tui Parakeets a couple of years to settle sufficiently in their quarters to start nesting in earnest, although a nestbox should always be supplied for roosting purposes.

72 **Black-headed Caique** *Pionites melanocephala*

Origin: *Colombia, Peru, Venezuela, Guyana, Guyane and Brazil*

Cock: 10in (25cm) Crown black, with green lores and a brownish-yellow back. Remainder of the upperparts green; throat and undertail coverts yellow. Underparts yellowish-white. Wings and tail green. There is a bare area of whitish-grey skin encircling the eyes. Iris reddish; beak blackish; legs and feet blackish.

Hen: Similar in appearance.

Few parrots are more playful by nature than caiques. They can be very amusing in the home, climbing deftly up curtain cords or playing on the floor with marbles, which they roll along the floor with their beaks. Their upright stance also gives them a slightly comical appearance.

Unfortunately, their loud screeching can be very annoying, especially at close quarters, but if this fault can be overlooked, young, hand-reared birds can develop into delightful companions. They may need to be watched, however, because in their enthusiasm they will sometimes nip fingers unexpectedly, and, obviously, this is not to be encouraged.

Their feeding requirements are quite straightforward, consisting of a good quality parrot seed mixture, supplemented with parrot pellets and with generous quantities of fruit and greenstuff. A supply of fresh branches must also be maintained for the caiques to gnaw, otherwise, their beaks will almost certainly become overgrown.

As aviary occupants, caiques may be kept in an outside aviary through-out the year, but they must have an adequate shelter. Pairs must be housed on their own, as they become very intolerant when breeding and will not hesitate to kill or maim other birds sharing their quarters.

71 White-bellied Caique (White-breasted Caique) *Pionites leucogaster*

Origin: *Brazil, Peru, Ecuador and Bolivia*

Cock: 10in (25cm) Head and neck brownish-yellow; sides of head, throat and undertail coverts yellow; remainder of underparts white. Upperparts, wings and tail green. Bare whitish skin encircling the eyes. Iris reddish; beak pale horn; legs and feet pinkish.

Hen: Similar in appearance.

Less well known in aviculture than the Black-headed Caique, this species requires similar care. For breeding purposes, the nestbox should be posi-tioned in a dark corner of the flight or in the aviary shelter itself. Otherwise, it is likely to be ignored. Breeding results have been recorded on various occasions, the first being from the USA in 1932.

Three eggs form a typical clutch, with the incubation period lasting about 26 days. In some cases, however, the adults do not prove ideal parents and may even attack their chicks while they are still young. If this happens the chicks will need to be removed for hand-rearing, while in future eggs may best be hatched in an incubator.

Pairs that do rear their chicks will normally take a wide variety of rearing foods, ranging from bread and milk, which should be supplied fresh every day, nectar and even cheddar cheese, to a wide variety of fruit and corn on the cob. The young caiques fledge when they are about 10 weeks old, and they may live for 40 years or more.

77 Blue-headed Parrot (Blue-headed Pionus) *Pionus menstruus*

Origin: *from Costa Rica south to Peru and northeast Brazil*

Cock: 12in (30cm) Head and neck dusky blue, with a black spot on the ear coverts. Remainder of the body green. There is a reddish area on the throat; undertail coverts red with blue flecking. Tail blue, with red at the base. Bare greyish area of skin encircles the eyes. Iris brown; beak blackish, with pale red sides on the upper bill; legs and feet greyish.

Hen: Similar in appearance.

Pionus parrots have become more popular in aviculture during recent years, and this is one of the most colourful and widely kept species. The coloration may vary quite markedly from bird to bird, and this should not be relied upon as a means of distinguishing the sexes.

Adult birds can be rather shy, and they have a rather disconcerting habit of wheezing and gasping when approached at close quarters. This could suggest the presence of the fungal disease aspergillosis, to which these parrots are susceptible. This condition can be diagnosed by an endoscopic examination, but other typical signs include lethargy, a progressive inability to fly and fluffed-up plumage.

An inadequate diet is a major predisposing factor in the development of aspergillosis. *Pionus* parrots must receive not only a good quality parrot food, but also parrot pellets and plenty of fruit, vegetables and greenstuff, to ensure they are not deficient in vitamin A. Pairs are generally quite ready to nest, with the first breeding results being recorded from France in 1890.

The hen lays about four eggs in a clutch, and incubates these alone until they hatch after a period of 26 days. The parrots ought to be left alone as far as possible during the breeding period, since they are susceptible to disturbance and may then neglect their chicks.

Assuming that all goes well, however, the young parrots will leave the nest when they are about 10 weeks old. At this stage, they can develop into very tame companions, being significantly quieter than Amazon parrots, although they can be taught to say a few words. In aviary surroundings, these parrots are quite hardy but are reluctant to use a nestbox to roost in, and so they must be encouraged to retire to the aviary shelter on cold nights. Placing the perches at a higher level here than in the flight can encourage this.

Cuban Amazon Parrot   *Amazona leucocephala*

Origin: *Cuba and other Caribbean islands*

Cock: 13in (33cm) Crown, lores and area around the eyes white. Ear coverts black; cheeks and throat rose-pink; belly maroon-red at the centre. Remainder of the plumage predominantly green, with the feathers having black margins. Blue coloration is apparent in the wings and tail. Iris brown; beak horn-coloured; legs and feet pinkish.

Hen: Similar in appearance.

For many years these beautiful Amazons have been better known in east Europe than elsewhere, but as a result of recent political changes, stock is now finding its way to breeders in other parts of the world. Even so, these Amazons are costly and rare, and are not, therefore, recommended for novice owners.

Their actual coloration is highly variable, with the rose-pink plumage on the throat extending down to the breast in some cases. Young birds in comparison are duller, with a reduction not only in the pink area, but also in the white plumage, which is replaced by green.

The first European breeding success was achieved in 1956 by E.J. Boosey, a well-known aviculturist of the period. He provided his breeding pair with bread and milk, hemp, carrots, boiled potatoes, spinach leaves and apples, and was rewarded with two youngsters. These birds took four years to mature and reach breeding condition themselves.

Four different subspecies of the Cuban Amazon are recognised, these having evolved in isolation on other islands. They are even rarer than the nominate race in captivity, and, at least in the case of the Cayman Brac Amazon (*A.l. hesterna*), the population in the wild has been adversely affected by hurricanes and development on its native island.

White-fronted Amazon Parrot (Spectacled Amazon Parrot)

Amazona albifrons

Origin: *Mexico south to Guatemala and Costa Rica*

Cock: 10in (25cm) Forehead and front of the crown white, with an area of blue behind. Lores and area of feathering encircling the eyes red. Uppertail coverts yellowish-green. Vent, primary coverts, upperwing coverts at the edge of the wing red. Tail green, tipped with yellowish-green. Bare whitish area of skin encircling the eyes. Iris yellowish-white; beak yellowish-white; legs and feet pinkish-grey.

Hen: Red coloration usually absent from the wings, being replaced by green plumage.

These small Amazons make attractive aviary occupants, although they are not a great deal quieter than their larger relatives. As pets, their size makes them easier to handle, and they can become very tame and devoted. Their talking abilities are highly rated.

They are easy to care for, requiring a diet based on a good quality parrot mixture, along with generous quantities of fruit and greenstuff. Corn on the cob is often favoured by these birds. Pairs have nested successfully on a number of occasions, with the earliest record coming from Japan, where chicks were reared in the collection of Prince Taka-Tsukasa during 1922.

They require a nestbox which is at least 10in (25cm) square and about 18in (46cm) deep. After preparing the nest by gnawing away wooden blocks in the base to make a soft lining, the hen will lay her clutch, which usually consists of four eggs. She sits alone, and the chicks should hatch about 24 days later. They fledge at around seven weeks old.

Red-lored Amazon Parrot (Yellow-cheeked Amazon Parrot)

Amazona autumnalis

Origin: *east Mexico south to parts of Colombia, Ecuador and Brazil*

Cock: 13in (33cm) Crown and neck green, tips of the feathers mauve with black margins; forehead and lores scarlet; cheeks golden yellow with a touch of red. Remainder of the plumage is green. Wings are green also, with some red and blue coloration evident here. Tail green and yellow. Iris orange; beak horn-coloured; legs and feet greyish.

Hen: Similar in appearance.

While adult birds of this species have a reputation for being rather timid and wild, this does not apply to young individuals, which settle well. As in most Amazons, juveniles can be recognised by their duller plumage and dark irises, which are brown in colour. In the past the Red-lored Amazon has tended to be better known in the USA, but it is now quite well represented in European collections as well. They are hardy birds and can winter out of doors if their shelter is adequately protected against draughts.

A diet based on a parrot food mix, augmented with other items such as parrot pellets, pine nuts and larger nuts, such as walnuts, will suit these and other Amazons. Corn on the cob is often a favourite, particularly as a rearing food, while generous quantities of fruit and vegetables such as carrots, peas in the pod and spinach should be offered regularly. They may also eat smaller seeds such as millet, although this should be provided in a separate food pot, because it will simply sink to the bottom in a mixture with larger items such as sunflower.

Festive Amazon Parrot *Amazona festiva*

Origin: *Venezuela, Peru, Ecuador, Guyana and Brazil*

Cock: 13in (33cm) Forehead and lores plum red; eyebrow stripe and chin blue. Lower back and rump red; upperparts green, with the underparts being of a slightly lighter shade. Wings green with black lacing on the feathers and blue flights. Tail green with yellow tips to the feathers. Naked greyish orbital skin. Iris orangish-red; beak black; legs and feet greyish.

Hen: Similar in appearance.

Young birds can be recognised very easily, because their lower back and rump are green, rather than red, and their irises are darker. If they are obtained at an early age, these lively Amazons can become both tame and affectionate, although overall this species is not well represented in aviculture, and breeding successes are relatively few.

Festive Amazons need similar care to that recommended for other members of the genus. They enjoy bathing, and will hang upside down off the aviary roof, calling excitedly with their wings outstretched during a rainstorm. Indoors, pet birds must be sprayed two or three times a week. A plant sprayer, which produces a fine mist, is ideal for this purpose. Direct the nozzle so that the water falls on to the bird from above, like a shower of rain. At first, it may be nervous, but will soon come to appreciate being sprayed in this fashion. Remove the food pot beforehand so that the contents do not become wet, and replace the cage lining afterwards. A spray of this nature, helps to keep the parrot's plumage in good condition and also dampens down the feather dust, which is otherwise likely to be spread further afield into the room.

73 Blue-fronted Amazon Parrot   *Amazona aestiva*

Origin: *Brazil, Bolivia, Paraguay and Argentina*

Cock: 15in (38cm) *Dark grass green on the upperparts, with black margins to the feathers, becoming lighter towards the rump and underparts. Forehead blue; crown, sides of head and throat yellow; sometimes the yellow extends over the entire head; feathers of the neck have black margins. Wings green, with red and yellow on the shoulders; red and blue on the flights. Tail green with reddish wash on the central feathers. Bare whitish area of skin encircles the eyes. Iris orange; beak blackish; legs and feet greyish.*

Hen: *Similar in appearance.*

The Blue-fronted Amazon has long been one of the most widely kept species in aviculture, both as a pet and as an aviary occupant. As with some other Amazons, there can be considerable variation in the markings, notably in this species in the extent of the blue feathering on the head. This particular characteristic is not unique to the Blue-fronted Amazon, however, being also associated with the Orange-winged Amazon.

Unfortunately, their raucous calls can be off-putting, particularly in urban areas. Like other Amazons, the Blue-fronted tends to have fairly specific periods when it calls, notably at first light and again towards dusk. This can create problems during the summer, particularly, when dawn may be as early as five o'clock in temperate areas.

Even hand-reared youngsters tend to show this instinctive behaviour, although they are also talented mimics. They will learn to imitate a wide range of sounds, and they will also learn to talk quite well, as well as becoming very tame. Their temperament may change somewhat, however, as they mature at around four years of age. They may become less friendly towards their owner and even attempt to bite. This is usually a reflection of a desire to breed, and under these circumstances, it may be better to arrange for a pet bird to be paired if possible. The introduction of a mate should be carried out on neutral territory, to reduce the likelihood of potential conflict.

Blue-fronted Amazons have been bred in collections since the 1880s. There is even a record of a tame pair which hatched and reared a chick on the floor of their parrot cage, but this result is exceptional. Hens may lay up to five eggs in a clutch. Blue-fronted Amazons are also long-lived birds; there are reliable records to show that some individuals have lived over 98 years.

Yellow-fronted Amazon Parrot (Yellow-headed Amazon Parrot)

Amazona ochrocephala ochrocephala

Origin: *west Colombia east to Surinam and north Brazil*

Cock: 14in (36cm) Dark grass green on the upperparts, with black margins to the feathers, becoming lighter towards the rump and underparts. Forehead stripe light bluish-green; crown, lores and chin yellow; feathers of the neck have black margins. Wings green with red and yellow on the shoulders, and red and blue apparent on the flights. Yellowish-green band present at the base of the tail. Bare white skin encircles the eyes. Iris orange; beak blackish, with red areas on the sides of the upper bill being well-marked; legs and feet greyish.

Hen: Similar in appearance.

There are a number of different races of *Amazona ochrocephala*, and identifying a pair on the basis of a slight variation in appearance is unreliable. You may well end up with two birds of the same sex, belonging to different subspecies. Pairs must be reliably sexed for breeding purposes. Variations between the races occur not only on the basis of their coloration, notably the extent of yellow plumage on the head, but also with regard to their size. The Panama Yellow-fronted Amazon (*A.o. panamensis*) for example, which occurs further north in Central America, has a pure yellow forehead, unlike the nominate race. It is also distinctly smaller in size.

Yellow-fronted Amazons all require similar care, and have long been highly prized for their mimicry skills. More recently, pairs have been kept for breeding purposes. As with other Amazons, they tend to have a fairly well-defined breeding period, rarely nesting until late April or early May in northern temperate areas. Hens usually lay only once, producing a clutch of up to five eggs. The incubation period may last for 26 days or so, and a proprietary rearing food should be supplied when there are chicks in the nest. They should fledge when they are around two months old.

Yellow-naped Amazon Parrot *Amazona ochrocephala auropalliata*

Origin: *south Mexico to northwest Costa Rica*

Cock: 14in (36cm) Grass green, rather paler on the underparts. There is a distinctive yellow patch on the nape, which may extend up to the rear of the crown. Red evident in the speculum of the wing; flights blackish with the outer webs green

*and the tips washed with blue. Tail green with a yellowish band and some red at
the base of the outer feathers. Bare whitish skin encircles the eyes. Iris orange; beak
blackish; legs and feet greyish.*

Hen: Similar in appearance.

These relatively large and attractive Amazons have become better known
in Europe in recent years, having previously been more common in North
American collections. The first breeding occurred in Australia in 1948.
Young birds can be easily recognised by the presence of just a few isolated
yellow feathers on the nape; their irises are dark brown. These birds are
highly valued as pets, having a reputation for being talented talkers, as
well as being gentle and affectionate by nature.

The Yellow-naped Amazon makes an attractive aviary occupant, but in
the past pairs have tended to be more reluctant to nest than other members
of the genus. A large flight, at least 15ft (4.5m) is recommended for them,
connected to a stoutly built shelter. Once acclimatised, they can remain
outdoors throughout the year.

Particular thought should be given to the access points into their aviary.
Amazons in general dislike being disturbed when they are breeding, and
may even attack you if you get too close to their nestbox. It is therefore a
good idea to be able to enter the aviary shelter directly, in order to feed the
birds there, rather than having to walk past their nestbox in the flight for
this purpose.

Among the various other members of the *Amazona ochrocephala* group,
one of the most colourful is the Double Yellow-headed Amazon (*A.o.
oratrix*). In this instance, yellow plumage extends over the entire head,
although in young birds it is restricted initially to the vicinity of the
forehead. More yellow feathering occurs over successive moults, with full
adult plumage being obtained when these parrots are about six years old.

Orange-winged Amazon Parrot *Amazona amazonica*

Origin: *north South America to the east of the Andes; also present on Trinidad
and Tobago*

*Cock: 12in (30cm) Predominantly green, greyer on the hindneck, with the
forehead, lores and a stripe above the eye being mauvish-blue; yellow coloration is
evident on the crown and cheeks. Orange coloration is apparent in the wing
speculum, and there is an orange patch at the base of the tail feathers. The bare
skin surrounding the eye is greyish. Iris orange, beak horn-coloured, darker at the
tip; legs and feet greyish.*

Hen: Similar in appearance.

One of the most commonly kept Amazons, the Orange-winged is sometimes
confused with the Blue-fronted Amazon, but it can be easily distinguished,

chiefly by its beak coloration. In addition, there are orange rather than bright red markings on the wings and, less evidently, on the tail. As with the Blue-fronted, however, there is considerable variation in the markings of individual Orange-winged Amazons. Although a popular pet, the calls of the Orange-winged can be just as harsh as those of larger species.

These parrots have been bred on various occasions, with the first British success being as recent as 1979. In this case, a young bird was reared from a pair kept as pets indoors. Three or four eggs are usually laid and incubated by the hen alone for 26 days. The young chicks, which are covered in wispy white down at first, develop quite rapidly and are able to fly by the time they are eight weeks old.

Although colour mutations are rare in the case of Amazons, a Lutino Orange-winged has been documented. It was kept at Paignton Zoo in Devon, England. In the case of all species within this genus the blue form of the Yellow-naped Amazon is probably the commonest mutation at present.

Senegal Parrot *Poicephalus senegalus*

Origin: *west Africa*

Cock: 10in (25cm) *Head, cheeks, ear coverts and throat dark grey; remainder of upperparts green. Flights and tail feathers brownish-black edged with green on the outer webs. Underparts yellow, shading to orange in the centre of the belly. There is a green band across the chest, and the flanks are also green. Dark area of orbital skin encircles the eyes. Iris bright orange; beak black; legs and feet blackish.*

Hen: Similar in appearance.

The depth of coloration on the underparts of these attractive parrots varies from yellow through orange to red, with birds of the latter race, which are known as *P.s. versteri* (Red-vented or Scarlet-bellied Senegal Parrot), originating from the Ivory Coast and Ghana and extending into western parts of Nigeria.

The relatively small size of these parrots, coupled with their quiet calls, makes them suitable for a garden aviary even in relatively urban surroundings. Unfortunately, adult birds may prove rather shy, especially at first, but they will soon settle in a suitable aviary. This should be made using 16SWG (standard wire gauge) mesh, because their beaks are quite powerful, and they will damage thinner mesh. A good supply of branches must also be provided as perches and replaced as necessary. Like other parrots, Senegals tend to become more destructive at the start of the breeding period. Details are as for other members of this genus.

Young Senegals, which are easily identified by their black and greyish irises and paler coloration, can in contrast become exceptionally tame and make magnificent companions. They were highly valued in this regard during the early 1900s, and they may even learn to say a few words. Their whistling calls do not, in any event, prove disturbing.

78 Meyer's Parrot *Poicephalus meyeri*

Origin: *widely distributed across much of Africa*

Cock: *10in (25cm) Head, back, wings and tail brown and grey, sometimes with a yellow stripe over the head. Edge and bend of wings, underwing coverts and thighs yellow. Underparts and rump green to greenish-blue. Bare greyish area of skin around the eyes. Iris orange; beak blackish; legs and feet blackish.*

Hen: *Similar in appearance.*

A number of races of this parrot exist, with quite striking colour variations between them. Some are far more colourful than others, notably with regard to the extent of yellow plumage and the coloration of the rump. These parrots need to be sexed in order to find a breeding pair, unless you are lucky enough to obtain a proven pair, which has already nested successfully.

Like the Senegal Parrot, young birds can become very tame and playful. They are suitable as pets because their calls are not especially loud, and they prove generally trustworthy with children. Breeding results have been obtained quite consistently, with one aviculturist in South Africa having kept this species successfully for over 50 years.

Just before egg-laying, hens will often flare their tail feathers while perching outside the nestbox. They will whittle away wooden blocks on the floor of the box to produce a lining for their eggs. Three or four eggs form the typical clutch, with incubation lasting for around 27 days. Assuming that all goes well, the young parrots will fledge around 10 weeks later. It is important to avoid disturbing these birds more than necessary when they are nesting, especially if the pair concerned have not bred before, because they may otherwise desert their eggs.

Ruppell's Parrot *Poicephalus ruppellii*

Origin: *southwest Africa, from south Angola into north Namibia*

Cock: *9in (23cm) Smoky-brown. Sides of the head and ear coverts silvery-grey. Rump and uppertail coverts dusky brown with darker edges. Bend and front edges of wing yellow, as are the underwing coverts and thighs. Iris orange; beak greyish-black; legs and feet also greyish-black.*

Hen: *Easily distinguishable by the bright blue coloration of the rump and uppertail coverts, with the undertail coverts being a pale, dull blue.*

Although young birds of both sexes tend to resemble the hen, they can be distinguished quite easily because their yellow coloration is confined to the underwing coverts, with a scattering of yellow feathers sometimes also in the vicinity of the shoulder. The beak is also paler, being grey.

Ruppell's Parrot has never been particularly common in aviculture, and in recent years it has become decidedly scarce. It is very similar to Meyer's Parrot in its habits, however, and requires identical care. A diet based on a good quality parrot mix will be required, with groundnuts being a particular favourite of these and other *Poicephalus* species. Pine nuts and parrot pellets can also be provided, along with fruit and greenstuff. Corn on the cob is often favoured as well.

For breeding purposes the nestbox must be sited in a secluded and darkened part of the aviary, even in the shelter itself. This will encourage the parrots to go to nest, and pairs must be housed on their own for this purpose. When rearing chicks, they may consume insects, such as greenfly, and it will be worth providing a suitable rearing food at this stage.

Other members of this genus which can be sexed visually include the Red-bellied Parrot (*P. rufiventris*), in which the plumage distinction is even more striking than in Ruppell's Parrot. Cocks have deep orange underparts, whereas those of hens are greenish. A less clear-cut definition applies with regard to Jardine's Parrot (*P. gulielmi*), in which the irises may indicate the bird's gender, being reddish-brown in cocks and a duller shade of brown in hens. No such means of distinction is apparent in the Brown-headed Parrot (*P. cryptoxanthus*), which is also seen in collections from time to time.

Grey Parrot (African Grey Parrot) *Psittacus erithacus*

Origin: *equatorial Africa*

Cock: 13in (33cm) *Predominantly grey, paler on the rump and belly. Tail and undertail coverts are bright scarlet. The plumage on the head and neck is margined with paler grey edges. A very broad bare area of whitish skin extends from behind the eyes around the cere. Iris straw-yellow; beak black; legs and feet blackish.*

Hen: *Similar in appearance.*

Throughout their wide range, the depth of grey coloration of these parrots varies distinctly. Those from the Cameroon, for example, are often described as Silver Greys, because of their light coloration. In the case of birds from the same region, it may be possible to distinguish cocks by the slightly darker coloration over the wings, as they have more dark pigment once they are mature. But this is not a reliable means of determining sex when the parrots are from a wider area.

The species has a very long avicultural history. It was known to the Egyptians and was almost certainly the first species of parrot ever to be kept in Europe. It is also the most talented of all parrots in terms of its powers of mimicry, and not only does it repeat words with unparalleled clarity, but frequently manages to say whole sentences with the right intonation, giving the impression that it correctly associates sounds with actions. Grey Parrots are capable of talking in sad, indignant or even querulous tones, and will imitate not only words, but other sounds as well.

You must seek a young, hand-reared parrot if you want a talking companion. At this stage, the irises are a dark grey in colour, but it is not easy to select a youngster that is likely to prove outstanding in terms of its powers of mimicry, since the talents of all birds vary to some extent. There are those which learn mainly to imitate the whistling of tunes; others are more adept at learning sounds such as coughing, sneezing, laughing or even the telephone ringing, while those most in demand, of course, are good talkers. This is not entirely a reflection of the bird alone, however, but also of the skills of the person responsible for teaching it. The more time that can be devoted to this purpose, the better will be the result. Grey Parrots may be slow to start talking, perhaps not uttering a word until they are six months old, but their vocabulary will then normally increase rapidly.

Grey Parrots can live to a great age and may be passed down from one generation to the next in the family, even speaking the language of a bygone age. If you have a bird that has acquired undesirable expressions, it is possible to cure it of this trait by placing it with another of its own kind. It should then forget the sounds it has learnt to mimic, and revert to its own natural language.

These parrots have a tendency to pluck their feathers; this is often due to a fault in their diet. In addition to a parrot mix containing items such as sunflower, peanuts, pine nuts, maize and groats, they should be offered parrot pellets. Fruit and greenstuff should also be provided on a regular basis.

Birds kept indoors must be sprayed twice a week or so, to ensure that their plumage remains in good condition. They are more likely to pluck themselves if it becomes dry and brittle. Plenty of exercise is also important for these intelligent parrots, and, as always with pet birds, a large flight unit is preferable to a small parrot cage when it comes to housing.

In recent years, Grey Parrots have been kept on a much wider scale for breeding purposes. It may take several years for imported birds to settle down sufficiently to breed, however, and the acclimatisation process also needs to be carried out gradually. Greys dislike damp, cold weather, and they must have an adequate shelter, complete with a safe heater if needed, where they can retreat when the weather is at its worst. Grey Parrots are sensitive birds, and dislike changes in their surroundings.

Compatibility is very important for breeding purposes. Swopping partners may be the only way to find a pair that will nest, once they have had time to settle in their new quarters. They will use either a nestbox or a hollow log, with the former usually being preferred since the interior will be easier to inspect, with minimum disturbance to the parrots themselves. As the breeding period approaches, the cock bird will start to feed his mate more frequently, while she flares her tail open on occasions, especially when close to the nest. They will be more destructive at this stage, and their perches may have to be replaced with increasing frequency.

The hen will lay three or four, sometimes five, eggs in a clutch. She incubates these on her own, and they should hatch after a period of 28 days or so. A good range of rearing foods should be provided at this stage, including egg food, corn on the cob and similar items. Pomegranates are often favoured.

The chicks should be out of the nest by the time that they are 11 weeks old, although they will be fed largely by the cock bird until they are fully independent. It will probably be four years before the young Greys are themselves likely to breed. They must always have a supply of cuttlefish bone available to ensure healthy bone development, because Grey Parrots are susceptible to calcium deficiency.

The slightly smaller and darker race, known as the Timneh Grey Parrot (*P.e. timneh*), needs identical care, although it tends to be less popular in aviculture. Interestingly, however, the upper bill is lighter in coloration, being horn-coloured with a darker tip in this case. Timneh Greys originate from Sierra Leone, Liberia, the Ivory Coast and south Guinea.

Lesser Vasa Parrot *Coracopsis nigra*

Origin: *Madagascar and neighbouring islands*

Cock: 14in (36cm) *Brownish-black overall, including the long and relatively wide tail feathers. Bare greyish area of skin encircles the eyes. Iris dark brown; beak variable through the year, being blackish after the moult, then becoming paler; legs and feet pinkish-grey.*

Hen: *Similar in appearance.*

These bizarre parrots, and the larger species known as the Greater Vasa Parrot (*C. vasa*), which averages 20in (51cm) in length, were almost unknown in aviculture until the 1980s. It is possible to sex them visually, when they are in breeding condition, not on the basis of differences in their plumage, but rather by means of a swelling that protrudes from the cock's vent, appearing rather like a prolapse. In addition, hens tend to lose the feathering on the back of their necks at this stage. The beaks of both species lighten in coloration.

They will eat a wide variety of seeds and other foods, being far less choosy in this regard than most parrots, and so they should be offered a varied diet, including plenty of fruit and greenstuff. Although Vasa Parrots do have a fairly penetrating call, this is not heard very often, unless they are alarmed. They also have a much softer series of whistles in their vocal repertoire. Active by nature, they should be housed in a suitably spacious aviary.

This species has suffered in collections from Psittacine Beak and Feather Disease (PBFD), the viral ailment which was originally reported in cockatoos. It is therefore recommended that they are not housed in the vicinity of cockatoos, and obviously the feathering of Vasa Parrots should be carefully checked for symptoms before purchase. The presence of white feathering in both the Greater and Lesser Vasa Parrot has been linked to PBFD, but this may simply be a metabolic disorder, rather like the odd yellow feathers associated with predominantly green psittacines, such as Ring-necks.

Breeding reports are now becoming more common, with hens usually producing clutches of two or three eggs. The incubation period is among the shortest of all psittacines, and Vasa Parrots themselves can be long lived, having a life expectancy in captivity of 50 years or more.

91 Madagascar Lovebird (Grey-headed Lovebird) *Agapornis cana*

Origin: *Madagascar*

Cock: 5in (13cm) *Mostly green, being lighter on the belly and darker on the wings. The head, neck and upper breast are grey. Tail green and black. Iris dark brown; beak pale horn in colour; legs and feet greyish.*

Hen: Lacks the grey plumage of the cock, being entirely green in colour.

These small parrots have a long avicultural history but have never been established to the extent of other species. Their availability tends to be rather sporadic, and they may be somewhat nervous by nature. Even so, it has been recorded that Madagascar Lovebirds can be taught to talk and become finger-tame, but this refers to home-bred chicks, which have lived indoors on their own from an early age.

In aviary surroundings these lovebirds are generally quiet, although the hen may become more aggressive during the breeding season. Pairs should be kept apart on their own. Because they often come into breeding condition during the winter months in the northern hemisphere, it is better to bring them indoors over this period. In any event, they are not entirely hardy, even when acclimatised.

These lovebirds build nests, but they are less bulky than those of some other species. Fresh willow twigs are traditionally provided to encourage breeding activity, with the birds stripping off the bark and using this to form the nest lining, but other materials will be taken for this same purpose if willow is unavailable.

Hens may lay as many as six eggs, with the incubation period lasting 23 days. The chicks can be sexed before fledging in the same way as adults, and fledging occurs when they are about six weeks old. Spray millet is a particularly important item in the diet of these small lovebirds, and it can be offered soaked as a rearing food during the breeding period. The first success was reported from Germany by Russ in 1872 and from Britain in 1882.

Red-faced Lovebird *Agapornis pullaria*

Origin: *northern and central parts of Africa*

Cock: 6in (15cm) Bright green, becoming more yellowish on the underparts. Face and crown orange-red. Rump bright blue. Bend of wing, shoulder and underwing coverts black; edge of wing bluish; flights dusky with green outer webs. Tail green with a band of red followed by a band of black towards the tip. Iris brown; beak red; legs and feet dark grey.

Hen: Red on the face is less bright and more orange in tone; rump paler blue; underwing coverts green; edge of wing yellowish.

Although this species used to be quite regularly obtainable and is reasonably easy to maintain, these lovebirds seldom produced young. In the wild they nest in ants' nests located on the branches of trees. Here, protected by the termites, they are reasonably safe from predators, while the nest itself benefits from the heat generated within the termite mound. As a result, these lovebirds do not sit as tightly as other species, with the consequence that in colder climates outside Africa, their eggs may be easily chilled.

Those breeders who have persevered with this species have used their ingenuity to achieve successful results. Arthur Prestwich, responsible for the first breeding of Red-faced Lovebirds in Britain, provided peat-filled barrels, into which the birds tunnelled to excavate their own nesting cavities. These extended back for approximately 6in (15cm) and ended in a larger nesting chamber, about the size of an orange, where the eggs were laid. A single youngster was then fledged successfully in 1955, being reared mainly on soaked millet sprays and apple.

More recently breeders have incorporated heat pads into the design of a nest box. Herr Blome, of Bremen, Germany, has pioneered this technique, achieving his first success in 1974, and rearing approximately 40 chicks using heat pads in under five years. The nestboxes themselves are 8in (20cm) square, and have an 18 watt heat pad, which is switched on and serves to maintain the internal temperature of the box at 86°F (30°C) once the chicks have hatched. It is not used beforehand, because the eggs will desiccate. Herr Blome also provides plenty of opportunity, by means of open containers of water, for hens to bathe. This appears to improve the humidity within the nest at the end of the incubation period, increasing hatchability.

Like the Madagascar Lovebird, this species tends to be rather nervous by nature and requires a fairly secluded environment. They must be acclimatised very carefully, and it is probably better to keep them indoors over the winter months, rather than leaving them exposed to the vagaries of the weather at this time.

93 **Abyssinian Lovebird** (Black-winged Lovebird) *Agapornis taranta*

Origin: *Ethiopia*

Cock: 6in (15cm) Forehead and area of plumage around the eyes red. Upperparts green; rump and undertail coverts lighter green, as are the underparts. Wing coverts and primaries brownish-black. Tail feathers green with a wide black cross band towards the tip. Iris brown; beak dark red; legs grey.

Hen: Resembles the cock, except that the red plumage on the head is replaced by green.

Since it is simple to select a true pair and the care of these lovebirds is straightforward, it is perhaps surprising that they do not enjoy more widespread popularity among breeders. In fact, Abyssinian Lovebirds are now quite scarce in aviculture, and obtaining stock can be difficult.

They soon become accustomed to new surroundings and, compared with the Madagascar and Red-faced Lovebirds, are quite bold. Abyssinian Lovebirds are also quiet by nature, which makes them ideal for a garden aviary. Once they are properly acclimatised they are relatively hardy, and can be allowed to remain in an outside aviary throughout the year, always providing that a dry shelter is available, with a nestbox provided there for roosting purposes.

In addition to a seed mixture composed mainly of millets, plain canary seed and groats, with a little sunflower added, they will also take fruit and greenstuff. For breeding purposes, pairs must be housed on their own. Compared with some other species of lovebird they construct a very small nest. It often consists of little more than a pad of feathers plucked from the female's breast. They also prefer a small nestbox, which may have dimensions of just 3in (7.5cm) square.

Pairs may take a year or so to settle in new quarters before they begin to breed. Three or four eggs are normally laid, hatching after about 23 days. The chicks are well protected against cold at this stage, being covered in a dense coat of white down. Their subsequent development is relatively slow, and they will not leave the nest until they are around seven weeks old. At this stage, their beaks are a dusky shade of yellow, often with darker markings at the base. It may be up to eight months before the red feathering on the heads of young cocks becomes visible. First breeding results were obtained in Germany in 1925 and in Britain in the following year.

92 **Peach-faced Lovebird** (Rosy-faced Lovebird)

Agapornis roseicollis

Origin: *Namibia and northwest Cape Province, South Africa*

Cock: 6in (15cm) Bright almond green, more yellowish on the underside. Forehead deep rose-red; side of head and throat paler rose-red. Rump and uppertail coverts bright blue; flights blackish; underwing coverts bluish-green. Tail green, with outer feathers orange-red at the base, with a black subterminal base. Iris brown; beak whitish-horn; legs and feet grey.

Hen: Similar in appearance.

The best known lovebird in aviculture, the Peach-faced is widely kept and has now been bred in a wide range of colour variants. Although its voice is louder than that of other species, it does not compare with that of other, larger parrots. In some parts of the world, notably Australia, these love-birds are kept in a colony system, but they can prove very aggressive. Indeed, if pairs are housed in adjoining flights, it is vital that each side of the framework is wired, so that they cannot reach each other's toes. This double-wiring will also need to be checked at intervals, to ensure that the mesh has not sagged on the frames. If these lovebirds are to be kept together in a group, they must all be introduced to the aviary at the same time, with nestboxes being positioned at the same height so that there will be no fighting between pairs keen to gain occupancy of the top box.

When they are breeding hen Peach-faced Lovebirds carry nesting material such as strips of bark to the box tucked in among their feathers. The resulting structure may be fairly bulky. On average she will lay five eggs, which will start to hatch after a period of 23 days. Young Peach-faced Lovebirds are covered in reddish down at first, and this is gradually replaced by grey. Fledging occurs when they are about six weeks old.

Feeding should be as recommended for other members of the genus. Although hardy, these lovebirds should be encouraged to roost, preferably in nestboxes or in the aviary shelter on cold nights, as they are rather susceptible to frost-bite. They may live for 10 years or so, and young hand-reared chicks in particular can develop into lively companions, although they are not especially talented as mimics.

The best-known of the Peach-faced mutations is the so-called pastel blue. This is not a pure blue, but retains a greenish tinge to its plumage, while its facial coloration is a very pale salmon. The first reports of this colour came from the Netherlands, where the mutation arose in a breeders' aviary in 1963.

The oldest mutation is the yellow form, which may have arisen in the USA as long ago as 1929, but whose recent development began in Japan during 1954. For a period, such birds were called Golden Cherryheads. This is a dilute form of the normal and is, as with the pastel blue, recessive in its mode of inheritance.

The blue rump of the yellow Peach-faced Lovebird serves to distinguish it from the pure Lutino, which is a rich, golden yellow with a white rump and red eyes. A sex-linked recessive mutation, it first came to prominence in the USA during the 1970s. Another American mutation is the pied, whose markings are variable in appearance, with no two individuals showing the same patterning. This originated during the 1960s.

The other major primary mutation in Peach-faced Lovebirds is the dark factor, which occurred in Australia, also in the 1960s. This is akin to the same mutation recognised in Budgerigars, giving rise to olive and dark green birds, with the latter being a slightly lighter colour. When transferred to pastel blues, the equivalent colours are described as mauve and cobalt.

Other colour combinations to have been developed include the Cremino, which is a pale lemon shade, and the 'white', which is not pure white, but actually a very light shade of grey. Although in recent years, there has been much interest generated by red pied Peach-faced Lovebirds, it is now clear the such birds are not the result of a genetic mutation. Instead, this pattern of markings can be induced by nutritional factors, notably a high level of fish oil in the diet. It is usually a transitory characteristic, varying in extent from one year to the next and often disappearing totally in the case of young birds once they moult out.

94 Fischer's Lovebird *Agapornis fischeri*

Origin: *south Kenya and north Tanzania*

Cock: 5in (13cm) Green, paler and more yellowish on the underparts. Forehead bright orange-red; crown dusky olive; nape orange; cheeks and throat paler orange slightly washed with olive. Rump and uppertail coverts bright blue; flights blackish with green on the outer webs. Tail green, central feathers tipped with pale blue, outer feathers orange at base, with a subterminal band of black and blue tips. Bare white naked skin encircles the eyes. Iris brown; beak coral red; legs and feet dark grey.

Hen: Similar in appearance.

These lovebirds can be easily kept by beginners and will give much pleasure, with pairs usually nesting quite readily. The major difficulty is actually identifying a cock and hen with certainty in the first instance, although reliable sexing methods have now made this more practical. Once acclimatised, they are quite hardy and can remain outside during the winter, although they must be encouraged to stay overnight in the shelter on frosty nights. They usually prefer to roost in a nestbox anyway.

The first breeding results were obtained by the Duke of Bedford in 1927. As many as six eggs are laid by the hen, and they should hatch after a period of 23 days. Fischer's Lovebirds build a rather dome-shaped nest in their box, which can make inspection difficult, but they usually prove reliable parents. They may pluck their chicks, however, and this is usually a sign that they are wanting to nest again. Providing a second nestbox as the chicks are feathering up may be useful in this regard, allowing the hen to build another nest while her first offspring are still in the other box.

Colour mutations of Fischer's Lovebird have been reported, but are not common. Various blue forms, a cinnamon, yellow and pied variants have all been documented, but have never achieved the popularity of the colour variants seen in the Peach-faced Lovebird.

Masked Lovebird *Agapornis personata*

Origin: *northeast Tanzania*

Cock: 6in (15cm) Head, including the ear coverts and cheeks, a dull brownish-black; a yellow collar extends around the nape of the neck to the breast, where it merges into the green of the body colour. Rump and uppertail coverts washed with grey-blue. Flights black with green outer webs. Tail green, outer feathers orange at the base and with a black bar and yellowish tips. Bare prominent area of white skin encircles the eyes. Iris brown; beak red; legs and feet dark grey.

Hen: Similar in appearance.

There is a school of taxonomic thought that groups all four lovebirds with white eye-rings into one species, *Agapornis personata*, with others such as Fischer's, for example, being considered as subspecies and becoming, in this case, *A.p. fischeri*. Although these lovebirds differ noticeably in their actual coloration, there is a clear similarity in their habits.

Masked Lovebirds have long been one of the most popular members of this group, with pairs usually breeding readily. Their diet should consist of a mixture of smaller cereal seeds, such as millets and plain canary seed, mixed with groats, and a little sunflower seed. Green food is often popular as is sweet apple. They build a fairly bulky nest, with breeding details being similar to those of Fischer's Lovebird.

Up to eight eggs have been recorded, while many pairs are double-brooded. The youngsters should be removed as soon as they are eating on their own so that they do not interfere with their parents' subsequent breeding activities. At this stage, they will be duller in coloration, while the upper bill is blackish at its base.

The blue mutation of the Masked Lovebird is widely kept, being developed from a single wild-caught cock bird imported by the London dealer, Chapman, in 1927. Subsequently, this lovebird bred at London Zoo, and so began the development of this attractive mutation. The beak in this case is affected – it is pale pink, – and white replaces the yellow on the breast; the remainder of the body is blue, aside from the characteristic black head.

The yellow mutation first arose in California during 1935. This is a dilute version of the normal, with the overall body coloration being paler, so that green becomes a yellowish shade of lime green, and the head is brown. Combination of the yellow and blue mutations has led to the development of a white form, although this is not pure in colour, being simply a much paler version of the blue form. Only one snow white Masked Lovebird has been recorded, from Denmark, and it apparently died without breeding.

Nyasa Lovebird (Lilian's Lovebird) *Agapornis lilianae*

Origin: *Malawi*

Cock: 5in (13cm) *Dark green on the back and wings, lighter green below, yellowish on the rump and uppertail coverts. Head, throat and upper breast salmon-pink, brighter on the forehead and pale on the cheeks. Nape yellowish-green, with flights being dusky green. Tail green, outer feathers orange at the base, with a black bar and green tips. Bare area of prominent white skin encircles the eyes. Iris dark brown; beak reddish; legs and feet greyish.*

Hen: Similar in appearance.

These rank among the smallest of all nine species of lovebird, and they have proved prolific in the past, although they are now less commonly seen in collections, certainly in Europe and North America, even though they are still quite often encountered in South African aviaries. Stock from South Africa is now becoming available elsewhere. They are not particularly difficult to keep, but are perhaps rather less hardy than the Masked Lovebird, for example, and so are best overwintered in a birdroom flight in temperate areas.

In other respects, Nyasa Lovebirds require similar care, although they may be somewhat less aggressive than related species, enabling them to be kept and bred more satisfactorily on a colony system. Some pairs prefer to nest during the winter months, which is a further reason for accommodating them indoors over this period. Their diet should not differ from that recommended previously for other lovebirds, with a rearing food being offered while there are chicks in the nest.

A Lutino form of the Nyasa Lovebird was first recorded in 1930, and it originated from Australia. Stock was subsequently exported overseas, and Lutinos were bred for a period in Britain, but this mutation now appears to have died out here, although odd individuals or pairs may be present elsewhere in Europe, and such birds have recently bred at Houston Zoo, Texas, in the USA.

Black-cheeked Lovebird *Agapornis nigrigensis*

Origin: *southwest Zambia*

Cock: 5in (13cm) *Predominantly dark green over the back and wings, becoming lighter on the underparts, and more yellowish on the rump and uppertail coverts. Mask is brown, with the ear coverts and cheeks being blackish. There is also a noticeably salmon-coloured area on the breast. A prominent area of bare white orbital skin encircles the eyes. Iris brown; beak dark red; legs and feet greyish.*

Hen: Similar in appearance.

One of the most recently discovered of all parrots, unrecorded until 1904, the Black-cheeked Lovebird has a very limited area of distribution. The first breeding results were obtained in Britain just four years later, and these lovebirds established a reputation for being prolific. Unfortunately, avicultural interest then tended to switch elsewhere, with the result that although a large number were imported during the 1920s, no serious attempt was made to establish them at this stage.

Once importations ceased they became quite rare, and the situation was worsened by the fact that remaining stock was often hybridised with other lovebirds, such as the Nyasa and Masked, and at least some of these hybrids themselves proved fertile. In recent years, much more emphasis has been placed on building up pure strains again, and there are now some thriving colonies, although the Black-cheeked still remains one of the rarer white-eye ringed lovebirds in aviculture. Their care and breeding is similar to that of other related lovebirds.

Mutations are essentially unknown in the case of the Black-cheeked Lovebird, apart from a blue individual bred in Denmark during 1981. As far as can be ascertained, this bird is of pure stock, and not the result of further hybridisation involving blue Masked Lovebirds.

6 Blue-crowned Hanging Parrot *Loriculus galgulus*

Origin: *Malaysia, Sumatra and Borneo*

Cock: 5in (13cm) Predominantly green with a distinctive dark blue spot on the crown, a triangular area of golden plumage on the upperback and a bright yellow band across the lower back. The rump and uppertail coverts are scarlet; there is also a large scarlet bib under the throat. Underwing and undertail coverts are bluish-green. Tail green with a yellowish tip. Iris brown; beak black; legs and feet greyish-brown.

Hen: Much duller overall, with no scarlet on the throat and no yellow band on the lower back.

When roosting, these small parrots hang upside down from suitable branches or from the roof of their aviary if this is of mesh. This unusual posture has led to them being called 'bat parrots', although they are better known as hanging parrots. They are relatively demanding in that their diet should consist of a nectar solution, supplied fresh each day, together with a good selection of fruit. Small seeds, such as millets, must always be available as well, and a dry nectar can also be provided, along with soft food.

Hanging parrots are, therefore, similar to lories and lorikeets in their feeding habits, although they most closely resemble lovebirds in terms of their breeding needs. They will use a small nestbox of natural log for this purpose, with hens cutting nesting material and transporting it to the nest site tucked in among the feathers of the rump and lower back.

It is also important to provide bathing facilities for these small parrots. Nectar should be provided only in a closed vessel, in case they try to bathe in this sticky solution. Their claws may also need trimming if the birds appear to become entangled on the mesh of their quarters when they are roosting. Otherwise, they could injure themselves as they climb around. Hanging parrots are very active, and like to clamber about the branches in their aviary, rather than flying.

Vernal Hanging Parrot *Loriculus vernalis*

Origin: *southwest India to Vietnam*

Cock: 6in (15cm) Green with an orange wash on the upper back. Rump and uppertail coverts red. Flights bluish on the inner webs. Throat with bluish patch, while there is a yellowish wash on the upper breast. Iris yellowish-white; beak dull red; legs and feet pale orange.

Hen: Tends to be of a more yellowish-green shade overall, with a dull green head, and the blue of the throat very faint or entirely absent. Iris usually dark.

Although less colourful than the better known Blue-crowned Hanging Parrot, this species still makes a fascinating aviary occupant. Pairs will thrive in a planted aviary, unlike other parrots, which are liable to destroy the vegetation if housed in such surroundings. Hanging parrots are not really suitable for keeping in cages, certainly on a permanent basis, because of their loose, sticky droppings. These will soil not only the perches, but also the surrounding area, both inside and outside the cage.

As with other species, breedings of the Vernal Hanging Parrot were rare until the 1970s. The first success was apparently recorded in Denmark in 1968. A small nestbox, well-concealed among the vegetation of the aviary, is likely to be preferred. Internal dimensions of 6in (15cm) square and 8in (20cm) in height should be adequate.

The first breeding in Britain involved a hen which was at least nine years old, which confirms the relatively long reproductive life of these small parrots. She had laid two clutches previously in 1974, before chicks were finally reared successfully in August of that year. All three eggs hatched, and the resulting chicks left the nest when they were just over a month old. They were soon roosting in the characteristic upside-down position.

The adult birds consumed mealworms when rearing their chicks, as well as their usual diet, which included sponge cake soaked in nectar, cheese and fruit. They were also observed feeding on the inner bark of silver birch logs present in their aviary.

Philippine Hanging Parrot *Loriculus philippensis*

Origin: *Philippine islands, extending to the Sulu Archipelago*

Cock: 5in (13cm) Predominantly green, darker on the wings and yellower on the underparts. Forehead and front of the crown red, merging into a yellow band, and a dusky yellow patch on the occiput. Red patch on throat and upper breast; golden-orange band on the nape. Rump and uppertail coverts bright red; pale blue feathering adjoining the rump. Iris dark brown; beak orangish-red; legs and feet pinkish.

Hen: Duller, without the red areas on the throat and breast. Lores show a distinctive bluish tinge.

There is often considerable variation in the appearance of these particular hanging parrots because a number of distinctive forms have evolved over the various Philippine islands where they occur. Less widely kept than either of the preceding two species, the Philippine Hanging Parrot nevertheless has similar requirements.

When starting out with these parrots, it is worth purchasing at least two pairs if possible. You will then have a basis for continuing a breeding programme, once your birds have, it is hoped, reared chicks successfully. Otherwise, it can be very difficult to track down odd individuals of the equivalent subspecies at a later date. There are approximately 11 of these recognised by taxonomists, some being much more colourful than others.

Three eggs form the usual clutch, and incubation lasts approximately 20 days. Sponge cake soaked in nectar is again often a favoured rearing food, as are mealworms, which the adult birds will crush in their beaks. Sieved shavings are a useful floor covering in the nestbox, in view of the liquid diet of these parrots.

Like other hanging parrots, the Philippine will not prove entirely hardy, and it is best kept in a planted indoor enclosure during the winter months, which can be heated as necessary. Under these circumstances, breeding may occur even at this time of the year. Recently fledged chicks can be distinguished not only by the greatly reduced area of red plumage on the forehead, but also by their bill coloration, which is dark yellow, with blackish markings near the base. Their legs and feet are also grey rather than pink at this stage. Similar distinctions apply to the young of related species.

Ring-necked Parakeet (Rose-ringed Parakeet)
Psittacula krameri

Origin: *widely distributed, being present in north Africa from Senegal to the Sudan, and across south Asia, from south India and Sri Lanka east to China*

Cock: 15in (38cm) A soft, rather greyish-green with a bluish sheen on the nape and central tail feathers; more grey on the underparts and yellowish on the underwing coverts. Outer tail feathers are yellow on the inner webs and green on the outer, all being tipped with yellow. There is a faint black line extending from the nostrils to the eyes, and a broad black band running downwards from the base of the beak and across the sides of the neck, with an adjoining rose-red collar behind. Orangish skin encircles the eyes. Iris pale yellow; beak dark red; legs and feet yellowish-grey.

Hen: *Lacks the black lines on the head, and the rose-red collar is replaced by a rather indistinct band of emerald green.*

Brought from India to Europe by the Greeks, this was one of the first species of parrot to become popular as a pet here. The Ring-necked Parakeet has the widest natural range of any psittacine, with the African race (*P.k. krameri*) being similar to the Indian form (*P.k. manillensis*) (Plate 79), which is as described above, except that its upper bill is blackish or slaty-purple and may be slightly smaller. It has become more common in aviculture during recent years.

Ring-necked Parakeets are easy to manage and quite hardy once they are properly acclimatised, although they are susceptible to frost-bite and should, therefore, be encouraged to roost in the shelter of their aviary, rather than choosing an exposed perch on a frosty night.

These parakeets will usually start breeding early in the year in the northern hemisphere, and a nestbox for this purpose should be hung up by November in a secluded and sheltered part of their aviary. The floor should be covered with some softwood blocks, which the hen can whittle away to make a nest lining. This preparation will take place over the course of several weeks.

There is no particularly strong bond between these or other related psittaculid parakeets. For much of the year the hen is dominant to her mate. He may be nervous about approaching her, and for this reason it is better to pair an older cock with a young hen, rather than vice versa, as there is then less likelihood of infertile eggs resulting.

A typical clutch is of three or four eggs, which the hen incubates alone for a period of about 24 days, until the chicks hatch. The cock will then play a greater role in caring for the offspring, helping to feed both them and his mate. In addition to their usual diet, which should be of a parrot seed mix and smaller items such as millet, you can offer greenstuff, carrot and fruit regularly, while bread and milk or soft food will be taken by some pairs when rearing their chicks. The first breeding results were recorded in Britain in 1902.

Colour mutations have now become quite common, especially the Lutino. These birds are entirely yellow, apart from the pink collar and white band seen in cocks, and they have been recorded in the wild in India. They were first bred there in 1932, followed by a blue mutation nine years later. Blue Ring-neck Parakeets are a rich shade of blue, which is particularly vivid on the head, contrasting with their red beak coloration, which is unaffected.

The combination of these two mutations has led to the development of the albino, which has become more common during recent years. There is no colour pigment present in this instance, and so even cock birds are pure, snow white, and they must be scientifically sexed in order to identify pairs with certainty. Other mutations that are now being developed include the cinnamon, a rather attractive grey and pieds.

2 Alexandrine Parakeet *Psittacula eupatria*

Origin: *Indo-China and Thailand, west to India*

Cock: 20in (51cm) Entirely green, with only the back of the head and cheeks having a grey-blue haze. A thin black line runs from the nostrils to the eye, while the lower sides of the cheeks show a black stripe, running to the lower mandible. The neck band behind is pink. Tail has green-blue feathers with yellow tips. There is a prominent, distinctive area of reddish-maroon on the wings. Narrow band of orangish skin encircles the eyes. Iris straw-yellow; beak red; legs and feet greyish.

Hen: Lacks the black facial markings and the pink neck band.

There is some variation in the size of these parakeets throughout their range, but they are invariably larger than the Ring-necked Parakeet and always show the red on the wing coverts. Alexandrines make impressive aviary birds, but they require a relatively strong flight, made of 16SWG (standard wire gauge) mesh, with the timber protected as far as possible from their stout beaks. Hens in particular, especially at the start of the breeding period, can be rather raucous.

They nest slightly later than Ringnecks, and again, if the first clutch of eggs fails to hatch, the hen may lay again, although the pair will not actually produce two rounds of chicks in a season. A pair should always be kept on their own for breeding purposes and require a somewhat larger nestbox, which will need to be well-supported because of its weight.

First breeding results were obtained in 1899, and although Alexandrines have bred regularly since then, some pairs prove to be much more prolific than others. Captain Veitch, of Garforth in Britain, owned a pair which bred consistently for 20 years and reared every chick that hatched. Two or three eggs form the usual clutch, with incubation lasting 28 days.

As with Ringneck Parakeets, young birds are similar to the adult hen when they fledge, except that their tail feathers are shorter. It will be at least two years before young cock birds obtain their characteristic markings. Blue and Lutino mutations have been recorded in the past, but are probably extinct. It is now hard to determine the validity of such Alexandrines, because hybridisation with Ring-neck Parakeets may have introduced these colours artificially. Hybrids in this case are often fertile.

Moustached Parakeet (Banded Parakeet) *Psittucula alexandri*

Origin: *north India east to Indo-China and south China*

Cock: 15in (38cm) Head blue-grey; line across the forehead and lores black, as well as a broad stripe running from the beak across the base of the cheeks; throat band bright green. Back green; breast rosy-lilac. Remainder of underparts green, often with a slight bluish tone. Wings green with a yellowish-green shoulder spot. Iris yellow; upper bill red, lower bill black; legs and feet greyish.

Hen: May show little variation in plumage, but is a trifle bluer in colour. Beak entirely black.

With eight different races of this species recognised throughout its wide range, there can be noticeable variation in the appearance of these parakeets. The most striking is perhaps the Javan subspecies (*P. a. alexandri*), in which the hen has a partially red beak just like the cock bird. In other instances, the extent of blue suffusion tends to be a significant distinguishing factor.

Moustached Parakeets have been available on a fairly regular basis but have never managed to arouse great enthusiasm in the avicultural community. Certainly, their calls can be rather raucous, and these birds may be destructive, but in spite of these difficulties, they are undeniably attractive.

They do not differ significantly from other psittaculid parakeets in terms of care. Careful acclimatisation is required in the first instance. Nesting occurs later than in the case of the Ring-necked Parakeet, with hens rarely laying before March in northern temperate climes. Outside the breeding period, they can be rather dominant towards their partners, and it is important to ensure that cocks are not excluded or persecuted at the food pot. It may be better to provide two well-spaced feeding containers within the shelter to minimise this risk.

Young Moustached Parakeets are predominantly green when they fledge, while possessing the characteristic black facial markings. Interestingly, the beak in both sexes is red at this stage, although of a less intense shade then in adult cocks. It then darkens to black, before the upper mandible lightens back to red in the case of young cocks. No colour mutations are established in this species.

81 Plum-headed Parakeet *Psittacula cyanocephala*

Origin: *India and Sri Lanka*

Cock: 14in (36cm) Yellowish-green with a rose-purple head progressing to violet-blue at the back, and with a narrow black collar edged with blue. Flights and long tail are shaded with yellow and pale blue, with the end of the central tail feathers being almost white. There is a dark crimson bar on the shoulder. Iris yellowish; beak yellowish on the upper bill, and black below; legs and feet pinkish grey.

Hen: Recognisable by dark lavender-grey head coloration.

These parakeets are beautifully coloured and relatively small in size. They have much in their favour as aviary occupants. Because they are tolerant towards other birds, they can be housed with foreign finches and doves in a large enclosure, although for breeding purposes, a pair should be given an aviary to themselves. Their calls are not harsh or unpleasant, and when kept as a pair, the voice of the cock is even quite melodious during the breeding season. Nor are they very destructive, especially when compared with other psittaculid parakeets.

Recently imported Plum-heads require careful acclimatisation. Millets, plain canary seed and groats form their normal bill of fare, varied with the addition of some sunflower seed, small pine nuts and hemp. Grass seeds, green food and plenty of fruit should also figure prominently in their diet.

A thick, small nestbox, about 8in (20cm) square and 12in (30cm) high, should be hung in the shelter for breeding purposes, lined with thin wooden offcuts or sieved shavings, which the birds can use as a nest lining. The hen lays between four and six eggs in a clutch, which takes at least 23 days to hatch. Unfortunately, although diligent parents, Plum-heads will cease brooding their chicks at night before they are fully feathered. As a result, they may be lost during cold weather. Positioning the box carefully will help in this regard.

A variety of rearing foods, including bread and milk, egg food and increased quantities of fruit and greenstuff will be required when the chicks are in the nest. They should be flying by just over six weeks old. At this stage, the young Plum-heads will be mainly green, and when they first moult, at around five months old, both sexes have grey heads. Odd plum-coloured feathers may then indicate males, as will their display.

Odd coloured variants have been recorded on occasions, but none is presently established. They have included a stunning Lutino and a blue form. Pieds are more frequently described, but these may be of nutritional rather than genetic origin. There is also a very similar form, known as the Blossom-headed Parakeet (*P.c. rosa*), from Indo-China and Burma (Myanmar). Cocks can be distinguished by the yellow tips to their long central tail feathers, with a paler head. Hens can also be distinguished from female Plum-heads by their red shoulder bars, corresponding to those seen in cocks.

Eclectus Parrot *Eclectus roratus*

Origin: *New Guinea and islands of eastern Indonesia*

Cock: 13in (33cm) Predominantly green, with sides of the body and underwing coverts red. Blue evident at the bend of the wing. Outer webs of primaries dark blue. Undersurface of tail greyish-black, with yellow tips to these feathers, with blue suffusion on the outer feathers. Iris orange; beak orange becoming yellower towards the tip; legs and feet greyish.

169

Hen: Easily distinguishable by combination of scarlet and maroon coloration, with prominent bluish-violet area on the underparts. Beak black.

These parrots represent the most extreme example of sexual dimorphism among the whole group. Indeed, it used to be though that the different sexes were actually separate species, because of the great variation in their coloration.

A number of different subspecies, varying between eight and ten depending on the taxonomy used, has evolved on the various islands where the Eclectus Parrot occurs. Rather strangely, although the cocks tend to be very similar in appearance, the differences in plumage between hens of these races can be quite marked.

Their calls can be quite loud, but these are not very noisy parrots by nature unless they are disturbed. They need a solidly constructed aviary and a diet that includes plenty of green food and fruit, as well as vegetables such as carrot and corn on the cob on a daily basis. Parrot seeds should also be offered, but these parrots require a fairly bulky, fibrous diet, as reflected by their long intestinal tract.

They are usually reliable breeders, with hens laying two eggs in the average clutch. Incubation can take 30 days, and until the chicks are several weeks old, the parents eat relatively little seed. Instead, items such as soaked raisins (well-washed before being offered to the birds), boiled rice pudding and egg food will all be valuable additions to their diet.

Young Eclectus Parrots can be sexed while they are still in the nest. They fledge at about 11 weeks old, and they should be removed from the aviary as soon as they are feeding on their own, and before then if the female appears to be hostile to them. She will probably want to lay again. Hens may also bully their mates, and care must be taken to ensure that they are able to feed in peace, with extra feeding stations being provided for this purpose. It is not unusual for pairs to produce chicks that are predominantly of one sex, for reasons that are unclear at present. Youngsters will need to be at least three years old before they themselves will nest.

83 Barraband Parakeet (Superb Parrot) *Polytelis swainsonii*

Origin: *east and southeast Australia*

Cock: 16in (41cm) Brilliant grass green. Forehead, throat and cheeks yellow with an orange-red crescent on the lower part of the throat. Wings greenish-blue, as is the tail. Iris orangish; beak pale orange; legs and feet greyish.

Hen: Pale green, lacking the yellow on the head and the red crescent.

These striking parakeets are quite hardy and can be kept in an outside aviary throughout the year, provided that there is adequate shelter.

Unfortunately, the Barraband is, like other Australian species, rather too flighty to be kept as a pet in the confines of the home.

Their diet should be formed mainly of smaller cereal seeds, such as millets and plain canary seed, augmented with some sunflower and a little hemp. Plenty of green food should also be offered whenever possible, particularly when there are chicks in the nest.

Barraband Parakeets are quite social by nature, and it has proved possible to breed them in groups in large aviaries, although there is always a risk of fighting breaking out under these circumstances. Breeding results were first reported from France in 1881 and from Britain in 1900.

A long flight, at least 12ft (3.7m) in length, is recommended, to enable the cock's display to be fully appreciated. A deep nestbox is also to be recommended for this species, ideally about 6ft (1.8m) tall. This can be supported on the aviary floor, provided that it cannot become soaked in heavy rain.

Chicks will fledge when they are about five weeks old, and young cocks in particular should be removed as soon as possible from the aviary, as they are liable to be attacked by the cock. They are unlikely to breed successfully until they are at least two years old.

Rock Peblar Parakeet (Rock Pebblar Parakeet, Regent Parakeet)

Polytelis anthopeplus

Origin: *southeast and southwest Australia*

Cock: 16in (41cm) Pale yellow overall, with a greenish tone; rump secondaries and entire underparts are yellow. Wings black with yellow and red on the shoulders. Tail black with a bluish sheen. Iris red; beak red; legs greyish.

Hen: More olive-brown rather than yellow, with brown tail coverts; tail feathers edged with salmon-pink.

Like other Australian species, these parakeets are powerful in flight and will appreciate a long aviary. Their diet should be similar to that recommended for the Barraband Parakeet, with sweet apple, twigs with buds and soaked seed representing other useful additions to the diet. Some pairs may even eat mealworms when they have chicks.

The deep nestbox can be positioned on the ground, attached by brackets if necessary to the aviary framework to give extra stability. The first breeding success occurred in 1865. Clutch size is typically four to six eggs, which start to hatch after an incubation period of about 19 days. Hens of this species are generally fairly tolerant of nest inspections, but a low door close to the base of the nestbox will be required for this purpose.

When the chicks fledge they resemble the adult hen, but young cocks may still show a more yellowish tone, notably on the head and breast. They will have moulted into adult plumage by the time they are about 15 months old. They are unlikely to breed until their second year.

84 Princess of Wales's Parakeet (Queen Alexandra's Parakeet)
Polytelis alexandrae

Origin: *central and western Australia*

Cock: 18in (46cm) Forehead, crown and nape light blue; hindneck, upper back, scapulas and inner secondaries olive-green. Lower back and rump blue; uppertail coverts light olive-green; two central tail feathers fading into bluish-green at the tips and edged with greenish-yellow at the base. The adjoining feathers here on either side are similar, but with the basal half of the inner webs pink; remainder pale bluish-grey broadly edged with rose-pink and tipped with greenish-yellow. Upperwing coverts yellowish-green, primary coverts indigo blue, innermost secondaries pale olive-green, remainder green on the outer webs tinged with blue at the tips and greenish-white on the outer edges; outer flights also tinged with blue. Lores and below the eyes yellowish-green; chin, cheeks and throat rose-pink. Remainder of the undersurface pale olive-green with a wash of grey-blue on the abdomen; thighs dull rose-red; sides of the flanks deep blue and lilac. Iris bright orange; beak coral red with a whitish tip; legs and feet dark grey.

Hen: Has a mauvish-grey crown, and a greyish tone to the plumage of the rump. Tail shorter; beak paler.

A strange feature associated with cock birds of this species is the presence of a spatule tip at the end of a primary feather on each wing, although these are relatively fragile and may break off. While Princess of Wales's Parakeets have been expensive in the past, stock is now available at much more realistic prices and also appears to be far less delicate.

These parakeets are at their most graceful in a large and roomy aviary, where they will usually settle down to breed. Their display is interesting, and members of a pair are devoted to each other. The cock flies up and down to attract his mate's attention, flaring the long tail feathers as he lands close to her on a perch. The pupils are then constricted so that his eyes appear bright red for a few moments, and this is followed by stretching, bowing and jumping on the spot to impress the female.

Breeding details are similar to those of the Rock Peblar Parakeet, and pairs may similarly have two clutches of chicks in a season. Their nestbox should also be deep, with a securely fixed ladder extending down towards the box. Young birds resemble the adult female at first, except that their tails are shorter, and the colour on the crown may be brighter in cocks, even at this early stage. Breeding is unlikely until they are two years old.

The blue mutation of the Princess of Wales's Parakeet is now quite well established, having first been recorded in the aviaries of an Australian

1 Chinese Painted Quail *Excalfactoria chinensis* (hen and cock)

2 Red-legged Partridge *Alectoris rufa*

3 Satyr Tragopan
Tragopan satyra

4 Temminck's
Tragopan
*Tragopan
temminckii*

5 Japanese Green
Pheasant
Phasianus versicolor

6 Himalayan
Monal
*Lophophorus
impeyanus*

7 Sonnerat's
Junglefowl
Gallus sonnerati

8 Red Junglefowl
Gallus gallus

9 Black-breasted Kalij *Lophura leucomelana* (cock and hen)

10 Silver Pheasant *Lophura nycthemera*

11 Edwards's Pheasant *Lophura edwardsii*

12 Swinhoe's Pheasant *Lophura swinhoiei*

13 Reeves's Pheasant *Syrmaticus reevesii*

14 Mikado Pheasant *Syrmaticus mikado*

15 Hume's Bar-tailed Pheasant *Syrmaticus humiae*

16 Lady Amherst's Pheasant *Chrysolophus amherstiae*

17 Golden Pheasant *Chrysolophus pictus*

18 Bornean Great Argus Pheasant *Argusianus argus grayi*

19 White Peacock *Pavo cristatus* (white form)

20 Indian Peacock *Pavo cristatus*

21 Indian Peacock *Pavo cristatus* (displaying)

22 Chinese Necklaced Dove
Streptopelia chinensis

23 White-crowned Pigeon
Columba leucocephala

24 Triangular-spotted Pigeon *Columba guinea*

25 Diamond Dove *Geopelia cuneata*

26 Green-winged Dove *Chalcophaps indica*

27 Zebra Dove *Geopelia striata*

28 White-winged Dove *Zenaida asiatica*

29 Common Bronze-winged
Pigeon *Phaps chalcoptera*

30 Luzon Bleeding-heart Pigeon
Gallicolumba luzonica

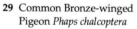

31 Crested Bronze-winged Pigeon *Ocyphaps lophotes*

32 White-faced Tree Duck *Dendrocygna viduata*

33 Muscovy Duck *Cairina moschata*

34 Red-billed Tree Duck *Dendrocygna autumnalis*

35 Group of Red-billed Tree Ducks *Dendrocygna autumnalis*

36 Common Pintail *Anas acuta* (drake)

37 Common Pintail *Anas acuta* (duck)

38 Common Shelduck *Tadorna tadorna*

39 Red-crested Pochard *Netta rufina*

40 Mandarin Duck *Aix galericulata* (duck and drake)

41 Carolina Duck *Aix sponsa* (duck and drake)

42 Hyacinthine Macaw
Anodorhynchus hyacinthinus

43 Red and Gold Macaw
Ara macao

44 Lear's Macaw
Anodorhynchus leari

45 Illiger's Macaw *Ara maracana*

46 Severe Macaw *Ara severa*

47 Green-winged Macaw
Ara chloroptera

48 Blue and Gold Macaw *Ara ararauna*

49 Noble Macaw *Ara nobilis cumanensis*

50 Swainson's Lorikeet
Trichoglossus
haematodus
moluccanus

51 Purple-capped Lory
Lorius domicella

52 Ornate Lorikeet *Trichoglossus ornatus*

53 Yellow-backed Chattering Lory *Lorius garrulus flavopalliatus*

54 Moluccan Cockatoo *Cacatua moluccensis*

55 Lesser Sulphur-crested Cockatoo
Cacatua sulphurea

56 Bare-eyed Cockatoo
Cacatua sanguinea

57 Head of Bare-eyed Cockatoo *Cacatua sanguinea*

58 Roseate Cockatoo *Eolophus roseicapillus*

59 Leadbeater's Cockatoo *Cacatua leadbeateri*

60 Cockatiel *Nymphicus hollandicus*

61 Cactus Conure
Aratinga cactorum

62 Cockatiel
Nymphicus hollandicus
(Lutino form)

63 Black-headed Conure
Aratinga nenday

64 Red-headed Conure *Aratinga erythrogenys*

65 White-eared Conure *Pyrrhura leucotis*

66 Brown-throated Conure *Aratinga pertinax*

67 Jendaya Conure *Aratinga jandaya*

68 Canary-winged Parakeet *Brotogeris versicolurus chiriri*

69 Tui Parakeet
*Brotogeris
sanctithomae*

70 White-winged
Parakeet
*Brotogeris
versicolurus
versicolurus*

71 White-bellied Caique *Pionites leucogaster*

72 Black-headed Caique *Pionites melanocephala*

73 Blue-fronted Amazon Parrot *Amazona aestiva*

74 Yellow-naped Amazon Parrot *Amazona ochrocephala auropalliata*

75 Senegal Parrot
*Poicephalus
senegalus*

76 Festive Amazon
Parrot
Amazona festiva

77 Blue-headed Parrot *Pionus menstruus*

78 Meyer's Parrot *Poicephalus meyeri*

79 Indian Ring-necked Parakeet *Psittacula krameri manillensis*

80 Grey Parrot *Psittacus erithacus*

81 Plum-headed Parakeet
Psittacula cyanocephala (cock and hen)

82 Alexandrine Parakeet *Psittacula eupatria*

83 Barraband Parakeet
Polytelis swainsonii

84 Princess of Wales's Parakeet *Polytelis alexandrae*

85 Crimson-winged Parakeet *Aprosmictus erythropterus*

86 Rock Peblar Parakeet *Polytelis anthopeplus*

87 Brown's Parakeet
Platycercus venustus

88 Green-winged
King Parakeet
*Alisterus
chloropterus*

89 Amboina King Parakeet *Alisterus amboinensis*

90 Australian King Parakeet *Alisterus scapularis* (cock and hen)

91 Madagascar Lovebird
Agapornis cana

92 Peach-faced Lovebird
Agapornis roseicollis

93 Abyssinian Lovebird *Agapornis taranta*

94 Fischer's Lovebird *Agapornis fischeri*

95 Masked Lovebird *Agapornis personata*

96 Blue-crowned Hanging Parrot *Loriculus galgulus*

97 Pennant's Parakeet *Platycercus elegans*

98 Stanley Parakeet
Platycercus icterotis

99 Turquoisine Grass Parakeet
Neophema pulchella

100 Adelaide Parakeet *Platycercus adelaidae*

101 Golden-mantled Rosella *Platycercus eximius cecilae*

102 Mealy Rosella *Platycercus adscitus*

103 Yellow Rosella
*Platycercus
flaveolus*

104 Red-rumped
Parakeet *Psephotus
haematonotus*
(yellow form)

105 Many-coloured Parakeet
Psephotus varius

106 Elegant Grass Parakeet
Neophema elegans

107 Red-rumped Parakeet
Psephotus haematonotus

108 Barnard's Parakeet
Barnardius barnardi

109 Bourke's Grass Parakeet
Neophema bourkii

110 Splendid Grass Parakeet
Neophema splendida

111 Budgerigars *Melopsittacus undulatus*

112 Budgerigar *Melopsittacus undulatus*
(yellow-faced sky-blue pied form)

113 Red-collared Whydah
Euplectes ardens

114 Yellow-backed Whydah
Euplectes macrourus

115 Giant Whydah
Euplectes progne

116 Jackson's Whydah
Euplectes jacksoni

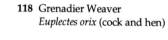

118 Grenadier Weaver
Euplectes orix (cock and hen)

117 Pin-tailed Whydah
Vidua macroura

119 Napoleon Weaver
Euplectes afer

120 Black-bellied Weaver
Euplectes nigroventris

122 Little Masked Weaver
Ploceus luteolus

121 Orange Bishop
Euplectes orix franciscana

123 Madagascar Weaver
Foudia madagascariensis

124 Taha Weaver
Euplectes afer taha

125 Speckle-fronted Weaver *Sporopipes frontalis*

126 Scaly-crowned Weaver *Sporopipes squamifrons* (cock and hen)

127 Village Weaver *Ploceus cucullatus*

128 Red-headed Quelea *Quelea erythrops*

129 Red-billed Weaver *Quelea quelea*

130 Crimson-rumped Waxbill *Estrilda rhodopyga*

131 Golden-breasted Waxbill
Amandava subflava

132 St Helena Waxbill
Estrilda astrild

133 Red-eared Waxbill *Estrilda troglodytes*

134 Blue-capped Cordon Bleu
Uraeginthus cyanocephala (hen and cock)

135 Red-cheeked Cordon Bleu
Uraeginthus bengalus

136 Peter's Twinspot *Hypargos niveoguttatus* (two hens with a cock in the centre)

137 Orange-cheeked Waxbill *Estrilda melpoda*

138 Yellow-bellied Waxbill *Estrilda quartinia*

139 Violet-eared Waxbill *Uraeginthus granatina*

140 Black-cheeked Waxbill
Estrilda erythronotos

141 Sydney Waxbill
Aegintha temporalis

142 Lavender Finch
Estrilda caerulescens

143 Green Avadavat
Amandava formosa

144 Strawberry Finch
Amandava amandava

145 Red-billed Firefinch
Lagonosticta senegala

146 Melba Finch *Pytilia melba*

147 Quail Finch *Ortygospiza atricollis*

148 Red-headed Finch
Amadina erythrocephala

150 Cut-throat *Amadina fasciata*

149 East African Cut-throat
Amadina fasciata alexanderi

151 Black-headed Mannikin *Lonchura malacca atricapilla*

152 Magpie Mannikin *Lonchura fringilloides*

153 White-headed Mannikin *Lonchura maja*

154 Three-coloured Mannikin *Lonchura malacca*

155 Bronze-winged Mannikin *Lonchura cucullata*

156 Common Spice Finch *Lonchura punctulata*

157 African Silverbill
Lonchura malabar
cantans

158 Indian
Silverbill
Lonchura
malaboric

159 Bengalese Finch *Lonchura domestica* (fawn and white form in front)

160 Bengalese Finch *Lonchura domestica*

161 Java Sparrow
    Padda oryzivora (white form)

162 Alario Finch
    Serinus alario

163 Java Sparrow *Padda oryzivora*

164 Cherry Finch
Aidemosyne modesta

165 Masked Grassfinch
Poephila personata

166 Star Finch *Neochmia ruficauda*

167 Chestnut-breasted Mannikin
Lonchura castaneothorax

168 Heck's Grassfinch
Poephila acuticauda hecki

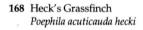

169 Long-tailed Grassfinch
Poephila acuticauda

170 Parson Finch *Poephila cincta*

171 Gouldian Finch *Chloebia gouldiae*
(red-headed form)

172 Gouldian Finch *Chloebia gouldiae*
(yellow-headed form)

173 Gouldian Finch *Chloebia gouldiae* (black-headed form)

174 Zebra Finch
Poephila guttata

175 Zebra Finch
Poephila guttata (pied form)

176 Zebra Finch *Poephila guttata* (white form; pied cock;
normal grey cock and fawn hens)

177 Painted Finch *Emblema picta*

178 Diamond Sparrow *Emblema guttata*

179 Pintailed Nonpareil *Erythrura prasina*

180 Bicheno's Finch *Poephila bichenovii*

181 Wild Canary *Serinus canaria*

182 Cape Canary *Serinus canicollis*

183 Green Singing Finch *Serinus mozambicus*

184 Grey Singing Finch *Serinus leucopygius*

185 Golden Song Sparrow *Passer luteus*

186 Saffron Finch *Sicalis flaveola*

187 Black-headed Siskin
Carduelis magellanica

188 Red Hooded Siskin
Carduelis cucullata

189 Crested Bunting
Melophus lathami

190 Common Rosefinch
Carpodacus erythrinus

191 Indigo Bunting
Passerina cyanea

192 Lazuli Bunting *Passerina amoena*

193 Rainbow Bunting *Passerina leclancheri*

194 Rainbow Bunting *Passerina leclancheri*

195 Nonpareil Bunting *Passerina ciris*

196 Versicoloured Bunting *Passerina versicolor*

197 Olive Finch *Tiaris olivacea*

198 Black-crested Finch *Lophospingus pusillus*

199 Cuban Finch *Tiaris canora*

200 Red-crested Cardinal *Paroaria coronata*

201 Virginian Cardinal *Cardinalis cardinalis*

202 Pope Cardinal
Paroaria dominicana

203 Yellow-billed Cardinal
Paroaria capitata

204 Black-tailed Hawfinch
Coccothraustes migratorius

205 Green Cardinal *Gubernatrix cristata*

207 Rufous-bellied Niltava
Niltava sundara

206 Blue Grosbeak
Guiraca caerulea

208 Shama
Copsychus malabaricus

209 Orange-headed
Ground Thrush *Zoothera citrina*

210 White-crested Jay Thrush *Garrulax leucolophus*

211 Oriental White-eye *Zosterops palpebrosa*

212 Pekin Robin *Leiothrix lutea*

213 Silver-eared Mesia *Leiothrix argentauris*

214 Golden-fronted Fruitsucker *Chloropsis aurifrons*

215 Red-vented Bulbul *Pycnonotus cafer*

216 Red-whiskered Bulbul *Pycnonotus jocosus*

217 White-cheeked Bulbul *Pycnonotus leucogenys*

218 Blue-throated Barbet *Megalaima asiatica*

219 Racket-tailed Drongo *Dicrurus paradiseus*

220 Common
Mynah
*Acridotheres
tristis*

221 Pagoda Mynah *Sturnus pagodarum*

222 Greater Hill Mynah *Gracula religiosa*

223 Lesser Hill Mynah *Gracula religiosa indica*

224 Red-billed Blue Pie *Urocissa erythrorhyncha*

225 Lanceolated Jay *Garrulus lanceolatus*

226 Violaceous Touraco *Musophaga violacea*

227 Cape Robin Chat *Cossypha caffra*

228 Wattled Starling *Creatophora cinerea*

229 Long-tailed Glossy Starling *Lamprotornis caudatus*

230 Green Glossy Starling *Lamprotornis chalybaeus*

231 Purple Glossy Starling *Lamprotornis purpureus*

232 Spreo Starling *Spreo superbus*

233 Malachite Sunbird *Nectarinia famosa*

234 Scarlet-chested Sunbird
Nectarinia senegalensis

235 White-bellied Sunbird
Nectarinia talatala

236 Mariqua Sunbird
Nectarinia mariquensis

237 Pucheran's Emerald Hummingbird
Chlorostilbon aureoventris pucherani (hen)

238 Pucheran's Emerald Hummingbird
Chlorostilbon aureoventris pucherani (cock)

239 Ruby Topaz Hummingbird *Chrysolampis mosquitus*

240 Yellow-winged Sugarbird *Cyanerpes cyaneus*

241 Purple Sugarbird *Cyanerpes caeruleus* (hen and cock)

242 Blue Dacnis *Dacnis cayana* (hen and cock)

243 Purple Sugarbird
Cyanerpes caeruleus

244 Superb Tanager
Tangara fastuosa

245 Mrs Wilson's Tanager
Tangara nigrocincta

246 Emerald-spotted Tanager
Tangara guttata

247 Bay-headed Tanager
Tangara gyrola

248 Silver-throated Tanager
Tangara icterocephala

249 Black Tanager
Tachyphonus rufus

250 Blue-grey Tanager
Thraupis virens

251 Scarlet Tanager
Ramphocelus bresilius

253 Green-billed Toucan
Ramphastos dicolorus

252 Scarlet-rumped Tanager
Ramphocelus passerinii

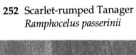

254 Toco Toucan *Ramphastos toco*

255 Spot-billed Toucanet *Selenidera maculirostris*

256 Chestnut-billed Emerald Toucanet *Aulacorhynchus haematopygus*

257 Mountain Bluebird *Sialia currucoides*

258 Red-winged Blackbird *Agelaius phoeniceus*

259 Baltimore Hangnest *Icterus galbula*

breeder back in 1951. It may subsequently have occurred spontaneously in Europe at the end of the 1950s. Lutinos are also known, but remain scarce at present.

5 Crimson-winged Parakeet (Red-winged Parakeet)
Aprosmictus erythropterus

Origin: *north and east Australia and south New Guinea*

Cock: 12in (30cm) Forehead and sides of the head light green; crown, nape and hindneck bluish-green. Back and shoulders black; lower back and rump ultramarine blue. Uppertail coverts yellowish-green; outerwing coverts rich crimson; secondaries and flights blackish, edged with dark green on the outer webs. Tail dark green tipped with pale yellowish-green. Underparts entirely rich green. Iris red; beak orange-red; legs and feet greyish.

Hen: General colour green, less intensive than the cock; lacks the black on the back and shoulders, with the crimson area on the wings replaced by red, most of the feathers being edged with dull green. Lateral tail feathers edged with pink on inner webs, with the undersurface being pale yellow. Beak dull orange.

Although not as widely kept as some Australian parakeets, these attractive birds are bred in aviaries each year. They may well prove consistent in this respect, with one pair being recorded as having reared 26 chicks over a period of nine years. Compatibility can sometimes be a problem, however, and it is better to start with young birds, rather than older individuals, which may already have proved to be a breeding liability.

Some cocks become exceedingly aggressive towards their partners during the breeding season, and fatalities are not unknown. If a cock does develop these savage tendencies, it is advisable to clip the flight feathers of one wing with care. This will handicap him sufficiently to allow the hen to keep out of his reach.

These parakeets are active by nature. They clamber and fly, and therefore need a large flight, at least 12ft (3.7m) long. Pairs should be housed individually and provided with a deep nestbox, at least 3ft (1m) high for breeding purposes. The clutch size may vary from three to six eggs, with incubation, which is carried out by the hen alone, lasting for 21 days.

Pairs should not be encouraged to breed too early in the year, because there is a real risk of their chicks becoming chilled. If all goes well, however, the young parakeets will leave the nest at about six weeks of age, and they should then be transferred to alternative accommodation as soon as possible, as the adult hen is likely to want to nest again.

Deworming is especially important with this species, as a number of losses among imported stock have resulted from tapeworm infestations and from roundworms, whose effects can be particularly severe in young birds.

Deaths caused by worm infestation soon after fledging are likely to indicate that the adults themselves may be infected, and regular treatment before the start of the breeding season, coupled with good aviary hygiene, is essential.

In addition to millets, plain canary seed, groats and lesser quantities of sunflower seed and hemp, soaked maize or corn on the cob can be provided. Plenty of variety in the diet is important, with fruit and berries being required, as well as green food, such as chickweed and seeding grasses. Once acclimatised, these parakeets are quite hardy, and they can remain outside both summer and winter, but they should have a shelter where they can retreat when the weather is at its worst.

88 Green-winged King Parakeet (Papuan King Parrot)

Alisterus chloropterus

Origin: *New Guinea*

Cock: 14in (36cm) Head and underparts scarlet, with an area of dark blue on the upper mantle, continuing into a small blue patch on the nape. Mantle greenish-black. A light yellowish-green band extends across the shoulders. Back, rump and uppertail coverts mauvish-blue; undertail coverts blue at the base, scarlet elsewhere. Tail bluish-black above and greyish-black on the lower surface. Iris orange; beak orange on the upper mandible, with a black tip, greyish-black on the lower mandible; legs and feet greyish-black.

Hen: Predominantly dull green, with throat and breast being olive-green. Black tip to the tail. Upper mandible brownish.

There are three species of King Parakeet, the island forms of which tend to be quite scarce in aviculture and invariably expensive. Imported birds need very careful management at first, and they must be offered a good, varied diet, which can include paddy rice seed, if this is available from a specialist seed supplier.

A vitamin and mineral supplement is also recommended, together with plenty of fruit and greenstuff. Warmth is also vital, and if necessary, a dull emitter infrared lamp, which does not emit light but only gentle heat, should be suspended over their quarters, although it is important to ensure that all the electrical cable is out of their reach.

These are active birds, and a long flight is to be recommended. It may take four years or even longer for imported birds to settle down and start breeding, and a deep nestbox is required for this purpose. They were first bred in Britain in 1945. The pair concerned had been resident in their aviary for nine years previously but had made no attempt to breed until then. They hatched and reared a single chick, eating nothing but buckwheat and oats, at this difficult time at the end of World War II, when all seed was virtually unobtainable.

In recent years small numbers of the Amboina King Parakeet (*Alisterus amboinensis*) (Plate 89) have become available from Indonesia. These birds require similar care, but they can prove nervous by nature.

Australian King Parakeet *Alisterus scapularis*

Origin: *east Australia*

Cock: 17in (43cm) *Head and underparts scarlet; nape band and rump blue. Back green. Wings green with blue and a light band across the shoulders. Tail black with olive-green edges. Secondaries dark olive-green, undertail coverts blue edged with scarlet. Iris yellow; beak reddish; legs and feet grey.*

Hen: *Head and upperparts green; throat, neck and upperpart of breast green with a dull red shading. Rump blue; belly scarlet; undertail coverts green. Neck and breast olive-green with a pinkish gloss. Tail green and black; beak grey.*

The best known species in Australian collections and also represented overseas, these King Parakeets require a long flight. Cocks can prove quite ferocious during the breeding period, and care must be taken to ensure that he does not harm his mate. Clipping the flight feathers on one wing may be necessary to cool his ardour.

A hen may sometimes refuse to use a nestbox, preferring instead to lay her eggs in a scrape in the floor of the flight or the shelter. She may even succeed in incubating the eggs and rearing her young there, but these conditions are far from ideal. This behaviour usually reflects a problem with the nestbox. It should be of the traditional 'grandfather clock' type, at least 36in (1m) deep and lined with thin pieces of softwood battening, which can be whittled away to form a soft bed for the eggs. The hen may lay four or five eggs, with the incubation period lasting for 21 days. The chicks should fledge when they are around eight weeks old and should be transferred to separate quarters once they are feeding independently.

At this stage, both sexes resemble adult hens, but the distinction in bill coloration soon becomes apparent, and young hens also tend to have less red plumage on their underparts. It will take over two years for these parakeets to acquire full adult coloration. Mutations are largely unknown. Although odd yellow individuals have been bred in various European collections, this colour form is still extremely scarce.

Pennant's Parakeet (Crimson Rosella) *Platycercus elegans*

Origin: *eastern south Australia, including Kangaroo Island*

Cock: 14in (36cm) *Predominantly deep crimson; cheeks violet-blue. Back black, with the feathers being edged with crimson. Flights black with blue on the outer webs; median secondaries edged with light blue; innermost edged with dull crimson; upperwing coverts blue. Central feathers of tail dark blue washed with green, outer feathers pale blue with whitish tips. Iris dark brown; beak greyish-white; legs and feet greyish-black.*

Hen: *Similar in appearance, but often with a noticeably smaller head.*

These stunningly colourful parakeets are, not surprisingly, very popular among breeders, but if you start out with an unsexed pair, try to obtain an agreement that one of the birds will be taken back if they subsequently prove not to be a pair. As a general rule, it is harder to obtain hens. The condition of the plumage is important in this species, because they are more susceptible to feather-plucking than other Australian parakeets.

Pennant's Parakeets make lively aviary occupants. They are always on the move, clambering on branches or amusing themselves busily on the floor, which must be kept clean. Their voice is usually heard towards dusk, and they have a fairly melodious whistle. They are also fairly reliable breeders, but a careful watch should be kept on the cock, since he may become rather aggressive at this stage, and he may persecute the hen, unless she accepts his advances readily.

It is not unknown for pairs to rear as many as seven chicks successfully, but not all pairs are so reliable. Egg-eating can be a problem in this species. It may be possible to cure this vice by placing dummy pigeon eggs in the nest immediately an egg is destroyed. These are indestructible, so that, it is hoped, the birds will become uninterested and the hen should incubate properly in the future.

Breeding and general care are as for other related species, with the first success occurring in Britain in 1880. These parakeets are quite hardy and can winter outside, if a well-insulated shelter is available for them.

Young Pennant's Parakeets can be surprisingly variable in the coloration of their plumage. Some are predominantly green, whereas others closely resemble their parents. Only one mutation is well-recognised at present. This is a blue form, which is actually far less colourful than the normal variety.

100 Adelaide Parakeet (Adelaide Rosella) *Platycercus adelaidae*

Origin: *south Australia*

Cock: *15in (38cm) Similar to the preceding species, but the brick red coloration of the Pennant's Parakeet is of a more yellowish-orange shade. The feathers of the back and upperparts are black, edged with buff and yellow. The tail is greener, slightly washed with blue. The blue of the cheeks is much paler. Iris dark brown; beak greyish-white; legs and feet greyish-black.*

Hen: *Similar in appearance but often with a noticeably smaller head.*

This rosella shows an obvious similarity to the Pennant's Parakeet, and it has been suggested that it arose as a result of natural hybridisation between this species and the related Yellow Rosella. Hybrids of this type have been produced in Britain, and their fertile offspring will continue to breed birds which also resemble Adelaides in appearance. Further support for this theory comes from the very limited area of distribution of the Adelaide Parakeet in the wild, which suggests that it is a local variant. There are two distinct populations, separated by an area of 45 miles (70km).

Adelaide Parakeets were displayed at London Zoo in 1863, and were first bred in Britain during 1892. These birds have never become very popular, although their care does not differ significantly from that of other rosellas. They tend to be single-brooded.

A Lutino mutation has been produced in Australia, with white plumage present on the wings, cheeks and tail, while orangish and yellow shades are retained. Unusually, this particular Lutino form is an autosomal recessive, rather than a sex-linked recessive mutation as is more common in the case of this colour variant.

03 Yellow Rosella *Platycercus flaveolus*

Origin: *interior of New South Wales and adjoining parts of Victoria and south Australia*

Cock: 13in (33cm) General coloration pale yellow. Feathers of the back and scapulars have black centres. Forehead has a narrow band of crimson immediately above the beak, with the lores and foreneck being slightly tinged with the same colour; cheeks blue. Wings and flights blackish with blue on the outer webs; outer secondaries edged with pale blue; inner ones and also innerwing coverts edged with pale yellow. Outerwing coverts pale blue and lesser coverts dark blue with a black patch. Two central tail feathers blue with a greenish tone at the base; next pair blackish with blue on the outer webs and tipped with blue; remainder blue, paler towards the tips. Iris black; beak horn-coloured; legs and feet greyish-black

Hen: Rather similar but with a smaller head and beak. In addition, the red frontal band may not be as clearly defined, and the plumage of the breast may be tinged with orange.

One of the duller members of the genus, the Yellow Rosella has, in consequence, become rather scarce in recent years, with breeders tending to concentrate on the more colourful species, such as Pennant's Parakeet. Yet this species is also quite hardy, and often proves to be relatively free breeding, sometimes being double-brooded. A single pair kept by the Duke of Bedford produced nearly 60 chicks over a period of less than 10 years.

Like other rosellas, they are lively and active birds by nature and should be kept only in aviary surroundings. Pairs should also be housed on their own. A diet based on the smaller cereal seeds, such as millet and plain canary seed, along with groats, a little sunflower, peanuts, small pine nuts and hemp should be offered. Greenstuff, such as chickweed and seeding grasses, is very popular, especially when there are chicks in the nest.

Young Yellow Rosellas can be recognised without much difficulty; they are significantly duller than adults, having a greenish-yellow body coloration overall. The scalloping on the back, which is a characteristic feature of this group of parakeets, is far less distinctive, and is even sometimes virtually absent. Chicks should be removed as soon as they seem to be feeding independently, since young cocks may be attacked by their father. This will also encourage the adult birds to nest again.

Eastern Rosella (Common Rosella) *Platycercus eximius*

Origin: *southeast Australia*

Cock: 13in (33cm) Head, sides of the neck and upper breast scarlet; cheeks white; nape yellow. Back and scapulars black, with feathers edged with greenish-yellow. Rump and uppertail coverts yellowish-green; flights blackish, dark blue on the outer webs; secondaries edged with light blue; primary coverts dark blue; lesser, median and outer series violet-blue, with a black patch on the inner series. Tail feathers dark blue, those in the centre washed with green, and the outer ones tipped with whitish-blue. Lower breast yellow, abdomen yellowish-green. Undertail coverts scarlet. Iris dark brown; beak greyish-horn; legs and feet greyish.

Hen: Somewhat duller in coloration, with the area of red on the head and breast reduced.

This species has been regularly bred in collections for over a century, and it is widely kept. Unfortunately, there was no attempt to keep the nominate race and the subspecies known as the Golden-mantled Rosella separate, in the early stages. This latter form, *P.e. cecilae* (Plate 101), is of similar size but is somewhat deeper in coloration and more brightly marked. The ground colour of the black-laced feathers on the back is golden-yellow rather than pale green, with the abdomen being golden with a reddish tinge. The undertail coverts are blue-green. It is now almost impossible to obtain really pure-bred birds of either race, although it might be feasible to recreate the Golden-mantled Rosella (often simply described as GMR) by careful selective breeding.

Pairs should always be housed on their own, because these parakeets can be aggressive, particularly during the breeding period. The call of the cock bird is a rather pleasing whistle, while the hen's call notes are shorter and less musical. A diet as recommended for the Yellow Rosella suits them well. They will also nibble at the bark and shoots of perches in their aviary.

These parakeets usually start nesting in the early spring. The hen alone will incubate the clutch of four to six eggs on average. When the young leave the nest, at about six weeks old, they are often extremely nervous, and disturbances in their vicinity must be kept to a minimum, otherwise they may well fly hard against the wire netting and injure themselves, perhaps even fatally. They soon become accustomed to the limitations of their aviary, however, and this nervous phase will pass within a couple of days.

Some, but not all, pairs are double-brooded and have been known to rear chicks when only a year old, but they have a long reproductive life, and may continue breeding even into their twenties. They should not, therefore, be encouraged to overtax themselves at an early stage. Youngsters will not gain adult plumage until they are about 15 months old.

In spite of the widespread popularity of these parakeets, colour mutations are surprisingly rare. A cinnamon form has been documented, and Lutinos have been reported, but none is especially common at present.

98 Stanley Parakeet (Western Rosella) *Platycercus icterotis*

Origin: *southwest Australia*

Cock: 10in (25cm) Crown, nape, breast and underparts crimson; cheeks and thighs yellow. Back black, each feather laced with green, yellow and sometimes crimson. Rump and uppertail coverts golden-green; shoulders blue; flights blackish with outer webs blue. Central pair of tail feathers dull green; the remainder are pale blue tipped with white. Iris dark brown; beak horn-coloured; legs and feet dull greyish-brown.

Hen: Generally duller in colour, with no red margins to the feathers of the back, except perhaps in old birds. Greenish head and underparts, although some red feathering is apparent here.

This is the smallest of the rosellas and also the only species which is sexually dimorphic. A pair should be kept on their own and initially given a choice of several nestboxes, hung up under cover in the outside flight. Unlike neotropical species, most Australian parakeets do not actually roost in their nestboxes, and if the nestbox is being used, it is a sign that breeding is likely to be imminent. The floor lining can be made up of sieved shavings or of small pieces of softwood battening, which the birds will be able to gnaw down to form their own nest lining. Once a nestbox has been chosen, you can close up the entrances to the others.

Stanley Parakeets typically lay four to six eggs in a clutch, and these are incubated by the hen alone. When the young have hatched, which will be evident from an increase in the food consumption of the adult birds, rearing foods including bread and milk, soaked seeds, such as millet sprays, and egg food should be provided fresh each day. Green food is also especially important at this stage, and fruit such as sweet apple may be eaten as well.

Avoid interfering more than is strictly necessary when the birds are nesting. Once the chicks have left the nest, the special rearing foods can be gradually reduced in quantity, as the youngsters start to feed on seed.

Millets, plain canary seed, sunflower and hemp should feature in their usual diet. Individual birds may enjoy nibbling peanuts, and chickweed is always a popular green food.

Youngsters must be removed from the aviary as soon as possible. This will increase the likelihood of another brood being reared. The young parakeets can be kept safely with others of their kind at first, but they will soon need to be separated. At first the juveniles are mainly green, with odd red feathers restricted to the forehead. By the winter, their coloration will be more clearly visible, but it will be a year before they moult fully into adult plumage.

Stanley Parakeets are hardy birds, and can be kept in an unheated aviary throughout the year, as long as they are provided with shelter.

102 **Mealy Rosella** (Pale-headed Rosella) *Platycercus adscitus*

Origin: *central Queensland and north New South Wales*

Cock: 13in (33cm) *Head pale yellow, deeper towards the base of the nape; hindneck, scapulars and upper back black, each feather edged with rich yellow. Lower back, rump and uppertail coverts pale greenish-blue. Upperwing coverts blue, darker on the shoulders. Secondaries and flights dark blue, with the latter being edged with greyish-white in some cases. Central pair of tail feathers dark blue with greenish wash at the base; next pair blackish with dark blue on the outer webs and tipped with white; remainder pale blue shading to darker blue at the base and again with white tipping. Cheeks white with blue wash on the outer border. Undertail coverts scarlet. Remainder of the underparts pale blue. Iris brownish; beak horn-coloured; legs and feet greyish.*

Hen: *A wing stripe of white spots is usually present on the underside of the wings, which becomes evident when the wing is opened.*

As in the case of the Eastern Rosella there has been considerable cross-breeding between the two races of the Blue-cheeked Rosella (*P.a. adscitus*), with the result that today such birds are invariably advertised as Mealy Rosellas. The Blue-cheeked, as its name suggests, showed more blue in its plumage, notably on the cheeks, which extended to the neck. Because this form was rarer in collections, its characteristics tend to have been lost, and the white-cheeked Mealy Rosella now predominates. Some reports suggest that the division between the white-cheeked and blue-cheeked forms was less clear-cut than is sometimes proposed. As a result, it may be possible to recreate the latter by careful selective breeding.

Their treatment does not differ significantly from that required for other similar species. A breeding pair should be housed on their own, and they may start nesting as early as February, although a later start in northern areas reduces the likelihood of eggs or chicks being lost as a result of chilling. First results were obtained in Belgium in 1899.

Interestingly, a study carried out by Dr Groen, a Dutch breeder, discovered that these rosellas were invariably more prolific when they are housed away from other rosellas. This may explain why some pairs are exceedingly prolific, while others may fail to breed, even when sexed to ensure the gender of the birds. Mealy Rosellas are usually single-brooded, but they may lay two clutches if the first fails to hatch or if the chicks die in the nest at an early stage.

Brown's Parakeet (Northern Rosella) *Platycercus venustus*

Origin: *north Australia*

Cock: 11in (28cm) Head and throat black; plumage of back black with a dull yellow edge to the feathers. Remainder of upper surface pale yellow. Cheek patches white with a blue edge. Wings blue and black. Tail light and dark blue, with white tips; undertail coverts red. Iris dark brown; beak greyish-horn; legs pinkish-grey.

Hen: Similar, but may be distinguished by smaller head and less prominent white cheek patches.

This rosella is costly and scarce in collections for several reasons. First, it can be difficult to persuade pairs to nest during the summer months as they are likely to be moulting then. If, however, hens lay in outdoor accommodation during the winter, they may then succumb to egg-binding or the eggs or chicks may be fatally chilled. There is also a further difficulty in that cocks can prove exceptionally aggressive, even murderous, towards their intended mates.

As a precautionary measure, it may be worth clipping the flight feathers on one wing of the cock initially, and when these are shed, the pair will, it is hoped, have settled down together. Once a compatible pair has been obtained, Brown's Parakeets can be quite prolific, and they frequently appear to be double-brooded. E.J. Boosey, at the Keston Foreign Bird Farm, Kent, in England, kept a pair which produced nine chicks in the course of two successive nests. Sadly, when the hen of this pair died, the cock refused to accept another mate, invariably attacking new females.

The earliest nesting success was recorded in Britain in the Duke of Bedford's extensive collection during 1928. A few pairs of Brown's Parakeets are still breeding in Britain and elsewhere at present. Experience has shown that they should be paired at an early age, as this greatly reduces the risk of aggression. Indoor accommodation may be recommended in some areas. The birds can then be encouraged to breed here, although they are quite hardy.

A typical diet as recommended for other rosellas will suit them well, although they are more insectivorous in their feeding habits. Mealworms and similar live food should be offered regularly, particularly to breeding pairs, and softbill food may also be taken.

108 Barnard's Parakeet (Mallee Ringneck Parrot, Buln Buln)

Barnardius barnardi

Origin: *from Queensland and eastern parts of Northern Territory down to south Australia*

Cock: 13in (33cm) *Forehead red; crown, ear coverts and cheeks verditer green, with the latter being edged with blue; nape with a dull bluish-brown band and a yellow band round the hindneck, broader at the sides. Back and scapulars dull greyish-blue, with a yellowish-green band down the centre of the upperwing coverts. Rump and uppertail coverts verditer green washed with yellow. Wing coverts and outer webs of flights deep blue, with the remainder being green. Central pair of tail feathers green, blue towards the tips; the remainder are dark blue at the base, fading to a pale blue towards the tips. Underparts verditer green with a broad band of orange-yellow across the breast. Iris blackish-brown; beak greyish-white; legs and feet pinkish-grey.*

Hen: *Duller in coloration, especially on the back and abdomen.*

Although they are similar to the rosellas in their requirements, the members of this genus tend to be less commonly seen in collections. They are quite hardy, and pairs will nest regularly. All are active birds and need a relatively long aviary so that they can fly freely.

Barnard's Parakeet itself was first seen in Britain in 1853, when a pair was exhibited at London Zoo. The species was bred in France in 1884, with six chicks being reared successfully from a single clutch of eggs. Incubation usually lasts about 21 days, with the hen sitting alone. The young parakeets have usually fledged by the time they are five weeks old. At this stage, they are duller than their parents, with a brownish crown and nape. It will be a year before they obtain adult plumage. Mealworms may sometimes be eaten by these parakeets, particularly, when they have chicks.

Mutations are essentially unknown, apart from two Lutinos, which were recorded as chicks in the wild in 1927. There are a number of subspecies, however, of which the Cloncurry Parakeet (*B.b. macgillivrayi*) is most distinctive. It originates from the eastern part of Northern Territory and northwest Queensland. The red frontal band in this case is confined to youngsters, being absent in adults, and the abdomen is pure yellow. This race has been maintained as a separate entity in aviculture.

The other member of the genus is the Port Lincoln Parakeet (*B. zonarius*), which has an entirely black head but is otherwise somewhat similar to the Cloncurry. The subspecies known as the Twenty-eight Parakeet (*B.z. semitorquatus*), so-called after the sound of its call, has a green rather than yellow abdomen and has a red area of feathering above the cere, making it relatively easy to distinguish from the nominate race.

⁊7 Red-rumped Parakeet (Red-backed Parakeet)

Psephotus haematonotus

Origin: *south and southeast Australia*

Cock: 11in (28cm) Green, with the cheeks and forehead being of a lighter shade, while the back is darker. Rump deep red. Underparts green shading to yellow towards the vent. Undertail coverts whitish. Wings bluish-green with a yellowish spot towards the shoulder and blue edging to the flights. Central tail feathers green, tinged with blue, while laterals are blue with white tips. Iris dark brown, beak blackish; legs and feet pinkish-grey.

Hen: Significantly greyer in coloration than the cock, and lacking the red on the rump, making her easily distinguishable. Beak grey.

These popular parakeets are usually keen to breed, and they have an attractive, musical call. Pairs should be housed on their own, because cocks can become very belligerent, particularly during the breeding season. They are not finicky about food: plain canary seed and millets, fresh green food, such as chickweed and seeding grasses, and, especially during the breeding season, soaked seeds should be offered.

Hens will lay during the early spring, with a typical clutch having five eggs. The incubation period lasts about 19 days, with the chicks leaving the nest about six weeks later. They can be sexed before fledging. Young cocks may sometimes be attacked and even killed in the nest by their father, and they must be removed from the aviary as soon as possible. The weaning period is very short in this species, and the hen is likely to nest again, with double-brooding being common.

First breeding results were reported in Britain in 1857 and from Germany in 1863. Several mutations have since emerged in captive stock, of which the best-known is the so-called yellow (Plate 104), which is actually a cinnamon version of the normal form, being a paler, more yellowish colour. The red plumage on the rump is of an orange shade in this form. Less common at present is the blue mutation, which is best known in Australian aviaries. Other colours which have been reported include the Lutino, which is particularly attractive, a genuine yellow and a pied form.

5 Many-coloured Parakeet (Varied Parakeet, Mulga Parakeet)

Psephotus varius

Origin: *south Australia*

Cock: 11in (28cm) Upper surface mainly emerald green, tinged with blue above the eyes and on the sides of the neck. Forehead, a band on the shoulders, sides and vent yellow. Back of the crown, rump, abdomen and thighs crimson. Throat and breast yellowish-green. Flights deep greenish-blue. Tail also greenish-blue; two *central tail feathers and bases of the remainder very dark, banded with black at the base, the outer ones tipped with pale blue. Iris dark brown; beak bluish-horn with blackish-tip; legs and feet pinkish-grey.*

Hen: *Head, back, throat and breast dull greenish-grey; no yellow on the forehead or wings, the patch on the wings being dull red; abdomen and undertail coverts pale green.*

The Many-coloured Parakeet resembles the Red-rumped Parakeet in habits and behaviour, but it is less hardy, and when it is first introduced to a new aviary it is inclined to be very nervous. It is especially necessary to ensure that it is not frightened suddenly, or it may fly wildly against the wire mesh and seriously injure or even kill itself.

A mixture of plain canary seed, millets and a small quantity of groats should form its main diet, together with a regular supply of green food and seeding grasses when available.

Many-coloured Parakeets usually nest quite readily, beginning early in the year in the northern hemisphere. A thick nestbox should be provided, which should help to raise the temperature in the box, because eggs and chicks at this time of year are prone to chilling. The hen alone incubates, with the cock feeding her at the nest, and he also plays a part in feeding the young. Incubation lasts about 19 days, and many pairs are double-brooded. When the young hatch, the adult birds can be supplied with bread and milk and soaked seed, especially millet sprays, which are usually eaten greedily. Grated carrot is often popular as well. Chicks can be sexed while they are in the nest, but it takes a year for them to obtain full adult plumage.

Once these parakeets are established in their aviary, it is not usually necessary to provide special conditions during the winter, but they must have a draught- and frost-proof shelter. Regular deworming, as recommended for other Australian parakeets, is also advisable with this species. They can be prone to digestive infections, and their quarters must be kept particularly clean, especially as they forage for food on the ground. This species was first bred in France in 1877 and in Britain in 1902.

106 Elegant Grass Parakeet *Neophema elegans*

Origin: *southwest Queensland, New South Wales, Victoria and southwest Australia*

Cock: *9in (23cm) General colour above is olive-green, with a golden wash; band across the forehead, extending in a narrow line over the eyes deep blue, edged with light blue behind; lores, fore part of cheeks and throat yellow. Upper breast and sides of body light golden-olive. Lower breast and abdomen yellow, sometimes with an orange patch at the centre. Undertail coverts yellow; underwing coverts dark blue. Central tail feathers greenish-blue shading to blue towards the tips; remainder yellow; blue at the base. Iris brown; beak blackish-horn; legs and feet pinkish-grey.*

Hen: Duller, with a narrower band on the forehead, less blue on the wings, no orangish patch on the abdomen and undertail coverts yellowish-green.

These and other *Neophema* parakeets are ideal occupants for suburban aviaries, being quiet, attractive and easy to look after, with pairs invariably keen to nest. Their diet should consist of roughly two parts of plain canary seed, two parts of mixed millets, one part of groats and a little sunflower, together with plenty of green food and seeding grasses whenever available. Soaked seed is also valuable, particularly when there are chicks in the nest.

A reasonably small aviary, with a flight at least 9ft (2.7m) long and 3ft (1m) wide will suffice for a pair, provided they also have a dry, snug, draught-proof shelter.

Elegant Grass Parakeets were first bred in Britain, when a pair received by London Zoo in 1859 nested successfully in the following year. They have since been bred on many occasions, with the hen usually laying a clutch of four or five eggs. These should take about 19 days to hatch, and the youngsters will fledge at about five weeks old.

When they first leave the nest, these parakeets are usually extremely nervous. Great care must be taken to ensure that they are not unduly disturbed or frightened until they become thoroughly accustomed to their surroundings. They should then be removed to separate quarters, enabling adult birds to breed again. At this stage they can be distinguished from their parents by the absence of a frontal band, and they gain adult plumage when they are about four months old. A Lutino mutation has been recorded, having first appeared in Belgium in 1972, but such birds are still quite scarce.

Blue-winged Grass Parakeet   *Neophema chrysostoma*

Origin: *Victoria, south Australia, Tasmania and some islands in the Bass Strait*

Cock: 9in (23cm) Olive-green upperparts, with the head being washed with yellow. Lores and orbital ring yellow; a band extending above the eyes across the forehead is dark ultramarine blue. Cheeks, side of the neck, throat and breast pale green. Abdomen, flanks, thighs, underside of tail yellow. Wings and upper coverts bright ultramarine blue. Primary coverts blackish, with outer webs of some of the flights pale blue. Central pair of tail feathers blue washed with green at the base, with next pair blackish with blue on the outer webs; remainder blackish, blue at the base and tipped with yellow, with the amount of yellow increasing in extent towards the outermost feathers. Iris brown; beak brownish; legs and feet pinkish-grey.

Hen: Duller in colour. Frontal band less pronounced and underside with less yellow on the abdomen.

Although not differing significantly in their requirements from other members of this group, the Blue-winged Grass Parakeet has not achieved such widespread popularity as, for example, the Turquoisine, possibly because its coloration is not as striking. Even so, they breed well, and the first success was recorded in France in 1879.

Their nestbox should have cork bark tacked on the front, below the entrance hole, as they like to cling to the opening here, rather than using a perch, although this should also be provided.

Blue-winged Grass Parakeets rarely lay before April in the northern hemisphere. Four to six eggs are normally laid, but as many as 10 have been recorded on occasions. One pair raised 70 chicks successfully over a 10-year period.

Chicks are usually less nervous than those of other *Neophema* parakeets when they first fledge. At this stage their beaks are lighter in coloration than those of adults, the blue frontal band is missing, and their wings are a dull shade of slaty-blue. It will take eight months or so for youngsters to acquire adult plumage.

99 Turquoisine Grass Parakeet *Neophema pulchella*

Origin: *from southeast Queensland to north Victoria*

Cock: 8in (20cm) General colour above is green. Occiput, ear coverts and sides of neck yellowish-green; lores, line of feathers above the eyes and cheeks turquoise; broad band across the forehead deep blue. Wings, upper coverts turquoise blue; inner series chestnut-red; primary coverts, secondaries and flights blackish-brown, dark blue on the outer webs of the former and greenish-blue on the outer webs of the flights. Under coverts dark blue. Central tail feathers green; remainder green at the base of the outer webs, dark brown on the inner webs and all tipped with yellow, with the extent of the yellow increasing towards the outermost feathers, which are almost entirely yellow. Throat, under surface and undertail coverts rich golden-yellow, the sides of the chest being washed with green. Iris brown; beak blackish-brown; legs and feet pinkish-grey.

Hen: Duller in overall coloration, and lacking the chestnut-red on the wing, with less blue on the face.

The Turquoisine Grass Parakeet is a bird of the twilight, becoming most active towards dusk. It is an ideal choice for a garden aviary, with pairs normally nesting readily, starting in the early spring. The affectionate behaviour of the birds is then a joy to observe, with the cock uttering his appealing soft, whistling song.

Breeding details are as for other members of the genus, but it is important to bear in mind that young birds are likely to be very nervous when they first leave the nest. They may not appreciate the obstruction formed by the aviary mesh, and may attempt to fly through it, sometimes with fatal consequences.

Encouraging climbing plants to grow up the sides, particularly at the end of the flight, is often an effective means of alerting them to the barrier here. Nasturtiums, which grow readily and rapidly from seed, are ideal for this purpose. They grow well even in poor soil, and their attractive flowers will enhance the aviary, while their leaves may be nibbled by the parakeets through the mesh, providing an additional source of green food.

A number of colour variants are now well represented in aviculture. There is an orange-bellied form, which has also been documented from the wild. It has proved possible to combine this with the yellow mutation of the Turquoisine, to create a stunningly attractive colour variant. More subdued is the dark factor form, which darkens the green coloration, giving rise to olive or dark green plumage. Other mutations include pied and cinnamon, and a red-fronted form has scarlet underparts.

Splendid Grass Parakeet (Scarlet-chested Grass Parakeet)

Neophema splendida

Origin: *interior of south Australia*

Cock: *8in (20cm) Head and sides of neck deep cobalt blue; remainder of upperparts green, with a bluish tone on the neck. Underparts yellow, with a prominent scarlet area on the breast. Wings green with brown and black evident. Iris brown; beak black; legs and feet pinkish-grey.*

Hen: *Underparts olive-green, brown on the upperparts. Sides of wings and head lack the blue markings seen in cocks. No scarlet on the breast.*

For many years the Splendid Grass Parakeet was exceedingly rare in aviculture. Although it was first seen at London Zoo in 1871, it remained unknown until 1933, when a pair was given to King George V. These birds, together with another pair obtained in the following year by the Duke of Bedford, were transferred to the Keston Foreign Bird Farm in Kent, where chicks were reared successfully in 1935.

Splendid Grass Parakeets became more widely available in the 1940s, and they are now among the most commonly bred of all parakeets, although they may still be rare in the wild. In addition to their attractive coloration, their quiet voice and lively disposition have helped to ensure their popularity.

They can be kept in an outside aviary throughout the year, but, like related species, they dislike damp, cold weather. Their aviary should be well protected against cold northerly and easterly winds, and the flight should be adequately covered on the sides and roof with translucent plastic to give additional protection.

Perhaps not surprisingly, in view of the numbers of these parakeets in aviculture, several colour mutations have arisen. The best known of these at present, is undoubtedly the blue form, although this is not a pure blue, being equivalent to the pastel blue variety of the Peach-faced Lovebird. In this form the red breast of the cock is transformed to a pale salmon shade of pink, while the green areas in both sexes become greenish-blue. There appears to be a factor associated with this coloration that means that these blues should not be paired together but rather with normal Splendid Grass Parakeets, with the resulting offspring being mated to produce further blues. There are also yellow, cinnamon, white-breasted and fallow forms, which appear to be becoming more numerous at present.

109 Bourke's Grass Parakeet *Neophema bourkii*

Origin: *interior of central and southern parts of Australia*

Cock: 9in (23cm) Greyish-brown above, darker on the rump and uppertail coverts. Head and neck tinged with salmon-red; forehead and eyebrow stripe pale blue, with the latter being white below, whitish below the eye and on the front of the cheeks; remainder of the cheeks otherwise rosy, each feather edged with brown. Wings, anterior upper coverts and outer webs of flights violet-blue. Six middle tail feathers brownish tinged with blue on the outer webs; outer feathers white with brown on the inner and blue on the outer webs at the base, under coverts pale blue. Feathers of the breast brown edged with rose-pink. Abdomen bright rose-pink. Flanks pale blue. Iris brown; beak dark brown; legs and feet pinkish-grey.

Hen: White feathering more prominent on the forehead, with the blue frontal band practically absent. Breast feathers buff rather than pink.

The soft pastel shades of the Bourke's Grass Parakeet, coupled with its beautiful dark eyes, make this one of the most appealing as well as most distinctive of the *Neophema* species. It also has an attractive voice, and it sings softly, particularly at the start of the breeding period in the spring. The large eyes of this parakeet indicate that it is a bird of the twilight and that it becomes most active at dusk.

First seen at London Zoo in 1867, this species remained scarce for a number of years, but breeding results started to be recorded regularly in the early 1900s. The first success in Europe was achieved in Belgium during 1877. Since then they have been widely bred, proving prolific and frequently double-brooded.

The hen typically lays five eggs, which should hatch after an incubation period of 19 days. The chicks will leave the nest for the first time when they are about four weeks old. Soaked seed is an important item in the diet of breeding pairs, along with green food. A seed mix based on the smaller cereal seeds, along with a little sunflower and hemp, suits them well.

An unusual but very attractive mutation of the Bourke's Parakeet arose in the Netherlands about 1970. Known as the rosa form, or sometimes as the opaline form, such birds have more pronounced soft, pinkish-red coloration on their backs and underparts. They can be identified in the nest by their pink feet just before they feather up. This is a sex-linked recessive trait.

Other, less popular mutations known in this species are the yellow and the cinnamon. Combinations have also been produced, such as the yellow rosa form, which shows very attractive pastel shades in its plumage, with the pink coloration being paler in this instance than in the rosa mutation. But individuals may well differ in their depth of coloration, a characteristic that applies even to normally coloured Bourke's Parakeets, with some being a deep shade of pink and certain cocks having more blue on their heads than others.

1 **Budgerigar** (Shell Parakeet) *Melopsittacus undulatus*

2 **Origin:** *Australia*

Cock: 7in (18cm) *Face and forehead yellow; with yellow and black barring on the sides of the head and on the neck, extending down over the wings. Blue cheek patch and three small black spots on each side of the face. Remainder of the body predominantly light green, with the tail being greenish-blue. Iris whitish; beak greyish-olive with a blue cere encompassing the nostrils above; legs and feet greyish.*

Hen: *Identical in plumage, but discernible by brown cere, paler when not in breeding condition.*

Millions of Budgerigars are kept around the world. They are the most popular of all pet birds in the home and also widely kept in aviaries for decorative and exhibition purposes. A huge range of colour mutations and varieties has been developed, and this process continues. Tracing their development is too vast a subject for this book. At present, the red Budgerigar remains unattainable for genetic reasons, and the black Budgerigar has yet to make its appearance.

These delightful parakeets were first seen alive in Europe when the famous artist and naturalist John Gould brought a pair back from Australia in 1840. They soon nested, and other pairs followed. Budgerigars were bred in Germany during 1855, and extensive breeding began in France, Belgium and the Netherlands. Huge colonies were first kept at Antwerp Zoo in Belgium, and this provided the impetus for the development of massive breeding facilities, such as l'Etablissement Bastide at Toulouse, France, where between 80,000 and 100,000 budgerigars were kept by late Victorian times, with their offspring being sold across Europe.

Budgerigars have now been domesticated for so long that recognised show standard, relating to deportment, shape, markings and colour, has been drawn up by societies. They are very easy birds to maintain, quite at home in an outside aviary throughout the year. They can be bred in such surroundings, although for show purposes, individual pairs are housed in special breeding cages, with nestboxes attached, so as to guarantee the parentage of the offspring.

If Budgerigars are to be kept on a colony system, it is essential that all the birds are paired up and that there are more nestboxes than pairs. This will help to avoid the likelihood of fighting. It is also vital that all nestboxes are positioned at the same height, otherwise, hens will squabble, often quite seriously, over the right to occupy the highest boxes. Even with all these precautions however, you will need to be alert to the possible presence of bad-natured hens, which will not only prove disruptive, but may well destroy the eggs of other pairs and possibly kill their youngsters as well.

Although Budgerigars will breed for most of the year, the nestboxes in outside aviaries should be removed in late autumn and replaced again only in the spring. Some hens may otherwise continue to lay through the winter, with an increased risk of egg-binding and breeding failure at this time.

Hens may lay as many as eight eggs or so in a clutch, although four or five is more usual. Incubation is carried out by the hen alone, and lasts approximately 18 days. The young birds fledge when they are about five weeks old, and are feeding on their own within a week or so of leaving the nest. They should be removed at this stage, because they may persist in returning to the nestbox and then soil the new clutch of eggs, which the hen is likely to have produced by this stage.

The basic diet is a mixture of millets and plain canary seed, but other items, notably green food, sweet apple and even a little carrot, which is a valuable source of vitamin A, should be provided regularly. Cuttlefish bone and grit must also be available, along with an iodine nibble. It is probably best to withhold carrot before a show however, because the orange juice may temporarily stain the feathering around the beak.

The native colour form of the Budgerigar is described as the light green. This has been darkened through the development of a dark factor mutation, which has created dark green and also a deeper olive-green variant. The corresponding colours in blue series budgerigars are sky blue, which is the lightest form, equivalent to the light green, the cobalt and the mauve, which, as the darkest variant of the three, tends towards soft purple in coloration. It has also proved possible to develop a violet form.

Yellow Budgerigars are perhaps less commonly seen these days, with the notable exception of the Lutino. This is a rich shade of pure butter yellow, with white throat patches and red eyes. It is justifiably popular. Albinos, which are entirely snow white with red eyes, have tended to be somewhat smaller in the past than other varieties seen on the show bench, but breeders are now producing larger individuals.

Pieds, which show variable areas of yellow and green or white and blue, are also popular. There is a genetically dominant form, originally bred in

Australia, which is larger than the Danish Recessive Pied. It can also be distinguished by the white iris around the pupil; Danish Pieds have darker eyes.

Alterations to the markings on the back and wings have also been recorded. There are now White-wings, Yellow-wings, Cinnamons and Opalines, with the latest Budgerigar mutation, known as the Spangle, also affecting this area of the plumage. This tends to give light centres and dark edges to the feathers, including the long flight feathers, although the basic body coloration is unaffected.

Crested mutations have also been developed. There are tufted, half-circular and full-circular forms, while the crest itself should be well positioned on the head. Again, crested Budgerigars can be bred in any colour.

When it comes to talking skills, coloration is not a significant factor. Generally, however, cocks make better mimics than hens, and they should be obtained as soon as possible, around six weeks old, once they are feeding on their own. At this stage, they will not have developed the white iris encircling the pupils, and their facial spots will be relatively small. There may be dark markings on the upper bill, and the bars, which are normally found on the crown of the adult bird, extend right down to the cere at this stage, so that young birds, before they moult for the first time at about 12 weeks old, are often referred to as 'barheads'.

It is harder to tell the sexes apart at this early stage, since their ceres are of a similar coloration, but generally, those of young cocks are of a deep purplish shade, and are more prominent than those of hens. Budgerigars may typically live seven or eight years, although on occasions, they have been known to live for over 20 years.

FINCHES, TOUCANS AND RELATED SPECIES

Paradise Whydah (Widow Bird) *Vidua paradisaea*

Origin: *central Africa*

Cock: 6 in (15cm) *Changes dramatically in appearance at onset of the breeding season: the two longest tail feathers become over 10in (25cm) long. Head, chin, throat, upper breast back, upper- and undertail coverts, thighs, wing coverts and tail black. White plumage in vicinity of the vent. Prominent ochre-yellow bar extends around the neck, and similar plumage on the underparts. Breast golden-brown, becoming paler towards the abdomen. Iris dark brown; beak black; legs and feet dark horn.*

Hen: *Resembles an out-of-colour cock, but generally distinguishable by lighter coloration. Crown black, with buff striping; sides of head and stripes above eyes sandy. Black stripe extends from behind the eyes to the ear coverts. Upperparts yellowish-brown, with black stripe. Underparts whitish, being rusty towards the throat.*

These birds make fascinating aviary occupants, although breeding can prove rather problematical. In the wild, these whydahs lay their eggs in the nests of waxbills, which hatch them and rear the chicks. Amazingly, each species of parasitic whydah tends to choose a particular species of waxbill, with which their young correspond roughly not only in the colouring of their feathers, but also in the reflecting papillae, which are visible in the mouth when the chicks beg for food. The unsuspecting foster parents then rear both their chicks and those of the whydahs together.

The Paradise Whydah usually deposits its eggs in the nest of the Melba Finch or a related species. In order to encourage breeding therefore, you will need to have several pairs of these finches nesting first. Breeding successes have also been recorded with the aid of the Red-billed Firefinches (*Lagonosticta senegala*) in aviary surroundings. As a result of their demanding requirements, there are only a few records of these whydahs having been reared successfully in aviaries.

When in breeding condition, cocks tend to become rather aggressive and restive. They should be kept apart at this stage, with the perches arranged so that their long tail feathers cannot be damaged by rubbing on the mesh of the aviary. It is also necessary to house three or four hens with each cock, because they are polygamous by nature. Their feeding and care should not differ from that of other members of the genus.

Pin-tailed Whydah *Vidua macroura*

Origin: *Africa, south of the Sahara*

Cock: 5in (13cm) In breeding plumage, forehead, crown and nape glossy bluish-black; cheeks and throat white, with the white being continued in a band round the neck. Upperparts mainly black with rump and uppertail coverts white. Underparts also white, apart from a black crescent-shaped area on the breast. Four long central tail feathers black, measuring up to 10in (25cm) in length, with other tail feathers and flights blackish-brown. Iris dark brown; beak light red; legs and feet greyish.

Hen: Resembles an out-of-colour cock. Centre of crown sandy, bordered on each side with black; mantle and scapulars buff heavily striped with blackish brown; rump brown with faint stripes. Flights and tail dark brown edged with buff. Throat whitish; remainder of underparts buff, darker on the breast and flanks. Beak pinkish brown; legs and feet light brown. Young birds also resemble the hen, but can be recognised by the horn-coloration of their beaks.

One of the most frequently imported whydahs, the Pin-tailed may be less colourful than the preceding species, but it is equally impressive and graceful when kept in a large, planted aviary. After careful acclimatisation, these whydahs are quite hardy, and can be kept outside for much of the year, although snug, frost-proof roosting quarters must be available when the weather is cold.

Various kinds of millet, plain canary seed, green food and soaked seed given regularly will ensure these birds remain in good condition. During the breeding season, small mealworms, whiteworms, softbill food and egg food can all be offered, and should help to condition the whydahs. When courting, the cock performs a hovering dance in front of a hen, using his tail feathers to maximum effect creating a striking impression. These whydahs are again polygamous, and should be kept in the company of several hens.

The Pin-tailed Whydahs use either the St Helena Waxbill or the Red-eared Waxbill as hosts for their young. Breeding and fledging periods correspond to those of the waxbills. The likelihood of success is greatly increased in spacious surroundings, where there is plenty of nesting cover available for the waxbills. Even if no successful results are achieved however, these whydahs make interesting aviary occupants and present a real challenge for the dedicated breeder.

Queen Whydah (Shaft-tailed Whydah) *Vidua regia*

Origin: *southern Africa*

Cock: 5in (13cm) In breeding plumage, crown, nape, scapulars and mantle glossy blue-black. Coverts and flights blackish; cheeks, throat, a narrow collar across the nape, and the whole of the underparts are a warm shade of tawny-buff.

193

Tail brownish except for the four central feathers, measuring around 8in (20cm) in length, which are extended as bare black shafts with glossy black webbing at the extremities only. Iris dark brown; beak coral red; legs and feet coral red.

Hen: *Resembles an out-of-colour cock. Warm brown on the upperparts, with variable heavy blackish-brown striations here. Head and neck buff, with a broad band of darkly striated feathers on each side of the crown. Underparts whitish, with the throat and flanks sandy-buff. Underwing coverts white; beak and legs brown. Young birds are similar to the hen, but paler overall, with less distinctive markings.*

One of the rarer species in aviculture, the Queen Whydah ranks among the most attractive members of its genus. The four elongated tail feathers consist of wire-like shafts, with feathery plumes at the tip. A cock should again be housed with several hens. In the wild an individual cock may have a harem of up to 20 females to himself. Although closely resembling Pin-tailed Whydah hens, they can be distinguished from this species by their red legs.

Queen Whydahs are easy birds to maintain, but breeding results are even less common with this species. This is because the relatively rare and costly Violet-eared Waxbill is the breeding host for this species. The first success in breeding Queen Whydahs in aviary surroundings was accomplished by a South African aviculturist in 1967. In Britain, chicks have been reared successfully by Red-cheeked Cordon Bleu Waxbills.

Fischer's Whydah (Straw-tailed Whydah) *Vidua fischeri*

Origin: *east Africa*

Cock: *4in (10cm) In breeding plumage, crown pale buff; remainder of head, neck, back and shoulders black. Rump and uppertail coverts light brown. Underparts cream-coloured, with the sides of the body finely barred with black. Wings brown-black. Tail brown-black, with four long, light cinnamon-yellow tail feathers, which may be 8in (20cm) long. Iris brown; beak red; legs and feet red.*

Hen: *Resembles an out-of-colour cock. Forehead reddish-brown; upperparts brownish with dark quills. White throat and light eyebrow stripe. Underparts and sides of head yellow-brown. Belly white in centre, with little dark stripes on the sides here.*

These whydahs are not regularly available, although they were first bred in Britain in 1911. Like other whydahs, they are active by nature and will not thrive in a cage, where the cock's magnificent tail plumes will inevitably be damaged. In the wild, they often occur in reedy surroundings and clamber up and down the stems, which helps to wear down their claws. Reeds and bamboo should be planted in an aviary for them, but you will need to ensure that their claws do not become overgrown. Additional cover can be provided by surrounding the sides of the flight with birch and willow branches, and you can create an artificial reed bed as well, using dry reeds. Cover a frame with narrow mesh netting at the base, and fill this with sand, having fixed the reeds in the netting. The sand will provide additional support for them.

As with other whydahs, this species feeds mainly on small grass seeds, with millet sprays in particular often being favoured.

The host species for breeding purposes for Fischer's Whydah is the Purple Grenadier Waxbill, another bird that is relatively scarce in aviculture. Sometimes however, Fischer's Whydahs may adopt the nest of Red-eared Waxbills for their eggs. Cock whydahs may show a remarkable ability to mimic the song of Purple Grenadiers and attract a hen to a likely nest for laying purposes in their vicinity.

3 Red-collared Whydah *Euplectes ardens*

Origin: *widely distributed across Africa*

Cock: *6in (15cm) In breeding plumage is black, with a wide red collar in front across the upper breast. Wings black. Long tail, up to 8in (20cm) long, black. Iris dark brown; beak blackish; legs and feet greyish.*

Hen: *Resembles an out-of-colour cock, but smaller in size, with less streaking. Upperparts black and brown streaks. Buff eye stripe; yellowish chin and throat, becoming whiter on the remainder of the underparts. Beak horn-coloured.*

A number of races occur in parts of this whydah's wide range, of which the most distinctive is probably the western form, *Euplectes ardens concolor*. Known simply as the Black Whydah, this subspecies is, as its name suggests, completely black, lacking the throat patch. In other cases, the depth of red coloration may vary, almost from yellow through to crimson. Colour-feeding prior to the nuptial moult may help to maximise the depth of red coloration here.

This is one of the non-parasitic group of whydahs, which build their own nests. Good breeding results have been obtained on various occasions, as their needs are more easily met than those of the parasitic species. It is best to give the cock and hens an aviary to themselves, because the male can become very aggressive towards other birds at the start of the breeding season, particularly birds with red in their plumage.

The nuptial display dance of the cock shows a remarkable resemblance to that of the Crimson-crowned Weaver (*Euplectes hordeacea*), and a German breeder has also commented on the aggression displayed by this whydah if it is kept in the company of these weavers. Both their calls and nesting habits show a remarkable resemblance to each other.

A densely planted aviary, preferably with long grass growing on the floor, will encourage breeding activity. The grass will be incorporated into the nest, being pulled over the top to help conceal its presence. Other nesting sites that have been used include low-growing shrubs and conifers.

195

Cocks may descend to the ground to display to their mates. Between two and four eggs form the typical clutch, and they should hatch after a period of about two weeks. The young will fledge around 16 days later, but avoid disturbing the nest if at all possible, because this may cause the adult birds to desert their offspring.

Red-shouldered Whydah (Fan-tailed Whydah)

Euplectes axillaris

Origin: *widely distributed across Africa*

Cock: 7in (18cm) *In breeding plumage is predominantly jet black. Red shoulder patches are a more orangish shade in eclipse cocks; wings black with brown lacing. Tail black. Iris brown; beak blackish; legs and feet black.*

Hen: Resembles an out-of-colour cock. Upperparts sandy coloured with black spotting; throat and centre of the belly white; shoulder areas black, enabling distinction between the sexes throughout the year. Wings and tail brownish-black, with light brown margins. Young birds can be recognised by their shoulder patches, which are black with characteristic buff edging.

Found over much of Africa, there are several recognised races, which tend to differ somewhat in terms of size and the depth of reddish coloration at the shoulders. The tail feathers are typically much shorter than those of related species. In breeding plumage the cock has a tail that is perhaps just 1in (2.5cm) or so longer than for the rest of the year.

Before mating, these whydahs perform an aerial ballet, with the cock flying low, flitting rather like a butterfly over the grass. His hissing, chattering calls merge with flute-like notes at this stage. A domed nest is built in a low shrub, with the cock remaining in close attendance and driving away any birds which approach here. The aviary should be planted as recommended for Red-collared Whydah, and two or three hens can be kept in the company of one cock bird.

The hen will lay from two to four eggs, which she incubates for 14 days. At first the hen will feed her chicks on small live foods, such as aphids, spiders, whiteworm and hatchling crickets, which can be dusted with a special supplement to improve their nutritional value. Soaked millet sprays, egg food and green food, such as chickweed or seeding grasses, can also be offered. The cock bird will remain in close attendance once the chicks have hatched. They will leave the nest when just over a fortnight old, and will soon be capable of feeding themselves.

The typical abbreviations used with this group of birds in advertisements still apply with this species: OOC means out of colour; while IFC confirms that the birds on offer are in full colour.

4 Yellow-backed Whydah (Yellow-mantled Whydah)

Euplectes macrourus

Origin: *west Africa*

Cock: 7in (18cm) In breeding plumage is predominantly black, apart from the mantle, which is vivid yellow. Brown feathering is apparent on the wings. Iris dark brown; beak black; legs and feet greyish-black.

Hen: Upperparts dull brown, with the feathers having black striations. The feathers on the back have yellow margins. Uppertail coverts brown. Sides of the head and flanks light brown, usually with dark striations. Throat and belly whitish. Wings and tail black with brown margins; yellow margins to the mantle feathers.

It may be possible to recognise cocks in eclipse plumage by odd yellow feathers in their wings, but this is not entirely reliable. Unfortunately, obtaining sufficient hens can be a frustrating task, but it is worth the effort because it will encourage an adult cock to display with greater vigour in most instances, enhancing the likelihood of breeding success.

A well-planted aviary, incorporating reeds if possible, and dense grasses as well as low-growing shrubs is to be recommended. These whydahs will eat a variety of cereal seeds, including plain canary seed, millets and paddy rice. They may also take live foods and insectivorous food, especially when nesting. Grit and cuttlefish bone should always be available.

Yellow-shouldered Whydah *Euplectes macrocercus*

Origin: *east Africa*

Cock: 7in (18cm) In breeding plumage is black, with yellow shoulder area. Brownish edges to the flight feathers. Long black tail feathers. Iris dark brown; beak black; legs and feet blackish.

Hen: Resembles an out-of-colour cock. Upperparts buff, with black streaks. Wings black with yellow shoulder patch. Buff underparts, becoming yellowish on the face and throat. Bill horn-coloured. As in other cases, it is often possible to recognise cocks of this species when they are out-of-colour by the more intense black markings on their upperparts, compared with hens. Young birds have fawn shoulder patches and paler beaks.

This species has never been very common in aviculture, and may be confused with the Yellow-backed Whydah; however, it lacks the yellow mantle, with this area being black. The tail feathers are also significantly longer, and a cock in breeding finery may be 10in (25cm) long.

Yellow-shouldered Whydahs are not particularly aggressive, and, indeed, they congregate together in large flocks in the wild outside the breeding period. Subsequently, however, cocks establish their own territories, being joined by several hens at this stage. These areas are defended vigorously, and in aviary surroundings, cocks must be kept apart at this time. They should also not be kept with other birds of similar colorations, because this may well provoke displays of aggression.

Their management presents no particular difficulties, and Yellow-shouldered Whydahs require similar care to that of other related species. They tend to dislike prolonged periods of damp weather, even when acclimatised, but are otherwise quite hardy, provided they have frost-proof accommodation available during the winter months.

115 Giant Whydah (Long-tailed Widow Bird) *Euplectes progne*

Origin: *east Africa*

Cock: 8in (20cm) *In breeding plumage is completely black, apart from vermilion coloration at the shoulder and white markings on the wings. Wing feathers have buff edges. Long tail feathers can measure 16in (41cm). Iris dark brown; beak blackish; legs and feet greyish.*

Hen: Resembles an out-of-colour cock, although tends to be smaller and has less pronounced black streaking on the upperparts. Mainly light brown above, with the underparts being of a lighter shade, showing dark striations, notably on the flanks. Lores, throat and belly are cream-coloured. Wings and tail brown, with orange and buff margins. Beak, legs and feet brownish.

This is a particularly majestic species but is rarely available. Although it was believed that this species was polygamous, studies carried out in Kenya have suggested that there may be only one breeding hen living in an area with a cock bird.

The claws of all whydahs and weavers need attention to ensure that they do not become overgrown, otherwise the birds may become caught up in their quarters. The claws of the Giant Whydah tend to grow quite fast and should be inspected and clipped regularly as necessary; take care not to cause bleeding by cutting them too short.

This species can also suffer from scaly-leg, which is caused by parasitic mites. In the past, it used to be necessary to catch the birds on a daily basis to keep them caged for treatment purposes. Today, however, the development of modern drugs such as ivermectin means that a single treatment may well be all that is required. The legs should be checked for signs of encrustation at the time of purchase; perches may form a reservoir where the mites can lurk, so that if a case develops in aviary surroundings, it is also advisable to replace the perches.

A large, well-planted aviary, with a flight of perhaps 20ft (6.1m) by 10ft (3m) wide will enable the cock to display his magnificent tail feathers to best effect. Even so, part of the flight must be well covered, because these whydahs can become waterlogged during heavy rain if their long tail feathers become saturated. Although peaceful for much of the year, when breeding it appears that cocks can become very aggressive towards any other birds sharing their quarters, which is another reason for housing them in spacious surroundings, where plenty of cover is available.

These whydahs hatch and rear their own chicks, with breeding details being similar to those of the Red-collared Whydah. The nest is usually built low down, close to the ground. Invertebrates are eaten greedily when there are chicks in the nest and should always be available, at least throughout the breeding period. A regular diet comprised of millets and plain canary seed suits these whydahs well, although they will also take green food in the form of chickweed and seeding grasses.

16 Jackson's Whydah *Euplectes jacksoni*

Origin: *Kenya and north Tanzania*

Cock: 5in (13cm) In breeding plumage is deep black, with brown wings which have yellow and brown margins. Black tail feathers can measure 8in (20cm), and are broad and distinctly curved in shape. Iris dark brown; beak blackish; legs and feet blackish.

Hen: Resembles an out-of-colour cock, but tends to be smaller with a less massive head. Light brown overall with dark striations.

Jackson's Whydahs are, unfortunately, not well-represented in aviculture. They require similar care to the Giant Whydah, with a good area of grass on the floor of their flight. Part of this will be selected as a display ground by the cock, which dances here to attract a mate, leaping up and strutting around, flattening the grass in his vicinity.

The distinctive tail feathers in breeding cocks of this species are carried upright, rather like those of a cockerel, and the longer feathers on the crown actually form a collar. Their display is fascinating to observe. With the crown feathers held erect and the neck stretched out, the cock jumps straight up from the ground, with wings fluttering and moving his legs as if he were cycling. The stiffly held tail is thrown forwards over the back, touching the crown of the head.

Displaying cocks are able to jump as high as 3ft (90cm) or more into the air, and they will create a circle of flattened grass on the ground, which can be 2ft (60cm) in diameter, while a clump at the centre here remains essentially untouched. The cock then runs round and round this raised area, pausing at frequent intervals to perform his display.

This species has been bred successfully in aviary surroundings on various occasions. A nest made of grass is typically suspended like a hammock from branches. Three eggs are likely to be laid here by the hen, who sits alone throughout the incubation period, which lasts about 12 days. Young may be reared almost exclusively on plain canary seed and millets in some cases, but live foods should be offered regularly throughout the breeding period, along with egg food and similar items.

These whydahs may become quite tame, even in aviary surroundings, although they are sometimes destructive towards growing vegetation here. Once acclimatised properly, they are quite hardy, but should be provided with a frost-proof shelter for the winter months.

Long-tailed Combassou (Steel-blue Whydah)

Vidua hypocherina

Origin: *east Africa*

Cock: 13in (33cm) In breeding plumage is black, with a greenish metallic sheen to his plumage. Wings glossy blackish-brown. The four central tail feathers may grow to 8in (20cm) long at this stage, with the other tail feathers being shorter, blackish-brown in colour with white edges on the margins. Iris brown; beak flesh-coloured; legs and feet brown.

Hen: Resembles an out-of-colour cock, with upperparts predominantly brown. A narrow light brown and a wider black-brown band extend along the sides of the head. Eye stripe buff, as well as the sides of the head. Throat, centre of abdomen and undertail coverts are white. Tail blackish-brown; bill horn-coloured brown.

It is possible to distinguish between this species and the Senegal Combassou quite easily, because the bill of the Senegal Combassou is pinkish, not white, its legs are brown not red, and, overall, the Long-tailed Combassou is larger.

There has been considerable debate about the status of the combassous, but it is now generally accepted that there are four recognisable species. None is especially popular in aviculture, because of their rather dull coloration and the difficulty in breeding them successfully. They tend to be parasitic in their nesting habits, like some other whydahs. Nevertheless, combassous are very easy to maintain in aviary surroundings, readily taking a foreign finch seed mixture augmented with seeding grasses, millet sprays and green food, such as chickweed.

Cocks display by fluttering in the vicinity of hens. The song of this species is a clear, flute-like note augmented with cheeping sounds. Firefinches (*Lagonosticta* species) are the host species for their eggs, and insects are important for the successful rearing of the chicks.

Combassous are quite hardy once acclimatised properly, and can winter outdoors provided their shelter is dry and snug and gives them adequate protection during cold weather.

Senegal Combassou (Village Indigobird) *Vidua chalybeata*

Origin: *widely distributed across Africa*

Cock: 5in (13cm) In breeding plumage is a beautiful steel-blue, with the wings and tail being an ashen shade. Iris brown: beak pinkish-white; legs and feet brownish.

Hen: Resembles an out-of-colour cock, but with lighter streaking on the crown. Here there is a pale central streak, with dark brown on the borders. Upperparts pale buff.

When in breeding condition, the cock becomes restless, displaying repeatedly by flying and hovering close to a potential mate, and calling at the same time. Senegal Combassous have been bred in aviary conditions on various occasions, but successes tend to be rare, largely because they are not kept in suitable surroundings. If breeding is to be attempted, a well-planted flight is essential, and both nesting material and diet should be as varied as possible.

These particular combassous may be parasitic in their nesting habits, with hens laying in the nests of the Red-billed Firefinch. Cock birds are able to mimic the calls of this species to perfection, and attract the female combassou to a suitable nest site for her eggs by this call. Alternatively, however, where there is no host available, these particular combassous (of which a number of different races are recognised, often on the basis of the coloration of their feet) are able to build a nest themselves, hatching and rearing their chicks in a more conventional manner. Old weavers' nests, artificial wicker nests or nestboxes, and a quantity of material such as horsehair and dried grass should be offered to provide a suitable choice, and there should be a variety of nesting sites, positioned at different heights in the aviary.

Several hens can also be accommodated with a single cock, because these birds are usually polygamous. Incubation of the eggs lasts about 12 days, with the chicks leaving the nest when they are about two weeks old. Breeding success is nevertheless most likely if these combassous are housed in the company of waxbills.

8 Grenadier Weaver (Red Bishop, Orix Bishop) *Euplectes orix*

Origin: *much of Africa south of the Sahara*

Cock: 6in (15cm) In breeding plumage forehead, crown, sides of the head, lower breast and abdomen are predominantly deep black. The remainder of the body is orangish-red, becoming browner over the mantle, and especially over the wings and tail. Iris brown; beak blackish; legs and feet pink.

Hen: Resembles an out-of-colour cock, being brownish with darker streaking, which is more clearly defined on the underparts of females.

In total, five races of this species are recognised, and they may be advertised under a wide range of different names, including the Red-crowned Grenadier (*E.o. sundevalli*), the Black-fronted Red Bishop (*E.o. nigrifrons*) and the Orange Bishop (*E.o. franciscana*) (Plate 121), which tends to be the most widely-kept race. It occurs in north Africa, extending across the continent from Senegal east to the Sudan. The head markings of the Orange Bishop are even more spectacular than those of the nominate race, which originates from southern Africa. The cock Orange Bishop develops a magnificent thick orange ruff of feathers on the back of his head at the start of the breeding season, while his head and abdomen become jet black. Outside this period, both sexes are a light, greyish-brown in coloration, with paler grey underparts. The choice of a pair is then difficult, because of the close resemblance of the cock and hen. It is only when males begin to don their nuptial plumage that there can be a certainty of obtaining a true pair.

A planted aviary is again to be recommended for these finches. In the wild they often occur in boggy areas and nest in reed beds, so similar plants should, if possible, be supplied in aviary surroundings. Alternatively, substitutes such as clumps of bamboo should be provided. Cocks tend to become very aggressive during the breeding period and will drive off potential rivals, while weaving nests to attract a mate.

Fresh grasses and strips of dried bark are favoured for the nest-building process. The nest itself will be egg-shaped, with a funnel-like entrance passage at the side, and will be larger and more carefully constructed than the nests of other weavers. It is usually suspended between two to four strong branches in a low-growing shrub or tree.

Although cocks may busily build nests, nothing much usually comes of attempts to breed in a communal flight. If a serious breeding programme is to be contemplated, it is recommended that one cock is housed with several hens as these birds are polygamous by nature. A single hen may be disturbed by the constant attention of a cock once she starts to breed.

A diet based on a mixture of millets and plain canary seed will suit them well. This should be augmented with greater amounts of soaked seed, such as millet sprays, and live food as the cock starts to moult into breeding plumage. In addition, colour feeding, using a water-soluble preparation given in the drinking water, is to be recommended throughout this period to ensure that the fiery orange plumage retains its depth of coloration. Without the use of a colouring agent, this is likely to fade over the course of successive moults. Eating grated carrot will also help the birds to ensure a good depth of coloration, because it contains a natural colouring agent, which will be taken up into the feathers at this stage.

First breeding results with this species were recorded in Britain in 1913. Successes since then have not been numerous, largely because breeders have not provided suitable conditions to encourage nesting. A possible solution is to plant corn on the cob in a corner of the aviary. These seedlings need to be planted quite close together, enabling the weavers to construct nests between the stout vertical stems. On occasions, open-fronted nestboxes have also been adopted, with the nest itself being woven in here.

Between two to seven greenish-blue eggs form the typical clutch, and these are incubated by the hen alone. The chicks should hatch after about a fortnight, and fledge after a similar period. The hen alone is responsible for rearing them, and will continue feeding them for a further two weeks until they are fully independent. By this stage, they will resemble out-of-colour adult birds, but they can be distinguished by the more prominent buff markings on their feathers, which make them appear somewhat paler overall.

Black-bellied Weaver (Zanzibar Red Bishop)
Euplectes nigroventris

Origin: *east Africa*

Cock: 4in (10cm) In breeding plumage crown of the head deep orange-red; entire underparts velvety-black, with the exception of the thighs, which are buff, and the undertail coverts, which are orange. There is no pronounced ruff on the nape, as in the case of the Orange Bishop, and this species is also somewhat smaller. Iris brown; beak blackish; legs and feet pink.

Hen: Resembles an Orange Bishop hen, but is smaller, and the underwing coverts and inner edges to the flights are a paler shade of buff.

Less frequently imported than the Grenadier Weaver, the Black-bellied Weaver is, nevertheless, a common coastal bird in east Africa, where it is usually seen in small parties. When it is out of colour, it is difficult to distinguish the cock bird from the hen, but it is, in any event, better to start with a group, in view of the polygamous nature of this species. Care is straightforward, and should be the same as outlined for the Grenadier Weaver.

While many nests may be constructed in a comparatively restricted area, each cock actually maintains his own limited breeding territory. The nests are usually built in tall grass, bushes or in clumps of reeds, in marshy areas. Each hen lays two or three pale blue eggs, which may be spotted with dusky-brown, and then hatches and rears the chicks on her own.

Crimson-crowned Weaver *Euplectes hordeacea*

Origin: *widely distributed across Africa.*

Cock: 6in (15cm) In breeding plumage sides of the head and upperpart of the throat black; back reddish-brown; remainder of upperparts and neck scarlet. The rest of the underparts black; undertail coverts brown. Wings and tail black, sometimes with lighter margins. Iris brown; beak black; legs and feet flesh-coloured.

Hen: Resembles an out-of-colour cock, but may have paler markings. Upperparts light brown with brown striations and light yellow eyebrow stripes. Underparts may vary from whitish to buff. Flanks and upper chest have dark striations on a light brown ground colour. Wings and tail brownish-black with lighter margins.

The depth of red coloration may vary in individual cocks, depending on their area of origin. On rare occasions, Crimson-crowned Weavers may have white wings and tail feathers, with the remainder of the plumage also being significantly lighter in coloration.

This species is not especially common in aviculture, but breeding successes have been recorded in Britain and elsewhere. The nests are built of grass, often against wire netting where branches and twigs have penetrated from bushes growing outside the aviary. They tend to be very dense, so that the eggs are not visible from the outside.

Breeding details for the Crimson-crowned Weaver are similar to those of related species, as is their general care. Young birds again resemble hens, but can be distinguished by the more prominent buff edging to their feathers. Although relatively hardy once established in their quarters, these birds should be protected from the worst of the winter weather and either provided with a heated shelter or transferred to a flight in birdroom surroundings until the spring.

119 Napoleon Weaver (Golden Bishop) *Euplectes afer*

Origin: *widely distributed across Africa south of the Sahara*

Cock: 5in (13cm) In breeding plumage, bright yellow extends from forehead to nape, and from the lower back down to the uppertail coverts. Bright yellow plumage also present around the sides of the neck down across the breast. The remainder of the feathering is black, sometimes with sporadic yellow feathers on the mantle. Wings and tail feathers black with buff edging. Iris brown; beak black; legs and feet pinkish.

Hen: Resembles an out-of-colour cock, but markings tend to be paler. Upperparts brown with dark striations, with the underparts being whitish-buff. Eyebrow stripe yellow-brown; beak horn-coloured.

Again, several races of this weaver are recognised through its wide range, of which the most distinctive is the Taha Weaver (*E.a. taha*) (Plate 124), which originates from southern Africa. Its appearance is duller than that of the nominate race, and the underparts are entirely black. An intermediate form is that found in Kenya and Tanzania and is recognised under the scientific name of *E.a. ladoensis*; slight traces of yellow feathering are present on the breast of this form.

There is a close similarity between the Napoleon Weaver and the Orange Bishop when these birds are in eclipse plumage. It is usually possible to distinguish them, however, because the Napoleon Weaver tends to display darker striping on the upperparts and has more yellowish coloration on its underparts. If you are buying birds and want to be certain about their species and gender, it is better to purchase them when they are in full colour, although they tend to be more expensive at this stage.

Cocks are liable to disagree when housed together during the nesting period, as they compete for mates, and this will cause disturbance in the aviary. An ideal system is to house them in groups of a cock with two hens. If required, these weavers will then usually live in peace with totally unrelated species such as Diamond Doves or Java Sparrows, which are of similar size. Weavers should not be housed in the company of waxbills, however, because they are likely to bully these smaller birds.

The yellow evident in the cock's plumage can again be improved by the use of a food that will enhance this colour. It will need to be given prior to and during the moult in order to be effective.

The cock will normally weave the nests himself, enticing the females to use them. These weavers frequently become quite insectivorous at this stage, and a good supply of suitable live food should help to ensure that the chicks, typically numbering two or three, are reared successfully. Breeding details are as for the Crimson-crowned Weaver, but Napoleon Weavers often prove readier to breed in aviary surroundings.

Yellow-rumped Weaver (Cape Weaver) *Euplectes capensis*

Origin: *widely distributed across Africa*

Cock: 6in (15cm) In breeding plumage has silky black plumage, with golden-yellow rump. Wings black with a yellow shoulder spot; flight feathers have lighter brown edges. Iris brown; upper bill black, lower bill horn-coloured; legs and feet light brown.

Hen: Resembles an out-of-colour cock, but is paler overall, with an olive-yellow rump. Light brown upperparts with black striations. Underparts dirty white with brown markings. Wings blackish-brown with whitish margins. Beak dark horn on upper bill, and paler below.

Five subspecies are recognised throughout the geographical distribution of this weaver, but none is especially common in collections. They are not imported regularly, and cocks often appear to predominate in consignments. Observations from the wild suggest these weavers are numerous but that they tend to be found at higher altitudes than other, more readily available species. Breeding results have been documented, especially in aviary surroundings containing tall grasses.

The cock bird builds nests quite low to the ground, with a well-concealed entrance at the front. They are usually positioned between stout vertical stems, and bamboo is, therefore, a good choice for inclusion in an aviary for these weavers, which become very insectivorous when they are breeding.

Up to four eggs may be laid by each hen, with incubation lasting about 14 days. Fledging takes place after a slightly longer interval, with young birds resembling females, but the yellow areas on the shoulders are missing, and the underparts are spotted rather than striped.

123 Madagascar Weaver (Madagascan Red Fody)

Foudia madagascariensis

Origin: *Madagascar, Mauritius, Seychelles and Reunion islands in the Indian Ocean*

Cock: 5in (13cm) In breeding plumage almost entirely crimson, with the feathers of the back, mantle and scapulars being marked with black, while the flights and tail are brownish. A black line is present on the sides of the head, running through the eyes. Iris brown; beak black; legs and feet pinkish.

Hen: Resembles an out-of-colour cock. Predominantly brown, with darker brown streaking on the upperparts, and more yellowish below, with brown suffusion on the breast and flanks. It is virtually impossible to distinguish between the sexes outside the breeding period.

Although at one time this beautiful weaver was frequently available, it has since become scarce. Stock is more numerous in mainland Europe than in Britain or North America, and this species is also still represented in Australian collections. Cock birds should be colour-fed at the start of their moult into breeding plumage and throughout the development of these more colourful feathers to maintain the fiery red shades.

Madagascar Weavers have a reputation for being quite quarrelsome in aviary surroundings, and they may even bully birds larger than themselves, especially during the breeding season. They are best kept in small groups on their own. If you are choosing stock in eclipse plumage, you may be able to detect cocks at this stage by the greyer tips to their bills.

The first breeding results were obtained in Germany in 1869. They build a typical nest in weaver fashion, suspended between the branches of low trees or among reeds. Clutch size averages between four and six blue eggs, which hatch after a fortnight. The youngsters then fledge about three weeks later. Suitable livefood must be offered to these birds when they are breeding, as they become largely insectivorous at this stage. In the wild Madagascar Weavers feed on grass seeds and insects, as well as causing damage to growing crops such as rice. They will thrive if provided with a diet as recommended for other weavers, and they may also eat paddy rice with enthusiasm.

Once acclimatised, these weavers are quite hardy, but they must have adequate shelter through the winter months.

2 **Little Masked Weaver** *Ploceus luteolus*

Origin: *widely distributed across much of Africa*

Cock: 5in (13cm) In breeding plumage has black head, with a light yellow superciliary eye stripe; remainder of the upperparts yellow to greenish-yellow. Sides of neck and underparts yellow; wings brownish, feathers laced with yellow-green. Tail brown with yellow-green sheen. Iris brownish; beak greyish-black; legs and feet pinkish-grey.

Hen: In breeding plumage has upperparts light olive-green, with yellowish uppertail coverts and dark striations along the back. Cheeks and underparts light yellow; lores white; beak grey. For the remainder of the year, the sexes more closely resemble each other, although hens tend to be paler white on their underparts, with traces of buff coloration on their breast and flanks.

Tending to be found more in wooded than in grassland areas, these weavers hunt for insects among the vegetation of a planted flight. Their song is soft and in no way disturbing. In spite of their wide distribution, they are not commonly available at present.

Their care is straightforward, however, with their diet consisting of a mixture of millets, plain canary seed and a little groats, augmented with softbill food, suitable live foods, such as small crickets, and green food, including seeding grasses.

Little Masked Weavers are liable to become aggressive during the breeding season, and they are not especially gregarious by nature. A cock should be housed with perhaps two hens. The nest is relatively small, with an entrance hole which is entered from below, via a small spout. The interior may be lined with softer material, such as feathers.

Two or three eggs form a typical clutch, and will hatch after a period of about 12 days, with both adults said to be involved in incubation duties and the rearing of young. Up to three clutches may be produced in succession during the course of a season.

These weavers are relatively hardy once acclimatised, but they will benefit from additional warmth and lighting over the winter period.

7 **Village Weaver** (Spotted-backed Weaver) *Ploceus cucullatus*

Origin: *widely distributed across much of Africa.*

Cock: 7in (18cm) In breeding plumage head and throat black, with this colour extending down to the upper breast; broad collar dark chestnut; mantle and back golden-yellow, with mantle being bordered by a black band which forms a V-shaped mark on the shoulders. Wing coverts and inner secondaries black edged with yellow; outer secondaries and flights dark brown, with narrow edging of yellow-olive. Rump yellow. Uppertail coverts olive; tail light brown with olive-yellow edging. Breast golden-yellow merging into chestnut where it joins the back of the *throat. Remainder of underparts bright yellow with chestnut tone on the flanks. Iris red; beak black; legs dark flesh-coloured.*

Hen: *Crown, nape and sides of neck olive with yellow stripe above the eyes. Mantle and back olive-brown, the feathers here being edged with grey. Rump olive. Wings brownish-black edged with yellow; primaries with broad yellow on the inner web. Tail brown with olive wash. Chin, throat and breast yellow; belly white; undertail coverts yellow. Iris warm brown; upper mandible brown, lower mandible pale horn. Although immature cocks resemble adult hens, there is otherwise a clear distinction between the sexes throughout the year, with mature males having yellower plumage on the head, and the upperparts are ash grey, with signs of darker streaking evident here.*

The name Village Weaver for this species stems from the fact that it is often found close to native villages in Africa, where it forms large and noisy colonies. One of the larger weavers, the bird is equipped with a powerful beak and has a justified reputation for being aggressive. Ideally, they should be housed on their own, or kept only with larger birds outside the breeding season.

Breeding successes are quite few, and often supposed hens will moult out as adult cocks, having been in immature plumage at the time of purchase. A small group of a cock and several hens gives the best likelihood of success if they are housed in a spacious, planted aviary. The cock may seek to suspend nests not from vegetation, but directly from the roof of the aviary, and although this can provide adequate support, there is a greater possibility of flooding if this happens. Covering the roof with translucent plastic sheeting reduces this risk from the outset.

Live foods, particularly mealworms, will be consumed in large quantities, especially when the chicks have hatched. The incubation period lasts about a fortnight, and several broods may be reared in one season. The first breeding success was recorded at London Zoo in 1905.

Their general care should not differ from that of other similar weavers. They are hardy once acclimatised and can spend the winter outside, if they are provided with a dry and well-insulated shelter.

Half-masked Weaver (Vitelline Weaver) *Ploceus vitellinus*

Origin: *north Africa from Senegal to the Sudan*

Cock: *5in (13cm) In breeding plumage has lores, ear coverts and cheeks black. Forehead chestnut fading into golden on the crown and bright yellow on the nape. Mantle and back olive; wings yellow, with the feathers here having blackish centres. Tail brownish. Chin and throat black shading into chestnut on the upper breast; rest of the underparts bright yellow. Iris yellow; beak black; legs and feet pinkish.*

Hen: Resembles an out-of-colour cock, being mainly brownish-olive, streaked with blackish-brown in eclipse plumage, becoming yellower when in colour, with buff suffusion on the underparts. It is usually possible to distinguish cocks because they tend to be more brightly coloured than hens, even outside the breeding period.

This relatively small species is usually more peaceable than other weavers, although they are better suited to aviary rather than cage surroundings, and will breed only in a large, planted flight.

Half-masked Weavers build a pouch-shaped nest, with a short entrance tunnel below, which is woven from grasses and fine rushes and suspended from the branches of low trees or shrubs. It is solidly and beautifully constructed. During the mating period, the cock dances around the hen, fluttering his wings and spreading his tail, and making hissing noises.

The two to four pale greenish-blue eggs, with brown markings, hatch in 12 days. As with other weavers, it is important to provide a good supply of suitable live food once the chicks have hatched, together with a softbill food, which may also be sampled.

This species is often considered to be one of the easiest species to breed successfully, and they may have more than one brood in a season. Half-masked Weavers also make entertaining aviary occupants. In a flight planted with oats for example, they will hop up and down the stalks, feeding on the seedheads as these fill out and start to ripen. They are hardy, having become accustomed to aviary life, and can winter out of doors when provided with suitable protection.

6 Scaly-crowned Weaver *Sporopipes squamifrons*

Origin: *southern Africa*

Cock: 4in (10cm) Black and white scale-like markings on the head. Lores black; back grey; sides of head greyish-brown; white cheek stripe, with a black stripe on the underside of the throat. Underparts whiter. Wings black laced with white. Iris red; beak pinkish; legs and feet light horn-coloured.

Hen: Similar in appearance.

The only means of telling these weavers apart is by the cock's song, which is heard with greater frequency at the start of the breeding season. It is quite pleasant and not loud. Scaly-crowned Weavers are liable to become aggressive at this stage, and pairs are best housed on their own, although it may be possible to keep them satisfactorily in the company of other birds of similar size, such as Cut-throats. They do show a tendency to disrupt the nests of companions, however, which is clearly not desirable.

Careful acclimatisation is necessary with Scaly-crowned Weavers, and they should not be placed in an outdoor aviary for the first time until they are well established and the weather should remain mild. They are lively and active by nature, and often prefer to roost in a suitable nestbox at night, sometimes retreating there during the daytime as well. If no additional heating is available, it may be better to bring them indoors over the winter as they are likely to thrive better in a birdroom flight during this period.

Although mainly seed-eaters, Scaly-crowned Weavers will readily take invertebrates during the breeding period, and these will be essential for the successful rearing of their chicks. A forked branch is often a popular site for the nest itself, and as many as five eggs may be laid. Alternatively, a pair may decide to use a nestbox, building a nest within, and they have been known to adopt the disused nest of another weaver, modifying it for their own purposes. Hatching will take 12 days, with both birds probably taking turns at incubation during the day and roosting together in the nest at night.

125 Speckle-fronted Weaver (Scaly-fronted Weaver)

Sporopipes frontalis

Origin: *north Africa*

Cock: *5in (13cm) Black beard stripe, with black and white scale-like markings on the head. Neck red-brown; back brown-grey; tail with white margins. Underparts white, with breast and sides showing a slight brownish suffusion. Iris brown; beak pink; legs and feet pinkish-horn in colour.*

Hen: *Similar in appearance.*

Neither of the *Sporopipes* weavers shows a change in plumage at the start of the breeding season, and the only difference between the sexes is in the cock's song. However, the Speckle-fronted Weaver proves to be a more docile bird than the Scaly-crowned species, often agreeing quite well with other birds outside the breeding season.

The requirements of the two species are similar, with a diet based on a mixture of millets, plain canary seed and similar small seeds suiting them well. They become more insectivorous at the start of the breeding period, and will also eat some green food such as chickweed.

Speckle-fronted Weavers can become quite tame and trusting, even in aviary surroundings, rarely flying off when approached and being generally less active than the Scaly-crowned Weaver. When housed in a planted flight, they will roost in a nestbox, which they will fill entirely with moss, pieces of grass and feathers. When living in groups, a number will share the same nest.

Live food is essential for the successful rearing of the chicks. They should hatch after an incubation period lasting 12 days, and will fledge around two weeks later, being fed for a further period by their parents until they are fully independent. Again, it is advisable to house them in a warm room in winter, as they are not especially hardy.

9 **Red-billed Weaver** (Red-billed Quelea) *Quelea quelea*

Origin: *widely distributed across Africa*

Cock: 5in (13cm) In breeding plumage forehead stripe, sides of head and throat black. Crown, sides of neck and underparts buff, with pinkish suffusion, becoming white on the abdomen. Undertail coverts white. Upperparts brownish, with black barring. Wings brown, with paler edges to the feathering. Red orbital ring encircles the eye. Iris brown; bill red; legs and feet pinkish.

Hen: Resembles an out-of-colour cock. Head brownish-grey; underparts paler, but with no trace of black feathering on the throat, and less streaking on the upperparts. When in eclipse plumage herself, the hen can be easily identified by her yellowish bill, which darkens to red only at the start of the breeding period.

Believed to be the commonest bird in the world and sometimes described as the 'feathered locust', millions of Red-billed Weavers are destroyed annually in Africa because of the damage vast flocks cause to ripening crops, devastating whole areas and bringing famine in their wake.

Rather surprisingly, however, they rarely nest as readily in aviary surroundings, possibly because they are not kept in large groups, but often simply in individual pairs. These weavers appear to need the stimulus of others of their kind to encourage successful breeding.

Cocks, in particular, are industrious by nature, being referred to in French as *travailleur*, meaning 'worker'. Soon after being introduced to an aviary, the cock, frequently assisted by a hen, will begin to build a nest. They start by making a hoop, which they extend each side to the shape of a ball, with an entrance hole located at one side. These weavers will use fresh, strong blades of grass for preference when constructing a nest, and a plentiful supply should be available for this purpose.

Constructing a nest does not necessarily mean that the pair will start breeding, however. They often destroy one nest, simply in order to begin building another, perhaps immediately next to the old one. If no material is available for this purpose, the weavers may worry other birds sharing their quarters, to the extent of attacking them and pulling out their tail feathers.

Fighting is unlikely to occur when Red-billed Weavers are kept in a colony, although they should all be introduced at the same time and in pairs if possible. This is because, unlike the *Euplectes* weavers, the *Quelea* species are monogamous, with a strong pair bond established between individuals in a flock. Breeding details and care are identical in this case to that for the Red-headed Quelea.

128 Red-headed Quelea *Quelea erythrops*

Origin: *widely distributed across west Africa*

Cock: 5in (13cm) In breeding plumage head and throat carmine, with the throat darker. Upperparts striated brown; underparts buff, being white in the centre, as may be the undertail coverts. Wings light and dark brown with yellow margins. Tail very dark brown, with light brown margins. Iris brown; beak black; legs pinkish.

Hen: Resembles an out-of-colour cock, but lacks any trace of red on the head and throat, which are brownish-white; upperparts light brown with white eyebrow stripes. Beak horn-coloured.

Although less common in aviculture than the Red-billed Weaver, these birds are equally easy to care for, and they can be recommended for those new to bird-keeping. A diet based on a foreign finch mixture will suit them well, along with millet sprays and green food. After the sprays are plucked clean of seeds, they are likely to be incorporated into the birds' nests.

The first breeding successes were documented from Germany in 1869. Keeping them in a colony should encourage meaningful breeding activity. They tend not to be aggressive in a mixed collection, but are perhaps less likely to nest successfully in such surroundings. In the wild they usually breed in reed beds, and stands of bamboo are likely to prove a suitable substitute in an outdoor flight.

Up to four eggs may be laid by the hen, and these will hatch after a period of 14 days. A good selection of live foods should be provided at this stage, otherwise the young birds may not be reared successfully. Assuming all goes well, they will leave the nest when they are nearly three weeks old.

Care must be taken to ensure that the claws of these birds do not become overgrown, because they may become caught up in their quarters or even inadvertently pull a young chick out from the nest.

Queleas are quite hardy birds by nature, and can remain in aviary surroundings both summer and winter, providing that adequate shelter is available for them.

Baya Weaver *Ploceus philippinus*

Origin: *India east to southeast Asia*

Cock: 6in (15cm) In breeding plumage crown of the head and breast golden-yellow. Narrow forehead stripe, lores, sides of head and ear coverts blackish-brown. Cheeks and throat are lighter. Lower underparts buff, with brown suffusion on the flanks. Wing coverts brownish-black, with paler margins. Tail feathers brown, with olive-yellow edges. Iris brown; beak horn-coloured; legs and feet pinkish.

Hen: Resembles an out-of-colour cock, but generally a paler shade of brown on the upperparts, which are streaked with black. Underparts yellowish-white, becoming whiter in the centre, with an ochre marking apparent on the breast.

These Asiatic weavers occur in several distinct subspecies through their extensive range, being found almost entirely in low-lying areas. They often attach their characteristic nests to the leaves of palm trees, but are quite adaptable, using other suitable vantage points in aviary surroundings.

Nest-building may take place throughout the year, even outside the breeding season. It is advisable to keep pairs separate at this stage, unless the aviary is very large, because they are likely to prove aggressive. Prior to mating, the cock will flutter near and above the hen, constantly uttering its hoarse, chattering song.

These weavers are probably the most talented of all species when it comes to nest-building. They tend to breed in the wild during the wet season, so that their nests are held so tightly together that the interior should remain completely dry. The birds enter by means of a tunnel beneath the nest. Up to five eggs may be laid by the hen, and these should start hatching after a period of 14 days, with the young birds leaving the nest after a similar interval. A good supply of insects is again vital during the rearing period.

Bengal Weaver *Ploecus bengalensis*

Origin: *Indian subcontinent*

Cock: 5in (13cm) In breeding plumage crown and nape yellow; remainder of upperparts dark brown, with the plumage of the mantle being heavily striated. Black-brown lines are present on both sides of the throat and chin. Underparts red-brown, darker on the flanks. Iris brown; beak black, legs flesh-coloured.

Hen: Upperparts brown with red-brown lacing. Underparts lighter with brown striations. Beak light brown.

During the winter, when he is out of colour, the cock simply has a yellow spot on both sides of the neck and a yellow stripe above the eyes. The Bengal Weaver can be difficult to distinguish from the Baya Weaver, although this species has a yellow breast for part of the year. It is invariably difficult to obtain a pair, not only because the hens of various species of weaver are very similar in appearance, but also because, in both eclipse and juvenile plumage, cocks and hens appear very similar to each other.

Bengal Weavers are best kept in a large aviary or birdroom flight, where they can build their remarkable nests, which may sometimes consist of two compartments. Success is most likely outside, during the summer months, although cocks may bicker at first over hens here. They should soon settle down and start nest-building in earnest. The material used will consist of soft blades of grass as well as strips of paper, raffia and similar items. Breeding details are similar to those of the Baya Weaver.

These weavers are easy to keep and quite hardy, being able to remain outside even through the winter if an adequate shelter is available. They require a varied diet, however, particularly during the breeding season when invertebrates such as mealworms should be offered on a regular basis. Green food and even some fruit may be eaten in addition to their regular seed diet. Soaked millet sprays are often a popular item when there are chicks in the nest.

135 Red-cheeked Cordon Bleu (Red-cheeked Blue Waxbill)

Uraeginthus bengalus

Origin: *central Africa*

Cock: 5in (13cm) Cheeks, throat, breast and flanks blue; eyes circled with blue. Upperparts fawn-grey; rump blue. Tail feathers darker blue. Distinctive wine-red ear patches, with some fawn-grey plumage on the underparts, often with a pinkish sheen in the centre of the abdomen. Iris reddish-brown; beak reddish-grey with black tip; legs and feet pinkish.

Hen: Lacks the red cheek markings and paler in terms of overall coloration.

Although these waxbills have a reputation for being delicate when first imported, they will usually settle down very well if they are carefully managed through these early stages, and they may then live for 14 years or even longer. Even so, they should not be exposed to the worst of the winter weather. They need to be housed in a moderately warm room through this period, preferably where the winter sun can penetrate.

Breeding has been achieved both indoors in a planted flight and also in similar aviary surroundings. Once established, the birds usually nest quite readily. The cock carries suitable material, such as pieces of grass, to the site, where the hen weaves the artistic nest, which she lines with soft grasses and feathers.

The nest is usually dome-shaped, with an entrance at the side, although in an aviary the birds may prefer to use a hollow log or small nestbox, filling it with suitable material. Fix the box relatively high up in the flight, under cover and in a position where the birds will be out of the line of general flight in the aviary. Otherwise, they may be disturbed and abandon the nest.

The cock executes an attractive little dance during the courting period, tripping around the hen with a piece of grass in his bill. His song is sweet and pleasant, but he is less likely to be well disposed to other blue waxbills sharing the aviary, and these birds should be housed apart for breeding purposes, although they will agree well with other waxbills. Their requirements do not differ significantly from those of closely related species.

An interesting and apparently localised variant of the Red-cheeked Cordon Bleu is an orange-cheeked form. In this case, the red patches are replaced by yellowish-orange plumage, with the remainder of the body coloration being unaffected. Although a small number of these birds were imported to Britain during the 1980s, nothing further appears to have been recorded about them to date. It is likely that this characteristic was a mutation, rather than a metabolic quirk, because of the very specific nature of this change and the fact that it was not confined to a single individual.

4 Blue-capped Cordon Bleu (Blue-headed Cordon Bleu)

Uraeginthus cyanocephala

Origin: *northeast Africa*

Cock: 5in (13cm) Whole of the head, throat, breast, flanks, rump, and uppertail coverts soft, clear blue. Mantle, back and wings earth brown. Centre of abdomen and undertail coverts buff-brown. Tail dark blue. Iris reddish-brown; beak dusky red; legs and feet pinkish.

Hen: Forehead, face, breast, thighs, rump and uppertail coverts soft blue, less brightly coloured than in the cock. Crown, nape, mantle, back and wings pale earth brown. Centre of abdomen and undertail coverts pale buff brown. Tail dark blue. In some individual hens, the blue on the forehead is replaced by earthy-brown coloured plumage.

Originating from fairly arid areas, these waxbills are seen in pairs or small parties. Their domed nest of dry grasses and other material is usually sited in a thorn bush, often close to a hornet's nest for added protection. It may be possible to persuade the birds to use a wicker nesting basket in aviary surroundings, and this will be lined with suitable material including feathers. Here the hen lays a clutch of between four and six eggs, which both members of the pair take turns at incubating for about 12 days.

Once the chicks hatch, live food becomes an increasingly important item in the diet of the adult birds. Greenfly, whiteworm and hatchling crickets will all be taken readily, with soaked seed being an important addition to their diet during this period. Assuming that all goes well, the chicks will fledge around 18 days old, when they will resemble adult hens, although their legs are brownish.

This is often considered to be the easiest of the blue waxbills to breed successfully, although the Blue-capped Cordon Bleu actually has a relatively short avicultural history. It does not appear to have been imported until 1927, with the first breeding being recorded from France three years later. The species then remained almost unknown until the 1960s, although it has become more common recently.

As with similar waxbills, the Blue-capped is not hardy, and should be overwintered indoors in temperate areas, with artificial heating and lighting being provided as necessary.

Blue-breasted Cordon Bleu (Angolan Cordon Bleu)

Uraeginthus angolensis

Origin: *southern Africa*

Cock: 5in (13cm) Area around the eyes, sides of head, throat, breast, abdomen, rump and uppertail coverts bright pale blue. Grey plumage evident on the abdomen. Upperparts fawn-grey. Tail deep blue. Iris reddish-brown; beak reddish-grey with a black tip; feet and legs pinkish.

Hen: Tends to be rather paler in colour, particularly in terms of blue coloration, which is often also more restricted in area.

Originating from a more temperate part of the world than the other blue waxbills, this species has a reputation for being somewhat hardier, but even so, the birds should not be expected to remain in unheated quarters over the winter. As with related species, they dislike prolonged periods of damp, wet weather, particularly foggy spells.

Their quarters should be designed to give them plenty of cover, which will also be useful during the breeding season to prevent nests from becoming flooded in heavy downpours, which may result in the loss of eggs and chicks. Ideally, a flight adjoining a birdroom should be provided for these and other waxbills. During periods of bad weather, they can be confined in the birdroom with heat and lighting, and allowed into the flight during the spring. In turn, this should ensure that the birds re-acclimatise more rapidly, so maximising the likelihood of breeding success.

Two broods, rather than just a single brood, of chicks may be reared during the summer months. It will be two or three weeks after fledging before the chicks are feeding independently. They are best removed to separate quarters at this stage, provided that this will not cause disturbance to other birds in the aviary that are nesting.

131 Golden-breasted Waxbill *Amandava subflava*

Origin: *most of Africa south of the Sahara*

Cock: 3in (8cm) Upperparts greenish-grey, with a red stripe over the eyes; lores black. Rump and uppertail coverts red. Underparts orangish with dark grey barring on the sides of the breast and flanks. Undertail coverts yellowish-orange. Iris orangish; beak reddish with darker markings; legs and feet pinkish.

Hen: Duller overall, lacking the red eyebrow stripe.

These small waxbills must be kept warm during the initial stages of acclimatisation, but they can then be housed in an outdoor planted flight during the summer, before being brought indoors again to overwinter in a sunny room, where the temperature will not fall below freezing. Small mesh is essential, because these tiny birds may otherwise escape.

A varied diet will help to ensure that even when they are housed within the confines of a cage, these waxbills do not become melanistic. This colour change occurs when their plumage is much blacker than normal from one moult to the next. Although the change is reversible, the altered feathers will be shed only during the subsequent moult, so it may take nearly a year for an affected bird to revert to its proper coloration.

A mixture of small millets and plain canary seed, augmented with green food, such as chickweed and seeding grasses, is to be recommended. Small insects are also an important part of the diet, particularly during the breeding period when there are chicks in the nest. The use of a vitamin and mineral supplements may also be recommended, particularly for newly acquired stock.

Golden-breasted Waxbills are quite adaptable by nature, and they will breed quite readily either in cage or aviary surroundings. At this time, cocks will often sing more readily, although their quiet calls, which resemble the clinking of glasses, are not especially musical. During the mating display the cock dances in front of his intended hen, proffering a stem of grass.

Breeding indoors may occur at virtually any stage, although it will take time for birds to settle down in aviary surroundings before they start to breed. A variety of small nestboxes should be provided for this purpose, and these waxbills will line the interior with a mixture of fine grasses, feathers and other material collected in the aviary. Although they are not especially tolerant at this stage, driving away other birds that approach too close, these waxbills are unlikely to disturb each other's nests, and so they can be kept in a group or in the company of other small birds.

The clutch is usually of four to six eggs, which are incubated by both parents alternately, hatching after about 12 days. It is important that the parents have become thoroughly accustomed to the rearing food beforehand. This should consist of hard-boiled egg or egg food, soaked seeds, small insects, such as hatchling crickets, aphids and whiteworm, and even perhaps some softbill food.

The young may remain in the nest for more than three weeks, and even after flying may return to the nest at night for some time longer, until they are fully independent. They can be recognised at this early stage by their predominantly yellow-grey plumage, with yellow-red tail feathers and black bills.

In spite of their small size, they may have a life expectancy of 10 years, and once they have started to breed, these waxbills may rear as many as four families in one season.

A slightly larger and more colourful form from southern Africa, known as the Cape Orange-breasted or Clarke's Waxbill (*A.s. clarkei*), is sometimes available. This needs similar care to its west African relative, which is at present better known in aviculture.

132 **St Helena Waxbill** (Common Waxbill) *Estrilda astrild*

Origin: *widely distributed across Africa*

Cock: 4in (10cm) *Upperparts fawn-grey, with pinkish suffusion on rump and undertail coverts and a dark wavy pattern covering the entire body. Lores red, extending in a line back beyond the eyes. Sides of head and neck greyish-white. Breast lightish shade of grey-brown, again with wavy markings and pinkish suffusion. Iris brown; beak red; legs and feet greyish.*

Hen: *Somewhat similar, but pink coloration on the underparts is usually paler.*

When in good health, the plumage of these birds is always tight and glossy, giving them a sleek appearance. Their song is insignificant, consisting only of a gurgling sound with some flute-like call notes, but during the mating period, the cock sings almost continuously.

Pairs will normally nest readily when they are given adequate seclusion. Pairs should, however, be kept apart from each other, because cocks are usually very pugnacious at this time, and outbreaks of fighting may lead to nests being deserted. They can be kept in the company of other unrelated waxbills, with far less risk of aggressive outbreaks.

When the birds are actively engaged in building a nest, they are fascinating to watch. It is usually constructed at a relatively high point in the aviary, and it will be domed in shape. A false, so-called cock's nest is built on top and may be lined with feathers, whereas the real nest is concealed below. This is a form of camouflage, helping to hide eggs and chicks from potential predators. Three to five rather pointed white eggs are laid, with the cock and hen sharing incubation duties.

The chicks should start to hatch after about 12 days, and will leave the nest when they are just over a fortnight old. Rearing usually presents no problems, provided that a good supply of live food is available. Young St Helena Waxbills are somewhat duller in coloration than adults, lacking the red lores and having black beaks. Again, they need warm winter quarters, and artificial lighting will be of value in prolonging the feeding period.

133 **Red-eared Waxbill** (Black-rumped Waxbill) *Estrilda troglodytes*

Origin: *central Africa*

Cock: 4in (10cm) *Upperparts greyish-brown with fine darker markings evident here. Lower side of the body light grey, becoming pinker towards the abdomen, with a prominent pink patch in the centre. Lores red, with a stripe extending behind the eyes; sides of the head greyish-white. Uppertail coverts and tail black. Iris brown; beak red; legs and feet brownish.*

Hen: *Hard to differentiate, although during the breeding season, the coloration of the cock becomes a darker, more intense shade of pink over the abdomen.*

Red-eared Waxbills are lively, tolerant birds by nature, and they may be satisfactorily kept in a mixed collection where they will usually live for many years. Although they will do well in an outside flight during the summer, they must be kept in a frost-proof room in the winter, where extra warmth may be required as well, particularly for recently imported or moulting birds.

The relatively loud, but not disturbing, 'chirrupy', flute-like notes, which are produced during his courtship dance, make the cock easily recognisable at this time. He dances around the hen with a blade of grass in his bill. Both members of the pair then utter a softer, gurgling song, with similar sounding call notes. Unfortunately, Red-eared Waxbills can prove rather nervous once they start nesting, and particular attention must be paid to providing them with quiet, undisturbed surroundings.

This species often nests relatively early in the spring, although better results may be obtained later in the summer. They like to use a nestbox in many cases, where they will construct a beautiful nest, with a narrow, hidden entrance passage. This is normally lined with softer material, such as feathers and wool.

A typical clutch is of three to five white and slightly pointed eggs. The birds rear the young largely on live food at first, so that a good supply of small invertebrates will be essential. Egg food and soaked seed may also be eaten, especially once the chicks start to fledge, when they are about a fortnight old. Soaking the seed makes it softer, so that it is easier for the young waxbills to crack and digest it. The fledglings are pale grey in colour at first, with black beaks.

Crimson-rumped Waxbill (Sundevall's Waxbill)

Estrilda rhodopyga

Origin: *northeast Africa*

Cock: 4in (10cm) Upperparts fawn-brown with a wavy body patterning. Crown grey. Wings brown with reddish edging to the feathers. Uppertail coverts and rump wine-red. Cheeks and throat whitish. Underparts pale brownish-yellow, with wavy body pattern, extending to the lower tail coverts, which are also suffused with pink. Iris brown; beak blackish with traces of red at the sides; legs and feet brownish.

Hen: Similar in appearance, but red area on the head and rump may be paler; eye stripes also smaller.

Although less commonly available than the Red-eared Waxbill, Crimson-rumped Waxbills usually prove quite ready to nest in aviary surroundings, although they may take a year or two to settle down before they attempt to nest.

A pair in my own collection built their nest on the floor in an indoor aviary. The completed nest was very large, and made from an assortment of feathers, hemp teasings, woollen threads, straw and grass. Their first clutch consisted of four eggs, which were abandoned. The second nest was made in a nestbox with a narrow entrance at the side. The eggs duly hatched, but a sudden change in the weather caused the parents to abandon their offspring without warning.

The third nest was even larger than the first, and again, four eggs were laid. These hatched, and the young were reared successfully by the adults, who were supplied with cut-up mealworms, grubs, ants' eggs and soaked seed.

Crimson-rumped Waxbills are relatively hardy, but should be brought inside for the duration of the winter in temperate areas.

137 Orange-cheeked Waxbill *Estrilda melpoda*

Origin: *west Africa*

Cock: 4in (10cm) Head bluish-grey; back and wings rosy-brown. Uppertail coverts and rump red. Distinctive orange-red cheek patches on the sides of the head, including the lores. Underparts bluish-grey, with yellowish centre to the abdomen. Tail black. Iris brown; beak red; legs and feet brownish.

Hen: Similar in appearance but may be slightly paler in coloration.

Orange-cheeked Waxbills are frequently available and relatively inexpensive. Once they have settled down, they will usually live for up to 10 years, but obviously the age of imported birds is unlikely to be known. Although breeding is not always easy, many satisfactory results have been recorded.

Both cock and hen have a soft 'chirrupy' song, with that of the male being louder than that of his mate. He dances and displays repeatedly while courting, fanning his tail wide while he bobs up and down in front of the hen. These waxbills are quite peaceable, but usually remain shy, concealing themselves in the vegetation of a planted flight.

They prefer to build in a nestbox in many cases, but may sometimes choose to construct a free-standing nest in vegetation. This will be domed in shape, and the sitting bird will draw blades of grass over the entrance hole to hide itself while incubating the eggs. Sometimes both adults may sit together in the nest, after the hen has laid three or four round-shaped white eggs.

Privacy is important with this species. The adult birds may be drawn off the nest whenever other birds approach too closely, and they must be provided with a quiet spot. Given suitable conditions, the eggs should hatch after an incubation period of about 12 days, and the chicks will be reared largely on small invertebrates at first.

They will fledge when just over two weeks old, but may return to the nest subsequently, especially at dusk, to roost overnight. The youngsters can be easily recognised at this stage by the virtual absence of the orange cheek markings. These become apparent only when they moult for the first time, around six weeks old. Their beaks are also blackish when they first leave the nest.

Dufresne's Waxbill (Swee Waxbill) *Estrilda melanotis*

Origin: *southern Africa*

Cock: 4in (10cm) Cheeks, throat and lores black; head grey; back olive; rump scarlet. Abdomen yellowish-white. Tail black. Iris brown; upper bill black, lower bill red; legs and feet black.

Hen: Less colourful, lacking the black markings on the head.

Less often seen than some species, these delightful waxbills are attractive and peaceable by nature. They can be kept in an outdoor aviary during the warmer months, but can also be housed indoors in a suitably spacious flight. Largely seed-eaters, feeding on a mixture of millets and plain canary seed, they become, like all waxbills, much more insectivorous when rearing chicks.

Dufresne's Waxbills often prefer to build their nest in a low tree or bush, and they may rear several broods in succession, provided that sufficient supplies of suitable live food can be maintained. The claws of adult birds should be checked at the start of the breeding period, and trimmed back if necessary, otherwise, young chicks may become entangled in the claws of a sitting bird and be inadvertently dragged out of the nest as it emerges into the aviary. This applies to other waxbills as well.

The incubation period lasts about 13 days, with the chicks fledging by the time they are three weeks old. They may return to sleep in the nest at night, and they will be fed by their parents for a period, until they are fully independent. They will be mature by the time they are a year old, and they can be expected to nest during the following breeding season. Four eggs form a typical clutch.

Yellow-bellied Waxbill *Estrilda quartinia*

Origin: *Ethiopia and southeast Sudan*

Cock: 4in (10cm) Head and breast grey; back olive-green; belly yellow; rump and uppertail coverts red. Iris brown; upper bill black, lower bill red; legs and feet blackish.

Hen: Paler overall.

A relatively rare species in aviculture, the Yellow-bellied Waxbill is friendly by nature. Care needs to be taken with recently imported individuals, and their acclimatisation to outdoor aviary life should not be rushed. They usually require additional warmth and should always be given spray millet for the first few weeks after arrival. Soaking a spray in warm water overnight is also recommended, because weaker birds will often eat this softened seed, even if they will not feed on dry seeds. It can literally prove a life-saver for these and other small finches.

Even once established, these birds prefer warm surroundings. They can only be kept in an outside aviary in the summer in temperate climates, and they should be housed only in the company of small, non-aggressive finches. Keep them in a moderately warm room in the winter.

Yellow-bellied Waxbills are quite suitable for an indoor aviary, and they may breed successfully in such surroundings. Pairs will normally roost together in a nestbox, and will also build a nest here, using fine grasses and lining the interior with soft feathers.

The three or four eggs laid should hatch after about 12 days. For the first week or so the chicks will be fed mainly on invertebrates, such as aphids and hatchling crickets. Fruit and greenstuff may also be taken, in addition to their usual seed diet.

The young waxbills will leave the nest for the first time when they are about three weeks old, being independent within a further fortnight. At this stage, they resemble their parents in terms of their plumage, but their beaks are black, and their legs and feet will be greyish.

140 Black-cheeked Waxbill *Estrilda erythronotos*

Origin: *eastern and southern Africa*

Cock: 5in (13cm) *Crown and nape grey with dark pencilling. Back vinaceous; rump and upper coverts carmine-red; tail black. Wings greyish to white with clearly marked black barring. Primaries brown with pale cross bars. Cheeks and chin black, with the remainder of the plumage here being shades of grey. Middle of the abdomen and undertail coverts black. The remainder of the abdomen grey, narrowly-barred and with a carmine sheen. Iris reddish-brown; beak black; legs and feet black.*

Hen: Similar, but usually distinguishable by greyish-brown undertail coverts, with paler red feathering on the flanks and vent.*

Although Black-cheeked Waxbills may be used to cold nights, coming from areas of Africa with wide temperature variations between daytime and night, they need to be kept warm, especially when recently imported. A dull-emitter infrared lamp suspended over a wire mesh flight close to a perch will provide them with a local heat spot, where they can warm themselves when required.

As with all waxbills a suitably wide variety of foods should be offered, although small seeds form the basis of their diet. Seeding grasses, chickweed, softbill food, a little grated cheese and a good supply of live food, which is especially important when there are young chicks in the nest, should all figure on the menu.

The song of the Black-cheeked Waxbill, like that of other species, is insignificant but melodious and low. The hen's call consists of two short, flute-like notes; her mate's call is of three notes, of which the last is prolonged and high pitched.

They are active birds by nature and will seek seclusion among dense foliage in a planted flight. These waxbills also enjoy basking in the sun, and they will rummage about on the floor of the flight in search of insects. Black-cheeked Waxbills also bathe readily, if an opportunity presents itself, but care should be taken over providing open containers of water in the flight, because young birds could become water-logged and may drown.

Pairs will nest in a large aviary and sometimes even in a spacious flight cage. They often choose to build their nest in a box, creating a well-concealed side entrance hole. The box itself should be well hidden by vegetation to give the birds more privacy. Breeding details are similar to those of other members of the genus. Bengalese Finches have been used successfully as foster parents for this species, but, obviously, it is better if a pair rears its own offspring. These birds should be overwintered in heated accommodation.

39 Violet-eared Waxbill (Common Grenadier Waxbill)

Uraeginthus granatina

Origin: *southern Africa*

Cock: 6in (15cm) Upperparts deep rich brown. Forehead and rump deep violet-blue; underparts chestnut; cheeks violet; tail, which is 2in (5cm) long, black. Iris brownish; beak red; legs and feet greyish.

Hen: Much lighter on the head, back and underparts; cheeks very pale violet.

These stunningly attractive waxbills are not commonly available, and they need particular care if they have been recently imported. They must be kept warm, with the temperature being reduced only very gradually. Plenty of small live food, as well as soaked seed, such as millet sprays, should be offered, along with greenstuff, softbill food, possibly a small quantity of grated cheese and even a little nectar, as well as pollen granules on occasions. This should help to ensure that the birds settle in well, and in due course, when the weather is mild and dry, they can be transferred to an outdoor planted aviary, for the summer months.

Although they can be kept with other small finches and softbills, only one pair of Violet-eared Waxbills should be housed in an aviary, because cocks are very pugnacious towards each other. It is also inadvisable to house them with closely related species, such as the Purple Grenadier (*Uraeginthus ianthinogaster*), which also has violet markings on the breast and abdomen, or with any of the Cordon Bleu group.

Violet-eared Waxbills have been bred successfully on a number of occasions since 1927. They will construct a typically domed nest, with a side entrance. Between three and five eggs form the usual clutch, and these hatch after an incubation period of about 13 days. Both parents sit during this stage, and once the chicks have hatched, the amount of live food required will rise dramatically. If supplies are insufficient, breeding disappointments will be inevitable.

Young Violet-eareds fledge at about three weeks old, at which stage they are considerably duller than their parents, being predominantly earthy-brown in colour. Their rump is dull blue, and the tail feathers are short and blackish. The tiny blue nodules, which guided their parents to feed them in the nest, are evident at the sides of the mouth at first, but these disappear soon after fledging. The young birds will be independent about two weeks later.

142 Lavender Finch (Grey Waxbill) *Estrilda caerulescens*

Origin: *west Africa*

Cock: 5in (13cm) Predominantly bluish-grey; rump, uppertail coverts and central tail feathers red. White spotting may be evident on the flanks. Lores black. Iris brown; beak black with reddish markings at the base; legs and feet black.

Hen: Slightly smaller; a less vivid shade of grey and red overall.

Although the distinction in plumage between males and females may not be especially clear, the cock will become easily recognisable during the mating season from his flute-like call notes. Lavender Finches are peaceable, and they can usually be kept without problems in the company of other small birds. They will play like tits, being full of curiosity, and will climb up and down branches. They soon become tame. When they go to roost, sitting in a row with their heads inclined towards each other, they sing a soft murmuring song, which finishes on a long, drawn-out note.

As with all waxbills, careful acclimatisation is required. If possible, these birds should not be accommodated in cages, for they are then most likely to pluck one another's feathers, so that they look ragged, even though they are not in poor health. When transferred to more spacious surroundings, their plumage should regrow.

Lavender Finches normally nest quite readily in an outside flight or an indoor aviary. They build a rounded nest, often in a box bush (*Buxus*), or will use a nestbox located in a secluded part of the aviary, partially hidden by vegetation, and taking a range of nesting material.

The hen lays about four white eggs, which should hatch after 12 days. Suitable live food, some of which the parents will obtain in a planted flight, is essential for rearing purposes. The chicks fledge when they are about a fortnight old.

It is best to overwinter these waxbills indoors in a suitable flight, and a birdroom will prove invaluable for this purpose.

Black-tailed Lavender Finch *Estrilda perreini*

Origin: *widely distributed in southern Africa*

Cock: 5in (13cm) Resembles the Lavender Finch but tends to be a darker shade of grey. Uppertail coverts red; undertail coverts and tail black. There may also be an area of black plumage on the chin. Iris brown; beak entirely black (another clear point of distinction from the Lavender Finch); legs and feet blackish.

Hen: Similar but distinguishable by her greyer undertail coverts.

In spite of their extensive area of distribution, Black-tailed Lavender Finches are not well known in aviculture. Their basic requirements do not differ from those of the Lavender Finch, but it has been shown that the availability of insects may influence the number of eggs laid in the first instance. Clutches of seven or eight eggs were produced by hens regularly provided with ant pupae prior to breeding, whereas in other cases, a maximum of five eggs were laid.

As in the case of other waxbills, the tail is used in their display. Both adults share the incubation duties, which last for about 13 days. The chicks may not fledge until they are nearly three weeks old. A generous supply of live food is vital to ensure breeding success.

These finches need to be kept warm and cannot be expected to overwinter outdoors. Instead, they will need to be brought into heated surroundings, before being carefully re-acclimatised in the spring. Alternatively, they can be kept in an indoor planted aviary throughout the year.

45 Red-billed Firefinch (Senegal Firefinch, Common Firefinch)
Lagonosticta senegala

Origin: *widely distributed across Africa south of the Sahara*

Cock: 4in (10cm) Pinkish-red overall. Rump, undertail coverts and underparts red, the underparts becoming browner towards the vent. The sides and flanks have white dots. Iris reddish; beak red with black on sides; legs and feet pinkish.

Hen: Significantly duller in colour, being mainly brownish, with red plumage confined to the rump, uppertail coverts and forming a narrow ring around the eyes. Underparts yellowish-grey.

Firefinches are often available, with their gorgeous coloration and pleasant dispositions ensuring their popularity. When they are first imported, however, they may be in poor condition, and they must always be acclimatised very carefully, as they are susceptible to any sudden fall in temperature. They also dislike damp weather. A diet as suggested for other related species suits them well.

Once settled, pairs will breed readily. They usually prefer to use a nestbox, rather than building in the open, but they may be persuaded to breed in a dense box bush (*Buxus*). As nesting material, they will take hemp teasings, small blades of grass and horsehair, in addition to commercially available nesting material. They are quite social by nature, and a number of pairs can be kept satisfactorily together.

Three or four eggs are normally laid, hatching after a period of 11 days. The young birds will then be reared on a diet of small invertebrates, and the adults may also take a soft food at this stage, which will be a valuable addition to their diet. The chicks will leave the nest for the first time when they are about 19 days old. At this stage, they are greyish-brown in colour and show only a little red on the tail feathers.

Heated winter quarters must be provided for these and other fire-finches, with the birds being removed from the outside aviary in the early autumn, before the weather turns cold.

Black-faced Firefinch (Masked Firefinch) *Lagonosticta larvata*

Origin: *west and central Africa*

Cock: 5in (13cm) *Crown and back of head dark grey. Above the beak is a dark stripe, which broadens over the eyes and cheeks. Throat and lower part of abdomen black. Back, breast and upper abdomen deep wine-red; there are a few white spots on the sides of the breast. Wings brown; tail feathers dark red. Iris brownish; beak grey; legs and feet grey.*

Hen: *Greyish-brown above with a reddish sheen; abdomen soft pink becoming beige. Head light grey.*

Although not regularly available, it is certainly worth obtaining pairs of this species. These members of the waxbill group are peaceful in a mixed flight, and they usually nest readily in suitable surroundings. Unfortunately, it can be difficult to recognise a pair with certainty, because they may be offered alongside other firefinches, and hens of other species are rather similar in coloration.

Careful initial acclimatisation is again essential, and in temperate regions these finches must be kept in a moderately heated area during the winter. A diet based on a foreign finch mix, composed of a variety of millets and plain canary seed, will suit them well, although a supply of live food is also important, particularly during the breeding season when there are chicks in the nest.

Breeding details are similar to those of the Red-billed Firefinch. These waxbills have an attractive, soft flute-like call, with the cock sometimes making clucking sounds as well. At first, young Black-faced Firefinches resemble adult hens, but by three months old, it will be possible to sex them with certainty, as males will by then have acquired their characteristic black facial markings.

Bar-breasted Firefinch *Lagonosticta rufopicta*

Origin: *west and central Africa*

Cock: 4in (10cm) Forehead, sides of head and lores pinkish-red. Crown and neck greyish-brown; back brown; uppertail coverts red. Wings grey-brown to brown; chin, throat and breast pinkish-red, with fine white dots on the breast. Remainder of underparts yellowish-brown. Iris brown; beak red; legs and feet brownish.

Hen: Rather similar, but usually pinkish-red areas paler.

Occasionally imported, these firefinches do not differ greatly in their requirements from the Black-faced Firefinch, and, like that species, they must be carefully acclimatised. Accurate identification, notably of hens, can again be difficult. The most obvious distinction between the Bar-breasted Firefinch and the Red-billed Firefinch is the presence of small white spots all over the breast of the Bar-breasted Firefinch, whereas these markings are confined to the sides of the body in the latter species. However, as there are nine or more differentiated races of the Red-billed Firefinch, the problem of identifying hens correctly is magnified. With their paler colouring and less definite markings, they vary very little from each other. In the case of the Bar-breasted Firefinch there are subspecies, *L.r. lateritia*, found in the south of Sudan and northern Zaïre, and *L.r. rufopicta*. The overall coloration of the plumage in this case is greyer, with more distinctive white transverse lines on the breast.

An interesting characteristic of the Bar-breasted Firefinch is the way in which it will apparently seek to hide on the ground, rather than flying off when it is disturbed. In addition, these firefinches often use a nest site for roosting purposes, whereas the Red-billed Firefinch usually prefers to spend the night on a perch.

Sydney Waxbill (Red-browed Finch) *Aegintha temporalis*

Origin: *east and south east Australia*

Cock: 4in (10cm) Forehead olive-grey; eyebrow stripes and lores red. Breast and belly whitish. Back olive; uppertail coverts and rump wine-red.

Hen: Similar in appearance.

Waxbills are generally an African group, except for the two *Amandava* species that occur in Asia. There is some uncertainty about the precise relationship of this species, however, in spite of its common name. Some taxonomists believe that it is more closely related to the grassfinches than to the waxbills, pointing to the fact that these birds predominate in Australia.

Difficulties in sexing can present breeding difficulties. Ideally, it is best to commence a breeding programme with several birds, which should ensure that you have at least one pair. The behaviour of cocks during the breeding season will provide further pointers, as they display to their intended mates holding a stem of grass. Interestingly, although young cocks can be quite easily distinguished from young hens because they sing at an early age, older cocks apparently may not utter a note.

These birds will build a nest of fine grasses in a nestbox or a dense shrub. The typical clutch of four or five eggs will be incubated by both cock and hen in turn, with this phase lasting for about 13 days.

The best rearing food for Sydney Waxbills consists of soaked millets, bread and milk, egg food and plenty of green food. They may also eat invertebrates at this stage. The chicks remain in the nest for about three weeks, and are soon feeding themselves.

One of the idiosyncrasies of these finches is that adults will also feed the young of other species sharing their quarters. Young Zebra Finches appear to be almost instinctively aware of this and often immediately attach themselves to Sydney Waxbills after fledging, allowing themselves to be fed by them.

Unfortunately, Sydney Waxbills are now scarce in collections in both Britain and North America, although they may be seen occasionally on mainland Europe as well as, of course, in Australian aviaries. This is a loss to aviculture, because these finches are both attractive and amenable by nature. They can stand northern temperate climates, but should spend winter nights in a snug shelter, only being allowed out into the flight during the day. In very cold weather, extra heating may be necessary.

Red Avadavat (Tiger Finch) *Amandava amandava*

Origin: *Indian subcontinent to China and Indonesia*

Cock: 4in (10cm) In breeding condition head and neck red, with a white line under each eye; lores black. Back dark brown, with red tipping to the feathers. Wings dark brown, with white spots, which are also present on the sides of the body. Underparts red; abdomen, lower tail coverts and tail black. Iris reddish; beak red; legs and feet brownish.

Hen: Resembles an out-of-colour cock. Greyish-brown upperparts, with the sides of the head being greyer; uppertail coverts and rump red; sides of the body brownish, with widely distributed patterning. Underparts whitish-yellow.

Only when adult and during the breeding season do cocks of this species sport their beautiful, predominantly red plumage. At other times, they resemble hens and can be distinguished only by their quaint song. Hens may also sing, but more softly.

When courting, the cock is very active, dancing around the hen and displaying with his tail spread. The birds will nest readily, but nearly always prefer to use shrubs, particularly box bushes (*Buxus*), where they build a hanging, pouch-shaped nest, sometimes with two entrances.

The hen lays from four to six eggs on average, and these should hatch after about 11 days. Small insects and an increased supply of green food are likely to be vital at this stage if the young chicks are to be reared successfully. Fledging occurs when they are about 18 days old. At this stage, the young are light brown, with dull spots on their wings and black bills.

Red Avadavats show to best advantage either in an aviary or a birdroom flight. In such surroundings they are less likely to develop melanistic plumage, when heavy black patches may cover almost the entire body, although this change may be only transitory. If their environmental conditions improve, the feathering will revert to normal at the next moult.

A slightly smaller and distinctive form of the Red Avadavat is known as the Strawberry Finch or Chinese Avadavat (*A.a. punicea*) (Plate 144), in spite of the fact that it originates from Indonesia as well as from Indo-China. In breeding plumage the cock's upperparts are darker, and there is a brighter shade of red on the underparts, with smaller white dots instead of black. The hen is also darker, like the cock in eclipse plumage.

There is a third race, known as the Yellow-bellied Tiger Finch (*A.a. flavidiventris*), which comes from the islands of Lambok, Flores, Timor and Sumba, Indonesia, as well as occurring in south China and Burma on the Asiatic mainland. The lores of the cock are red, and the abdomen is orange-yellow. The small white spots also appear on the breast and are not confined just to the sides of the body. The upperparts tend to be lighter overall, with the underparts being a more yellowish shade. Their care should not differ from that outlined previously.

3 Green Avadavat (Green Munia) *Amandava formosa*

Origin: *India*

Cock: 4in (10cm) Head and uppertail coverts yellowish-green; upperparts olive-green. Underparts mainly yellow, with white horizontal lines on the olive-green sides here. Tail black. Iris brown; beak red; legs and feet brownish.

Hen: Less brightly coloured, being more greyish with the abdomen a paler shade of yellow.

These avadavats are not considered to be as hardy as the Red Avadavat. Although they may be kept outside in the summer, they must be brought indoors during the winter. Once they are acclimatised, however, they can live to a considerable age, perhaps for 10 years or more.

In addition to a foreign finch seed mixture, composed mainly of millets, Green Avadavats must also be provided with a regular supply of invertebrates. They are quiet by nature, with similar breeding habits to those of their red relative. It may be a good idea to grate a little cuttlefish bone with a sharp knife, because hens have a reputation for being susceptible to egg-binding. This can be caused by a calcium deficiency, and hens may have difficulty in nibbling pieces off the bone with their small beaks.

They should also be prevented from breeding early in the year, when the weather may suddenly turn cold, as chilling is another factor that may be implicated in egg-binding. Assuming that all goes well, however, chicks should be reared successfully. They can be distinguished from their parents after fledging by their coloration. Young Green Avadavats are duller, being predominantly greyish-green, with black beaks.

136 Peter's Twinspot (Peter's Spotted Firefinch, Red-throated Firefinch) *Hypargos niveoguttatus*

Origin: *east Africa*

Cock: 5in (13cm) Head brown-grey; back red-brown; uppertail coverts, neck, sides of the head and chin carmine red. Underparts black with white spotted markings on the flanks. Wings reddish-brown to black-brown. Tail black, with reddish markings on the tips and bases of the outer feathers, centre feathers are entirely black. Iris brown; beak blackish-grey; legs and feet horn-coloured.

Hen: Has less red on her head, is paler and has less evident spotting.

These beautiful finches are only irregularly available, and they are always rather expensive. They must be acclimatised with care, especially if they are in poor feather condition, which will render them susceptible to chilling. They like the sun and must be kept warm at first. Later on, once well-established, they can prove quite hardy, but they should always be provided with warm, frost-proof winter accommodation.

Peters' Twinspots will thrive on a typical waxbill diet, including spray and loose millet, which can be soaked on occasions, particularly for birds that may be slightly off-colour or rearing chicks. Green food, egg food and small invertebrates should also be offered, especially when they are rearing chicks. Fruit, such as sweet apple or grapes, may also be popular, along with bread and milk.

In a reasonably well-sheltered and planted aviary, these birds will hunt for insects themselves, often hopping about on the grass under shrubs for this purpose. They like to make their nest, for which grasses, coconut fibres and similar material should be provided, just above ground level in a dense shrub such as box (*Buxus*) or a dwarf conifer. The entrance is carefully concealed by a tunnel of grass, although occasionally a pair may prefer to use a nestbox.

The cock bird displays to his mate on the ground, carrying a feather or a blade of grass in his beak, dancing around the hen with outspread wings and an upstretched neck. She will respond by moving her tail swiftly from side to side. During the nesting period, a pair will drive other birds away from the vicinity of the nest, although they do not become especially aggressive at this stage. There is a risk that repeated intrusions may cause them to abandon their nest, so the aviary must not be overcrowded. Pairs may also resent nest inspections, and they are best left alone at this stage.

After a period of 13 days, the chicks hatch and will fly in a further three weeks. Between three and six offspring form the typical brood, and live food is particularly vital during the rearing phase. Youngsters show some similarity to adult hens, but their heads are more brownish with a hint of red evident on the back and wings.

Aurora Finch (Crimson-winged Pytilia) *Pytilia phoenicoptera*

Origin: *west and central Africa*

Cock: 5in (13cm) *Head and back grey, with the back and rump showing a red suffusion. Uppertail coverts carmine red, as are the central tail feathers, with the remainder being blackish-brown. Red and brown are apparent on the wings. Breast narrowly barred with white; underparts grey. Iris red; beak black; legs and feet pinkish.*

Hen: *Decidedly more brown with more wavy brown markings on the underparts; legs and feet reddish-brown.*

These steady and confiding waxbills will settle well, and they can be kept quite satisfactorily in an indoor flight, although breeding is more likely in a planted aviary. They require careful acclimatisation, and even when they are established they will need heated winter surroundings. The song of the cock bird is soft and short, but melodious, and is usually heard towards the evening. When courting, he will hop with raised tail round and round his hen, bowing and uttering a quiet song.

Aurora Finches like to build their nest in a box bush (*Buxus*), but they will also use a nestbox. The nest itself is constructed in an untidy fashion from grasses, hair and fibres, with the inside usually lined with small feathers. A typical clutch consists of four eggs, which are incubated by both adults and which hatch after about 12 days.

The young birds will fledge from the age of about 18 days onwards, and at this stage they resemble adult hens, although the red plumage is much lighter and their beaks are greyish. Live food, such as fruit flies and whiteworm, is again vital for rearing purposes, and pairs may well prove prolific under suitable circumstances, rearing perhaps four broods in a season.

There is a slightly larger, more localised form of the Aurora Finch, restricted to a small area of northeast Africa, which is known as the Abyssinian or Red-billed Aurora Finch (*P.p. lineata*). Apart from its size, these birds can also be distinguished by their red bills. They are not common in aviculture.

146 Melba Finch (Green-winged Pytilia) *Pytilia melba*

Origin: *widely distributed across Africa*

Cock: 5in (13cm) *Forehead, cheeks and throat scarlet. Lores, head and neck grey; back and wings olive-green. Abdomen whitish with black barring sometimes broken up into spots; yellow band on the lower edge of the breast. Tail red. Iris reddish-brown; beak red; legs and feet yellowish-brown.*

Hen: *Lacks the red markings on the head, which is entirely grey; paler overall.*

A number of distinctive races occur through the wide range of this species, differing not only in their plumage, but also in their song. Studies have revealed local variations, rather like dialects.

Attractive aviary birds, Melba Finches, like other *Pytilias*, need careful acclimatisation, and a dull-emitter infrared lamp suspended over their quarters indoors can be helpful as a local heat source. If these or other waxbills appear slightly fluffed up on arrival, an increase in the temperature of their surroundings may be required. The advantage of the dull-emitter is that it gives off heat only, rather than light, which can be controlled independently. Approximately 12 hours light is recommended initially, so that the birds have adequate opportunity to feed. Their small size relative to their surface area means that they are vulnerable to hypothermia if they do not have an adequate intake of food.

Live food should be offered regularly, especially to new arrivals and breeding birds. The use of a probiotic can also be recommended, being most easily administered in the drinking water. This will help to stabilise the beneficial bacteria in the intestinal tract, so lessening the risk of enteritis or other similar complaints, which can be rapidly fatal in small birds.

Although Melba Finches will live in harmony with birds of other species, they may prove very aggressive during the breeding period, especially towards their own kind. More than one pair should not be kept together. Pairs prefer to build a domed nest in a dense shrub, although they will sometimes use a nestbox.

Breeding details do not differ significantly from those of related species, with the young birds being fed for about a fortnight after fledging before they are fully independent. They moult for the first time after four weeks, and acquire full adult plumage by the time they are seven months of age. Two or three clutches may be reared in the course of a season, and the birds should then be brought into heated quarters for the duration of the winter, before being allowed back into the aviary once the weather warms up again in the following spring.

Quail Finch *Ortygospiza atricollis*

Origin: *a distinctive population occurs in west Africa; the species is found over a wide area of east and south Africa*

Cock: 4in (10cm) *Head and throat black, with a small white chin spot. Upperparts greyish-brown; lower parts brown with black and white barring on the breast and along the flanks. Iris brown; upper bill black, lower bill pinkish-red; legs and feet pinkish.*

Hen: *Lacks the black coloration on the head, which is brownish-grey; plumage paler overall.*

This description applies to the west African race. The widely distributed eastern race, *O.a. muelleri*, can be distinguished by the white orbital ring around the eyes, white lores and the much larger chin spot.

Quail Finches differ from other finches in that they are almost entirely terrestrial, scrabbling in sand and taking dust baths. If their aviary is turfed, they will conceal themselves in the grass. Their acclimatisation needs to be carried out carefully, and hens have a reputation for being particularly delicate. They need warmth, an opportunity to bathe and dry moss in the corner of their quarters. A double breeding cage can be used for this purpose in the early stages.

Once they can be transferred outdoors Quail Finches will develop into fascinating aviary occupants, but their accommodation must be carefully prepared. They dislike prolonged periods of wet weather, and their flight should be well screened to protect them from the elements. A good covering of grass on the floor is also recommended. At night, they will normally roost in a clump of moss or a branch off the ground.

Care must be taken because they are rather nervous birds by nature and will fly vertically if disturbed, colliding with the roof of their quarters. They are very quick when moving across the floor of the flight, like true ground birds such as quails. Sometimes when they sense danger, they flatten themselves on the ground, with their mouths wide open to conceal their presence further.

Quail Finches will live in harmony with other birds and can be kept in groups. During the breeding period, there may be mild disputes between cocks, but serious fighting is unlikely. Their quarters must be kept clean however, and a close watch maintained on their feet. It the toes become caked with dirt, this must be soaked off before harm results. It is better to use a good covering of sand and gravel in those parts of the flight that is not turfed, because wet mud is more likely to cake around the feet and dry there.

Although mainly seed-eaters, Quail Finches will eat not only a mixture of millets and plain canary seed, but will also consume green food and insects. For breeding purposes, their aviary should contain tussocks of grass. They will build a round nest, well concealed under or between clumps, using grass blades, coconut fibres and similar material and incorporating a narrow entry passage. The cock and hen incubate the two or three eggs alternately, and these should hatch in 14 days. The chicks are reared largely on small insects, as well as some seeds and greenstuff. They fledge when they are about three weeks old.

150 Cut-throat (Ribbon Finch) *Amadina fasciata*

Origin: *central and east Africa*

Cock: 5in (13cm) Upperparts of the body yellowish-brown, with a greyish sheen and small dark brown horizontal markings. Wings greyish-brown, with black streaks and yellow dots. Uppertail coverts and rump light brown with paler edges. Tail black, with white markings. Throat and sides of the head white, with a large carmine-red area below. Breast and flanks dotted with black; underparts yellowish-brown, with a more prominent chestnut area in the centre here. Vent whitish. Iris brown; beak pinkish-grey; legs and feet pink.

Hen: Easily distinguishable by the absence of the red throat band.

There is also a race from east Africa, *A.f. alexanderi* (Plate 149), which is sometimes available. Cocks of this subspecies have very dark barring and a particularly prominent, wider area of red feathering on the neck. Their basic coloration is a deeper shade of beige-brown, with the scaly markings also being more extensive. Hens are also more boldly-marked. These popular finches are widely kept and bred, and care is identical for both races.

Although the cock's song is not especially loud, even at the start of the breeding period, he may often be seen singing with his throat feathers puffed out. Cut-throats are quite assertive by nature, becoming more aggressive generally at the start of the breeding season, and they are not really suitable companions for smaller waxbills. They can be accommodated with weavers or Java Sparrows.

A close watch should be kept on hens, because they appear to be particularly susceptible to egg-binding. Pairs should not be encouraged to breed until the weather is warm, and cuttlefish bone must be freely available throughout the year. A shortage of cuttlefish bone may contribute to a calcium deficiency, which is probably the underlying cause of most cases of egg-binding. A general supplement can also be given by sprinkling it over green food or soaked seed.

Cut-throats will breed in nestboxes, and they build a nest here with any suitable material, ranging from leaves to feathers. Items can be provided for this purpose. The hen will lay between four and six eggs, which the parents take turns to incubate. Hatching should take place about 12 days later, when insects become a more significant part of the birds' diet.

The first recorded breeding success was achieved in France in 1770, and Cut-throats have even nested successfully in budgerigar-type breeding

cages, although failure through disturbance is more likely in these surroundings. When the chicks fledge at about three weeks old, young cocks
will already be displaying their characteristic throat marking. They are
hardy birds once acclimatised as necessary, and will live for years in an
outside aviary with snug roosting quarters.

❽ Red-headed Finch (Paradise Sparrow) *Amadina erythrocephala*

Origin: *southern Africa*

Cock: 5in (13cm) *Scarlet plumage extends from the top of the head down to the
throat; lores whitish-grey. Upperparts greyish-brown, with black and cream
markings on the wing coverts and black streaks also apparent on the wings. Throat
greyish-white; breast a purer shade of white, broken by brown and black speckling.
Abdomen reddish-brown, becoming white around the vent. Tail brownish-black
with white tipping. Iris brown; beak steel grey; legs and feet pinkish.*

*Hen: Easily distinguishable by the absence of red on the head; underparts also
lighter.*

Although they are less often available than the Cut-throat, these finches
tend to be of a more placid disposition. It may, however, be better to house
pairs individually in small flights, not because they are aggressive, but
rather because they are easily disturbed when nesting and may abandon
their attempts.

On their own, Red-headed Finches will readily build in a nestbox. They
may even occupy an old nest, built by weavers perhaps, and refurbish it
for their needs. Their breeding habits are similar to those of the Cut-throat,
with insects being in demand particularly when there are chicks in the nest.
The young birds will fledge at around three weeks old, by which time cocks
will be showing the characteristic red plumage on their heads. They may
be mature by the time they are six months old. These finches are somewhat
less hardy than Cut-throats and may have to be brought inside over the
winter months.

Bib Finch (African Parson Finch, Madagascar Mannikin)

Lonchura nana

Origin: *Madagascar*

Cock: 4in (10cm) *Forehead, lores and uppertail coverts light olive-brown. Tail
black; underparts light brown with pink margins and scaly markings. Undertail
coverts grey with yellow-brown margins. Iris brown; upper bill black, lower bill
horn in colour; legs and feet pinkish.*

Hen: Similar in appearance.

Few breeders keep this species today, and it has become one of the rarer African munias in collections at the time of writing. Even so, it makes a desirable addition for those keen to breed, for it is one of the most prolific members of the group. Broods of six chicks, produced in three or four successive nests, are no exception.

Given the obvious initial difficulty in sexing Bib Finches, it is advisable to purchase several in the first instance. In time, you will be able to distinguish pairs, as cocks perform their nuptial dance and sing their pleasant song. During the breeding season, they will chase other birds from the nest and even persecute them. They should, therefore, be kept apart from species such as waxbills, being housed either in a small planted aviary or a large flight cage. Breeding is most likely to occur in the former surroundings. Their nest is built in any suitable receptacle, such as a nestbox or basket, and is constructed from fibres or grass and lined with feathers.

The birds incubate alternately during the daytime, with both staying together at night in the nest. Incubation lasts 12 days, and the young birds will remain in the nest for a further three weeks. After a further 10 days they will be entirely independent, and they should not disturb their parents, which are likely to be breeding again. Their diet should be the same as for other munias. Although these finches may be able to overwinter in the shelter of an outside aviary, a frost-proof room will be better.

155 Bronze-winged Mannikin (Bronze Mannikin, Hooded Finch)

Lonchura cucullata

Origin: *widely distributed across Africa*

Cock: 4in (10cm) Head and neck black, with a greenish sheen. Wings and back dark brownish-grey, with a black mark and a green sheen on the scapulars. Uppertail coverts and rump whitish, with dark patterning here. Sides of the breast marked with black, with the greyish-brown sides having horizontal white stripes; underparts otherwise white. Tail black. Iris brown; upper bill black, lower bill greyish; legs and feet blackish.

Hen: Similar in appearance.

Although breeding results are not always easily accomplished with this species, the attractive markings and lively nature of these mannikins have helped to ensure their popularity. The song of the cock bird may be barely audible, but this is the only certain way by which to distinguish the sexes.

For breeding purposes, a planted flight is recommended, although occasionally, pairs have nested in cage surroundings. A variety of nesting boxes and baskets should be provided, along with a good selection of suitable material, such as moss, grass stems and similar items. These mannikins cannot be housed alongside waxbills, as they can be rather aggressive, and they are best kept in groups on their own. If kept in the company of other munias, they may hybridise with them, which is not to be recommended.

When breeding, Bronze-winged Mannikins construct a simple nest, and the hens lay four to six eggs. These should hatch about 12 days later, with incubation duties being shared. In addition to their usual diet of foreign finch seed and green food, these finches will also eat a variety of small live food when rearing their chicks. The young birds will moult into adult plumage by the time they are about six months old.

Black and White Mannikin (Rufous-backed Mannikin)
Lonchura bicolor

Origin: *widely distributed across Africa*

Cock: 4in (10cm) Head and breast black; back and wings brown; belly white. Whitish barring is apparent on the wings, while the rump and the uppertail coverts have white transverse stripes. Tail black. Iris brown; beak greyish; legs and feet black.

Hen: Similar in appearance.

Although there may be differences in the plumage of individual birds of this species, this is a reflection of their area of origin, rather than a means of distinguishing the sexes. Variations in the markings on the flanks are typically evident between the different races. For breeding purposes, a group should be purchased in the hope of obtaining one or more pairs. These mannikins tend to be quite peaceful by nature, at least when kept in a colony. Fighting may be more likely to break out within the confines of a cage.

The song of the cock bird is of lower pitch than that of the hen and not as sharp. He often displays while singing, fanning his tail in front of his intended mate and moving his head at the same time. Breeding results are more likely to be achieved in aviary surroundings, and these birds may prefer to construct their own nest in a dense bush rather than in a nestbox. Their general care and breeding details are similar to those of other African mannikins. Young birds in nest feather can be identified by their paler coloration. They have brownish rather than black plumage.

Magpie Mannikin *Lonchura fringilloides*

Origin: *central and eastern Africa*

Cock: 5in (13cm) Head, neck, rump and uppertail coverts black; wings and back dark brown, with white lines evident on the scapulars. Underparts white, with black plumage evident on the sides of the breast and rusty-brown markings below. Tail black. Iris reddish-brown; upper bill black, lower bill dark grey; legs and feet greyish.

Hen: Similar in appearance.

The common name of these birds stems from their predominantly black and white plumage, although young Magpie Mannikins are browner when they leave the nest. Their beaks are quite large and powerful, and it is inadvisable to mix them with smaller, weaker companions. Kept in a flight with birds of similar size, however, they tend not to be aggressive. Although relatively hardy once established, these mannikins must, like the other species, be properly acclimatised, and they may benefit from additional heating and lighting in particularly cold periods of weather.

Magpie Mannikins tend to prove more ready to nest in aviary surroundings than the Bronze-winged Mannikin. They are quieter by nature, and the cock is recognisable only by his song (which is almost inaudible) and his behaviour during the mating season. Pairs should have adequate space for breeding purposes, because they may otherwise engage in territorial disputes, which can lead to nests being abandoned.

A simple nest is usually constructed in a nestbox, and between four and six eggs form the typical clutch, hatching after a period of about 12 days. The young are normally reared without problems, although disturbances should be kept to a minimum at this stage. The adults will often take live food and egg food when they have chicks, but they have also been known to rear their offspring successfully on nothing other than white bread softened in a nectar solution, and their usual diet of millets and other small seeds.

Pairs may often breed several times in rapid succession. Young birds will take several months to acquire adult plumage, and they are usually tolerated by their parents, even after they are feeding independently.

158 Silverbill *Lonchura malabarica*

Origin: *west and central Africa; in Asia, east to the Indian subcontinent*

Cock: 4in (10cm) Upperparts light brown; the rump and lower tail covert white, with some black evident on the outer feathers. Flight feathers and tail black. Sides of the head and underparts fawn. Iris brown; beak greyish; legs and feet pinkish.

Hen: Similar in appearance.

There are two distinct subspecies of this popular finch, with the description above referring to the nominate race, which comes from Asia. The African Silverbill (*L.m. cantans*) (Plate 157) can be distinguished by the difference in its rump coloration, which is blackish rather than white. The requirements of both races are otherwise identical.

Silverbills are frequently available, and they rank among the easiest of all finches to breed and rear successfully. They have also been used as foster parents on occasions, hatching and caring for chicks of other species. These birds are worth keeping for this purpose in case a nest of eggs is neglected by more nervous birds; both Red-eared Waxbills and Cordon Bleus, for example, have been reared successfully by Silverbills.

In order to obtain a pair of Silverbills you will probably need to purchase a group. In time, the soft song of the cock will become apparent; they will usually start to sing once they have settled down in new surroundings, even outside the breeding period.

Although their plumage is not as colourful as that of other foreign finches, the behaviour of Silverbills is so charming that they are a real pleasure to keep, and they will thrive in indoor quarters. Indeed, it may be best to breed them in cage surroundings so that they are not disturbed by other birds. Silverbills are not hardy, and they should be brought indoors for the duration of the winter.

They will build in a nestbox or nesting basket, constructing a narrow slip-in entrance and lining the interior with feathers. Alternatively, if they are in aviary surroundings they may adopt the nest of other birds. A weaver nest often proves popular, although these birds, being too large and boisterous, are not suitable companions.

Indian Silverbills tend to lay much larger clutches than those of their African relatives, often up to 10 eggs. Incubation lasts for 12 days in both cases, and the young will fledge about three weeks after hatching. They are quite social when breeding, and tend to have several broods in succession, so that it is certainly not exceptional for as many as 20 offspring to be reared by one pair in a single season.

Feeding presents no difficulties. They will thrive on a normal foreign finch seed mix, comprised mainly of millets, green food and spray millet, which can be soaked, providing valuable variety to the diet, especially when there are chicks in the nest. At this stage, egg food and small invertebrates should also be provided on a regular basis, with cuttlefish bone and grit being available throughout the year, as for all finches.

Common Spice Finch (Nutmeg Finch, Spotted Munia)

Lonchura punctulata

Origin: *Indian subcontinent east to Indonesia and China*

Cock: 5in (13cm) Head and neck brownish-red, becoming lighter on the sides of the neck and lower parts. Abdomen white, with brownish tinge towards the lower tail coverts. Breast and flanks have blackish and brown edges, creating a wavy pattern. Dark brown wavy pattern on uppertail coverts and flanks. Tail brown with grey edges. Iris reddish-brown; beak dark grey, lighter on the lower bill; legs and feet bluish-grey.

Hen: Similar in appearance.

Because this species has such a wide distribution, there are differences in coloration between individuals from different parts of the range. The nominate race described above occurs on the Indonesian islands of Java and Bali. For breeding purposes, therefore, it is better to start with a group from one source, which are likely to be of one race, rather than choosing odd birds.

Spice Finches have been widely kept for centuries. They are easy to keep, feeding chiefly on small seeds, and they can remain in a well-protected outside aviary through the winter once they are properly acclimatised.

Cocks can be identified by their peculiar humming and buzzing song, and their behaviour during the breeding season will confirm their sex. Breeding details are similar to those of other mannikins, and the cock's display consists of jumping up and down in front of the hen, with a blade of grass in his beak. Spice Finches should be kept on their own at this time, as this will dramatically increase the likelihood of success. They will build a nest high in the aviary in suitable vegetation, or they may be persuaded to use a well-concealed nestbox. Disturbances at this stage must be kept to a minimum, because these finches may desert their nest. If this happens, it may be possible to use Bengalese Finches as foster parents.

159 **Bengalese Finch** (Society Finch) *Lonchura domestica*

160 Origin: *does not occur in the wild*

Cock: 5in (13cm) *Variable in coloration, with distinctive colour forms having been bred as the domestication process has proceeded.*

Hen: Impossible to distinguish by visual means.

It is believed that these finches were developed in Japan over 200 years ago, from stock imported from China, and they are considered to be a domesticated form of the Sharp-tailed Munia (*Lonchura striata acuticauda*). This munia is mostly dull brown, with faint striations on its body; the breast and rump are buff-white, and the tail feathers are blackish, with the longer central ones extending to a narrow point.

Today, Bengalese Finches occur in a wide range of colours. There are self (pure-coloured) forms, such as the fawn, chestnut and the darker chocolate, the lower breast and abdomen being paler in colour in all cases. There is also a pure white form, which was the first of these birds to be seen in the West, reaching London Zoo in 1860. More common are the pied versions of the solid dark colours, with their coloration being broken by areas of white plumage, which are variable in extent. A crested form has also been established, and this characteristic can be introduced to any colour variant.

As a guide, darker colours are dominant over lighter colours, and, as in other species, when a crested mutation arises, these birds should not be paired together but with uncrested individuals. A percentage of the resulting offspring will themselves be crested. Colour development of these finches is continuing, with dilute forms, which are paler than the original colour, growing in popularity. Almost black forms have been created by crossings involving Bronze-winged Mannikins, but these are not widely kept.

These birds are ideal for beginners, and they also offer a challenge for more experienced breeders keen to exhibit their stock. Judging standards are laid down for the various varieties, and these encourage breeding for coloration or patterning as well as for type (appearance). Another reason for the universal popularity of the Bengalese Finch is its readiness to act as a foster parent for the eggs of offspring of other species.

The song serves to distinguish cock from hen. When displaying, he puffs himself up until he resembles a ball of feathers and then sings his characteristic rattling song. Bengalese will usually build their nest in a box, using various materials. They prefer an enclosed rather than a half-fronted box, entirely enclosed apart from a small entrance hole at the front so that the birds are hidden completely while incubating. Bengalese are better bred in cages rather than in flights alongside other finches, because their tame and gentle natures mean that they may be driven off a nest by a more determined bird.

Up to eight eggs may form a typical clutch. They take about 14 days to hatch, with the chicks leaving the nest approximately three days later. In addition to their usual seed diet, comprised mainly of millets, the adult finches may also eat egg food while rearing their offspring, as well as green food and, possibly, small live food as well. The young birds themselves will be able to breed when they are eight months old, and two or three clutches may be reared by a pair during a season.

Bengalese Finches that are housed indoors will appreciate the opportunity to bathe regularly. If they are kept permanently in a cage, their claws may become overgrown, even if thick branches have been provided, together with perches of a more traditional width. These long nails will need to be clipped back on occasions, taking care to ensure that this does not cause bleeding, or the birds flying from the nest may become entangled with the nesting material and accidentally drag young hatchlings out of the nest.

In spite of their small size, Bengalese Finches are quite long lived, with a life expectancy of seven or eight years.

Javanese Mannikin (Black-beaked Bronze Mannikin)
Lonchura leucogastroides

Origin: *Indonesia*

Cock: 4in (10cm) Upperparts chocolate-brown, with fine wavy markings. Head and breast black; belly white. Rump and tail brownish-black. Iris brown; beak greyish, black on upper bill, and lighter below; legs and feet bluish-grey.

241

Hen: Similar in appearance.

First seen in Europe in 1879, these mannikins are very easy to care for. They live mainly on seed, with various millets, plain canary seed and green food forming the basis of their diet, and even the chicks are reared largely on seed, although a wider range of foods should be offered at this stage, including some live food.

The habits of the Javanese Mannikin are very similar to those of other related species. Cocks can be distinguished by their characteristic song, which sounds rather like prolonged humming. Breeding results have been achieved in both cage and aviary surroundings, and these mannikins have also been used as foster parents on occasions.

It is advisable to keep them in a group on their own to prevent any risk of hybridisation, which is not recommended. Emphasis should be placed on establishing pure aviary strains, even though such hybrids may be fertile.

153 White-headed Mannikin (White-headed Nun, Maja Finch)

Lonchura maja

Origin: *Thailand, Malaysia and Indonesia*

Cock: 5in (13cm) Head, throat and neck white, with brownish suffusion apparent over the nape and throat. Upperparts chestnut; uppertail coverts and rump lighter shade of reddish-chestnut. Breast, abdomen, thighs and lower tail coverts black, with the sides of the body being dark chestnut. Flight feathers blackish-brown; wings brown. Iris brown; beak grey; legs and feet brownish-grey.

Hen: Similar in appearance.

It may sometimes be possible to recognise hens by their slightly smaller heads, but the song of cocks provides a more reliable guide to distinguishing between the sexes. Although they are quite friendly and tolerant by nature and will live well in a group together, the White-headed Mannikin is not easily induced to breed. Success is more likely if these birds are kept in a colony in a well-planted aviary. First breeding results were obtained in Germany, about 1870.

A dark location is usually preferred for nesting purposes. Dense bushes may encourage pairs to build their own nests, using suitable material such as dried grasses and strips of paper. A nestbox may be used, especially if it is well camouflaged by branches of conifers, for example.

Hens lay between three and five eggs in a clutch, and these are incubated by both hen and cock for about 13 days. When the young hatch, a range of rearing foods should be supplied, including some live food, and in addition to a regular seed diet of millets and plain canary seed, it may also be worth offering paddy rice, which is often eaten by these mannikins in the wild.

They are, in fact, regarded as pests in some areas, with flocks causing serious crop damage.

Fledging takes place when the chicks are about three weeks old, and they are fed by the adults for a further fortnight or so. At this stage, the youngsters can be distinguished by their dark brown upperparts and black beaks. They moult into adult plumage by the time they are four months old, and can live for well over 10 years.

4 **Three-coloured Mannikin** (Tri-coloured Nun)

Lonchura malacca

Origin: *India east to the Philippines and Indonesia*

Cock: 4in (10cm) Head and neck jet black; upperparts dark chestnut; rump and uppertail coverts reddish-brown. Abdomen white, with vent area and undertail coverts black. Iris brown; beak light grey; legs and feet dark grey.

Hen: *Similar in appearance.*

It is possible to distinguish between the nominate race described above and the subspecies known as the Black-headed Mannikin (*L.m. atricapilla*) (Plate 151) very easily, because the underparts of the Black-headed Mannikin are chestnut with no white present. There is also a black area evident in the middle of the abdomen. Other subspecies are also recognised, but the distinctions are less clear cut.

The Three-coloured is one of the most frequently available of all mannikins. It is quite hardy once acclimatised and may be kept outside through the winter months, provided that a snug shelter is available. They are also easy to keep on a diet of millets and canary seed with perhaps some groats or paddy rice added to the regular seed mixture. Green food, such as chickweed or seeding grasses, should also be supplied regularly when available, along with egg food and live food, particularly in the breeding season.

Unfortunately, as with the White-headed Mannikin, breeding results are not common. This may be partly because many people keep these mannikins as members of a mixed collection, rather than on their own in a small group, when breeding success is more likely. Similar management as recommended for the White-headed Mannikin for breeding purposes is required for these birds.

In the wild, these mannikins live in reedy surroundings in long grass and near rice fields, often building their nests here, hidden and hung between sturdy stems. If bamboo or rushes are planted in the flight, in addition to ordinary shrubs, the birds may be encouraged to nest here. Sometimes they will take over an old nest and rebuild it.

They are friendly, quiet and not normally a disturbing influence in a mixed collection. They like perching high up in the flight. Their song is barely audible.

243

163 Java Sparrow (Rice Bird) *Padda oryzivora*

Origin: *Indonesia*

Cock: 6in (15cm) *Predominantly dove-grey. Head and tail black, with a white cheek patch. Lower breast has a bluish tinge; belly and undertail coverts brownish, becoming whiter. Iris brown; beak rose-pink with whitish edging; legs and feet pinkish.*

Hen: Similar in appearance.

The simplest means of distinguishing between the sexes is by noting the song of cock birds, which is pleasant and not too loud. In addition, the cock's bill may be slightly larger.

One of the most widely kept of all munias, the Java Sparrow is usually kept in groups on its own, or in the company of Cockatiels, because its larger size and heavy, powerful beak mean that it can prove a liability in the company of smaller, weaker birds. A distinct pecking order will evolve within a small group of Java Sparrows, and it may well be that only the dominant pair will nest, especially in the confines of a fairly small aviary, although disputes between individual birds are not common. Introducing new birds to an established group is, however, likely to result in fighting. All the birds should be placed in the aviary at the same time in order to minimise this risk. Their quarters must also not be overcrowded so that there can be adequate space between the nests, with hollow logs or nesting baskets being preferred for this purpose. They should be about 3ft (1m) apart to enable each pair to establish its own territory.

A variety of nesting material will be used, ranging from grasses to moss and coconut fibres. If a pair decides to build its own nest, it is usually located close to the aviary roof, in dense vegetation, and shaped like a ball. Hens typically lay from four to seven eggs, with incubation lasting for approximately 13 days. At this stage, in addition to their regular diet, a mixture of millets, plain canary seed and paddy rice, it is advisable to provide typical rearing foods, including live food and egg food. It is also advantageous to provide a softbill food and fruit at intervals throughout the year, if the birds will eat such items.

The young Java Sparrows will leave the nest when they are nearly four weeks old, and it will be a further two or three weeks until they are fully independent. At this stage, their beaks are blackish; by the time they are about three months old, they will be indistinguishable from adult birds.

Strangely, grey Java Sparrows have a reputation for being slow to nest, but this usually applies to pairs kept on their own. It may take two or three years before imported birds will start breeding.

Once they are acclimatised, they can be allowed to overwinter in an outside aviary, with a suitable shelter. The hours of darkness in winter can be shortened by providing artificial light until about 7 o'clock in the evening with the lighting being switched on again, automatically if required, at about 7 o'clock the following morning. Finches living outside during the winter should not be left in darkness for over 12 hours, especially if the weather is cold, as they need to eat regularly to maintain their body temperature.

The coloured varieties of the Java Sparrow will usually breed far more readily than the natural form. White Java Sparrows (Plate 161) may have originated in China, but they reached Europe from Japan where they have been bred for centuries. Like the normal form, these birds are invariably sleek in appearance, with wax-like plumage.

It is not unusual for White Java Sparrows to show odd grey markings, and parti-colour pied individuals are not uncommon. White chicks always have some dark markings on fledging, but their beaks are usually red; pied Java Sparrows have dark beaks at this stage.

The other mutation that has become more popular in recent years is the fawn. This originated in Australian aviaries during the 1950s and has since been introduced to European and North American collections. In these birds, the black and grey plumage is replaced by corresponding shades of fawn, although the beak coloration and the red circle of skin encircling the eyes are unaffected. Fawn pieds are also established now as well.

Pectorella Finch (Pectoral Finch) *Lonchura pectoralis*

Origin: *north Australia*

Cock: 5in (13cm) Cheeks and throat black; fawn line over the eyes. Upperparts grey-brown; upper chest white, with black barring; lower parts pinkish-brown, with white spots on the back and flanks. Tail brownish-black. Iris brown; beak bluish-grey; legs and feet pinkish.

Hen: Easily distinguishable by brownish plumage of the ear coverts and throat, as well as the black and white barred appearance of the foreneck.

Although they were first bred back in 1892, Pectorella Finches are quite rare in aviculture today, certainly outside Australia, although they can be sexed easily. Their care also presents no particular problems. A diet based on a mixture of millets and plain canary seed, as well as green food including seeding grasses, and a suitable rearing food during the breeding period should be provided. Grit and cuttlefish bone should also be provided.

The song of the cock bird, a series of chipping notes, is quite insignificant. His display is rather more elaborate, however. It takes place on the ground, and he bows to his intended mate, fans his tail, drops his wings and hops round the hen. Both birds then perch quietly beak to beak for a period, after which they will diligently search the ground together, picking up grasses and small twigs.

In the wild, Pectorella Finches nest in clumps of grass. In aviary surroundings they will hunt for a secluded corner in the flight, building a nest in a shrub just off the ground. Alternatively, they may use an open-fronted nestbox, which they will fill with grass and other material, making a shallow depression that they will line and partially cover.

The four to six eggs are incubated by both parents alternately, with the hen undertaking much of this task. The young will hatch after 13 days and will leave the nest in a further three weeks. A fortnight later they will be independent. The fledglings are greyish-brown and have browner underparts than adults.

167 Chestnut-breasted Mannikin *Lonchura castaneothorax*

Origin: *Australia and New Guinea*

Cock: 5in (13cm) Top of head and nape cinnamon, with grey tips to these feathers; upperparts otherwise lighter. Rump and uppertail coverts straw-yellow. Black plumage predominates on the sides of the head and throat, with brownish streaks evident here. Upper breast and sides of neck light cinnamon, with a narrow black stripe below. Flanks, thighs and undertail coverts black; remainder of abdomen white. Black and white barring may be evident on the sides of the body. Wings cinnamon with greyish-brown flight feathers. Central tail feathers yellow, with the remainder greyish-brown. Iris brown; beak bluish-grey; legs and feet pinkish-grey.

Hen: Similar in appearance.

First kept at London Zoo in 1860, the Chestnut-breasted Mannikin is similar in its requirements to other *Lonchura* species. Sexing is difficult by visual means, but hens tend to be slightly duller in coloration. Again, it is the song of the cock that is diagnostic, and these mannikins have a more audible song than other members of the group.

Breeding has been achieved successfully on a number of occasions. Pairs often prefer to nest close to the ground, where, in dense vegetation, they may build a purse-shaped nest from grass and other fibres. The young birds may be rather nervous when they first fledge. At this stage, their upperparts are dark brown with cream underparts, with adult plumage being gained when they are about four months old. A varied diet should help to ensure breeding success.

Yellow-tailed Mannikin (Yellow-rumped Finch)

Lonchura flaviprymna

Origin: *north Australia*

Cock: 5in (13cm) Head and neck whitish-grey, becoming paler on the throat. Upperparts chestnut; uppertail coverts ochre-yellow. Wings chestnut, with greyish-

brown flight feathers. Breast has ochre-yellow sheen; lower parts yellowish-white. Tail brown with yellow edges. Iris brown; beak grey; legs and feet grey.

Hen: *Similar in appearance.*

Resembling the Chestnut-breasted Mannikin in some respects, this species can be distinguished by its whitish cheeks and plain buff underparts. First seen in Britain in 1904, Yellow-tailed Mannikins bred shortly afterwards. Their care is straightforward, and breeding details do not differ significantly from other members of the genus.

In the wild they often nest close to water, using grasses and the leaves of *Pandanus* palms, to create a bottle-shaped structure. These mannikins show a great liking for grass and weed seeds, which should figure in their diet whenever possible.

As with other mannikins, a watch should be kept on their claws to ensure that they do not become overgrown and twisted, as may happen, particularly in cage surroundings. Otherwise, apart from the risk of the birds becoming caught up in their quarters, this could also result in the loss of newly hatched chicks, which may accidentally be dragged out of the nest in the parent birds' claws.

This is one of the rarer mannikins in European and North American collections today, and every effort should be made to maintain their numbers, as they make an attractive addition to aviculture. Yellow-tailed Mannikins are certainly better represented in Australian aviaries, and they appear to be quite common in the wild.

4 Cherry Finch (Plum-headed Finch) *Aidemosyne modesta*

Origin: *east Australia*

Cock: *5in (13cm) Forehead purplish-red; lores red; chin reddish-black; sides of head white with brown lines. Remainder of head and upper body brown. Rump and uppertail coverts show whitish lines. Tail feathers black with white tips. Iris brown; beak black; legs and feet pinkish-brown.*

Hen: *White plumage evident on chin and throat, with less red on the forehead.*

The quiet nature of these Australian finches have helped to ensure their popularity, although they can become more aggressive during the breeding season. Pairs have nested successfully both in cages and aviaries. In a planted flight, they may build a round, domed nest, or they may decide to construct their nest in a box.

The typical clutch is composed of four to six eggs, with both adults sharing the task of incubation, which lasts about 12 days. The chicks should fledge at approximately three weeks of age and will be independent within a fortnight.

As well as a regular seed diet, based on millets and plain canary seed, egg food, invertebrates and green food, such as seeding grasses, make a good rearing diet when there are chicks in the nest. Breeding and rearing is not always straightforward, however, because Cherry Finches are very susceptible to disturbance and may then abandon their eggs. If the eggs are not chilled they may be fostered to a pair of Silverbill or Bengalese Finches, both of which can hatch the eggs of the Cherry Finch and rear the chicks successfully.

It may be best to overwinter Cherry Finches in a birdroom, although they can prove relatively hardy, having been bred consistently in northern climates for over 30 years. All stock available in Europe, as in the case of other native Australian species, will be captive-bred.

169 Long-tailed Grassfinch *Poephila acuticauda*

Origin: *north Australia*

Cock: 7in (18cm) including 3in (7.5cm) tail Top and sides of the head light bluish-grey, extending to the neck; lores, chin and throat area black. Upperparts creamy-brown; white rump clearly defined by a black stripe across the base of the back. Tail black, with the central tail feathers terminating in shafts. Lower parts of wing brown, with white plumage around the vent and undertail coverts; white edging present on the outer flight feathers. Iris reddish-brown; beak yellow; legs and feet pinkish.

Hen: Similar in appearance, but may be slightly smaller, with a reduced area of black plumage on the throat.

The nominate race described above can be distinguished quite easily from the subspecies known as Heck's Grassfinch (*P.a. hecki*) (Plate 168) by the coloration of its beak, which is black rather than red. Heck's Grassfinch occurs in the northwest of Australia, and its plumage may also be of a somewhat darker shade. Both subspecies need similar care.

Sexing can create difficulties, and it is probably safest to rely on the birds' behaviour to distinguish a compatible pair. If a number of these finches are housed together, a cock will select a hen and sit close to her, distending his throat in a wheezing, almost silent song, as well as bobbing up and down on the perch at intervals.

Once identified, it is preferable to keep breeding pairs on their own, either in a spacious breeding cage or a small aviary, as they can become very aggressive when nesting and may even kill smaller birds. A hen will use a nestbox, having constructed a lining from moss, grasses and other nesting material. She may lay five eggs, which start to hatch after a period of about 13 days.

Rearing food should consist of egg food, small live foods and plenty of green food. Soaked seed, such as millet sprays, and ripening seedheads are also valuable additions to the diet at this stage. The young birds will fledge when they are about three weeks old, and will then be fed by their parents for perhaps a further month.

Weaning should not be carried out too quickly, and the rearing foods must be offered to the fledglings until they are eating a diet based mainly on seed. Losses may otherwise occur. Their quarters must also be kept very clean to minimise the risk of enteric diseases, with any spilt egg food, for example, being removed together with its container before it can turn sour.

Long-tailed Grassfinches can be prolific, rearing two or three broods in a season. Unfortunately, especially when they are kept indoors, they may attempt to breed throughout the year, which is not to be recommended. Nesting facilities should be withdrawn at the end of the summer, and, if necessary, the sexes can be kept apart in a flight cage or indoor aviary. Under these circumstances cocks should be kept as far apart from hens as possible, because if they can still see and hear them, they may become quarrelsome towards each other.

Colour mutations are far less common in this species than in some other Australian finches, notably the Gouldian Finch. Even so, a fawn mutation is known, although it is not widely kept at present.

Parson Finch (Black-throated Finch) *Poephila cincta*

Origin: *east Australia*

Cock: 5in (13cm) Head and neck ash-grey, lighter on the sides of the face. An area of black plumage extends from the chin and throat down to the chest. Uppertail coverts and rump white. Black band here extends around the sides of the body. Vent, thighs and lower tail feathers white. Tail black, with central feathers having slightly elongated central shafts. Iris dark brown; beak black; legs and feet pinkish.

Hen: Similar in appearance, but may be distinguished by smaller bib.

Quite well-represented in collections today, the Parson Finch has proved ready to nest, and pairs are usually reliable parents. Their sex can be determined with certainty only during the breeding period by the cock's display, and a bird that appears to be a duller looking hen may turn out to be a young cock.

A pair usually prefers to adopt a nestbox for breeding purposes. Here the birds will fashion a round, domed nest using blades of grass, teasings of nesting material and even small roots, lining the interior with feathers and hairs.

The typical clutch, of between four and eight eggs, is incubated by both birds sitting alternately, with the rearing duties also being shared. Breeding details and care are similar to those of the Long-tailed Grassfinch. Bengalese Finches can be used as foster parents, but Parson Finches will normally rear their own offspring without problems provided they are given a varied diet.

The young birds should be separated from their parents once they are fully weaned. By this stage the adults are likely to be ready to nest again. They can have three broods of chicks during a season, but as these finches can prove something of a disturbing influence in a mixed flight, it is better to keep pairs apart. They will breed most satisfactorily in a large breeding cage.

Parson Finches can be overwintered in unheated surroundings indoors, but the provision of extra warmth during cold spells in temperate areas is recommended.

165 **Masked Grassfinch** *Poephila personata*

Origin: *north and east Australia*

Cock: 5in (13cm) *A band across the forehead, lores, face, chin and top of throat black. Remainder of body predominantly brownish, but lighter on the sides of head and underparts. There is a large black band at the top of the rump, which extends down the sides of the body. Rump, upper- and undertail coverts and an area of the lower abdomen white. Iris brown; beak yellowish; legs and feet pinkish.*

Hen: *Similar in appearance.*

Recognising pairs outside the breeding season can prove very difficult, and the cock's song again serves as a distinguishing feature. This species was first kept in Germany in 1899, and it does not differ significantly in its requirements from other members of the genus. Masked Grassfinches are very lively birds, however, and they often do best in aviary surroundings rather than in cages.

Masked Grassfinches are usually not very aggressive, and they may prove rather nervous by nature; disturbances, particularly during the breeding season, should, therefore, be kept to a minimum. A pair will choose a nesting site close to the ground, using either a nestbox or building an open nest in vegetation. If their nest is abandoned, any eggs or chicks can be fostered to Bengalese Finches, which underlines the value of keeping several pairs of these delightful domesticated finches, even if your main interest is in Australian finches.

A regular seed diet, composed mainly of millets and plain canary seed, is recommended, together with green food and possibly some live food as well, particularly when they are breeding. In addition, besides grit and cuttlefish bone, it will be worth offering charcoal. This can usually be obtained from specialist seed suppliers, and is actually present in some grit mixes. Although the finches may not eat the charcoal, it is often carried to the nest, where it is thought to serve as a deodoriser.

ˈ1 **Gouldian Finch** *Chloebia gouldiae*

ˈ2 **Origin**: *north Australia*

ˈ3 Cock: *5in (13cm) Three different head colours are recognised from the wild – black, red and yellow (the least common). This area is separated from the neck by a bluish line, becoming yellowish-green. Wings and back grass green; rump and uppertail coverts bluish; breast violet, with a relatively orange area separating this from the yellow underparts. Tail feathers black, with central tail feathers long and pointed. Iris brown; beak pinkish-white with a redder point; legs and feet pinkish.*

Hen: *Distinguishable by paler colour and underparts.*

One of the most beautifully coloured of all finches, the Gouldian is widely kept. However, its requirements are reasonably specific, because these birds are not hardy. They dislike cold, damp surroundings, and although it may be possible to house them in an outdoor aviary during the warmest months of the year in temperate areas, they must be brought inside for the winter.

Many breeders of finches not surprisingly specialise in Gouldian Finches, accommodating them in birdrooms that are equipped with heating and lighting controls. Pairs can be bred in cages, and as colour mutations have emerged this has become particularly important in order to ensure the parentage of the offspring. Non-breeding stock are accommodated in flights.

A diet based on millets and canary seed, together with other seeds such as maw, rape and niger, will suit these finches well. Green food should also be offered regularly, with seeding grasses often being especially popular. As always, small amounts should be offered frequently, rather than large quantities intermittently, which are more likely to precipitate digestive upsets.

Before the breeding season, cocks and hens take little interest in each other. They will chase each another away from the highest roosting perches, although they are not aggressive. As soon as the cock starts to sing at the beginning of the courtship period, the hen becomes far more receptive. She will remain sitting close to him as he begins his dance, which includes deep bowing towards her. The hen usually remains passive throughout, but sometimes their bills will touch.

They will use a nestbox or a hollow log, in which they will build a nest, often preferring to use dark materials, such as roots, grasses, moss and coconut fibres, for this purpose. The interior may be lined with both feathers and pieces of charcoal. Up to six eggs may be laid, with the incubation period lasting 16 days. The chicks have the typical phosphorescent spots within their bills, which enable their parents to find their mouths within the dark nest.

Rearing food should consist of egg food, soaked seed, green food (especially chickweed if it is available) and small live foods. The relative scarcity of Gouldian Finches in the past and the fact that pairs are not always reliable parents, has meant that widespread fostering of eggs to Bengalese Finches occurs, notably in Europe and North America. Australian breeders, however, not only allow their birds to rear their own chicks, but also breed Gouldian Finches in colonies, which reflects a totally different management approach.

Fostering can be advantageous when Gouldian Finches are infected with air-sac mites. These parasites are found in the respiratory tract, causing wheezing and ill-health. They are spread from the parents to their offspring during the rearing period, and if Bengalese Finches are used to hatch the eggs and care for the chicks, there is no risk that these mites will be passed on from one generation of Gouldian Finches to the next. Until quite recently, effective treatment of air-sac mites was not possible, but a new drug, ivermectin, which is applied in drop form to the skin on the bird's neck and absorbed from here into the body, allows these parasites to be overcome. Unfortunately, the mites are threatening to decimate the wild population of Gouldian Finches, whose treatment is very difficult.

Weaning of Gouldian Finches can be problematical, and it should not be carried out hurriedly. Weight loss, often described as 'going light', may well occur, stunting the development of affected individuals. There can be other causes of this condition, however, and if any young birds are lost at this stage, it would be advisable to have autopsies performed. If the cause is infectious, suitable treatment can be given to safeguard the other birds.

A range of colour mutations has been developed in recent years. These include a white-breasted form, in which the lilac plumage on the breast is replaced by white feathering; the remainder of the body coloration is largely unaffected, although the abdomen may be a paler shade of yellow. White-breasted Gouldians can be bred in all three head colours, and as in other cases, the red-headed form is dominant to the black-headed. Among other less common colours are the blue-breasted and yellow-backed and even a rare Lutino form.

180 Bicheno's Finch (Owl Finch, Banded Finch) *Poephila bichenovii*

Origin: *north and east Australia*

Cock: 4in (10cm) *Forehead black, with a black stripe extending above the eyes, down on to the cheeks, giving rise to a black collar across the chest. There is a second black band lower down the body, across the lower breast. Top of head, neck and back brownish-grey, with fine wavy black markings. Chequered patterning apparent on the wings. Rump white, with black stripe on the lower back; tail brownish-black. Sides of face and throat white; breast and abdomen yellowish-white. Undertail coverts black. Iris brown; beak lead-grey; legs and feet grey.*

Hen: Similar in appearance.

There are two distinctive races of Bicheno's Finch, with the nominate race being as described above. This is by far the most commonly available subspecies in aviculture, and breeding stocks are well established. In comparison, the Black-ringed Finch (*P.b. annulosa*) has become very scarce, possibly as the result of hybridisation in the past. It can be distinguished by its black rather than white rump, but crossings between these two forms apparently produced offspring that were identical to the Bicheno's Finch – that is, with a white rump. Only when such birds were paired did the black characteristic appear again and in just a quarter of the offspring, being clearly recessive in its mode of inheritance. As domestication has proceeded, the Black-ringed Finch has largely disappeared, but there is always the possibility that such birds could recur in a nest of apparently pure Bicheno's, with their genes still being present within the captive population.

These are lively birds by nature, moving rather like tits, and they will show to best effect in an aviary where they are likely to build a neat little nest in a bush, take over an abandoned nest or adopt a nestbox for breeding purposes. The nest will be lined with soft materials, including wool and feathers.

A typical clutch is of from four to six eggs, with the incubation period lasting for about 12 days. The chicks will leave the nest when they are approximately three weeks old, and it will be a further fortnight before they are fully independent.

As a rearing food, hard-boiled egg and powdered rusks mixed with a few drops of cod liver oil and a little honey, or a proprietary egg food can be given, along with small live food. Plenty of green food and soaked seed are also recommended at this stage. If necessary, the eggs of these finches may be hatched by Bengalese Finches, which will prove very suitable foster parents. Although Bicheno's Finches can overwinter in a frost-proof bird-room, they should ideally be kept in a temperature of about 64°F (18°C).

Zebra Finch *Poephila guttata*

Origin: *Australia, especially the interior; also the Indonesian islands of Flores, Sumba and Timor*

Cock: 4in (10cm) Top of head and neck light grey, becoming darker on the back and wing coverts. Flights grey. Uppertail coverts long and black, with white barring at the tips. Front of cheeks white, with thin black vertical lines on each side of the face. Large ear patch chestnut-brown; sides of neck silvery-grey, as are throat and upper chest, which show the black horizontal stripes reminiscent of a zebra's markings. A broad black horizontal band extends across the chest. Flanks chest-nut-brown, with white round spots evident here. Underparts whitish, becoming fawn towards the vent. Iris brownish; beak coral-red; legs and feet pinkish.

Hen: Lacks the ear patches, as well as the markings on the flank and chest. Cheeks, throat and upper breast are a uniform shade of grey. Beak orangish-red, paler than that of the cock.

These popular finches are very easy to care for, and they will breed well in groups. A whole range of colour forms has been developed in recent years, and there is now a considerable interest in exhibiting Zebra Finches, with judging standards being laid down for many of these varieties. For breeding show stock, it is usually preferable to house pairs individually in breeding cages so that the parentage of the offspring can be identified. If they are bred in a flight or aviary it will be harder to produce the required colours, as the birds will pair up at random.

The feeding of Zebra Finches presents no difficulty. A mixture of panicum millet and plain canary seed can be used as the basis of their diet. Green food, such as seeding grasses and chickweed, should also be supplied on a regular basis, although during the breeding period, it should be chopped up finely to deter the birds from adding it to their nest, where it may turn mouldy. Millet sprays are also popular, and particularly valuable when soaked as a rearing food at this stage. Grit and cuttlefish bone should also be supplied throughout the year, and some breeders also offer a little powdered charcoal to assist the digestive process.

Zebra Finches will breed through much of the year, especially if they are housed indoors. They are relatively unfussy about the choice of a nest site, readily adopting nesting baskets or nestboxes for this purpose. In aviary surroundings, however, there should be many more nesting sites on offer than pairs of birds to minimise the risk of bickering and disturbance.

A variety of nesting material, such as coconut fibres, dried grass, moss and feathers, will be used. Zebra Finches seek to cram their nest full, which can create problems if they begin with an empty nestbox. The hen will lay a clutch of about five eggs on a foundation of nesting material, but the nest-building activity will continue during the incubation period, which is likely to result in these eggs becoming buried and chilled. Another nest will be built on top of these eggs, and the process will repeat itself, sometimes until three nests have been lost. Finally, the eggs laid close to the roof of the box will have the greatest likelihood of hatching. Once settled, Zebra Finches are very reliable parents, incubating diligently and rarely being disturbed by periodical inspection of the nest. However, the hen will have exhausted herself by laying a dozen or more eggs in rapid succession prior to this stage to no avail. The nestboxes must, therefore, be filled up beforehand, and no more nesting material should be supplied, when the eggs have been laid to avoid this problem arising.

Breeders often prefer to use nestboxes with a half-open front, the inside of which should be filled with nesting materials to just under the entrance. Once they are in use, the nests should be checked occasionally. It is better not to let a pair incubate more than half a dozen eggs, because the nest may become too full and eggs will be chilled during the incubation period, reducing the overall hatching rate.

Both members of the pair share the task of incubation, which lasts for approximately 12 days. The young birds leave the nest after only 20 days. Although they learn to eat by themselves quite quickly, the youngsters allow themselves to be fed for some time by the cock. When they are independent, the Zebra Finches should be transferred to a large flight, where they will not interfere with their parents.

Care should be taken to ensure that they do not begin nesting too soon. No boxes should be provided in the flight because the young birds may start breeding at just three months old, before they are fully mature, and this is likely to harm their development. The adults should not be allowed to rear more than four broods during a season. If they are permitted to breed excessively, hens will continue to lay and are then at great risk of succumbing to egg-binding.

Zebra Finches are quite hardy and are able to live outside in an aviary in both summer and winter, provided there is an adequate shelter. A little gentle heat can be beneficial during very cold spells, however, together with artificial lighting to lengthen the feeding period. These finches will not only breed in nestboxes but they will also roost in them throughout the year, and so the boxes should not necessarily be taken away during the winter. In order to prevent breeding during the winter months, cocks should be separated from hens. Alternatively, you can remove the boxes, and the birds can roost quite well on perches in the aviary shelter.

Indoors, the breeding period of Zebra Finches can be extended, provided that they have a few months' rest during the late summer. An even temperature is to be recommended, although it can be allowed to drop a little at night. The birds must be kept in a light place in the home, although not in direct sunlight, and they should be housed in pairs only for breeding purposes.

A number of different colour forms is now well established. These include a dark-eyed white mutation, which first appeared in 1921. Both hens and cocks have pure white plumage, but they can still be distinguished by the paler colour of the hens' bills. There is also a chestnut-flanked white form, often described under the abbreviation CFW, which can be distinguished by the markings.

Fawn Zebra Finches are also widely kept today. Fawn coloration replaces the grey plumage of the normal cock bird. Like the chestnut-flanked white, this is a sex-linked recessive mutation. There are two different forms of the silver mutation, one of which is recessive in its mode of inheritance, the other being dominant. The recessive silver form tends to be darker, with the cocks having deeper orangish cheek patches, than the dominant form. The same distinction serves to separate the recessive cream and its dominant counterpart.

A pied mutation is well established, and this feature can be combined with any of the solid colours (apart from pure white). The markings of individual pieds may be very variable, and their plumage may range from being almost entirely white at one extreme to just showing odd flecks of white feathering in among their normal coloration. For exhibition purposes, pairs should be well matched, with balanced markings.

The crested form of the Zebra Finch is another mutation that can be combined with any colour. This is a dominant characteristic. Pairs should consist of only one crested parent, because pairing two crested birds means that a percentage of the resulting chicks is unlikely to survive.

Some mutations are still being developed, including the attractive orange-breasted, in which the typical zebra patterning is largely replaced by orange and white. Among other colours, there is also a less common black-breasted form, which has, as its name suggests, a solid black breast. The penguin Zebra Finch, of which the cocks have white breasts, is now more common. Orangish markings are retained in this instance, but even the black tear marks are lost in these birds.

One of the more unusual Zebra Finch mutations recorded to date does not affect the body coloration or feathering but the beak. Yellow-beaked Zebras first appeared in the 1960s, and although they attracted interest at the time, they have since become quite scarce. The legs and feet are also paler than normal, being a yellow or orange shade. This change is a recessive genetic trait and can occur in any colour form. Interestingly, the beaks of hens are still a paler shade than those of cock birds.

166 **Star Finch** (Red-tailed Grassfinch) *Neochmia ruficauda*

Origin: *east Australia*

Cock: 4in (10cm) Forehead, lores and side of face down to throat red. Small white dots are evident around the eyes and on the sides of the neck. Upperparts brownish-green; uppertail coverts red. Tail brown and red. Underparts greenish-grey, becoming yellowish on the abdomen and undertail coverts. Iris reddish; beak red; legs and feet yellow.

Hen: Duller in coloration, with the red on the chin, forehead and cheeks being a paler shade.

Unless the origins of the birds are known, it can be difficult to recognise a pair of Star Finches with certainty because there is the risk of mistaking a young bird for a hen.

Their attractive coloration has meant that Star Finches are popular avicultural subjects. Not only are they peaceable and lively, but pairs usually nest quite readily if they can be kept in a separate enclosure where they are unlikely to be disturbed. They will breed in spacious cages, rearing two or three broods in a season here.

The young – usually up to four in number – are hatched after an incubation period of 13 days and will fledge in a further 25 days. A nestbox rather than a basket is often favoured for nesting purposes. A dome-shaped nest with a narrow entrance is made from suitable material such as coconut fibres and dried grass. Alternatively, in aviary surroundings, twigs of broom suspended in the outside flight will attract the birds to construct a free-standing nest.

On the whole, results are more satisfactory when pairs are kept separately. They should be kept together only when not breeding and during the winter. They will then have adequate space for exercise. As soon as the young birds are independent, they should be transferred to a large flight, so that they have good opportunities to develop their flight muscles. They should not be paired up too early.

Attempts to breed from birds less than a year old are likely to end in failure. Even if fertile eggs are laid, the rearing of young is not frequently successful, and the eggs are best transferred to Bengalese Finches, which are suitable foster parents for this species. Mature pairs of Star Finches may produce three rounds of chicks in succession, but the hens should never be encouraged to breed in cold weather, because they are then liable to suffer from egg-binding.

Crimson Finch (Blood Finch) *Neochmia phaeton*

Origin: *north Australia and New Guinea*

Cock: 5in (13cm) Mostly red, with a brown suffusion over the wings. Top of the head blackish-brown, becoming reddish-grey over the neck. Sides of face bright red, as are throat, breast and sides of the body, where there are also small white spots. Abdomen black. Iris brown; beak red; legs and feet yellowish.

Hen: Duller in coloration, being olive-brown, with dull crimson on the sides of the face, throat, lores and rump.

There is a white-bellied form of the Crimson Finch, which is confined to areas of northern tropical Australia and the southern part of New Guinea. These birds are easily identifiable by their white abdomens and paler upperparts. Neither type of the Crimson Finch is common in collections outside Australia, however, and stock is usually quite expensive. Imported birds require a careful period of acclimatisation, but subsequently these finches do not prove particularly delicate, and they can withstand moderately cold weather.

Millets, plain canary seed, niger seed and especially spray millet should be given as the basic diet, together with seeding grasses and other fresh items such as chickweed. Soaked seed is especially valuable with recently acquired stock, and probiotics may also be useful at this stage. Live food of suitable size must be provided, since these birds are insectivorous.

Unfortunately, Crimson Finches should not be kept with other birds in an aviary because they are rather aggressive by nature. The cock of a pair may even need to be separated from his hen when they are not breeding because he may start to bully her. A well-planted and spacious aviary will reduce this possibility, although even here, young birds will probably have to be caught and transferred elsewhere as soon as they are feeding themselves, because they may be attacked by the adult birds.

Once Crimson Finches start breeding, they are likely to nest several times in succession. Dried grass, coconut fibres and similar material will be used in the construction of the nest, which is often built in an open-fronted style of nestbox. Some fine feathers should be supplied for a nest lining.

The typical clutch of four or five eggs should hatch after a period of about 12 days, with the cock and hen each taking turns at incubation. After a further three weeks, the youngsters will leave the nest. In addition to soaked seeds, small live foods, such as aphids, whiteworm and hatchling crickets, must be given.

177 Painted Finch (Painted Firetail) *Emblema picta*

Origin: *Australia*

Cock: 4in (10cm) Forehead, lores, chin and throat red; upperparts brown; rump and uppertail coverts red. Tail brownish-black. Underparts black with large white dots, with a red band evident in the middle of the breast. Iris light yellow; beak black and red; legs and feet pinkish.

Hen: Less brightly coloured, with less prominent red markings on the head. Denser distribution of white spotting on the underparts.

These beautiful finches are quite common in some parts of Australia, where they prefer arid country. They have benefited from the presence of artificial irrigation in these areas, which guarantees them a constant supply of drinking water. Feeding mainly on grass seeds, they will also consume insects, particularly when they are breeding and have chicks in the nest.

Painted Finches were originally seen in Britain in 1869, but it was not until 1910 that the first breeding results were recorded here, and they have never been especially common in aviculture. They have nested successfully in both cage and aviary surroundings, however, and Bengalese Finches serve as suitable foster parents if required.

The incubation period appears to last about 15 days, and the chicks are brooded closely for a further 10 days, before fledging at around 25 days. Soaked seed, egg food and live food must be provided, in addition to green food.

An unusual feature of Painted Finches is that they may hide away in the grass on the floor of a planted flight; this is especially the case with recently fledged birds. Not surprisingly, in view of their natural range, they dislike damp, cold weather and should be overwintered in heated accommodation. Their aviary should be well shielded to protect them against driving wind and rain during the warmer months of the year.

Red-eared Firetail Finch *Emblema oculata*

Origin: *southwest Australia*

Cock: 5in (13cm) A narrow black band extends over the forehead to the lores and encircles the eyes. There is reddish-scarlet plumage behind each eye. Upperparts olive shade of greyish-brown, with slight dark brown horizontal lines evident here. Rump and uppertail coverts bright red. Throat and upper breast a yellowish shade of olive-brown with light black horizontal markings. Abdomen black with white horizontal lines, broad on the sides of the body and forming large dots here. Iris red; beak red; legs and feet horn-coloured.

Hen: Less brightly coloured than the cock.

This species and the closely related Fire-tailed Finch (*Emblema bella*), are best known in Australian aviculture, although even there, they are not often seen in collections.

Red-eared Firetail Finches have a very limited distribution, frequenting the eucalyptus forests in the coastal area of southwest Australia. They make very frail nests of long, wiry grasses, often with little or no lining and usually in the forked branch of a tree, 10ft (3m) or more off the ground.

In aviary surroundings, they have been bred in well-planted, spacious enclosures. They feed on a diet of small seeds, but live food is important, especially when there are chicks in the nest. Aphids appear to be a particular favourite, but these finches may also take soft food.

78 Diamond Sparrow *Emblema guttata*

Origin: *central Australia*

Cock: 5in (13cm) Top of the head and nape of the neck silvery-grey; back and wings dark brown. The sides of the head are white, becoming greyer towards the back; lores in the form of a black line. Rump and undertail coverts bright red. Lower part of the body white, with a black line across the lower breast, extending down the sides and becoming spotted with white here. Orbital skin reddish. Iris brown; beak red; legs and feet brownish-grey.

Hen: Virtually identical, but sometimes smaller and duller.

First seen in Germany in 1870, Diamond Sparrows are one of the more easily bred Australian species, and stocks are frequently available. It can be difficult to select a pair, but the song of the cock serves to distinguish the sexes. These finches are generally unsuitable for keeping in a cage for any length of time, because they need room in which to exercise;

otherwise, they tend to become obese and breeding results suffer accordingly.

Diamond Sparrows are inclined to breed throughout the year, and it is better to restrict their breeding period to spring and summer if possible. After this, nesting facilities should be withdrawn. Pairs may choose to build their own nests in suitable vegetation or to use a nestbox. They will construct a fairly substantial domed structure, using thick stems of dried grass and fibres, and line the interior with softer material such as feathers.

Between four and six eggs are usually laid, and these are incubated alternately by the hen and cock, with the resulting young then normally being reared without problems. Hard-boiled egg mixed with rusk, plenty of green food and small invertebrates should be provided, as well as both soaked seed and millet sprays.

If, when they first breed, the Diamond Sparrows do not feed their young, the chicks can be fostered by Bengalese Finches, but avoid placing more than three chicks in a nest. Young Diamond Sparrows often seem to need more food than other small birds, and a pair of Bengalese Finches may find it difficult to cope with a complete brood of such gluttons.

By the time they are four months old, the youngsters will be indistinguishable from the adults, but they need not be separated if the flight is large enough, because they are peaceable birds and may even be housed with other finches during the breeding season. In a small enclosure young Diamond Sparrows may sometimes be chased, and if this happens, they must be caught and transferred elsewhere.

They are relatively hardy and may not need winter heat, although they are probably best kept in frost-free quarters. A fawn mutation is known, in which black feathering has been replaced by brown.

Blue-faced Parrot Finch (Three-coloured Parrot Finch)

Erythrura trichroa

Origin: *New Guinea and nearby Indonesian islands*

Cock: 5in (13cm) Sides of the head and forehead blue; lores blackish. Upperparts dark green; wings green and brown. Uppertail coverts and rump red. Tail blackish-brown with reddish edging. Lower parts more brownish-grey. Iris dark brown; beak black; legs and feet brown.

Hen: Similar in appearance, but often duller overall with less pronounced blue coloration on the head.

At present this is the best established parrot finch in aviculture. It was first bred in Germany in 1887. They may be persuaded to use a nestbox or they may prefer to build their own nest in suitable vegetation. Both birds share in the task of constructing the nest, with the cock chasing his mate on occasions, but this rarely develops into any serious display of aggression.

The typical clutch is of four to six eggs, which should hatch after an incubation period lasting about a fortnight. The development of the young birds is quite slow, with their plumage starting to emerge by the time they are 12 days old. Fledging occurs when the chicks are three weeks old, after which they will be fed by the cock bird for a further fortnight or so.

A diet of millets and similar small seeds, augmented with quantities of green food, small live food and soft food is recommended, with soaked seed being particularly valuable once the chicks have hatched. A settled pair may breed two or three times during a season, rearing perhaps 14 youngsters during this period.

Young birds are significantly duller than the adults, being predominantly green, with a greatly reduced area of blue feathering on the head; their beaks are yellowish. They will have moulted into adult plumage by the time they are five months old.

If they are kept in an inside flight, some cover should be provided, because they can be nervous by nature. Conifer branches suspended from the roof and sides of their quarters will provide suitable retreats.

The related Red-headed Parrot Finch (*Erythrura psittacea*) has similar requirements; it is distinguishable by its red facial coloration. There is also a rare Lutino form in which the blue plumage of the Blue-faced Parrot Finch is replaced by white, with the remainder of the body coloration being yellow, apart from the red feathering over the lower back region. The beak is pinkish in this case.

Pintailed Nonpareil (Pintailed Parrot Finch) *Erythrura prasina*

Origin: *southeast Asia and Indonesia*

Cock: 5in (13cm) Forehead, sides of the head and throat blue; lores black. Upperparts grass green; wings a combination of green and brownish-black. Underparts light cinnamon, with a red patch in the centre of the abdomen. Tail brownish-black; central tail feathers red and elongated, ending in a fine point. Iris brown; beak black; legs and feet brownish-horn.

Hen: Head coloration entirely green, with no trace of blue feathering. Lower parts brownish-grey; short central tail feathers.

Unfortunately, since young cocks resemble adult hens, it is possible to have what is believed to be a pair, only to discover that the birds are, in fact, both cocks. Careful acclimatisation is required with this species, and paddy rice should figure prominently in their diet, especially when they are first obtained. This can be supplemented with other, small cereal seeds such as plain canary seed and millets. Soaked seed is very valuable in the early stages, along with limited amounts of green food.

These finches will benefit from plenty of space, especially as they are very lively by nature. Confined to a cage, they will be far less active and will be susceptible to obesity. Pintailed Nonpareils can be housed satisfactorily with Zebra Finches and will soon follow their feeding example.

During the mating period, the cock will dance around the hen, flirting his tail up and down, singing to her and displaying with a stem of grass. The nest is sometimes built in a nestbox or it may be sited in a bush or other vegetation in the aviary which provides similar cover. Incubation and fledging details are similar to those of the Blue-faced Parrot Finch.

It will be six months before the young birds acquire full adult coloration. Outside the breeding period, Pintailed Nonpareils may be kept together in groups in suitably spacious surroundings. Although they might chase each other occasionally, this rarely results in any conflict.

181 Wild Canary *Serinus canaria*

Origin: *Canary Islands and Madeira*

Cock: 5in (13cm) Predominantly greyish-green, with black streaks on the upperparts. Forehead and rump greenish-yellow. Area above the eyes, throat and breast yellow, with the abdomen also being yellowish. Iris dark brown; beak greyish-pink; legs and feet greyish.

Hen: Similar, but rather duller in overall coloration.

It is over 400 years since the Wild Canary was first brought to Europe by the Portuguese; since then, its descendants have become well known around the world. They can be broadly divided into three groups. There are breeds, such as the Roller and American Singer, which have been evolved primarily for their singing skills; others, such as the Belgian Fancy, the Gloster, Border and Fife breeds, and the Norwich have been bred for their appearance, with type standards, specifying the qualities on which judges assess the birds, being established for them. The third and final category is the most recent in terms of development. These are the New Coloured Canaries, bred, as their name suggests, primarily for their coloration, although some emphasis is also placed on type. The most desirable of these are red factor birds, which arose through hybridisation involving the Black-hooded Red Siskin from South America during the 1920s.

Today, canaries are still crossed with other finches. The offspring of pairings involving a British finch such as the Goldfinch are described as mules. Although normally infertile, mules or indeed other Canary hybrids often have an attractive appearance and possess the singing skills of their Canary ancestor.

Wild Canaries themselves are essentially unknown in aviculture today however, although they are still kept in their native islands, largely for their song. Only cock canaries sing, which provides the easiest means of distinguishing the sexes. Hens utter a series of cheeping calls, which are far less mellifluous.

33 Green Singing Finch *Serinus mozambicus*

Origin: *widely distributed across Africa*

Cock: 5in (13cm) *Areas of yellow plumage evident above and below the eyes, and also on the throat, extending down on to the breast. Back and wings greenish-grey with darker markings. Rump yellowish; underparts greenish-yellow. Iris dark brown; beak greyish-pink; legs and feet greyish.*

Hen: Recognisable by the necklace of dark spots across throat and somewhat duller overall coloration.

The Green Singing Finch is closely related to the Canary, and hybrids have been obtained by mating a cock with a small Canary hen. They require a similar diet, composed of a good quality canary seed mixture, and they are partial to soaked seed and millet sprays. Green food should also be included regularly in their diet, and during the breeding season egg food must be provided for rearing purposes; live food may also be eaten at this time.

These finches are graceful and lively by nature, and they are suitable companions for other small finches, although pairs should not be housed together, as they can prove rather territorial. The song of the cock bird is quite delightful and will be heard frequently, especially during the breeding period.

Their flight is silent and butterfly-like. Unlike many finches, they do not huddle together during the day, but they will readily share a communal roosting perch high up in the aviary at night. Kept by themselves in a breeding cage, a pair will make a nest in an open-fronted nestbox or they may be persuaded to use a canary nestpan. They like fine woollen threads and hemp teasings as nest materials.

In an aviary, Green Singing Finches may alternatively build an open, cup-shaped nest in the flight, usually high up in a tree or shrub. The hen alone is responsible for its construction, while the cock sings diligently near the nesting site and, later, sits close to the hen. Four eggs form the typical clutch, and these hatch after a period of 13 days. The chicks fledge about three weeks later, and are then fed largely by the cock bird until they are fully independent. They must then be separated from their parents, which will probably have started to nest again and are likely to resent the continual interference of their earlier offspring.

Since they tend to breed in Africa from September to January, recently imported birds housed indoors during the winter should be provided with nesting facilities. They may well attempt to nest during this period in a cage or indoor flight where an even and reasonably warm temperature can be maintained. Once acclimatised, Green Singing Finches are relatively hardy, and are also long lived, with a life expectancy of 20 years or more in such surroundings.

184 Grey Singing Finch *Serinus leucopygius*

Origin: *west and central Africa*

Cock: 5in (13cm) *Upperparts greyish-brown; head purer shade of grey, transversed with pale brown lines. Wings dark brown, with dull white edging. Rump white. Underparts grey with white plumage in the centre of the abdomen. Iris brown; beak pink-horn; legs and feet pinkish.*

Hen: *Heavier streaking evident on the underparts.*

The dull grey appearance of this little finch is fully compensated for by its extraordinary singing qualities. A cock, even if kept by himself, will sing for practically the whole year, stopping only during the moult. Although at first sight, Grey Singing Finches appear insignificant, they will soon win an aviculturist's heart with their lively, bold natures. They can be quickly tamed, are always active and prove quite hardy once acclimatised.

Their care is similar to that recommended for the Green Singing Finch. They agree well with most birds of their size, but are not social with their own kind, with pairs soon establishing their own territories. They breed quite readily, often choosing a locality high up in the flight.

In a nestbox the hen will build a nest, which is a work of art, and she will defend it fiercely against all other birds. She carries out this building work on her own, while the cock sings nearby and feeds her by regurgitation. Breeding details do not differ from those of the Green Singing Finch, although hens may be more vulnerable to egg-binding. A readily accessible supply of cuttlefish bone should be available therefore, and a supplement including vitamin D3, which is responsible for mobilising the body's calcium stores, should also be provided to breeding birds housed indoors. Here they will not be able to synthesise their own vitamin D3 under the influence of sunlight. It is also important to prevent the finches going to nest when the weather is cold, as this dramatically increases the likelihood of egg-binding.

St Helena Seedeater *Serinus flaviventris*

Origin: *east and southern Africa*

Cock: 5in (13cm) *Upperparts olive-green; head and back striated with black; forehead band and eyebrow stripe yellow; ear coverts yellow-green. Underparts and part of the cheeks yellow, with olive-green moustached stripe. Wings black with yellow margins. Iris brown; upper bill dark, lower bill horn-coloured; legs and feet blackish.*

Hen: *Upperparts grey-brown, striated with black; rump greenish-yellow; forehead and eyebrow stripe dull white. Cheeks and underparts white, with the breast and sides of the body being brownish, with black markings on the flanks. Wings have yellow and white margins.*

These birds, which should not be confused with the *Sporophila* seedeaters from the New World, are not regularly available, but again, cocks prove exceptionally melodious songsters. Their song sounds rather like that of a lark. They will thrive on a mixed canary seed mixture, which includes a little hemp, plus green food. During the rearing period their diet should also include a suitable egg food, along with soaked seed and small invertebrates.

St Helena Seedeaters have nested successfully in aviary surroundings on a number of occasions. They make a cup-shaped nest, like that of the Canary, in dense shrubbery, often close to the ground. Alternatively, they may prefer to build in a nestbox, using woollen threads, fine twigs, dried grasses, coconut fibres and horsehair, if available.

Four or five eggs form the clutch, with incubation lasting about 13 days. Cocks should be watched particularly during the breeding period, to ensure that they do not persecute their mates, as they can prove rather aggressive at this time, especially in the confines of a cage. Young birds resemble adult females on fledging but have a more dense patterning. They can stay in an outside aviary throughout the year, if an adequately protected shelter is provided.

Cape Canary *Serinus canicollis*

Origin: *east and southern Africa*

Cock: 5in (13cm) Forehead and crown yellow; neck olive-grey to grey; back and rump olive-yellow striped (except on the rump) with dusky grey. Ear coverts grey; lores black; cheeks brownish-yellow; breast yellow merging into white on the belly. Undertail coverts yellow. Wings black with yellow; tail brown-yellow. Iris brown; beak greyish-horn; legs and feet horn-coloured.

Hen: Chin to chest greyish, and usually more distinctly striped on the upperparts.

Relatively unknown in aviculture outside southern Africa, the Cape Canary has a very attractive song. Although these finches are sometimes delicate when they are first obtained as imported stock, they soon settle well in aviary surroundings. They are active and lively by nature and will live satisfactorily in a mixed collection alongside birds of similar size.

Cape Canaries will eat a typical canary seed mixture, together with green food, seeding grasses and occasional live insects. They appreciate insectivorous food or a canary-rearing food, especially when they are breeding or rearing their chicks, and soaked seed is also especially popular at this stage. Breeding details are similar to those of other *Serinus* species, with young birds being heavily streaked with brown and black on their upperparts, with buff and black on lower parts of their body. During cold weather, Cape Canaries are best kept in a fair sized cage or indoor aviary, where heat can be provided as necessary.

162 Alario Finch *Serinus alario*

Origin: *southern Africa*

Cock: 5in (13cm) *Head and neck black; upperparts reddish-brown; wide black bands along the flanks. Wing coverts reddish-brown; remainder of wings black. Underparts white. Tail reddish-brown. Iris brown; beak horn-coloured, with lighter lower bill; legs and feet blackish.*

Hen: *Greyish-brown, with dark striations on the reddish-brown upperparts; back lighter in colour, underparts dull buff-white. Tail red-brown, with centre of each feather dark, almost black.*

There is a distinctive race of the Alario Finch, known as *Serinus alario leucolaema*, which differs from the nominate race described above in having white stripes above the eyes and, in the case of cock birds, white plumage on the throat and chin. Hens are distinguishable by their paler coloration. It occurs in the southwest Africa, including Namibia.

Alario Finches are relatively tame and steady by nature, but unfortunately they are rarely available to aviculturists outside Africa. The cock, which has a soft and pleasant song, sings all year round. He may even mimic other songbirds on occasions.

The care of the Alario Finch appears to pose no particular problems. A mixed diet of canary seeds, augmented with green food and the usual rearing foods should suffice. They may not consume insects regularly when rearing young, but these should be provided as they may be sampled and will increase the level of protein in the birds' diet.

185 Golden Song Sparrow *Passer luteus*

Origin: *north Africa, including Somalia, and southern Arabian Peninsula*

Cock: 5in (13cm) *Head and underparts canary yellow; mantle and edges of inner secondaries chestnut. Wings dark brown to blackish, with chestnut edging, with a white bar across the secondaries; rump yellowish. Iris brown; beak black when in breeding condition and horn-coloured for the rest of the year; legs and feet pinkish.*

Hen: *Head, mantle and rump buffish-brown with a few black or dark brown streaks on the mantle; flights and tail dusky brown with lighter edges, white bar on secondaries less conspicuous. Underparts buff washed with yellow. Beak horn-coloured.*

The cocks are particularly colourful, but they are certainly not talented songsters as their name would suggest. Golden Song Sparrows are best kept in a group, especially for breeding purposes. A planted aviary suits them well, and hanging pieces of gorse in the aviary will further encourage breeding behaviour. Bold and restless by nature, these finches often prefer to hide in dense undergrowth.

Breeding presents something of a challenge, as they do not breed freely. In suitable surroundings, however, pairs may be persuaded to build a relatively slovenly nest in an open-fronted box or nesting basket. Alternatively, they may build a free-standing structure in vegetation. It is domed, with an entrance at the side. All kinds of material may be used, such as dried grasses and coconut fibres, and the interior will be lined with soft down and feathers.

The hen incubates her clutch of three or four eggs alone, for about 13 days. Once the chicks have hatched, a much higher proportion of live food must feature in the diet, and small caterpillars, hatchling crickets and similar items will be required. Green food and soaked seeds are also very important at this stage. If all goes well, the chicks should fledge when they are about two weeks old. At this stage, both sexes resemble the adult hen, but tend to have paler underparts.

These sparrows favour a basic diet of mixed millets and plain canary seed. They are quite hardy but need to be properly acclimatised before being expected to overwinter in an outside aviary. Even so, there must be a suitable shelter here, with lighting and heating available, particularly if the weather turns very cold. It may be better to bring them indoors into a birdroom flight in winter.

The depth of yellow on cocks can vary from bird to bird. It is possible to improve this by the use of a suitable colouring food just prior to and during the moulting period. Birds showing the deepest natural yellow plumage originate from the east of the species' range, and these are sometimes referred to as the Arabian Golden Sparrow (*P.l. euchlorus*). The mantle is also yellow in cocks of this race, while hens have ashy rather than brown upperparts as in the nominate race.

Common Rosefinch *Carpodacus erythrinus*

Origin: *north Europe and Siberia; winters further south in India and Burma (Myanmar)*

Cock: 6in (15cm) Predominantly crimson, most brilliant on head, throat, breast and the lower part of the rump. Upper back, mantle and wing coverts have dusky centres; remaining wing feathers and tail dark brown with rosy margins; abdomen bright rose, fading to buff-white on undertail coverts. Iris brown; beak horn-brown; legs and feet horn-brown.

Hen: Generally brown, darker on the crown, nape, wings, tail and throat, with the back and rump having a slightly olivaceous tone.

Colour-feeding is necessary to preserve the beautiful rose coloration of this and other species of rosefinch, otherwise the cock's plumage will fade over successive moults. These birds feed mainly on seed, taking a canary seed mix, with maw, niger and hemp. Green food is also important in their diet, and flower buds of fruit trees and hawthorns as well as young leaves, followed by berries later in the year, will all be consumed. Insects are also eaten, particularly during the breeding season when there are chicks in the nest.

Their nest is usually located fairly low down, concealed in climbing plants or small bushes, and made from dry grasses lined with horse hair or rootlets, as well as feathers. The eggs, typically between four and six in number, are pale blue, with black and light red spotting.

Incubation lasts approximately 12 days, and the young fledge about a fortnight later. A good selection of rearing foods should be offered at this stage. Once acclimatised, Rosefinches are hardy, and may be wintered outdoors in an aviary with a suitable shelter.

186 Saffron Finch *Sicalis flaveola*

Origin: *much of South America*

Cock: 6in (15cm) Forehead and crown bright orange; sides of head yellow. Upperparts greenish-yellow, with indistinct dusky streaks. Underparts clear yellow. Iris brown; beak horn-coloured; legs and feet brownish-yellow.

Hen: Duller in coloration than the cock, with orange on the crown being less pronounced. Upperparts more brownish-grey; throat grey.

These colourful finches are a popular choice for an aviary, although they can also be kept in a spacious cage. Saffron Finches are easy to maintain on a diet of canary seed and all kinds of millet, as well as insects and plenty of green food. They may also take insectivorous food, and they are particularly fond of ripening grass seeds, which should be supplied whenever possible, particularly during the breeding season.

These finches are not usually aggressive by nature, even when nesting. Cocks have a clear, sweet voice, which is most likely to be heard at this time of year. For breeding purposes, nestboxes or even the abandoned nests of other birds may be used. Saffron Finches typically construct an untidy nest, using whatever materials are available and lining the interior with wool and feathers.

Incubation lasts a fortnight, and the adults require a variety of rearing foods, such as rusk crumbs mixed with egg yolk or a proprietary egg food, soaked seeds and green food for their chicks. When they fledge at about 16 days old, the youngsters have greyish-brown upperparts, with an olive wash and blackish streaks. The underparts are greyish-white, with yellow plumage restricted to their undertail coverts and thighs.

Towards the end of their first year, they develop a yellow band across the throat and chest, and it may be three years before young cocks attain their full colouring. They are likely to breed before this stage, however, while still in immature plumage.

Saffron Finches may nest two or three times during a season, and it is advisable to remove the young birds as soon as they are feeding independently, which will be by about a fortnight after fledging. If they are not moved, they may be persecuted by the cock bird.

There are four separate races of this finch, of which the most distinctive is probably Pelzeln's Saffron Finch (*S.f. pelzelni*). This is found in the southern part of the species' range, in Brazil and Argentina. Such birds can be recognised by the presence of dark markings on the sides of the body.

Rufous-collared Sparrow (Andean Sparrow)

Zonotrichia capensis

Origin: *Central and South America*

Cock: 6in (15cm) Crown grey, with black dividing lines. Eyebrow stripe grey; ear coverts black with white markings. Neck chestnut-brown; back and shoulders brown streaked with black, remainder of upperparts brown; underparts whitish-grey. Wings brown with grey markings. Tail brown. Iris brown; beak brown; legs and feet dark pink.

Hen: Similar in appearance but may be slightly smaller.

Although it is intermittently seen, like many neotropical finches, the Rufous-collared Sparrow occurs over a vast area in the wild, and as many as 25 subspecies are recognised by taxonomists. In spite of the name, these are actually considered to be American buntings, although they are not talented songsters, unlike other members of the group.

Their care is reasonably straightforward, and a diet based on a mixture of millets and plain canary seed will suit them well. They will also eat green food, some insects and even a little fruit. Once they are acclimatised, Rufous-collared Sparrows can prove quite hardy, but they must always have a snug shelter forming part of their aviary.

Adequate seclusion is vital for breeding purposes. A pair will construct a cup-shaped nest, often low down and hidden in a bush. Several broods may be raised here in succession, provided that the birds are left undisturbed. If they are disturbed, however, they may desert their nest and abandon any eggs or chicks. A typical clutch is of one to three eggs, which are greyish in colour with dark splodges and a rusty band.

Incubation lasts about 11 days on average, but the chicks develop slowly and are unlikely to fledge until they are at least three weeks old. They are protected by their parents, who will attack other birds that approach them. At this stage, the youngsters are duller in coloration, lacking the characteristic rufous collar. Their underparts are also more heavily streaked.

187 **Black-headed Siskin** *Carduelis magellanica*

Origin: *South America*

Cock: 5in (13cm) Black head, neck and throat. Rump, uppertail coverts and whole of underparts yellow. Wings and tail black, with greenish-yellow and white margins; remainder of upperparts striated greenish-yellow. Iris brown; beak black; legs and feet brown.

Hen: Head and upperparts olive-grey; underparts grey; belly white. Tail blackish-brown.

This species is decidedly rare in aviculture at present, and because a majority of cock birds was available in the past, it was difficult to establish breeding stock. In view of their wide distribution, however, it is possible that these siskins may become available again. They need to be carefully acclimatised to new surroundings, and their diet is most important at this stage. These birds require extra warmth and clean water for bathing purposes.

Canary seed and millet, as well as maw, rape, niger, linseed and a little hemp should be supplied as part of their diet, along with green food and some live food. Soaked seed provides valuable variety, and is particularly important for recently imported birds and during the breeding season.

At first they should be housed indoors in a flight containing either growing shrubs or natural branches. They can be transferred to an outside aviary when the weather is warm.

Black-headed Siskins are very active by nature, and like to clamber about high up in the aviary where they will hang from branches and from wire netting. The top of their flight should be covered with plastic sheeting to protect them from cats and other predators. A branch can then be suspended under this covering so that the birds cannot damage their tails on the wire when displaying their trapeze skills. The song of these siskins is reminiscent of that of the Goldfinch.

When breeding, a pair will build a cup-shaped nest, which is lined with wool and feathers. Their four to five eggs take 13 days to hatch, and the parent birds will become more insectivorous when rearing their chicks.

188 **Red Hooded Siskin** *Carduelis cucullata*

Origin: *northwest South America*

Cock: 4in (10cm) Head and throat black; sides of neck and lower parts bright scarlet. Back and scapulars brownish-scarlet, with orange-red feathering on rump and uppertail coverts. Wings black, with the wing coverts having red edges and tips. Abdomen and thighs white. Flight feathers and tail have a black base. Iris brown; beak dark horn; legs and feet greyish.

Hen: Predominantly grey on the upperparts with a wash of vermilion on the back and bright vermilion on the rump. Underparts orange-red, with white on the thighs and abdomen.

These birds have declined in numbers in the wild where they are strictly protected. Captive-bred stock, however, is occasionally available.

In the past these siskins were hybridised with canaries in order to introduce the highly desired 'red factor'. Although during the 1920s, when such pairings were first made, the resulting offspring were usually infertile, this problem has since been overcome, and red factor canaries are now well established. It did not prove possible to produce pure red birds, however, as the geneticists who started this programme had hoped. Young cock birds tended to be an attractive reddish-brown, while hens more closely resembled the siskin hen.

Red-hooded Siskins are lively by nature, and both sexes will sing, although the cock tends to be more mellifluous.

During the breeding season, the cock stays close to his mate and often feeds her. The hen alone incubates the eggs in a cup-shaped nest, built in an open-fronted nestbox or in the open, using dried grasses, coconut fibres and similar materials. She also feeds the young unaided until they leave the nest, when the cock takes over. Throughout the rearing period, egg food should be provided, along with green food and soaked seed. Insects may be given but are rarely consumed.

The chicks are typically independent by the time they are six weeks old, and they will begin to moult at about four months of age, obtaining full adult coloration two months later. The adult birds may produce two rounds of offspring in rapid succession. They will benefit from heated winter accommodation.

Black-headed Bunting   *Emberiza melanocephala*

Origin: *southeast Europe to India*

Cock: 8in (20cm) Upperparts chestnut-brown and grey, with lighter margins and dark striations. Crown and sides of the head black. Wings blackish. Rump yellow; underparts bright yellow. Iris dark brown; beak dark grey; legs and feet pinkish-brown.

Hen: Head dusky-brown; breast pale yellow, fading almost to white on the belly and with no striations on the flanks. Undertail coverts bright yellow.

One of the biggest buntings, cock Black-headed Buntings have a very attractive song and are not aggressive by nature. Pairs will breed in a well-planted aviary, provided that insectivorous food is supplied in addition to seed. A cup-shaped nest is built in thick shrubbery, with incubation of the four or five brown-spotted green-blue eggs lasting 13 days. The young are reared mainly on live food, at least in the early stages, and suitable items such as aphids, spiders and small crickets should be freely available to the adult birds at this time.

Black-headed Buntings are one of the hardiest species if they are properly acclimatised. They can overwinter in an outdoor aviary, as long as there is a frost-proof shelter to roost in at night.

Red-headed Bunting (Brown-headed Bunting)

Emberiza bruniceps

Origin: *central Asia to India*

Cock: 8in (20cm) Upperparts, head and throat olive-brown; breast and belly yellow, with a brown sheen. Rump yellow, with the wings and tail coverts having lighter margins. Iris dark brown; beak dark grey; legs and feet pinkish-brown.

Hen: Paler in terms of overall coloration. Upperparts brownish-grey with dark striations. Underparts dull yellowish-white.

Closely related to the Black-headed Bunting and requiring similar care, the Red-headed Bunting is also now much scarcer in aviculture than was formerly the case. Nevertheless, it can still be seen in some collections, and it has been bred on a number of occasions. The first success to be achieved in Britain took place at Chester Zoo in 1973. A pair built a nest in a honeysuckle bush in a large planted flight and reared their offspring on both insects and seeds.

189 Crested Bunting *Melophus lathami*

Origin: *Indian subcontinent to China*

Cock: 7in (18cm) Overall glossy blue-black with prominent crest; tail coverts cinnamon at the base. Wings and tail dark cinnamon with dusky tips. Iris dark brown; beak blackish, with flesh-coloured base to the lower mandible; legs and feet pinkish.

Hen: Dusky brown above, with the feathers having paler edges. Wings and tail paler cinnamon than the cock. Lores and area around the eyes whitish; cheeks ashy; throat yellowish-white. Underparts dull brown with black streaks. Undertail coverts reddish with black streaks. Crest less developed.

Although they are rare in aviculture, these buntings make interesting aviary birds. The cock has a quite musical call, often choosing a prominent position to display to his intended mate. She builds the nest on her own. When feeding, Crested Buntings hunt for insects on the trunks of trees, and live food is a vital part of their diet, particularly if a pair go to nest. In addition, they should be provided with a mixture of seeds, green food and suitable rearing food when breeding. They will thrive in a planted aviary after being carefully acclimatised, but they should receive adequate protection against the cold during the winter months.

Cinnamon-breasted Rock Bunting *Emberiza tahapisi*

Origin: *north and central parts of Africa through to southern Arabian Peninsula*

Cock: 5in (13cm) Head and throat black, with white stripes above and below the eyes. Upperparts cinnamon, with dark brown striations. Wings rust-coloured and brown-black. Underparts cinnamon.

Hen: Browner and duller in coloration.

Although this species is not especially popular with aviculturists, possibly because of its relatively dull coloration, it nevertheless has a particular charm. These birds are lively and not shy by nature, and although they are not great songsters, they have a floating, butterfly-like flight. They also walk or hop about the floor of their quarters, hunting for food.

Normally peaceable, Cinnamon-breasted Rock Buntings may become more aggressive during the breeding season. Their nest is sometimes built in a nestbox or a nesting basket placed high up. The exterior is constructed using moss and grasses, with the interior being lined with softer materials. Four eggs form the typical clutch, and these will take 12 days to hatch. The chicks fledge at about two weeks of age and will be independent after a similar interval.

A canary seed mixture, along with a little groats, hemp and millet should form the basis of their diet, along with a little insectivorous food and live food. When there are chicks, a canary-rearing food and soaked seed should also be supplied each day.

These buntings, which originate from a relatively arid part of the world, thrive in warm weather. They dislike damp, wet conditions and so should be brought indoors to heated surroundings over the winter period.

Indigo Bunting *Passerina cyanea*

Origin: *Canada to Venezuela and islands in the Caribbean*

Cock: 5in (13cm) In colour during the spring and summer in the northern hemisphere, distinguishable by the overall predominantly bright blue coloration, which is darker on the crown and with shades of violet on the side of the head. Wings and tail are a combination of black and chestnut. Iris brown; beak greyish; legs and feet black. It is sometimes possible to recognise cocks outside the breeding season by the presence of odd blue feathers near the shoulder and on the tail.

Hen: Resembles out-of-colour cock but generally a paler shade of dull brown.

Indigo Buntings have become scarce in aviculture over recent years, but their care presents no particular problems, and they make an attractive addition to any collection.

When they are first imported, these birds can be rather delicate and need special care. They soon settle down well, if provided with a varied diet. Soaked seeds and invertebrates are valuable at this stage, and green food and fresh leaf buds should also be supplied whenever possible, along with softbill food. A standard canary seed mix, as well as other seeds such as millets will be needed.

It appears that the regular provision of live food helps to ensure the full beauty of the cock's coloration. Mealworms, crickets and similar insects can be used for this purpose, and fresh fruit, ranging from cherries and various berries to apples and pears, will also be beneficial.

The cock Indigo Bunting is aggressive during the breeding season, and if they cannot be housed in a flight on their own it is best to keep them with larger species. Cocks will always fight each other, so pairs must be kept apart. In the late afternoon through to dusk, the male's clear, melodious song will be heard frequently through the spring and summer. Being migratory by nature, you may notice that these birds become more restless than normal about October.

It is not easy to breed this species, but a pair may nest in a well-planted aviary, sometimes using a box placed not too high up above the ground. Alternatively, they may build their nest low down in thick shrubbery. The nest itself is constructed of grass stems, hemp fibres and roots, although proprietary nesting material as sold by pet shops for Canaries would doubtless prove satisfactory as well. Three or four eggs form the typical clutch, with incubation lasting about 13 days. During the winter months, Indigo Buntings should be housed in frost-free quarters.

192 Lazuli Bunting *Passerina amoena*

Origin: *western USA to Mexico*

Cock: 5in (13cm) Head and rump bright blue; remainder of upperparts bluish-grey. Wings slate-grey with a whitish bar and greater coverts tipped with white. Throat and sides of breast bright blue; upper breast pale warm brown; remainder of underparts white. Iris brown; beak bluish-black; legs and feet blackish.

Hen: Mainly dull brown, with a blue wash on the crown, wings and tail. Underparts pale buff-brown.

This species requires similar care to that recommended for the Indigo Bunting. Its song is also similar and can be heard throughout the summer, with a cock choosing a prominent position in the aviary as a singing post. Pairs must not be housed in the company of other buntings, as cocks in particular may prove aggressive, especially when in breeding condition.

Rarely seen in aviculture, the Lazuli Bunting has never proved to be a prolific species in the past. In the wild, the nests of these birds are found about 3ft (1m) above ground in thick shrubbery, and they are made of grass lined with soft hairs and fibres. In a large flight, which is thickly planted with shrubs, and given a varied diet, which includes plenty of live food, a pair may be persuaded to nest. They are likely to be highly insectivorous during the rearing period if chicks are hatched successfully. Once acclimatised, these buntings require snug, frost-free winter accommodation.

5 Nonpareil Bunting *Passerina ciris*

Origin: *USA to Central America*

Cock: 5in (13cm) Head and shoulders blue; an area of red feathering may encircle the eyes; mantle and back yellowish-green, becoming greener over the wings. Throat and entire underparts reddish. Iris dark brown; beak greyish; legs and feet greyish.

Hen: Lacks the blue coloration on the head, with the red on the underparts replaced by dull yellowish-green.

When Nonpareil Buntings were more freely available cocks tended to outnumber hens, and obtaining true pairs could, therefore, be problematical. Young cocks resemble hens, but selecting individuals with the whitest throat and necks was recommended, as such birds were the most likely to be hens. The red coloration of the cock fades over successive moults, and colour feeding immediately prior to and during the moulting period is recommended to prevent this loss of colour.

The Nonpareil Bunting has acquired a reputation for being the most enthusiastic member of its genus to breed in aviary surroundings. Pairs may even rear three broods during a season. They soon become quite tame and remain steady even when nesting.

The nest itself may be built in a well-branched shrub or sometimes even in a nestbox with a partially open front. Stems of dried grass, coconut fibres, strips of paper and moss will be used to make the cup-shaped structure, which is lined with soft materials such as feathers.

The hen will incubate alone, and the eggs should hatch in about 13 days. The chicks will be reared largely on live food, along with egg food and even softbill food in some cases. A regular seed diet should also be given, and a regular supply of green food provided.

Assuming all goes well, the young buntings will leave the nest after about 10 days, and will be fed by both parents if the hen has not started to nest again. If the hen is nesting again, the cock will be responsible for caring for the offspring until they are independent. Pairs are likely to be aggressive through the breeding season. Compared with other species, the song of the cock Nonpareil Bunting is rather restricted.

193 Rainbow Bunting *Passerina leclancheri*

194 Origin: *Mexico*

Cock: 5in (13cm) *Upperparts sky blue, with a greenish tinge on the mantle; crown and tail bluish-green; ear coverts and sides of the neck cobalt. Cheeks and underparts bright orangish-yellow. Iris brown; beak greyish, darker on the upper bill; legs and feet blackish.*

Hen: Olive-green, being more yellowish on the underparts and with bluish wash on the tail.

In spite of their beautiful coloration, Rainbow Buntings invariably prove to be shy birds in aviary surroundings. They often hide away in the bushes and rarely show themselves, except when feeding and occasionally in the grass. They are not especially nervous birds, however, and cocks have a soft but melodious song.

An avicultural rarity at present, like other *Passerina* species, the Rainbow Bunting closely resembles the Nonpareil Bunting in its requirements. They can be kept with other birds in a well-planted outside aviary during the summer but should be moved into a frost-free birdroom through the winter.

If they are provided with a varied diet, these buntings will retain their attractive pastel coloration through the moult. Lack of breeding successes in the past was probably often the result of incorrect feeding. Live food, soft foods and green food should form their main diet during the breeding period, while seeds assume much less significance at this time.

196 Versicoloured Bunting (Varied Bunting) *Passerina versicolor*

Origin: *northern and Central America*

Cock: 5in (13cm) *Purplish above; back of the crown and orbital ring scarlet; throat purplish. Underparts purplish-blue and grey. Iris dark brown; beak greyish-horn in colour; legs and feet blackish.*

Hen: Dull brown, paler on the underparts. Flights and tail washed with dull blue. Wing coverts edged with pale buff.

A decidedly uncommon species in aviculture, this attractively coloured bunting is confined mainly to Mexico, but is also seen across the US border in Arizona and Texas. It is shy by nature and spends much of its time on the ground, seeking out insects.

Versicoloured Buntings need particular care when they are first obtained, as they can prove rather delicate. A good supply of live food must be offered, particularly as they seem more insectivorous than related species. Even so, they should be encouraged to take a balanced diet and must not be allowed to gorge themselves on mealworms, as they may otherwise do. They must be overwintered in relatively warm surroundings. At this time of the year, the cock's plumage will be duller than in the breeding season, but it is still possible to sex these buntings at this stage without difficulty.

Diuca Finch *Diuca diuca*

Origin: *Chile and Argentina*

Cock: 7in (18cm) *Upperparts grey; lores black; cheeks and throat white. Breast and sides of the body light grey, with the belly being white with a chestnut spot. Undertail coverts white with chestnut margins. Wings grey and greyish-black. Tail black. Iris brown; beak black; legs and feet grey.*

Hen: *Similar to the cock, but browner with less distinctive markings.*

Like other South American finches, the Diuca is only intermittently available, and cocks tend to predominate in most consignments. These birds have soft voices, and they chirrup and chatter readily. They are attractive by nature and soon settle down well, even in a cage, becoming quite tame.

Feeding presents no particular problems, as they are very undemanding birds in terms of diet. A basic seed mix, composed of millets and plain canary seed, should be offered, along with a range of green food, live food and softbill food on occasions. Fruit can also be given from time to time.

Breeding has been successfully achieved both in cage and aviary surroundings where adequate cover is available and a good supply of live food for rearing the chicks is provided. The cup-shaped nest, which is made from small twigs, dried grass, rootlets, coconut fibre and feathers, is usually constructed in a nestbox.

Three or four eggs, with brownish or blue spotting on their surface, will be laid and will hatch after about 13 days. Both cock and hen feed their offspring with a selection of live food, such as hatchling crickets, and other items such as egg food. Unless suitable supplies of insects can be maintained, the chicks are likely to be neglected. After 16 days, however, assuming that all has gone well, the young Diuca Finches will leave the nest, being fed by their parents for another 10 days or so, by which time they will then be fully independent.

Pileated Finch *Coryphospingus pileatus*

Origin: *northern South America*

Cock: 6in (15cm) *Upperparts grey, with scarlet crest edged with black; lores whitish. Underparts pale grey; tail black. Iris dark brown; beak greyish-horn; legs and feet greyish.*

Hen: *Smaller, blackish crest, with sandy shade to the upperparts. Breast streaked with blackish-brown.*

These lively crested finches soon settle down and are easily tamed, even to the extent that they may be persuaded to nest in a cage, although better results may be anticipated in aviary surroundings. It is best to house a pair on their own in a small aviary planted with dwarf conifers, the dense branches of which will form a secure basis for the nest. This will be constructed from stems of dried grass, coconut fibres, moss and similar material. The nest tends to be relatively bulky, and it is built by the hen alone. Her mate remains in close attendance, however, and will frequently raise his chest to his partner in display. These finches are not always recommended for a communal flight because of their potentially aggressive natures, particularly during the breeding season.

Their breeding cycle is very fast, with the hen incubating alone. The clutch size is typically three eggs, and these should hatch after just 11 days, with a similarly short fledging interval. A suitable supply of small live food is critical at this time, and if it is not provided the chicks will almost certainly be neglected. Mealworms are generally too large, but hatchling crickets, along with other invertebrates such as aphids and small spiders, will be ideal. A rearing food should also be supplied.

Red-crested Finch *Coryphospingus cucullatus*

Origin: *much of South America*

Cock: 6in (15cm) Upperparts reddish-brown; underparts vinous. Crest carmine with black edges; chin whitish. Wings black; tail brownish. Iris dark brown; beak grey, darker on the upper bill; legs and feet greyish.

Hen: Predominantly light brown, becoming bright vinous on the underparts. Crest smaller and brown, and relatively inconspicuous compared with that of the cock.

Very similar in its requirements to the Pileated Finch, this member of the bunting group should be offered a mixed diet of seeds, including plain canary seed and millets, as well as green food, live food and a little fruit. The birds will benefit from having access to an outside aviary during the warmer months of the year, but they should be brought inside to overwinter in frost-free surroundings, even when they are acclimatised.

Red-crested Finches are relatively peaceful by nature, but the best breeding results are likely to be obtained if these birds are housed in a flight on their own where they will not be disturbed and where they are unlikely to be faced with a shortage of live food, which may happen in a mixed collection when other birds will be competing with them for insects.

Breeding details are similar to those of the Pileated Finch, with the young being reared almost entirely on live food. They will fledge before they can fly and are watched closely by the adults, with the cock then being responsible for feeding their offspring, as the hen starts nesting again. The youngsters resemble the adult hen in appearance, but are duller in coloration with only a trace of vinous on the breast. As many as three broods may be produced by a pair during the course of the summer.

It has been said that cock Red-crested Finches were paired with hen Canaries as part of the attempt to produce red Canaries. Their red coloration is darker than that of the Hooded Siskin, which is most often used for this purpose, but details of such matings are sketchy and do not appear to have been carried out in recent years.

8 Black-crested Finch (Pygmy Finch) *Lophospingus pusillus*

Origin: *Bolivia, Argentina and Paraguay*

Cock: 5in (13cm) Crown and prominent crest black, with a black spot also on the throat, and a black line extending through the eyes, with white plumage above and below here. Back greyish-brown, becoming greyer over the rump; wings ashy-grey, while the wing coverts are partially white. Tail black, with white tips. Underparts entirely ashy-grey, apart from the whitish area at the centre of the abdomen. Iris dark brown; beak greyish-horn, darker on the upper bill; legs and feet greyish.

Hen: Tends to be paler, with a greyer crest, and a whitish throat, with no black marking here.

These attractive members of the bunting clan may not be especially colourful, but they are lively and often nest quite readily. They have reasonably straightforward requirements. A diet based on plain canary seed and millets, along with softbill food, some live food and green food suits them well. Black-crested Finches are not entirely hardy, and they need to be kept in moderately warm winter quarters, even when acclimatised.

Breeding results have been obtained in both indoor flights and outdoor aviaries. These birds can be aggressive, particularly at this stage, and they are best housed on their own in individual pairs. The hen will make a cup-shaped nest, often adopting a canary nesting pan for this purpose. This will be lined with soft hair and small feathers. Alternatively, a relatively flimsy nest of twigs and rootlets lined with finer materials and built in some twiggy branch close to the main stem of a shrub or pine tree may be preferred.

The hen will lay two or three greeny-grey eggs, which take 12 days to hatch; the young fledge after a similar interval. Insects are vital for rearing purposes, forming almost the entire diet of the young birds while they remain in the nest. Inert foods are likely to be ignored, but should be provided in the hope that they may be sampled, which will add to the protein level of the diet. After fledging, the youngsters are fed on a variety of food by the cock until they are independent at about three weeks old.

Subsequently, when the adult birds show signs of nesting again, remove these youngsters, or they may be plucked by their parents, with their feathers being used to line the new nest. The fledglings resemble the hen

279

in terms of coloration, but they are usually slightly paler. After five months they will have moulted into adult plumage, and the difference between cocks and hens will then be clearly apparent. If they are to be housed with other birds, larger species such as weavers should be chosen as their companions and not small waxbills.

201 Virginian Cardinal (Scarlet Cardinal, Virginian Nightingale)

Cardinalis cardinalis

Origin: *Much of USA, eastern Canada and Central America*

Cock: 8in (20cm) Completely red, apart from a black area around the beak, extending down on to the throat. Erect crest. Iris brown; beak red; legs and feet reddish.

Hen: Entirely brown, paler on the underparts.

There may be some variation in the size of these spectacularly coloured cardinals through their wide range. The great difference in coloration between the sexes means that it is easy to select a true pair, and successful breeding results have been recorded on a number of occasions.

The alternative common name of Virginian Nightingale is something of an exaggeration of the singing abilities of these birds. Their song is certainly melodious and loud and can be heard for hours on a moonlit night, but it does not attain the variety and richness of that of the Nightingale. The hen, as well as the cock, sings during the breeding season.

A seed mix based on the small cereal seeds, with other seeds such as rape, hemp and some sunflower, is recommended, but the oil seed content of the diet should not predominate because these cardinals are susceptible to obesity.

They are best kept in a large flight where they can have plenty of exercise, rather than in a cage. Their liveliness, tail movements and alert demeanour make them a constant source of pleasure to watch. Although they are often shy at first, Virginian Cardinals will soon come to recognise their owner and rapidly learn to catch mealworms that are thrown to them.

Pairs should be kept in a flight on their own for breeding purposes, otherwise there is likely to be constant bickering and fighting. The hen will build a nest of grasses and other fibrous material in a shrub or conifer. Two or three bluish-green eggs will be laid here, and these should hatch after a period of about 13 days, with both parents feeding the young.

The chicks develop very rapidly. They will leave the nest after just 10 days, when they are barely covered with feathers. For rearing purposes, the adults should be offered a limitless supply of live food, as well as egg food, grated carrots and fruit such as apples. A shortage of live food will almost inevitably lead to breeding disappointment.

As two or even three broods may be produced in a season, young birds should be removed from the flight as soon as they are feeding independently, which is usually about a fortnight after fledging. Colour feeding and a varied diet are important in maintaining the cock's fiery red coloration. Virginian Cardinals are quite hardy once they are established, and they can be kept in an outside aviary throughout the year as long as they have a snug shelter in bad weather.

5 Green Cardinal *Gubernatrix cristata*

Origin: *Uruguay and Argentina*

Cock: 7in (18cm) *Upperparts olive-green, streaked with dusky black. Crest, chin and throat velvety-black. A broad streak over the eyes and on the sides of the throat is bright golden-yellow. Breast greenish-yellow; belly and undertail coverts bright yellow. Tail bright yellow with the two centre feathers blackish. Iris dark brown; beak greyish, darker on the upper bill; legs and feet blackish.*

Hen: *Streak over the eye is pure white as are the sides of the throat. Breast brownish-grey, with the yellow colouring being less vivid.*

Generally considered to be more willing to nest than other cardinals, the Green Cardinal is not a difficult bird to care for as it feeds on a range of seeds, green food, berries and fruit, as well as live food, which is especially vital during the breeding period.

It is much better to keep pairs by themselves, especially when nesting, because Green Cardinals are liable to prove very pugnacious. Although they may be persuaded to use a nestbox, they often prefer to build their nest in a thick bush or hedge, where an artificial mesh base or a wicker basket has been concealed. They favour grass stems for this purpose.

Incubation lasts about 13 days, with the chicks fledging after a similar period. As many as six eggs may be laid, but a typical clutch is three or four eggs, although more than one brood of chicks may be reared during the summer months.

0 Red-crested Cardinal *Paroaria coronata*

Origin: *southern South America*

Cock: 8in (20cm) *Head and crest brilliant red, extending down on to the throat and upper breast. Upperparts grey, with lighter edging to some of the feathers here. Sides of neck, and remainder of underparts white, becoming more greyish on the flanks. Iris dark brown; beak light horn, darker at the tip; legs and feet greyish.*

Hen: *Similar in appearance, but often said to be smaller and slimmer, with the red on the head area being less extensive.*

The simplest means of sexing these cardinals is during the breeding season, when the cock's song will be frequently heard. They are hardy and robust birds when they are acclimatised and are lively by nature. Unfortunately, Red-crested Cardinals are aggressive, and pairs should be housed on their own in a suitable planted aviary.

They will soon begin to breed, building a rather untidy nest from material such as dried grasses and heather. A pair may adopt an artificial nest, located at least 3ft (1m) off the ground in a thick box bush or privet hedge. The hen will lay three or four eggs, which she incubates largely on her own. The chicks should hatch about two weeks later, and at first are fed almost exclusively on small insects, augmented with egg food and similar foods. Fledging occurs after a similar period. A selection of seeds, green food and fruit, as recommended for other cardinals, should also be offered to these birds. Colour-feeding is also useful just before and during the moult to maintain the fiery red head coloration. Although it has been said that hens can be recognised by their paler red plumage, this is more likely to be a reflection of their diet rather than their gender.

202 Pope Cardinal (Red-cowled Cardinal) *Paroaria dominicana*

Origin: *northeast Brazil*

Cock: 7in (18cm) *Resembles the Red-crested Cardinal but lacks the crest. Head brilliant red, extending down to the throat. Upperparts dark grey, with white edging to some of the feathers. Underparts white, becoming more greyish on the flanks. Iris brown; beak horn-coloured darker on the upper bill; legs and feet greyish.*

Hen: *Similar in appearance but may be slightly smaller.*

This species has a long avicultural history, and although it is not at present available from its native range, it is possible to obtain captive-bred stock. It needs identical care to the Red-crested Cardinal. The song of the Pope Cardinal is fairly melodious, although it does not compare with that of the Virginian Cardinal. Compatibility can sometimes be a problem when it comes to breeding, and ideally the birds should be allowed to pair up on their own. When a bond is apparent the pair can be moved to separate accommodation and provided with breeding facilities there.

Although Pope Cardinals tend to be somewhat less aggressive than other species, this difference is relative, and pairs are best kept on their own for breeding purposes. Some individuals can be particularly pugnacious. Breeding details are the same as for the Red-crested Cardinal. The cock may help in the construction of the nest and will assume responsibility for feeding the chicks after they have fledged.

▶3 Yellow-billed Cardinal *Paroaria capitata*

Origin: *Brazil, Argentina, Paraguay and Bolivia*

Cock: 7in (18cm) Head intense carmine, with black throat mark running down to a point on the breast. Nape pure white with small black crescent marks. Remainder of upperparts black; underparts snowy white. Iris brown; beak yellow; legs and feet yellow.

Hen: A duller shade of brick red on the head, with the mantle being greyer.

The more pointed beak of this species indicates that it is more insectivorous in its feeding habits than the cardinals already discussed. The Yellow-billed Cardinal will take more live food as part of its regular diet but will also feed on seeds and green food. The buds of fruit trees, provided they have not been sprayed with chemicals, are particularly popular with these birds.

The nest is usually concealed in a dense bush and is cup-shaped, with the foundation being made of thin twigs and coarse grasses and lined with moss and other soft materials. Breeding details do not differ significantly from those of related species. The young are reared largely on insects and require almost unlimited quantities of soft-bodied invertebrates. Egg food may also be eaten and will assist in rearing the young, as will a supply of chickweed.

Young birds can be distinguished by their sandy-buff heads and brown throats. Their beaks are also stained with slate-grey. Less hardy than other cardinals, the Yellow-billed may need to be brought inside over the winter.

▶4 Black-tailed Hawfinch (Chinese Hawfinch, Yellow-billed Grosbeak) *Coccothraustes migratorius*

Origin: *eastern Asia, from Amur to China*

Cock: 8in (20cm) Head entirely black, as is the throat. Upperparts greyish-brown; uppertail coverts white. Tail black with a bluish gloss. Breast grey becoming white on the abdomen. Wings black with white tips. Iris brown; beak yellow with darker base and tip; legs and feet pinkish.

Hen: Lacks the black coloration on the head, which is drab grey. Upperparts greyish-brown, lighter below with a white belly and yellow flanks.

Similar to the Black-headed Hawfinch (*Coccothraustes personatus*), which occurs both in north and west China and further east in Japan, this species is somewhat smaller in size. In addition, its head is entirely black, whereas that of the rather incorrectly named Black-headed Hawfinch has grey plumage on the ear coverts, with black feathering being restricted to the crown, lores, base of the cheeks and the chin.

Both species require similar care. Their diet should be based on a mixture of cereal and oil seeds, including millets, plain canary seed, groats, rape, hemp and sunflower seed. Small pine nuts are also appreciated. Since hawfinches can be rather prone to obesity, particularly in cage surroundings, hemp, sunflower and other seeds with a high fat content should be fed in restricted amounts. A regular supply of fruit such as apples should be offered throughout the year, as well as various twigs from which the buds will be eaten. Live food is also important.

When these birds sing, they make a pleasant whistling sound with peculiar long-lasting notes. It can sometimes be difficult to obtain a pair because cocks tend to predominate in most consignments. They are not especially popular with aviculturists, in spite of the fact that these birds can make fascinating aviary occupants. Their powerful beaks mean that a pair should be housed on their own and never in the company of smaller birds.

A planted aviary is recommended for hawfinches. They will often begin to build a nest right at the end of the winter, favouring a site high up in the aviary, typically in a dense shrub or ivy. A cup-shaped nest is produced, consisting of thin twigs as a base, with an inner lining woven from dried grasses, fibres and horsehair.

The typical clutch of four bluish-green eggs will be incubated by the hen alone, and they should hatch after 12 days. The cock will feed the hen on the nest and will later share in the rearing of the youngsters. Rearing foods should consist of assorted live food, which can include mealworms, softbill food and egg food. Soaked seed is also valuable, particularly as a weaning food once the chicks have left the nest. They are best removed to separate quarters once they are feeding independently in case the adult birds want to nest again.

Cocks should be watched carefully during the courtship period to ensure that they do not attack their mates in their ardour. A densely planted aviary and a choice of feeding sites should help to prevent this. Hawfinches are quite hardy once they are acclimatised, and they can usually be overwintered without extra heat, provided a dry, well-lit and draught-proof shelter is attached to their flight.

206 Blue Grosbeak (Northern Blue Grosbeak) *Guiraca caerulea*

Origin: *south USA, through Mexico and Central America down to Nicaragua and Costa Rica*

Cock: 7in (18cm) Forehead, chin and lores black. Flights and secondaries blackish, edged with blue; median wing coverts chestnut. Remaining upperparts deep, shining cobalt blue, with softer greyish-blue underparts. Iris brown; upper bill almost entirely black, lower bill greyish-blue; legs and feet greyish-black.

Hen: Upperparts olive-brown, becoming more rufous on the crown; hindneck faintly streaked with buff. Median wing coverts tawny-buff; tail dusky edged with blue. Underparts paler brownish-buff; chin and throat whitish.

During the winter the cock's coloration is duller, with the bright blue plumage being replaced by less conspicuous feathering. The whitish-buff and yellowish-brown edging to the plumage serves to obscure the blue areas almost completely, creating a scalloped effect.

This is a charming species, which will become quite tame, but unfortunately cocks in particular are inclined to bully other birds of their own size or smaller, and pairs are best kept on their own. They are comparatively hardy once acclimatised, and as long as the weather does not become too severe they can remain in an unheated aviary throughout the year, if there is a well-built, draught-free shelter.

Their diet should consist of a seed mixture containing canary seed, white and panicum millet, groats, sunflower, buckwheat and a little hemp. They also appreciate apple, from which they will often first extract and eat the pips, and they may also take rose hips, hawthorn and elderberries. They display little interest in green food.

Breeding results are uncommon, but were first obtained at London Zoo in 1921. Details are similar to those of the Brazilian Blue Grosbeak, with live food again being vital for rearing purposes.

Brazilian Blue Grosbeak *Cyanocompsa cyanea*

Origin: *South America*

Cock: 6in (15cm) *Deep blue, lighter towards the tail. Forehead, chin and lores black. Crown and ear coverts cobalt blue. Abdomen and tail black. Iris brown; beak black; legs and feet black.*

Hen: Upperparts yellowish-brown; underparts warm brown, wings and tail brown.

In spite of their name, these grosbeaks occur over a much wider area of South America than Brazil. Intermittently available, the duller coloured hens are less often seen than cocks. They have a pleasant, relatively quiet voice. A diet based on a mixture of seeds as recommended for the Blue Grosbeak suits them well, and it should be augmented with live food and softbill food, as well as some fruit and greenstuff. In a cage, these birds can be prone to obesity, and the oil seed content of their diet should be reduced accordingly. Fruit and seasonal items, such as buds on twigs and green peas, should be provided whenever possible.

Brazilian Blue Grosbeaks show to best effect in an aviary. Although they tend to be less aggressive than their northern relative, their companions should be chosen with care, particularly if it is hoped to breed them successfully. A pair may well start nesting in dense shrubbery, where they may build a cup-shaped nest from grass stems and other plant fibres, lining the inside with moss and other softer material.

The typical clutch of four eggs is incubated by the hen alone, and they should start to hatch after a period of 13 days. During the nesting period, the cock sings continually. The young leave the nest after just 12 days, being fed for some weeks by their parents until they are fully independent. Soaked seed, live food and canary-rearing food should be provided daily during the breeding period. These birds like bathing, and they may be kept in an aviary throughout the year, provided that they have a suitable shelter where they can, if necessary, be confined during bad weather.

Parrot-billed Seedeater *Sporophila peruviana*

Origin: *Ecuador and Peru*

Cock: 4in (10cm) Head and upperparts grey, suffused with brown, becoming darker on the wing. White area on the wings, and at the base of the primaries. Throat black, with a white crescent below on the sides of the throat. Upper breast black, with remainder of the underparts being dull white. Iris brown; beak horn-coloured; legs and feet pinkish.

Hen: Similar to the cock, but has greyish-buff rather than black on the underparts.

The very stout, stocky beak of this species has given rise to its common name. Like other *Sporophila* finches, the Parrot-billed is not well represented in aviculture, but it has become somewhat better known during recent years. Again, hens may often be in short supply, which can make obtaining a pair difficult. It is worth persevering, however, because these finches are interesting aviary occupants. They are easy to maintain on a diet composed largely of mixed millets and plain canary seed, supplemented whenever possible by seeding grasses and other green food. Softbill food and some live food may also be eaten, while soaked seed is especially valuable during the breeding period.

At this time pairs become very pugnacious and will harass other birds, especially those of their own species. They should, therefore, be housed in a small planted flight on their own and never in the company of smaller birds such as waxbills. Breeding details are similar to those of other *Sporophila* species.

Plumbeous Seedeater *Sporophila plumbea*

Origin: *much of south America*

Cock: 5in (13cm) Ash-grey, lighter on the rump. Lores black; neck and upper breast ash-grey; breast, abdomen and undertail coverts white. Wings and tail black with grey margins. Iris greyish; beak black with lighter tip; legs and feet horn-coloured.

Hen: Light brown with a small white spot on the cheeks; underparts paler and whiter towards the abdomen.

This tends to be one of the better known *Sporophila* species, but the birds are often not very popular, possibly because of their rather drab coloration.

The pair bond is not especially strong, and disagreements between cock and hen may sometimes be seen; they rarely perch together in the same way as waxbills, for example.

Plumbeous Seedeaters may be less aggressive than other related species however, even when nesting, but breeding results will almost inevitably be better if a pair is housed on its own in a planted flight. They often like to build in a conifer, constructing a fairly deep nest from a variety of materials. They may tolerate occasional inspections, although disturbances should be kept to a minimum, especially in the case of a pair which has not bred before.

The hen will lay two or three eggs in a clutch, with both adults sharing the task of incubation, which lasts for 12 days. The chicks will be fed for three weeks or so before they are fully independent. One pair may raise three or four broods in a season. The song of the cock is shrill, but not unpleasant.

They have a long potential lifespan, having lived for more than 10 years in aviary surroundings.

Double-collared Seedeater (Bluish Finch)

Sporophila caerulescens

Origin: *southern South America*

Cock: *5in (13cm) Upperparts greyish-blue; forehead, lores, ear coverts and throat black. White moustachial stripes; narrow black crescent on upper breast. Underparts white. Wings grey-brown; uppertail coverts have a brownish suffusion. Iris brown; beak horn-coloured; legs and feet grey.*

Hen: *Upperparts olive-brown; underparts yellowish-brown; abdomen yellowish-white, somewhat browner on the flanks. Wings and tail brown.*

There are approximately 27 different species of *Sporophila* finches recognised by taxonomists, but avicultural records for most of these are rather sparse. This genus offers plenty of scope for the specialist who is keen to add to species that are well-established in aviculture. Part of the problem in obtaining pairs is not only that there is a shortage of hens but that young birds of both sexes resemble hens. It is relatively common for a supposed pair to develop into two cock birds after a moult!

The Double-collared Seedeater is quite tolerant of other unrelated species, but it is likely to prove aggressive towards members of its own genus. These birds will bathe regularly and are sufficiently hardy to be kept in an outside aviary if there is an adequate shelter.

Lined Finch (Variable Seedeater) *Sporophila americana*

Origin: *northern South merica*

Cock: 5in (13cm) Upperparts black, with head and back being glossy. There is a narrow white line running through the centre of the crown. Cheeks white; throat and chin black. Breast and centre of abdomen, as well as undertail coverts white. Base of flights white but this white is often concealed when the wings are closed. Tail black, tipped with grey. Iris brown; beak grey; legs and feet blackish.

Hen: Upperparts olive-grey; rump brown; underparts buff and brown; beak and legs horn-coloured.

A popular species as a songbird in its homeland, the Lined Finch may have a continuous or broken black line in the vicinity of the throat depending on the race concerned. When they sing, cocks usually raise the feathers of their rump and back. Breeding success does not yet appear to have been achieved with this particular species, but it is likely that its requirements at this stage are similar to those of related species. Plenty of green food should feature in their diet, including seeding grasses whenever available.

Collared Seedeater *Sporophila collaris*

Origin: *eastern Brazil and Argentina*

Cock: 5in (13cm) Upperparts black; throat white with a black band across the upper breast; abdomen light brown. Iris brown; beak horn-coloured with a yellow tip; legs and feet light horn-colour.

Hen: Upperparts brown with olive wash on head and back. Wing and tail feathers dark brown with paler margins. Sides of the head and underparts pale tawny-buff, deeper on undertail coverts. Underwing coverts buffish-white.

Sporophila finches can tend to resemble each other, and it is often difficult to distinguish among them without reference to a specialist field guide. In this case, there is also a slightly smaller race, *S.c. cucullata*, which can be distinguished by the presence of a prominent white spot between the cheek and lower bill. Sometimes called the Rusty-collared Seedeater, it also tends to be browner on the upperparts than the nominate race described above.

Their relatively powerful beaks enable the Collared Seedeater to tackle larger seeds, such as groats. Paddy rice is also often taken quite readily, as is plain canary seed, millets, rape, hemp and maw. Apples, pears, green food and even insectivorous food will also usually be eaten, along with live food.

The cock's voice is soft and melodious, and he sings frequently, sometimes being joined by the hen. The birds have a chirruping call. They will nest readily in a well-planted flight, choosing a thick shrub where they will make a cup-shaped nest from thin plant fibres and other material. Breeding details are similar to those of other *Sporophila* species.

Cinnamon Warbling Finch (Pretty Warbling Finch)

Poospiza ornata

Origin: *northwest Argentina*

Cock: 5in (13cm) Grey upperparts, becoming dark ashy-grey on the crown and uppertail coverts. Cinnamon eye stripe, with black plumage above. White bar on the wings. Underparts cinnamon, being a darker, richer shade on the breast and becoming paler towards the undertail coverts. Iris brown; beak horn-colour, with darker base to the upper mandible; legs and feet pinkish.

Hen: Significantly paler in overall coloration.

Warbling Finches are another group of neotropical buntings that are not well-represented in aviculture. In total, there are about a dozen species, none of which is brightly coloured. In fact, their coloration is reminiscent of the *Sporophila* finches, but their beaks are significantly narrower.

All the species require similar care and are not difficult to maintain on a basic diet of seeds, such as millets, plain canary seed, rape and maw. The shape of their beaks reveals the insectivorous nature of these birds, however, and live food should also figure regularly in their diet, together with an insectivorous food. They will also take fruit, and often search for food on the ground.

Warbling Finches are liable to be aggressive, and the cock often proves particularly belligerent during the breeding period, so it is best to house pairs on their own in a well-planted aviary. A pair will build a cup-shaped nest, with the hen undertaking most of the construction work, while the cock gathers material for her.

Three eggs would appear to form a typical clutch. The hen sits alone and is fed during the incubation period at least in part by the cock, which remains in close attendance. The chicks should hatch about 13 days later, and they will grow rapidly, being reared mainly on small, soft-bodied live food such as spiders.

They fledge after a similar interval, looking like the adult hen at first. Once they are independent, the young Warbling Finches should be removed to separate quarters, because the adult birds may nest two or three times in a season. The birds will need to be brought indoors to heated accommodation during the winter months, as even when established they are not entirely hardy.

Cuban Finch *Tiaris canora*

Origin: *Cuba*

Cock: 4in (10cm) Head black becoming olive-green on the mantle; remainder of upperparts having a brownish suffusion. Bright yellow crescent-shaped markings start above the eyes and widen across the breast. Underparts otherwise olive, becoming greyer behind the vent. Iris brown; beak black; legs and feet greyish.

Hen: *Duller in coloration, with a brown face and paler yellow markings.*

Quite well established in aviculture, particularly in Australia, Cuban Finches have been bred for many generations in aviary surroundings. Although they appear to be quite docile, they can become aggressive, especially during the breeding season. Pairs are best housed on their own, therefore, in a small, planted flight, or with slightly larger companions such as weavers. They should not be placed with waxbills.

Their song consists of an insignificant chirping and twittering. These finches are extremely lively, and they will soon begin to build a nest, although if they are kept in the company of other birds, they may steal one and adapt it for their own purposes. A pair will construct a dome-shaped nest, with a concealed entrance low down at the side. The passage may be 4in (10cm) long.

The eggs are greenish-white in colour, with reddish-brown dots. Clutch size is often quite small, with only two or three eggs being laid. They are incubated by the hen alone, for about 12 days. The chicks should fledge about two weeks later and are usually capable of feeding on their own within a further fortnight.

Once the youngsters leave the nest, the hen will probably lay another clutch of eggs almost immediately, with the cock then completing the rearing of their offspring until they are independent. They must then be removed to separate quarters without delay, because they may be attacked by their parents. As many as six broods have been reared successfully during a season.

The likelihood of chicks being produced will be greatly increased if the birds are allowed to nest with minimum disturbance, because any unnecessary interference may cause the hen to desert the nest, setting back the whole breeding process. Cuban Finches have been bred successfully in cage surroundings, however, when a pair may be persuaded to use a nesting basket or an open-fronted nestbox as the basis for their nest. Feeding should be as for the Olive Finch, with live food being of relatively little significance for rearing purposes, although it will be beneficial.

197 Olive Finch *Tiaris olivacea*

Origin: *parts of Central and South America, Cuba, Haiti, Jamaica and other West Indian islands*

Cock: *4in (10cm) Upperparts olive; cheeks black; eyebrows and throat orange-yellow. Abdomen olive-grey, with black chest. Iris dark brown; beak blackish; legs and feet blackish.*

Hen: Paler in coloration with no black on the chest and less prominent orange-yellow throat markings.

Cocks of this species often have a variable amount of black plumage on their chest, depending on the race concerned, but it is still possible to recognise hens without difficulty.

A diet based on a mixture of plain canary seed, millets and other small seeds suits these birds well. They will also eat seeding grasses readily, as well as other green food. Soaked seed is especially valuable during the breeding season, as are egg food and small live food, including ant pupae if these are available, although the chicks may be reared largely on seeds.

Their breeding habits are similar to those of the Cuban Finch. Chicks must again be removed from the adults once they are feeding independently. Breeding in a cage has been achieved successfully, but it is more likely to occur in a flight that is planted with box bushes and conifers. Olive Finches may prove aggressive, and it is probably best to house individual pairs separately if possible.

Jacarini Finch *Volatinia jacarini*

Origin: *Central and much of South America.*

Cock: 4in (10cm) Almost entirely black, with dark blue reflection, especially on head and nape. During flight, the white underneath the wings becomes visible. Iris brown; bill black; legs and feet blackish.

Hen: Earthy brown on the upperparts, ashy on the head. Underparts pale brown.

These birds are tolerant by nature, and they will sing in a very cheerful manner. Sexing is straightforward because of the differences in plumage. Breeding in aviary surroundings was first achieved in Britain in 1910, and since then a number of aviculturists have been successful with this species.

Cock and hen will build a cup-shaped nest in a low shrub together or they may use an artificial nestpan, adding hemp teasings and grasses. The hen will incubate alone for about 12 days. The young are fed by both parents and will fly after a period of just 10 days. Although only two or three chicks may be produced in a single clutch, as many as six to eight broods of chicks have been reported in a season. Live food and chickweed, with fresh ants' pupae if available, are indispensable for rearing the young. Jacarini Finches are classified with Olive and Cuban Finches in a group sometimes described as Grassquits. Seed forms the basis of their regular diet.

Care must be taken to ensure that their chicks, which fledge in a relatively immature state, do not become chilled in a shower of heavy rain, which will also leave them unable to fly. Jacarinis are best kept in heated winter accommodation, but pairs should never be housed together, because fighting is then likely to result, particularly when the birds are in breeding condition.

Japanese White-bellied Blue Flycatcher

Muscicapa cyanomelana

Origin: *Japan and Korea, overwintering in Malaysia, Indonesia, the Philippines and other parts of southeast Asia*

Cock: 6in (15cm) Cap sky blue merging into cobalt blue on the back; neck, lores and sides of head black. Rump ultramarine. Wings and tail very dark blue, bordering on black. Underparts white. Iris dark brown; beak black; legs and feet greyish.

Hen: Upperparts brown; breast grey-brown; abdomen white; chin and throat light brown.

There is invariably a shortage of hens of this species because most consignments are composed mainly of cock birds. They soon become quite tame, and their song is pleasant and melodic. Careful acclimatisation is necessary, and a good range of live food must be offered. As their name suggests, these birds are largely insectivorous, and a good quality softbill food should also be provided for them, together with egg food on occasions and a little cooked beef heart.

Once established, a pair will settle well in an aviary for the duration of the summer months. In temperate areas they should be brought into heated accommodation for the winter. When breeding, these flycatchers will build a nest of moss, grass stems and other material in a concealed place, such as a partially open-fronted nestbox. The clutch is of three to five eggs, with incubation lasting about two weeks. A limitless supply of small live food, such as hatchling crickets, should be provided for rearing purposes.

207 Rufous-bellied Niltava *Niltava sundara*

Origin: *Himalayas to China and Thailand*

Cock: 7in (18cm) Forehead, sides of head and throat black; crown, nape and mantle, as well as the wing coverts, rump and tail bright blue. Underparts bright chestnut. Iris dark brown; beak black; legs and feet greyish.

Hen: Entire upperparts russet-brown; underparts dull brown. There is a white crescent on the throat, and a tiny spot of brilliant pale blue on each side of the neck. This area of blue is often concealed, except when the bird is alert, with its head raised.

This extraordinarily beautiful flycatcher is imported rather infrequently, and it needs careful management when first obtained. It has a very peaceable nature, except with its own kind, and can be kept in an aviary alongside other small insectivorous birds.

If the Rufous-bellied Niltava is kept in anything other than a planted flight, fresh, supple branches should be provided regularly as these will help to keep the bird's feet in good condition and also ensure that the perches remain clean. Within the confines of a flight cage, absolute cleanliness is essential. The tray at the bottom of the cage should be covered with sheets of paper that are changed daily. A clean pot of water must also be provided for bathing purposes every day; this will help to keep the plumage in good condition.

Live insects are very important, particularly in the case of newly acquired moulting or breeding birds. Waxmoth larvae are often favoured, but crickets, a few mealworms and similar invertebrates can all be provided. A good quality insectivorous mix is also required, to which extras such as egg yolk, grated carrot, pieces of apple, steamed and grated beef heart and even small prawns can be added. This food should be prepared fresh each day, and the food pots themselves must be washed thoroughly.

When they are provided with a good, varied diet, Rufous-bellied Niltavas can be maintained without difficulty, passing through the moulting period rapidly. In the late spring, once the weather is warm, a pair can be allowed into a secluded outside aviary. Here they will tend to occupy the lower areas, becoming most active towards dusk as they hunt for flying insects.

Reasonably hardy once properly acclimatised, a pair may choose to nest in such surroundings. The first breeding success was recorded in England in 1962. Rufous-bellied Niltavas will build a shallow nest of plant fibres, usually concealing it well in the vegetation, sometimes using an open-fronted nestbox for this purpose.

A breeding pair should be housed on their own to increase the likelihood of success. A typical clutch has four eggs, which hatch after two weeks. The chicks will not thrive unless they have a constant supply of live food. Fledging takes place after a further two weeks, and the young birds are soon independent. A birdroom flight, where heat can be supplied, is recommended as winter accommodation.

8 Shama (White-rumped Shama) *Copsychus malabaricus*

Origin: *Indian subcontinent to Indonesia*

Cock: 10in (25cm) Entire head, back, throat and upper breast glossy black. Flights and long central tail feathers black, with the former being edged with brown on the inner webs. Outertail feathers and rump pure white. Underparts deep rich chestnut. Iris dark brown; beak black; legs and feet pinkish.

Hen: Those parts that are black in the cock are dull grey; underparts warm buff. The white on the rump is less prominent. Tail noticeably shorter.

Probably the finest singer of all foreign birds, the Shama's song is infinitely varied and liquid in tone. It quickly learns to imitate the runs and trills of the Blackbird and the Nightingale. This talent makes it essential to keep the Shamas away from creaking doors, bleating sheep, cackling geese or turkeys, however, because these noises will also be copied, with a less desirable effect. Even a cock bird which is housed on its own will sing fluently, pausing only during the moulting period, which will last for a few weeks.

The active nature of these birds means that they should be housed in indoor flights, rather in than cages, when they are kept indoors. This will also help to keep their plumage from becoming soiled. Shamas are very elegant birds, and will jerk their long tails up and down whenever excited by any unusual sight or sound. This action is accompanied by their sharp 'tek-tek' alarm call.

When they feed Shamas tend not to scatter their food around their quarters. A good quality softbill food, a range of finely diced fruit, grated carrot and live foods, such as mealworms, crickets and small locusts or waxmoth larvae, will all be eaten readily. These birds often become quite tame, even in aviary surroundings, and they may be persuaded to take insects almost from the hand.

It is best to keep a breeding pair of Shamas on their own, although if they are in a very large aviary other species may be tolerated. Pairing can be a rather fraught time, because the cock is likely to chase the hen almost continuously. They must be accomodated in a roomy flight that is furnished with ample cover, so that she can escape from her mate when his attentions become too pressing.

The hen usually builds the nest on her own, preferring a nestbox with a half-open front for this purpose. She fills the box with moss and twigs, lining the cup of the nest with softer material such as feathers and fine hair. Here she will lay up to five eggs, which should hatch after an incubation period of 13 days. The cock does not incubate, but shares in feeding the young. Live food should figure more prominently in the diet when the birds are rearing chicks.

Fledging occurs when the young Shamas are about 17 days old. At this stage, both sexes are predominantly brown in colour and heavily mottled, but later they become much like the hen. After the first full moult the distinctive differences in their plumage will be apparent. It is advisable to remove the early chicks once they are independent, so that the parent birds can begin a second brood.

Once Shamas are properly acclimatised, they are relatively hardy, but although they will not need to be kept very warm, they will still require adequate protection from the elements. It may be useful to be able to confine them to the shelter of their quarters when the weather is at its worst, as well as supplying some heating at this time.

Magpie Robin (Dhyal Bird) *Copsychus saularis*

Origin: *Indian subcontinent to Indonesia, and parts of China*

Cock: 8in (20cm) Head, neck and upper breast black; belly, undertail coverts and wing bars white. Tail black and white. Iris brown; beak black; legs and feet pinkish.

Hen: Greyish-brown where cock is black; white areas in cock greyish.

There may be considerable variation in the coloration of the Magpie Robin, as 17 distinctive races occur through their wide range. This tends to be reflected in the relative proportions of black and white feathering, with members of one subspecies being entirely black, apart from the wing barring. Although it is a less accomplished songster than the Shama, the Magpie Robin nevertheless has a melodious and pleasing song. It is also often rather shyer at first, but will settle well in a flight, and can become quite tame in these surroundings.

A diet as recommended for the Shama will suit these birds well, although the two species should not be kept together in the same aviary. For breeding purposes, Magpie Robins are best housed on their own. Their nest building is similar to that of the Shama, and, similarly, the hen incubates on her own, while the cock bird shares in feeding the young. Rearing foods should include a high proportion of live insects, such as waxworms and crickets.

During the winter months acclimatised Magpie Robins can be kept in unheated quarters, but it is better to keep them in surroundings where artificial heat is available if required.

09 Orange-headed Ground Thrush (Dama Thrush) *Zoothera citrina*

Origin: *Indian subcontinent to Indonesia and parts of China*

Cock: 8in (20cm) Head, breast and abdomen orange-brown blending into yellowish-white. Bluish-white line behind the eyes. Remainder of upperparts bluish-grey. Median wing coverts spotted with white. Iris brown; beak black; legs and feet pinkish.

Hen: Upperparts greenish-grey, with the orange coloration of the head and breast being far less brightly coloured than in the cock.

Although it is more gaudily coloured, this bird is similar in behaviour to a Song Thrush, and the songs of the two birds are also similar. It spends much of its time on the ground searching for worms and insects, turning over fallen leaves and other debris for this purpose with its beak. Quiet by nature, cock Orange-headed Ground Thrushes will often sing continuously for periods while resting on one leg.

They are easy to cater for, requiring a good quality softbill food, mealworms and similar invertebrates, as well as a varied selection of fruit.

Hard-boiled egg and bread and milk can also be supplied occasionally to provide variety in the diet.

Because they prefer to feed on the ground, these thrushes can be housed with other larger birds, and they will hunt for food under bushes and in grass. The floor covering must be kept clean. They should be provided with a separate food supply on the ground, because they may otherwise bully other birds which descend to feed here.

A pair may breed in well-planted surroundings. Their nest is constructed from leaves, small twigs, grass, moss and rootlets, often cemented together with damp mud, which should be provided in a pot in the flight for this purpose. The interior is lined with fine grasses and fibres. The cock normally sings more than the hen, and his song is particularly melodic during the breeding period.

The typical clutch is of two or three eggs, which are blue with darker spots, and these are incubated by the hen alone. Incubation lasts 13 days. A good supply of live food is especially vital while the chicks are being reared. They should fledge when they are about 17 days old, with two broods often being produced in a season.

These birds like bathing. Once acclimatised, they can remain in an aviary throughout the year, but they must be encouraged to remain indoors during the worst of the winter weather.

Hoami (Spectacled Jay Thrush, Chinese Nightingale)

Garrulax canorus

Origin: *China and northern Indo-China*

Cock: *9in (23cm) Crown, nape and back brown; forehead rust-coloured. Sometimes marked with fine black stripes along the nape of the neck. Cream line above the eye, which is surrounded by white. Abdomen lighter, fading to grey. Iris dark brown; beak yellowish-horn; legs and feet pinkish.*

Hen: *Similar in appearance.*

Although these birds are not regularly available and are not especially colourful, they are popular avicultural subjects because of the cock birds' exceptional singing abilities. The range of the song is such that birds are able to sing both deep and very high notes, producing a really wonderful melody. If a Shama or another songster is nearby, the Hoami is likely to start singing and imitating the song of these birds, blending it with its own.

Unfortunately, they are often very aggressive by nature. For breeding purposes pairs should be housed on their own in a well-planted aviary where there is plenty of cover. Several feeding points should be included if the cock bird starts to prove domineering towards his intended mate, as may happen at the start of the breeding period.

Hoamis are easy birds to cater for, feeding on a mixture of softbill food, fruit and insects, such as mealworms and locusts, with live food becoming increasingly important during the breeding season. Small dead mice, sold for reptiles as 'pinkies', and even small fish may be eaten as well. The bird will hold the fish in its claws, tearing it to pieces with its beak, and there is little doubt that small companions in its quarters would be liable to suffer a similar fate. A little seed, such as groats and canary seed, may also be eaten, along with some green food.

These birds will bathe frequently, and suitable facilities must be provided for this purpose if they are housed indoors. The Hoami will be quite hardy once acclimatised however, and can winter outdoors without artificial heat, provided there is a suitable shelter. These birds soon become quite confident with their owner, but remain noticeably shy of strangers. Breeding details are similar to those of the White-crested Jay Thrush.

10 White-crested Jay Thrush *Garrulax leucolophus*

Origin: *Himalayas to Indonesia, Thailand and Indonesia*

Cock: 12in (30cm) Graceful white crest, usually carried erect. Head and the area to the upper breast white, apart from a black facial band incorporating the eyes. Coloration brighter on the forehead, as well as the throat and chest, becoming tinged with grey on the hind crown. Remainder of plumage brownish, being redder where this joins the white areas. Tail darker brown. Iris brown; beak black; legs and feet greyish.

Hen: Similar in appearance, but may have a slightly smaller, greyer crest.

These relatively large jay thrushes have distinctly soft feathering, but the coloration varies somewhat through their range. The Sumatran race, *G.l. bicolor*, for example, has darker plumage, with blackish shades in the areas of brown plumage.

To be seen to best advantage, a pair should be kept in a planted aviary on their own. They are exceedingly active birds and are likely to prey on any smaller species housed with them, and once a pair bond is formed they will also attack other members of their own kind.

White-crested Jay Thrushes are among the most entertaining birds to keep, although they do not become very tame. During the day they play together, tumbling over each other with a constant cackling, which sounds rather like human laughter. At night, a pair sleeps together side-by-side, covering each other with their wings.

Their song, which is powerful, consists of a variety of not unpleasant flute-like notes. They will eat the same type of food as the Hoami, including a good selection of fruit, and are able to overwinter in an outside aviary once they are acclimatised.

Breeding has been achieved successfully on a number of occasions. A bowl-shaped nest, made from grasses, twigs and similar material, is constructed in a suitable conifer or shrub. Four eggs form the typical clutch, and these hatch after 13 days or so. The critical period is the first week after the chicks have hatched, because they may be eaten by their parents. Live food is essential, but simply placing this where it is easily accessible appears to encourage the adults to consume their offspring. Instead, it should be scattered around the floor of their quarters so that the birds have to hunt for it. Rearing is more likely to be successful under these circumstances. Assuming that all goes well, the young birds should fledge when they are around three weeks old. They should be removed once they are feeding independently.

Golden-eyed Babbler *Chrysomma sinensis*

Origin: *Indian subcontinent to Indo-China, China and Thailand*

Cock: 7in (18cm) Head and neck reddish-brown. Cheeks, areas round the eyes, lores and stripe above the ear coverts white; ear coverts brown; throat and breast white. Abdomen creamy in colour. Wings rust-brown; tail brown with rust-coloured margins. Iris yellow; beak black with yellow nostrils; legs and feet golden-yellow.

Hen: Similar in appearance.

The distinctive eye coloration of these babblers is emphasised by the orange-reddish skin here. Although they are not regularly available, they make attractive aviary birds, being peaceable by nature and having a soft, pleasant song. A careful period of acclimatisation is required, with the temperature of their quarters being reduced gradually. A good varied diet should be provided. Fruit laced with softbill food, a generous supply of live food and nectar will all be valuable. Bathing facilities must also be provided, and drinking water should be given in a sealed vessel as in the case of nectar.

These babblers should only be kept in flights, in view of their active natures. They will thrive in a sunny aviary during the summer months, but require heated winter-time accommodation, even when they are acclimatised. Breeding results do not appear to have been recorded as yet, but the sexing methods now available should enable a true pair to be distinguished without difficulty. Breeding may occur in a planted aviary.

Yellow-cheeked Crested Tit *Parus xanthogenys*

Origin: *India and the Himalayas*

Cock: 6in (15cm) Head, a bar extending from the beak, passing through the eyes and extending to the nape, and the neck itself black. Eyebrow stripe, sides of head and spot on neck yellow. Crest black, backed with yellow. Upperparts olive-grey. Wings black with white spots. Tail, throat, breast and abdomen black. Remainder of underparts yellowish-green. Iris brown; beak black; legs and feet greyish.

Hen: *Similar in appearance.*

Like other related species, Yellow-cheeked Crested Tits are lively by nature, intensely inquisitive and readily become tame. Their song is insignificant however, consisting of soft chirps and twitters.

Insects of various kinds and spiders should feature regularly in their diet, along with softbill food. Green food can also be given, as can the occasional sunflower seed, although these should not be provided on a regular basis because they are likely to result in obesity.

These birds may need particular care at first, but for those experienced in keeping softbills, this species is an attractive addition to their collection. Recently imported birds must be kept warm, and an infrared heat lamp may be necessary. Although these tits can be housed in an aviary during the summer months once they are acclimatised, they are not hardy and need to be kept in heated surroundings in the winter-time. Bathing facilities should always be provided.

Breeding results do not appear to have been recorded for this species to date, but there is no reason this should not be possible once a pair is established in its quarters. A nestbox is likely to be favoured, and an ample supply of small live food will be essential when the chicks are being reared. They are likely to leave the nest before they are fully able to fly and so should be watched accordingly, particularly during wet weather, in case their plumage becomes saturated.

Chestnut-flanked White-eye *Zosterops erythropleura*

Origin: *Manchuria, Korea and southeast China; also migrates to parts of Burma (Myanmar), Thailand and Cambodia*

Cock: *5in (13cm) Upperparts grey-green with a circlet of white feathering surrounding the eyes. Chin, throat and breast yellowish, becoming greyish-white on the rest of the underparts. Distinctive chestnut feathering on the flanks. Tail dark green. Iris brown; beak black; legs and feet dark grey.*

Hen: *Similar in appearance.*

Over 80 different species of *Zosterops* are known but distinguishing among them can be difficult, although the chestnut feathering on the flank of this species makes identification straightforward. As a rough guide for sexing purposes, choose the darkest and lightest coloured individuals on offer, in the hope of obtaining a pair; alternatively, if possible obtain a small group. White-eyes are amenable birds and will live together well in a colony outside the breeding period. The only reliable way of distinguishing the sexes is by means of the cock's song, which becomes more powerful and persistent when the birds are nesting.

When they are first acquired the birds' plumage may be in poor condition. The provision of bathing facilities should lead to a rapid improvement. They are one of the easiest softbills to cater for and can be recommended as an introduction to this group of birds. Fresh nectar should be provided every day, along with small live food, fruit and a softbill mixture. A varied diet can be given without too much difficulty. *Zosterops* often appreciate half an orange or dates cut into small pieces, while ripe banana, grated apples, grapes and pear will also be eaten. Fruit flies and, occasionally, small mealworms, tebos, crickets and waxworms are taken readily, but these need not be supplied daily outside the breeding season. Hard-boiled egg, grated carrot and canary-rearing food also serve to vary the menu.

On a range of such foods, white-eyes will moult without problems and should remain in excellent condition for many years. They will appreciate it if their food is not placed on the ground but raised or hung up, because they will usually spend most of their time climbing around the branches in their quarters.

Once acclimatised, white-eyes are quite hardy, but it is best to provide at least some additional warmth during the worst of the winter weather.

Breeding details for the Chestnut-flanked White-eye are as for the Oriental White-eye.

211 Oriental White-eye (Indian Zosterops) *Zosterops palpebrosa*

Origin: *India eastwards to China, Indo-China and Indonesia*

Cock: 4in (10cm) *Upperparts dull shade of olive-green. Bold eye ring of white feathering. Throat and upper breast yellowish; lower underparts dusky grey. Iris brown; beak black; legs and feet dark grey.*

Hen: *Similar in appearance.*

All white-eyes need a similar diet, and they usually settle well, often breeding, especially in a planted flight, where they can be housed on their own or in the company of quiet finches. A deep cup-shaped nest will be made, either in a partially open-fronted nestbox or in a thick shrub, suspended from a forked branch. Fine grasses, hair, coconut fibre and woollen threads may all be used for this purpose.

A quiet spot is essential. When the hen is sitting on her bluish eggs she will be well-concealed, with only her slender beak, white feathering around the eyes and tail visible. She is constantly on the look-out for danger, and during bad weather may pull a large feather or leaf over herself for protection. The incubation period lasts for about 12 days, and the young should fledge after a similar interval. A wide variety of small live foods, such as aphids and spiders, should be provided during the rearing period.

Young birds should be removed as soon as they are feeding independently, because young cocks in particular may be persecuted by the adult male at this stage. Several broods are likely to be reared in succession, but an entirely new nest will be made on each occasion, often using material from the old one. Disturbances must be kept to a minimum through the rearing period.

2 Pekin Robin (Red-billed Leiothrix) *Leiothrix lutea*

Origin: *from the Himalayas to China*

Cock: 6in (15cm) *Head olive, becoming greyer over the rest of the upperparts. Wings show both bright reddish-orange and yellow markings, particularly when folded, with the remainder being a dull shade of olive-slate. Chin and throat bright yellow, forming a dark rusty-orange band below; remainder of underparts greyish-olive. Area around the eyes olive-buff, with a greyish area over the ear coverts. Iris dark brown; beak bright red; legs and feet pinkish-grey.*

Hen: *Rather similar, but may be slightly duller in coloration.*

The song of the cock provides the most reliable means of distinguishing the sexes. It is varied and strong, but pleasant to listen to and never disturbingly loud. The smooth, sleek appearance of the plumage and beautiful coloration have also helped to establish this species as an avicultural favourite. Despite its common name, it is not a robin as such.

Inquisitive by nature and easily tamed, the Pekin Robin will soon take mealworms from the hand. These birds are not finicky about their food and will eat a variety of small seeds, such as millets and canary seed, as well as softbill food, fruit, some live food and green food. Elderberry and other berries, as well as pieces of fig and peas are all greatly enjoyed.

Only a single cock or a pair should be housed in the same flight, because they will become rather aggressive during the breeding period. Pekin Robins will agree with other birds however, but they cannot safely be kept with smaller species during the breeding period, because they may steal their eggs. Although they cannot swallow eggs whole, they will hold them under one foot and peck them to pieces.

A pair will become very affectionate as the breeding season approaches and build a cup-shaped nest of grasses, fine twigs, mosses and similar materials. They will also accept artificial linings fixed in nestboxes. The boxes themselves should be concealed behind high shrubbery in the aviary. The typical clutch is of three or four eggs, with both incubation and fledging periods lasting about a fortnight. Live food will feature prominently in the diet of breeding birds, but a proprietary rearing food can also be supplied at this stage.

Pekin Robins delight in bathing, which helps to keep their plumage in good condition. They usually moult without difficulty in the autumn. Once acclimatised, they can live outdoors in an aviary with a suitable shelter throughout the winter. They should be encouraged to roost here, even if this means shutting them in during cold spells.

213 Silver-eared Mesia *Leiothrix argentauris*

Origin: *Himalayas to Indochina and Indonesia*

Cock: 7in (18cm) Head black; ear coverts silvery-white; throat and nape orange-red. Similar coloration present on parts of the wings and rump, with the rest of the upperparts being greyish. Remaining underparts are bluish-grey. Iris dark brown; beak horn-coloured, darker towards the base of the upper bill; legs and feet pinkish.

Hen: Duller in overall coloration.

It is usually possible to house Silver-eared Mesias safely in the company of other softbills of similar size, including Pekin Robins. The cock's song, which has as many as seven distinct notes, is stronger and sharper than that of its relative. Their requirements are virtually identical. The inclusion of bamboo in a planted flight for these birds will often encourage them to build a nest here, usually relatively close to the ground. Breeding details do not differ significantly from those of the Pekin Robin.

Black-headed Sibia *Heterophasia capistrata*

Origin: *Himalayas*

Cock: 10in (25cm) Head entirely black, with an orangish-brown collar, matching the colour of the underparts. Back and tail brownish-grey, the tail feathers themselves edged with greyish-blue, with a broad subterminal band of blue barred with black. Wings greyish. Iris dark brown; beak black; legs and feet pinkish.

Hen: Similar in appearance.

Although the song of these Sibias is not very pronounced, they are attractive birds, showing well in a planted aviary. Their care is quite straightforward. They require a diet of softbill food, diced fruit and live food, with mynah pellets providing valuable variety to the diet when available. These should not be fed to the exclusion of other foods, however, in case they may predispose the birds to liver problems.

In aviary surroundings, Black-headed Sibias will often clamber about on bark and twigs hunting for beetles, spiders and other invertebrates. Breeding results are uncommon, however, possibly because of the difficulty in recognising a pair in the first instance. They will construct a cup-shaped nest, often using pine needles, and line the interior with softer materials. Four eggs form the typical clutch, with the incubation period lasting a fortnight.

Live food must be supplied in adequate quantities if the chicks are to be reared successfully. They fledge after about two weeks in the nest. Once acclimatised, these birds are relatively hardy. They are best kept on their own, however, and never with smaller species, which are otherwise liable to be bullied.

Blue-whiskered Fruitsucker *Chloropsis cyanopogon*

Origin: *southeast Asia and Indonesia*

Cock: 7in (18cm) Upperparts shades of green; lores, cheeks and throat black; moustachial stripes cobalt. A thin yellow band of feathering extends around the eyes and throat. Underparts light green to yellow. Wings green with black flights; tail dark green. Iris dark brown; beak black; legs and feet greyish.

Hen: Lacks the black markings present in the cock.

It is difficult to obtain pairs, because cocks are favoured for their song and are often taken from the nest and hand-reared for this purpose in their native lands.

The care of this species does not differ from that of related species, but these birds are not social by nature, and under no circumstances should they be housed together or serious fighting will be inevitable.

Hens are equally likely to be persecuted by intended mates, and so plenty of seclusion is vital if breeding is to be attempted. The problem of compatibility has handicapped breeding of these and other fruitsuckers, and for this reason, these birds represent a real challenge for the dedicated aviculturist.

Hardwick's Fruitsucker (Orange-bellied Fruitsucker)
Chloropsis hardwickei

Origin: *Himalayas to China and southeast Asia*

Cock: 8in (20cm) Forehead, orbital stripe and ear coverts yellowish-green; lores, sides of head and neck black. Golden sheen on the crown, and a wide light blue band extends across the cheeks. Upperparts green, becoming brighter near the rump. Underparts lighter, running into orange-yellow near the vent. Primaries and coverts cobalt, with the remainder of the wings green. Tail green with outer feathers blue. Iris brown; beak black; legs and feet greyish.

Hen: Has less black on the throat, no blue on the wings and more yellowish-green feathering on the underparts.

Like other fruitsuckers, this species can be housed in a flight with other medium-sized softbills, including larger tanagers, but it should not be kept with its own kind. The song of the cock is varied and not too penetrating.

303

It is only when the bird is alarmed – by a cat, for example – that it utters harsh, unpleasant sounds.

These fruitsuckers are active by nature. They are fond of bathing and will jump and climb about branches in their quarters for much of the day. Moderate heat must be supplied during the winter months, even when they are well established.

Successful breeding has apparently yet to be recorded, but it is known that the clutch size is usually two or three eggs. Incubation then lasts for 13 days, with the chicks fledging after a similar period. A diet as recommended for the Golden-fronted Fruitsucker will suit these birds, with live food possibly being more significant during the rearing period.

214 Golden-fronted Fruitsucker (Golden-fronted Leafbird)

Chloropsis aurifrons

Origin: *Himalayas to southeast Asia and Indonesia*

Cock: 10in (25cm) Forehead to the middle of the crown rich orange-yellow; lores, sides of face and upper breast velvet black; throat blue. Orange band separates the black plumage from the pale green underparts. Upperparts darker green. Flight feathers and tail blackish-brown. Iris brown; beak black; legs and feet greyish.

Hen: Distinguishable by green forehead, and reduced areas of black feathering.

Suitable companions for birds such as bulbuls or orioles, these fruitsuckers are quite easy to maintain. They are primarily frugivorous in their feeding habits, and they must, therefore, be provided with a good range of fruits and berries, sprinkled with softbill food. Soaked mynah pellets may also be added to their fruit mixture. Some live food, such as waxworms, will also be eaten, along with egg yolk and ants' pupae. Nectar is also appreciated. They dislike descending to the ground to feed.

Unfortunately, these fruitsuckers are often very aggressive to each other, even when kept in pairs. A densely planted aviary will help to lessen the likelihood of aggression, and, if possible, members of a pair should be housed in adjacent flights. Once they appear reasonably compatible, the cock can be introduced under supervision to his potential partner. This method offers the best hope of successful breeding.

A pair will construct a relatively shallow, cup-shaped nest, and they should be left undisturbed as far as possible. The song of the cock will be heard with increasing frequency during the breeding period. It is varied, starting softly and gradually rising to a crescendo. Although generally considered to be slightly hardier than related species, these fruitsuckers really need warmth during the winter months. They dislike damp, cold weather.

Fairy Bluebird *Irena puella*

Origin: *India through southeast Asia to Indonesia and the Philippines*

Cock: 10in (25cm) *Distinctive glossy blue coloration extends from the crown, narrowing over the nape, before broadening across the shoulders. It then extends down over the secondary wing coverts, the rump, uppertail coverts, as well as the undertail coverts, which are elongated almost to the tip of the tail, which is black, as is the rest of the body and wings. Iris ruby red; beak black; legs and feet black.*

Hen: *Entirely soft blue, with slight greenish suffusion.*

The male Fairy Bluebird is stunning to look at although his song is not particularly melodious. These birds are generally not aggressive, and they make ideal occupants of a planted aviary. Indeed, in the wild, they live in small groups before splitting off into individual pairs at the start of the breeding season. Recently imported birds need careful acclimatisation and must be allowed to become accustomed to an artificial diet, which should include a variety of fruit, laced with softbill food and mynah pellets, as well as live food. Once they are established, Fairy Bluebirds are relatively hardy, but they do need to be protected from frost and so are better overwintered in heated accommodation.

If they are kept in a well-planted aviary, breeding can be anticipated. A pair will construct an open, cup-shaped nest, usually relatively high up and carefully concealed in suitable shrubbery. Two predominantly olive-grey eggs will be laid here, and they should hatch 13 days later. Live food again assumes greater importance in their diet during the rearing period, with the chicks fledging after approximately a fortnight. It is vital, especially when these birds are being housed indoors on artificial perches, that the perches are clean at all times. The relatively small feet of Fairy Bluebirds are susceptible to infections acquired from soiled perches.

Red-vented Bulbul *Pycnonotus cafer*

Origin: *Indian subcontinent*

Cock: 8in (20cm) *Head and front of neck black; remainder of neck and back dark brownish-grey with lighter margins. The black on the neck merges into dark brown on the breast, and then into the light brown of the abdomen. Rump brownish-grey; uppertail coverts white; undertail coverts red. Wings and tail feathers grey-brown, also with lighter edges. Iris dark brown; beak black, legs and feet blackish.*

Hen: *Similar in appearance.*

The name 'bulbul' is the Turkish word for Nightingale, but the song of these birds is not quite like that of the Nightingale, as it consists of only three melodious notes constantly repeated. These bulbuls are lively birds, but they can soon be tamed and will eventually take mealworms from the hand. They should not be kept in the company of birds smaller than themselves, and pairs need to be given a flight to themselves where they may well breed successfully.

The nest will often be built in a nestbox from stems of grass, small twigs, moss and coconut fibres. Alternatively, it may be concealed in vegetation, and the bottom is then often lined with leaves. The hen will hatch her two or three eggs after approximately 12 days, with the young fledging when they are about a fortnight old. The cock shares in the task of rearing the family. Their feeding should be identical to that recommended for other species.

216 **Red-eared Bulbul** (Red-whiskered Bulbul) *Pycnonotus jocosus*

Origin: *India to China and southeast Asia*

Cock: 8in (20cm) Head and prominent crest black. A black band extends from lower bill across the cheeks to the neck. Cheeks white, with a red spot; breast white. Undertail coverts red; back brown. Iris dark brown; beak black; legs and feet greyish.

Hen: Similar in appearance but sometimes slightly smaller.

The feathering of these and other bulbuls is very soft, and any birds in poor plumage will need particularly careful acclimatisation, as they will be sensitive to cold. Once they have moulted successfully, however, these birds will thrive in an aviary, often living for 10 years or more in such surroundings. They will soon lose their initial nervousness, especially if fed with mealworms from the hand.

A diet based on fruit and berries, mynah pellets (if available) and a good quality softbill food is recommended. Live food should also be provided regularly, especially if a pair start nesting. The nuptial display by the cock consists of a dance with crest erect, tail spread and wings drooping. Breeding details are similar to those of the Red-vented Bulbul.

217 **White-cheeked Bulbul** *Pycnonotus leucogenys*

Origin: *from Iraq to the Indian subcontinent*

Cock: 8in (20cm) Upperparts grey-brown. Head feathers narrow and elongated, with those in the centre forming a crest. Lores black. Eyebrow stripe, ear coverts and cheeks white. Dark brown-black spot immediately behind the ear coverts. Wings brown-grey with olive margins. Undertail coverts yellow; Uppertail coverts brown-white, becoming white in the middle. Tail brown to black, with a white tip. Iris brown; beak black; legs and feet greyish.

Hen: Similar in appearance.

Once settled in aviary surroundings, these bulbuls are relatively hardy. They can often winter outside provided a good shelter is available, although some heat may be required during severe spells of cold weather.

It is best to house pairs on their own. In a mixed aviary, cocks can be aggressive, especially during the breeding season, and hens may disturb the nesting activities of other birds.

The White-cheeked Bulbul was first bred in Britain as long ago as 1910. It does not differ significantly from other species in its requirements. A pair may choose to build a cup-shaped nest in a bush or use a nestbox. Live food is vital for rearing the chicks successfully.

Chinese Bulbul *Pycnonotus sinensis*

Origin: *China, offshore islands and Vietnam*

Cock: 9in (23cm) A small black crest on the head, with a wide, white eyebrow stripe above each eye. Lores grey; cheeks black with a black spot. Neck white; remainder of upperparts olive-grey. Breast grey; abdomen dirty white. Wings brown with greenish margins. Iris brown; beak black; legs and feet greyish.

Hen: Similar in appearance.

It is inadvisable to house these bulbuls with other, smaller birds, especially during the breeding period, for there is always the risk that eggs or chicks may be eaten. Other related species are also likely to be a cause of friction, and this will hamper breeding results. However, various species of dove can be kept in their company.

Chinese Bulbuls will soon settle into aviary surroundings, but they should not be housed in cages if at all possible because they are active by nature and may become rather overweight if they are deprived of the opportunity for adequate exercise.

As the breeding season approaches, their song is more likely to be heard. This resembles the calls of the Linnet but is generally not as loud and typically consists of chattering and chirruping sounds only, which are not very melodious. Even so, these are not noisy birds.

A pair may well nest successfully, although the first recorded breeding of this species occurred only as recently as 1975 in Britain. The cock displays by spreading his tail, lowering his wings and bowing his head. These bulbuls tend to be quite shy during the breeding season, and they should be left alone as much as possible at this stage. Plenty of live food and a good quality rearing food should be supplied when the young have hatched. Breeding details are similar to those of other species.

Yellow-vented Bulbul *Pycnonotus aurigaster*

Origin: *southeast Asia, Indonesia and China*

Cock: 8in (20cm) Head black; ear coverts white; neck grey and brown; throat black. Upperparts brown; rump and uppertail coverts white. Underparts greyish-brown, with a yellowish suffusion; undertail coverts yellow. Tail brown, with white markings at the tips. Iris brown; beak black; legs and feet greyish.

Hen: *Similar in appearance.*

These bulbuls are reasonably peaceful by nature, and they were first kept at London Zoo in 1865. Pairs can sometimes be recognised by the cock's song, and they are among the most talented songsters of the group. An open-fronted nestbox or a canary nestpan, well concealed in a planted flight, may encourage breeding activity, although in these surroundings the birds may prefer to construct their own nest. Grass stems, moss and coconut fibres should be provided for this purpose. Between three and five eggs will be laid in the resulting cup-shaped structure. These should hatch after 13 days, with the chicks leaving the nest for the first time after a similar period.

A good selection of insects should be provided, especially while the chicks are in the nest but also on a regular basis throughout the year. Diced fruit and softbill food otherwise form the bulk of the diet. A nectar solution is also often appreciated, and it can be particularly valuable for newly acquired birds.

Red-eyed Bulbul (Yellow-rumped Bulbul) *Pycnonotus nigricans*

Origin: *southern Africa*

Cock: *7in (18cm) Head and throat black; upperparts brownish-grey. Breast brownish-white; abdomen pure white; flanks greyish-brown; undertail coverts yellow. Tail blackish-brown. Eyelids red. Iris red; beak black; legs and feet black.*

Hen: *Similar in appearance.*

Out of the 120 different species of bulbul, it is the Asiatic species, including the Collared Finchbill Bulbul (*Spizixos semitorques*), that are best known in aviculture. African species, such as the Red-eyed Bulbul, are scarcer. Others species that may be encountered occasionally include the Cape Bulbul (*Pycnonotus capensis*), which is approximately 8in (20cm) long and is greyish-brown, with darkest coloration on the head, wine red eyelids and reddish-brown eyes. Another very similar form is Layard's Bulbul (*P.c. layardi*), which shows less black on the head and throat, but more white on the abdomen; the eyelids are black.

These birds require similar care to the Asiatic species. Once they are acclimatised they can overwinter in a frost-proof birdroom or even in the outside aviary if there is a good shelter there. They are lively by nature, yet easy to tame and also prove to be good songsters.

Red-eyed Bulbuls are mainly frugivorous, but they also take live food readily. They will eat a wide variety of fruit, including apples, pears, plums, berries, soaked raisins and currants. The fruit should be diced into small pieces and laced with a suitable softbill food. Mynah pellets also add useful variety in the diet, and mealworms, which are readily accepted, can be used to help tame these birds. Nectar is also often appreciated.

Their breeding habits are similar to those of other species. Insects may be used almost exclusively as rearing food, yet nestlings have also been reared successfully on a mixture of finely chopped meat, grated carrot, stale bread and mulberries, although other soft fruit and other more easily obtainable berries may be substituted for the latter.

8 Blue-throated Barbet *Megalaima asiatica*

Origin: *Indian subcontinent to Indonesia and China*

Cock: 9in (23cm) *Crown of head red, with a red spot also on each side of the throat, with a narrow stripe extending over the head and continuing along the black and yellow ear coverts. Orbital stripe blue; throat and cheeks green-blue; upperparts and wings green. Primaries black with yellow margins. Underparts lighter green; cere orange. Iris brown; beak horn-coloured with black tip; legs and feet bluish-green.*

Hen: *Similar in appearance.*

This group of softbills is notable for the 'beard' or tuft of narrow, elongated feathers at the base of the beak, which is the origin of their common name – 'barbet' meaning 'bearded'. A range of species is often available, with those from forested areas tending to be more frugivorous in their feeding habits than others, such as Levaillant's Barbet (*Trachyphonus vaillantii*), which occurs in relatively open country. This family has a wide distribution, and representatives may be found in the New World as well as in Africa and Asia.

Blue-throated Barbets are colourful and lively birds, with smooth, glossy feathering. They enjoy bathing and will roost in a nestbox. Their calls, which are not often heard, have a peculiar clucking sound. Fruit, ranging from diced apple to cherries, grapes and even soaked currants, should figure prominently in their diet, with softbill food sprinkled over the moist surfaces of the fruit. Live food, such as mealworms and even locusts, must be offered regularly.

Barbets appreciate having a log of rotting wood in their quarters. They will hammer this with their stout beaks and may even create their own roosting cavity there. Breeding results are not commonly achieved, however, not only because of the difficulty of distinguishing a pair but also because of the cock's aggressive nature, and it may even be necessary to separate potential pairs for this reason. Not surprisingly, barbets are unsuitable for a community aviary, as not only are they pugnacious and destructive, but they may actually kill and swallow smaller birds.

Great Barbet (Giant Barbet) *Megalaima virens*

Origin: *Himalayas to China and Thailand*

Cock: 12in (30cm) Head black, with slight bluish-green suffusion. Upper chest and back olive-brown, with yellowish streaks sometimes evident on the mantle. Wings, rump and tail feathers green, with brownish markings sometimes evident on the edges of the flight feathers. Underparts dull yellow, with darker streaking evident here. Some green is evident on the flanks and at the centre of the abdomen. Undertail coverts bright red. Iris dark brown; beak pale horn in colour, with darker markings on the upper bill; legs and feet greyish.

Hen: Similar in appearance.

These giant members of the barbet family need to be housed on their own. Surgical sexing can be used to distinguish a true pair, but unfortunately breeding is very difficult because of their aggressive natures. It is often impossible even to keep a pair together without fighting taking place, although a large and densely planted enclosure may help to prevent outbreaks of aggression.

Great Barbets are bold by nature, and they will soon settle down. They need to be handled carefully, because their bills are powerful and can crush a finger quite painfully. Like related species, they will hammer away at rotting wood, often pulverising this with their strong beaks.

Generally quiet, these birds do possess a harsh and loud voice, however, and they may occasionally call on bright moonlit nights. Great Barbets usually roost in nestboxes. They are relatively hardy, although they should not be exposed to the worst of the winter's weather, being kept in a stout indoor flight at this time. They can easily hammer their way through hardboard sheeting as well as thin plywood, and this must be borne in mind when constructing accommodation for them.

Fire-tufted Barbet *Psilopogon pyrolophus*

Origin: *Malaysia and Sumatra*

Cock: 10in (25cm) Predominantly green, darker on the upperparts and paler below. Blue and black is evident on the edges of the flight feathers and tail. Forehead, crown and nape black, becoming mixed with maroon on the hindneck. There is a characteristic bristly tuft of red feathers around the base of the beak. A band of greyish-white plumage crosses the crown, and forms an eyebrow streak. Cheeks greyish. A yellowish band encircles the upper breast, extending to the sides of the throat, with a black band below. Iris brown; beak pale yellowish-green, with a black area encircling it about halfway along its length; legs and feet greyish-green.

Hen: Similar in appearance.

These attractive barbets show to good effect in an aviary which includes thick tree trunks. Here they will hop up and down, probing with their beaks as they search for insects. A dish of water should also be provided in their quarters for bathing purposes. They will frequently bathe every day, if given the opportunity, and this helps to keep their relatively fine plumage in good condition.

Although Fire-tufted Barbets can be housed outdoors during the warmer months of the year, they will need to be brought inside to heated accommodation during the winter. Even indoors, however, a flight should be provided for them, as these birds are active by nature and will not thrive in the confines of a cage.

Breeding results have not been frequently obtained, but a pair may decide to nest in a secluded aviary. Again, they should be watched closely to ensure that the cock does not harass his intended mate excessively. In terms of their feeding habits, Fire-tufted Barbets are relatively frugivorous.

Levaillant's Barbet (Crested Barbet) *Trachyphonus vaillantii*

Origin: *southern Africa*

Cock: 8in (20cm) Crest black; forehead, sides of head, throat and breast lemon-yellow, with some signs of red spots. Mantle, wing coverts and tail, plus a band across the breast bluish-black, with variable white markings on the wings and tail. Underparts yellowish; undertail coverts red. Iris brown; beak greenish-yellow with a darker tip; legs and feet greyish.

Hen: Similar, but may be slightly duller in coloration.

Occurring in relatively arid areas of scrubland, these barbets are more insectivorous in their feeding habits than the Asiatic barbets. They may nest in termite mounds in the wild and have even been known to tunnel into the aviary floor to excavate a nesting chamber. This should be discouraged if possible because of the risk that it will collapse on the birds or become flooded during wet weather.

Levaillant's Barbets are used to relative extremes of temperature, and they are reasonably hardy once acclimatised, although they should be protected from frost. A shelter that forms part of a birdroom, where heating is available, is recommended.

For breeding purposes, pairs should be housed on their own, although they have nested successfully in the company of other birds, notably Black-cheeked Lovebirds (*Agapornis nigrigenis*), whydahs and weavers. On this occasion, the barbets made their own nest in a log, boring a nesting chamber. The young take two weeks to hatch, and fledge just over three weeks later. At this stage, they are duller than adult birds, with browner feathering. Up to five chicks may be reared, and an almost limitless supply of live food must be maintained, along with a suitable rearing food, to assist the adult birds in this task.

Black-naped Oriole *Oriolus chinensis*

Origin: *India to China, the Philippines and Indonesia*

Cock: 10in (25cm) Back yellow with a slight green sheen. A wide black band extends from the nostrils around and above the eyes, uniting over the nape. Wings black with yellow and white on the flight feathers; tail feathers are similarly coloured. Underparts yellow. Iris reddish-orange; beak reddish-pink; legs and feet greyish.

Hen: Mantle and back are somewhat greener than in the cock.

Variations in plumage occur through the range of these orioles, and there are, in fact, 23 different recognised forms. Young cocks may take three years to acquire their full adult coloration, and colour-feeding at the start of the moulting period and during the time that the feathers are being replaced may be helpful in increasing the depth of yellow coloration, which may otherwise fade over successive moults.

These orioles are easy to maintain on a diet based on a mixture of fruits and softbill food, augmented with some live food. They can be given soaked raisins, currants and even pieces of fig to add variety to their diet.

A planted aviary is recommended, particularly as orioles often prove nervous by nature until they have settled in their quarters. Breeding results do not appear to have been recorded to date, but there is no real reason a pair should not nest successfully in aviary surroundings.

The flute-like song of the cock is especially melodious and powerful. These and other orioles are not hardy and must be kept in an indoor flight in temperate areas during the winter months. They are reasonably peaceable with other softbills of similar size, and they can, therefore, be included in a large communal aviary.

219 Racket-tailed Drongo *Dicrurus paradiseus*

Origin: *India to Thailand and Indonesia*

Cock: 14in (36cm) Predominantly black, with a steel-blue gloss and narrow elongated feathers on the crest, nape and breast. Outer tail feathers extend into long, bare quills carrying a tuft of plumage at the very tips. Iris brown; beak black; legs and feet black.

Hen: Similar in appearance.

Drongos, with their dull coloration, have never been popular avicultural subjects, but the unusual tail plumes of this particular species are highly distinctive. Adept at catching flying insects, drongos should be given a predominantly insectivorous diet. This can include items such as mealworms, waxmoth larvae and tebos, as well as crickets and locusts, which they may catch in flight. Fruit and softbill food should also be offered.

Racket-tailed Drongos settle well in aviary surroundings, and they can be kept in the company of other, similarly non-aggressive species. They often prefer to rest high up in the branches, and if housed indoors, these birds will probably need to be sprayed to maintain their plumage in good condition, as they are reluctant to bathe in a bowl of water. Although reasonably hardy, they may require moderately heated winter accommodation.

Drongos soon become quite tame. Their song is usually melodious and flute-like, but if they are alarmed they also have more unpleasant harsh call notes. These birds may prove talented mimics as well, incorporating the song of other species such as Shamas into their own singing patterns.

Should a pair go to nest, a constant supply of live food must be available if the chicks are to be reared successfully.

21 Pagoda Mynah (Pagoda Starling) *Sturnus pagodarum*

Origin: *Afghanistan, India and Sri Lanka*

Cock: 8in (20cm) Black head with a long crest. Cheeks striped with white; loosely hanging neck feathers grey and white. Upperparts otherwise greyish-blue; underparts reddish-fawn. Tail black with a white tip. Iris greenish-white; beak bluish at the base, becoming yellow half-way along its length; legs and feet yellow.

Hen: Similar in appearance.

Easy to maintain, like other species of mynah, the Pagoda Mynah is a bold, companionable bird, which can be readily tamed and may imitate various sounds, including the call notes of other birds. Even so, unlike the Hill Mynah it cannot be considered a talented 'talking' species. These birds should be housed only in the company of other species of similar size, as they can be aggressive, and for breeding purposes, pairs should ideally be kept on their own.

A large nesting box should be provided, with those used for parakeets being ideal. Pagoda Mynahs will collect a wide range of material ranging from stems of grass to feathers from around the aviary and create a lining for their eggs. Between four and six form a typical clutch, with incubation lasting for about a fortnight. Plenty of live food should be available during the rearing period, and the chicks will fledge when they are about 25 days old. The general care of these mynahs does not differ from that of related species.

Malabar Mynah (Malabar Starling) *Sturnus malabaricus*

Origin: *Indian subcontinent to Thailand and China*

Cock: 8in (20cm) Head and neck greyish-pink; back grey. Wings and tail coverts darker, merging into black with brown tips. Breast and abdomen brownish-pink, with a greyish sheen. Iris yellowish-white; beak blue at the base, with a yellow tip; legs and feet flesh-brown.

Hen: Similar in appearance.

These birds have long been popular among aviculturists, and surgical and other reliable sexing methods have made it much easier to establish breeding pairs. In the past, identifying pairs of these and other starlings was largely a matter of trial and error, although cocks often appear more dominant by nature. The first breeding success with the Malabar Mynah was obtained in Britain in 1900, long before there were specialist diets available for such birds. They are, in fact, quite adaptable in their feeding habits, being related to the Common Starling (*Sturnus vulgaris*), which has become such a common sight in cities around the world.

A mixture of diced fruit laced with softbill food, and some mynah pellets if available will help to maintain Malabar Mynahs in good condition. Live food should also be offered regularly. Hardy once established, these mynahs are quite able to overwinter in an outside aviary, provided that they have a snug shelter.

Pied Mynah (Pied Starling) *Sturnus contra*

Origin: *Indian subcontinent to Thailand and Indonesia*

Cock: 9in (23cm) Head and neck black, with a greenish sheen. Back brownish-black. Area under the eyes, extending to the ear coverts whitish. Long, narrow bar of white feathering present on the scapulars. Throat and breast black. Remaining underparts greyish, becoming white on the undertail coverts. Uppertail coverts black. Bare orbital skin yellowish-red. Iris brown; beak relatively long and yellow; legs and feet yellow.

Hen: Similar in appearance.

Considered to be one of the most mellifluous of the starlings, this species may occasionally utter a few harsh notes, typically when disturbed, but otherwise it has a flute-like song. It sings persistently, with much bowing and flapping of the wings when displaying.

Although young Pied Mynahs can become very tame and are sometimes kept in the home as pets, they are usually too messy to keep in these surroundings. They scatter their food around and splash water when bathing, which they do frequently. All starlings kept indoors should have a bowl of water because regular bathing helps to keep their plumage sleek and immaculate.

Breeding details for this species do not differ significantly from other members of the genus. Pied Mynahs were first kept at London Zoo in 1871 and bred there for the first time back in 1900. Since then they have nested successfully in aviary surroundings on a number of occasions. Although they may agree in a group outside the breeding season, pairs should be housed on their own for nesting purposes. Young birds must also be removed once they are independent, because they are liable to be attacked by the adult cock in particular. This applies to all starlings.

Mandarin Mynah (Mandarin Starling) *Sturnus sinensis*

Origin: *China and Indo-China to Malaysia*

Cock: 8in (20cm) Front of the head cream-coloured, becoming grey towards the back of the crown; chin and ear coverts cream. Back grey; rump and upper part of uppertail coverts creamy-white. Breast pale grey, becoming whiter on the underparts. Prominent white shoulder patches. Iris whitish; beak bluish-grey; legs and feet grey.

Hen: Similar in appearance, but crown may be greyer, with the white on the wings being less prominent.

The song of these starlings, which is not unlike that of the Common Starling (*Sturnus vulgaris*), consists of a mixture of chattering, fluty, grumbling and gargling notes. Inquisitive by nature, the Mandarin Mynah often lives close to people in China and elsewhere through its range, and even in aviary surroundings pairs often become quite tame. Because of their active natures they must have a spacious flight cage if they are kept indoors.

Successful breedings have been recorded on various occasions, with pairs typically using a nestbox. They will amass grass, feathers and other material, and they often become shyer at this stage, so disturbances should be kept to a minimum. The hen usually lays four azure blue eggs in a clutch. These are incubated by both adult birds for 13 days, by which time the young mynahs should have begun to hatch. Live food must be freely available at this stage, along with other nutritious foods such as hard-boiled egg and a proprietary rearing food. A shortage of suitable food is liable to result in the chicks being thrown out of the nest.

Two or more broods may be reared in succession under favourable conditions. Chicks should, therefore, be removed as soon as they are independent, because they are liable to be attacked if the adults are nesting again.

Bank Mynah *Acridotheres ginginianus*

Origin: *north India and Pakistan*

Cock: 9in (23cm) Black head, with the predominant coloration being dusky grey. Wing coverts black with a greenish sheen. Rump and uppertail coverts light grey; undertail coverts yellowish-grey; underparts reddish-grey. Tail feathers black with yellowish-grey tips. Bare orbital skin reddish. Iris orangish; beak orange with a yellow tip; legs and feet orangish-yellow.

Hen: Similar in appearance.

As their name suggests, Bank Mynahs often live near areas of water, and they dig deep holes in steep banks by rivers, where they can nest in relative safety from predators. Some breeders have created similar surroundings in an aviary for them by constructing a wall and leaving bricks out to encourage the birds to tunnel. This is not, however, strictly necessary, because these mynahs are very adaptable and will readily breed in a nestbox instead. The box needs to be positioned quite high up in the aviary. Breeding details are as for the Common Mynah.

A mixture of softbill food sprinkled over fruit, such as diced apple and small grapes, will suit these mynahs well. Live food should also be provided, particularly when a pair are rearing chicks. Soaked currants and raisins can also be provided, and these are particularly valuable as a source of energy during the winter months.

Bank Mynahs prove hardy when acclimatised and can remain in a well-sheltered aviary or birdroom through this period.

220 Common Mynah *Acridotheres tristis*

Origin: *Occurs naturally from India across southeast Asia, but has been introduced in other parts of the world*

Cock: 10in (25cm) Head black; upperparts a warm shade of brown. Wing patch, undertail coverts, vent and tips of the tail white. Underparts rufous-brown. A bare area of yellow skin encircles the eyes. Iris orangish; beak yellow; legs and feet yellow.

Hen: Similar in appearance.

If a young bird can be obtained, it will soon become tame and can become a very pleasant pet. Common Mynahs hiss, whistle and chatter, and they have good powers of mimicry (although nowhere near those of the Hill Mynah) and can often be taught to whistle a short tune and even speak a few words. The specific name *tristis* refers to their dull coloration, and the liveliness and friendliness of these mynahs is in direct contrast to its name.

Even in the wild, Common Mynahs are naturally found near areas of human habitation, and they are frequently seen hopping around in meadows and on arable land in the company of farmstock, looking for insects and worms. During the hottest part of the day, they will perch in trees and on roofs, with widespread wings and ruffled feathers, singing loudly at times.

Common Mynahs are easy to cater for, requiring a similar diet to the Bank Mynah. A pair will nest quite readily if supplied with a cockatiel-type nestbox. They build a simple nest, using grasses, feathers and similar material, but will prove rather secretive during the breeding season, and they should be left alone as much as possible.

The hen will lay up to five eggs, with incubation lasting about two weeks. Plenty of live food is essential while rearing is taking place, and the resulting chicks should fledge just over three weeks later. Once they are feeding on their own, they should be removed to separate quarters. These mynahs are liable to prove aggressive when breeding, and they are best kept on their own. They are quite hardy once acclimatised.

22 Greater Hill Mynah *Gracula religiosa*

Origin: *Indian subcontinent to Indo-China and Indonesia*

Cock: 10–13in (25–33cm) *Almost entirely black, with a greenish or purplish gloss most apparent in good light over the back of the neck. White areas on flight feathers. Vivid yellow naked folds of skin, known as wattles, behind the eyes and along the ear coverts. Iris dark brown; beak orange, becoming more yellowish towards the tip; legs and feet yellowish.*

Hen: *Similar in appearance.*

There is some variation in the size of these mynahs through their wide range, with the largest individuals usually originating from the Indonesian island of Java. Smaller races include the Lesser Hill Mynah (*G.r. indica*) (Plate 223), which comes from India.

Few birds have a longer history of being kept as companions, and Hill Mynahs were known as sacred grackles in ancient Greece, because of their ability to mimic the human voice. In some respects, these birds are superior to parrots in their powers of mimicry, imitating noises such as a ringing telephone without any difficulty. Their speech also tends to be clearer than that of most parrots, even though their vocabulary is rarely as large. Some Greater Hill Mynahs are even able to mimic the human voice so well that they can repeat parts of a conversation between two people with such distinctive intonation that a listener would not realise that the bird was talking on its own.

A young Hill Mynah, known as a gaper because of its habit of begging for food, will develop into a good companion, whereas older birds will remain shy. These are active birds by nature, and a pet bird must be kept in a large cage, so that it does not become obese, with a consequent curtailment of its lifespan.

An indoor flight provides the best option, but it must be easy to clean, because these birds are very messy, both when feeding, when they scatter food everywhere, and when bathing, which they do frequently. Cages for mynahs are designed in the box-style, rather than being open on all sides. Suitable screening around the flight cage will also be required, and it should be possible to wipe this clean without too much difficulty. Although they are relatively hardy, they dislike damp, cold weather, and should be provided with heated accommodation through the winter.

Hill Mynahs are easy birds to feed. They require a mixture of diced fruit, grapes, cherries and similar items, augmented with a softbill mixture and mynah pellets if available, although these should not be fed to the exclusion of other items. Live food must also be offered, and 'pinkies' (dead day-old mice sold for snakes and other reptiles) are readily taken as an occasional treat.

In recent years, with the advent of reliable sexing methods, there has been greater interest in keeping these mynahs in aviary surroundings for breeding purposes. Pairs must be kept on their own, because they can prove aggressive, particularly when breeding. At this time they will build a loose nest in a suitable box. The hen will lay a clutch of two or three eggs, which should hatch after 15 days. The young mynahs, reared largely on insects in the early stages, should leave the nest when they are about a month old. As soon as they are eating on their own, the youngsters must be transferred elsewhere, because they are liable to be attacked by their parents.

Young cock birds are particularly vulnerable to aggressive outbursts from their father, and it may even be necessary to take the young mynahs away before they are fully independent to ensure their safety. Hand-rearing at this stage is not especially difficult however, because the fledglings will usually gape readily for food when they are hungry. They may live for 10 years or more.

Yellow-billed Blue Pie *Urocissa flavirostris*

Origin: *Himalayas eastwards to Vietnam and China*

Cock: 27in (69cm) Head, neck and breast black, with a slight greenish sheen. Back and wings blue, with some white also evident on the wings. Underparts pale yellow. Very long tail feathers predominantly blue, barred with black and with yellowish-white tips. Iris dark brown; beak orangish-yellow; legs and feet orangish-yellow.

Hen: Similar in appearance.

These very large corvids can be kept satisfactorily only in a large flight, with pairs preferably housed on their own or else in the company of other birds of similar size. In addition to their very colourful plumage, their liveliness and curiosity, they also have the ability to mimic, which they quickly learn to do, and they also become tame.

They are very hardy birds, and can stay outside throughout the year once they are acclimatised. However, they should be encouraged to roost in the aviary shelter at night, especially during the winter.

Feeding presents no problems. Yellow-billed Blue Pies will eat fruit, live food, softbill food and mynah pellets, as well as 'pinkies', green food and some seeds, such as sunflower. Protein should figure prominently in their diet, and locusts, crickets, tebos and other bigger live foods become increasingly important should a pair decide to nest and subsequently hatch chicks successfully.

The Yellow-billed Blue Pie is much scarcer in aviculture than the Red-billed Blue Pie, and breeding results do not yet appear to have been recorded, at least in Britain, but their habits probably do not differ significantly.

4 Red-billed Blue Pie (Red-billed Magpie)
Urocissa erythrorhyncha

Origin: *Himalayas to China*

Cock: 27in (69cm) Head and neck black, with the feathers on top of head tipped with blue. There may be a white area on the nape and shades of brown on the mantle. Back and wings rich blue, with white edges to some of the feathers here, and black markings as well. Tail feathers are long and have whitish tips. Iris orange; beak red; legs and feet red.

Hen: Similar in appearance.

These magnificent birds require a spacious aviary that is well furnished with perches so that they can hop speedily from branch to branch. They also need adequate flying space. They like to rest relatively high up in the aviary and watch all that goes on below them with a keen interest. Red-billed Blue Pies are not safe companions for smaller species, which they are liable to kill and eat. Jays or larger Australian parakeets may be suitable to be kept with them, but, certainly for breeding purposes, pairs should be housed on their own.

Red-billed Blue Pies have nested successfully on a number of occasions. They build a loose nest of sticks, twigs and other material, and between three and six eggs form a typical clutch. Incubation lasts 17 days. Once the chicks hatch, there is a risk that they may be eaten by the adult birds, which may happen if there is a shortage of live food. Alternatively, it may be linked to boredom, and to encourage the birds to hunt for their own food, the live food should not be supplied at a single place but scattered around the floor of the aviary. The chicks are at greatest risk from cannibalism in the first week or so after hatching. Disturbances should be kept to the absolute minimum at this stage, because the birds may eat their young if they are upset. Assuming all goes well, the young will fledge when they are just over three weeks old. At this stage, they resemble their parents, but are duller in coloration and have shorter tails. Once they are feeding independently, they should be transferred to separate accommodation.

A varied diet as recommended for the Yellow-billed Blue Pie suits them well. They prove equally hardy once properly acclimatised.

319

225 **Lanceolated Jay** *Garrulus lanceolatus*

Origin: *western Himalayas and India*

Cock: 13in (33cm) *Head black; throat black with white striations. Back grey with a reddish tone; wings grey and black with white tips. Tail blue with black cross bands and white tips, margined by wide black bands. Underparts dark reddish, merging into grey towards the throat. Iris black; beak greenish-horn in colour, with black base; legs and feet greyish.*

Hen: Similar in appearance.

Several kinds of jay are occasionally seen in aviculture, and reliable sexing methods have helped to enhance their popularity by increasing the likelihood of breeding success. All jays have basically similar requirements, and they are not difficult to maintain and usually prove quite hardy when they are established in their quarters. Pairs are best housed on their own, but in spacious surroundings they can be kept in the company of other large birds, such as the blue pies.

The Lanceolated Jay first appears to have been maintained in the collection at Berlin Zoo in 1885. The initial breeding success was reported in 1954, but it has faded from the avicultural scene in recent years. A pair will build a fairly loose nest in a tree or bush in their quarters, and they can sometimes be persuaded to use a nesting platform to provide additional support.

The hen will lay three or four eggs, which hatch after about 16 days. A wide variety of live food is eaten when the birds are rearing their chicks. They parents may prove aggressive near to the nest itself, and it is inadvisable to approach too closely. The chicks should fledge around three weeks old, remaining close to the nest at first. At this stage they can be distinguished by their pale, flesh-coloured beak and legs.

Jays are personable birds, soon becoming tame in aviary surroundings. Encouraging them to hunt for food should help to prevent cannibalism just after the chicks have hatched. In addition to invertebrates, they should also be provided with fruit laced with softbill food, mynah pellets, some green food, 'pinkies' and even acorns, which are a particular favourite of many jays.

Red-billed Lark *Calandrella conirostris*

Origin: *South Africa*

Cock: 5in (13cm) *Upperparts brown to rust-brown, with the feathers being flecked with black. White stripe below the lores and eyes. Throat and chin white; underparts yellowish-brown, darkest near the crop, spotted with black. Wings dark brown with light brown and white margins. Tail dark brown. Iris brown; beak reddish-brown; legs and feet pinkish.*

Hen: Similar in appearance.

These birds are not commonly seen in collections, but their care is reasonably straightforward. Although Red-billed Larks can be housed with other birds, their habit of flying suddenly upwards is liable to disturb other aviary occupants. Adequate cover on the ground of their quarters should help to prevent these birds being frightened and flying upwards, when they may injure their heads on the roof of the aviary, and soft mesh should be strung across here at first as a precautionary measure. Once settled into their quarters, these birds will be quite steady. They are quiet by nature and spend most of their time on the ground, sometimes singing while perched on a rock or tree stump.

A thick layer of sharp river sand should be included on the floor of their aviary. Perches should be placed above this, and a few sizeable rocks added, together with an old tree stump. Preferably this should be located in a reasonably sunny spot, where the lark will sit and sing continuously. Their food dish should also be placed on the floor.

They will eat a wide variety of food, including various kinds of millets, canary seed and groats. Green food, such as chickweed, is also appreciated, and an insectivorous mixture, along with hard-boiled egg or egg food, live food and ants' pupae will all be eaten avidly.

These larks like to bathe in sand, which may help to overcome parasites. Even so, they should be treated with a special avian ectoparasite spray when first obtained, as they may be rather vulnerable to mites and lice.

This species has never been bred in aviary surroundings to date, although nests have occasionally been made in a shallow hollow in the ground. Eggs have been laid, but they have not hatched successfully. It is likely that if they did, a good supply of small live food, such as hatchling crickets and a proprietary rearing food, would be needed for the chicks.

Grey Plantain-eater (Grey Go-away Bird) *Crinifer piscator*

Origin: *west Africa*

Cock: 19in (48cm) Head and neck brown; wings grey with brown quill stripes. Elongated feathers on the nape of the neck have white margins. Tail brown and black. Underparts whitish with brownish-black markings. Iris brown; beak yellow; legs and feet greyish-black.

Hen: Similar in appearance.

These rather plainly coloured members of the touraco family are not especially popular, but the development of sexing methods allows pairs to be distinguished without difficulty and breeding is becoming more commonplace. These birds are active by nature, and need a large aviary. Unfortunately, Grey Plantain-eaters will eat vegetation, with buds and young leaves being especially favoured, and any plants in their enclosure must be sufficiently hardy to withstand these depredations.

When they are breeding, Grey Plantain-eaters construct a simple platform-type nest of twigs and sticks. This is often fairly flimsy, and so they should be encouraged to build on a mesh or wicker support. Two or three eggs form the typical clutch, and the task of incubation is shared by the adult birds. This stage lasts for about 28 days, with the chicks usually fledging in a relatively immature state, before they can fly properly, when they are only three weeks old. Care should be taken to ensure they do not become saturated in rainy weather, since this could be fatal.

A variety of fruit and green stuff, cut into pieces if necessary and sprinkled with softbill food, should form the basis of their diet. It can be difficult to persuade these and other touracos to take sufficient protein in their diet, and mynah or parrot pellets can be helpful in this respect.

226 Violaceous Touraco *Musophaga violacea*

Origin: *west Africa*

Cock: 19in (48cm) *Dark glossy blue-black overall, darkest on the back and underparts. The silky head plumage is purplish-red. Upperparts violet-blue. A white stripe runs below the cere and naked red orbital skin, with a green sheen over the crop area. At rest, red plumage in the wings just evident. Iris orangish-brown; beak yellow with red tip; legs and feet greyish.*

Hen: *Similar in appearance.*

One of the larger touracos, these attractive birds need a spacious flight. A diet as recommended for the Grey Plantain-eater suits them well, and breeding results have also become more frequent during recent years. Unfortunately, as with other related species, the cock may persecute his intended mate quite savagely at the start of the nesting period, and it may be necessary to trim the flight feathers on one wing to cool his ardour. Providing several different feeding stations around the aviary should also mean that the hen can feed unmolested by her mate.

Winter accommodation also needs to be thought out carefully, because touracos often prefer to roost in the open part of the flight, where they are liable to suffer from frost-bite. Although they are quite hardy once they are acclimatised, they must have snug roosting quarters. Positioning the perches in the roost higher than those in the flight itself should help to encourage them inside. If necessary, however, they may need to be shut inside here on cold nights. They are not particularly noisy birds, with the calls of the cock bird during the mating period resembling those of a cock pheasant. Green stuff should feature prominently in their diet.

Hartlaub's Touraco *Tauraco hartlaubi*

Origin: *northeast Tanzania and Kenya*

Cock: 16in (41cm) Head predominantly glossy blue-black, with a white spot in front of the eye and a narrow white line below and extending to the ear coverts. Bare orbital skin, bright red. Wings, rump and tail violet-blue. Mantle green, as are the underparts from the neck to the abdomen. Red feathering apparent in the flight feathers. Lower abdomen darker shade of green. Iris dark brown; beak olive-red; legs and feet blackish.

Hen: Similar in appearance.

One of the best known touracos in aviculture, Hartlaub's Touraco shows the typical characteristics of the family. Its toes are flexible, so that they can perch with either three or two toes directed forwards, keeping either one or two behind the perch. This may help them to maintain their balance on thin branches, where they have ventured to pluck fruit or berries. They also have the unique copper-based turacin pigment, which is responsible for the red coloration of the wings.

Again, they should be offered a mixture of fruit, berries and chopped green stuff. Avoid using cabbage-type greenstuff as far as possible, because this contains a goitrogenic component, which may depress the functioning of the thyroid glands over a period of time. In addition to wild green foods, such as chickweed, you can grow cress quite easily in the home for these birds. Softbill food should also be sprinkled over their food. Live food may well be largely ignored outside the breeding period.

White-cheeked Touraco *Tauraco leucotis*

Origin: *Ethiopia and southeast Sudan*

Cock: 16in (41cm) Predominantly green, with a dark blue crest. A distinctive area of white is present on the hind cheeks and visible in front of eyes. Wing coverts and rump bluish-grey. Iris dark brown; beak orange-red; legs and feet black.

Hen: Similar in appearance.

Another species now quite well established in aviculture, the White-cheeked Touraco is often the most willing species to breed, building a nest on a suitable platform. Here, the hen will lay her clutch of two eggs, which should hatch after a period of three weeks. The young develop quite rapidly, fledging when a month old. At this stage, they are easily distinguishable by their dark beaks. It is important to provide support for the nest, because of the typically flimsy way in which touracos build, and which may result in the loss of eggs and chicks.

Plenty of perches should be supplied in the aviary, so that the birds can bound from one to another. These must be kept clean, however, because touracos are liable to develop localised foot infections, often described as bumblefoot. Effective treatment can be difficult, and prevention is far easier than cure.

227 Cape Robin Chat *Cossypha caffra*

Origin: *South Africa*

Cock: 8in (20cm) Upperparts olive-brown with a grey sheen; rump red-brown. White eyebrow mark extends back behind the ear coverts; cheeks black; throat red-brown edged with white. Breast and flanks grey. Centre of abdomen white, with the remainder being rust coloured. Wings reddish-brown and grey. Tail brown. Iris brown; beak black; legs and feet brownish.

Hen: Throat creamy in colour. Breast reddish-brown with more white on the abdomen.

While the song of these birds is usually soft and melodious, it may also contain some harsher notes. Active by nature, Cape Robin Chats will jump from perch to perch and through branches, as well as running about on the ground, diligently hunting for food.

They feed largely on softbill food, fruit, which should be diced into small pieces, and insects. Chopped-up hard-boiled egg may also be eaten. Little known in aviculture outside South Africa, it is likely that Cape Robin Chats would need adequate protection against the winter weather in northern climes. This particular species does not appear to have bred successfully in aviary surroundings as yet.

228 Wattled Starling (Locust Bird) *Creatophora cinerea*

Origin: *east and southern Africa*

Cock: 8in (20cm) In the breeding season, the head is bright yellow and devoid of feathers, with well-developed wattles over the eyes and on the throat. During the non-breeding season, the wattles are much reduced in size and, apart from a small yellow orbital patch, the head is covered in pale grey feathers. Upperparts grey-brown, with a lighter rump and uppertail coverts. Underparts lighter, merging from grey to white. Tail black, with the wings being a combination of black and white. Iris brown; beak yellow; legs and feet pinkish.

Hen: Retains plumage on the head even in breeding condition, but develops two small wattles on the throat at this stage.

Although widely distributed in the wild, this species is an avicultural rarity. They are, however, interesting, lively aviary occupants, which were first bred successfully in Britain during 1971. They are highly insectivorous in their feeding habits, and in the wild they can be seen in large flocks, hunting for locusts and following locust swarms. They also nest in areas where locusts have laid, usually in colonies, with the young then being reared on hoppers (immature locusts). Locusts and crickets should therefore figure prominently in their diet, together with a range of other invertebrates. Softbill food, mynah pellets and some diced fruit can also be offered for variety.

Their nest is often built close to the ground, with twigs and grasses, although a pair may also be persuaded to use a nestbox. The hen lays four or five bluish eggs, and the incubation period lasts approximately two weeks. Live food must be freely available during the rearing phase, with the chicks fledging around three weeks old. Young birds of both sexes are similar to the hen, but browner in coloration.

Long-tailed Glossy Starling *Lamprotornis caudatus*

Origin: *west Africa*

Cock: 20in (51cm) *A gleaming, steely green overall, being more bronze-coloured on the head and neck, with a blue gloss on the rump and tail. Black spots present on the tail as well as the ear coverts and lores. Underparts have a blue gloss, being suffused with bronze on the belly. Iris yellow; beak black; legs and feet black.*

Hen: Similar in appearance.

In the sunshine, the sheen and glossy coloration of these birds is a glorious sight. Their tail feathers are very long, with the central ones being typically slightly longer in the cock than in the hen. Their initial shyness soon wears off, and in time they will immediately recognise and come to meet their owner and be persuaded to take mealworms from the hand.

A softbill food mixed with a variety of diced fruit, mealworms and other live food should be provided fresh each day. Mynah pellets are also usually appreciated, and they may even eat a little seed on occasions. Unfortunately, these starlings cannot be kept safely with other birds. Everything may seem to run smoothly at first, and then there will be a sudden attack, usually resulting in the death of the victim. Unpaired starlings are also vulnerable, and pairs should be housed on their own for breeding purposes.

A nest made of grass stems, coconut fibres and other material will be prepared in a roomy nestbox. The eggs hatch in a fortnight, and plenty of live food must be provided for rearing purposes. The young birds, which are duller in coloration and lacking the sheen of their parents, will fledge about three weeks later. They also will need to be removed before they are attacked; they are most at risk just after they are feeding independently, although they may be attacked before then in some cases.

Long-tailed Glossy Starlings will bathe frequently, and suitable facilities must be provided for this when they are housed indoors, which is usually recommended for the winter period. The perches in their flight or aviary will need to be carefully positioned, so that they will not damage their long tail feathers on the mesh as they land. The song of these starlings is not particularly attractive, consisting as it does of constant cheeping, hissing and screeching sounds, but it is not particularly loud.

230 Green Glossy Starling *Lamprotornis chalybaeus*

Origin: *much of Africa south of the Sahara*

Cock: 8in (20cm) Upperparts glossy metallic green. Ear coverts, rump and uppertail coverts blue. Abdomen deep blue; tail glossy metallic blue-green. Iris golden-yellow; beak black; legs and feet black.

Hen: Similar in appearance.

All glossy starlings require a considerable amount of space because of their active natures. Like their long-tailed relatives, the short-tailed Green Glossy Starlings are unpredictable in terms of temperament, and sudden outbreaks of aggression can occur, both with their own kind and with other species of similar size. They tend not to molest the larger parakeets, however, nor such birds as the White-crested Jay Thrush, which is not the sweetest-tempered species itself.

A diet as recommended for the Long-tailed Glossy Starling is suitable for all members of the genus. Breeding details are also similar, with clutch size usually varying from three to five eggs.

Purple-headed Glossy Starling *Lamprotornis purpureiceps*

Origin: *across Africa south of the Sahara*

Cock: 8in (20cm) Head black, with a distinctive purple gloss. Sides of head and chest black, with a pinkish sheen. Remainder of the plumage black with a blue and green sheen. Iris brownish; beak black; legs and feet black.

Hen: Similar in appearance.

The darker eye colour helps to distinguish this species from the Purple Glossy Starling, and the entire head is purple. Surgical sexing can be used to identify a breeding pair with certainty, and a cockatiel-size nestbox will be ideal for breeding purposes.

These starlings are generally quite robust, but they do require adequate acclimatisation before they can be expected to overwinter outside. Ideally, they must have access to a heated shelter, which can form part of a birdroom when the weather is at its worst. They can be aggressive and disruptive in an aviary alongside other birds, not hesitating to rob nests and eat eggs or chicks.

1 **Purple Glossy Starling** *Lamprotornis purpureus*

Origin: *widely distributed across Africa south of the Sahara*

Cock: 9in (23cm) Head and underparts violet-purple. Wings and back metallic glossy-green and blue, with a short, violet tail. Iris golden-yellow; beak black; legs and feet black.

Hen: Similar in appearance.

One of the most commonly available members of the genus, the care and breeding of these starlings does not differ form that of related species. They bathe frequently, and when they are housed indoors they should be provided with a heavy ceramic bowl for this purpose (a dog bowl is ideal). The bathing water will need to be changed frequently, and drinking water should be provided separately.

Pairs nest quite readily and may rear two broods successfully during the breeding season. The early youngsters must be removed as soon as they are feeding independently. The juveniles lack the glossy sheen to the plumage that characterises the adult birds and that is most visible in sunlight. The bird's coloration may actually appear to change as it moves, depending on the light.

2 **Spreo Starling** (Superb Starling) *Spreo superbus*

Origin: *east Africa*

Cock: 9in (23cm) Glossy black plumage, with blue and green iridescence on the head, extending to the upper chest; back and wings metallic green. Velvety-black spots on the wing coverts. A white band separates the black area on the chest from the chestnut plumage of the abdomen. Vent and undertail coverts white; tail blackish. Iris metallic-straw; beak black; legs and feet black.

Hen: Similar in appearance.

One of the most beautiful of all African starlings, the Spreo is usually sufficiently tolerant for it to be safely kept with most other birds of similar size in a communal flight. Although its song is rather loud, it is not particularly attractive, but there is the added compensation that these birds soon become tame.

Their dietary needs are straightforward. Softbill food, diced fruit and live food should be provided each day. Live food assumes greater importance in the diet during the breeding period. Pairs will use a nestbox, typically rearing two or three chicks in a brood. Hatching takes 13 days, with the chicks fledging when they are about three weeks old. At this stage they can be recognised by the dark coloration of their eyes. Once they are acclimatised, Spreo Starlings are quite hardy, and then can be kept outside throughout the year, provided they can roost in a snug, dry shelter.

Royal Starling (Golden-breasted Starling) *Cosmopsarus regius*

Origin: *east Africa*

Cock: 14in (36cm) *Head, nape and back metallic green; ear coverts, wings, rump and uppertail coverts purplish-blue. Upper chest with violet gloss, while the lower chest and abdomen are brilliant golden-yellow. Long, slender and graduated tail is golden-brown, with blue and purple iridescence. Iris whitish; beak black; legs and feet blackish.*

Hen: *Similar in coloration.*

These stunning starlings are highly insectivorous by nature, and this should be reflected in their diet, which must incorporate plenty of live food. Crickets are especially useful for this purpose, because it is possible to obtain special supplements to sprinkle on them to improve their nutritional value. Berries are another popular item with these starlings, which need particular care when first obtained. They are vulnerable to gapeworm and other parasites of this type, and deworming may be advisable at this stage.

Once the weather is mild, Royal Starlings can be transferred to an outdoor aviary. Provided with a suitable nestbox or hollow log, they may breed here. The hen may lay as many as six eggs, with the incubation period lasting around two weeks. A good range of rearing foods must be provided for the chicks.

When they fledge, the young birds are much duller than their parents, resembling the related Ashy Starling (*C. unicolor*), being ashy-brown in colour. These starlings are not hardy, and should be brought inside to heated quarters for the winter.

233 Malachite Sunbird *Nectarinia famosa*

Origin: *southeast Africa*

Cock: *6in (15cm) In breeding plumage it is entirely shining metallic green. Coppery on the back; wings and tail blackish. The two central tail feathers are considerably lengthened, and on the flanks (usually concealed when the wings are folded) are tufts of silky yellow feathers. Iris dark brown; beak long, slender, curved and black; legs and feet black.*

Hen: *Resembles out-of-colour cock, being olive-grey, lighter on the underparts, with yellowish eyebrows and facial stripes. Also lacks the elongated tail feathers. It is possible to distinguish cocks outside the breeding season since they retain green plumage on the rump and wing coverts. Immature birds can be recognised because although they also resemble hens, they have noticeably shorter beaks.*

This is one of the largest species. Occasionally, a related form, known as the Scarlet-tufted Malachite Sunbird (*Nectarinia johnstoni*), is available.

These birds can be distinguished by the bright scarlet rather than yellow tufts on their flanks.

Like other sunbirds, the Malachite Sunbird requires a diet based on nectar and small insects. The long, curved beaks are adapted for thrusting into flowers, from which they extract nectar, and their tongues can also be easily projected, being equipped with a tube at the end. By feeding in this fashion, sunbirds play an important part in the fertilisation of various plants since pollen sticks to their beaks and is transferred from one flower to another.

Specially designed feeding tubes should be used when providing nectar for these birds. These must also be cleaned very thoroughly between feeds, because sunbirds can be prone to the fungal disease candidiasis, which may be acquired and transmitted via contaminated feeders, with the nectar providing an ideal culture medium for the *Candida* yeast-like micro-organism responsible for this illness. Treatment with specific antibiotics is possible, but prevention should always be the aim. Since a low level of vitamin A can predispose birds to candidiasis, it is worth adding a specific supplement to the nectar of newly acquired sunbirds as a precautionary measure. Bottle brushes can be used with soapy water to keep the tubes clean, after which the drinkers should be rinsed thoroughly before being refilled.

334 Scarlet-chested Sunbird *Nectarinia senegalensis*

Origin: *east and southern Africa*

Cock: 5in (13cm) Crown of the head, upper throat and streaks on sides of head brilliant green. Lower part of throat and breast deep crimson. Remainder of plumage a combination of velvety black and dark brown, with a violet spot at the fold of each wing. Iris black; beak long, curved and black; legs and feet black.

Hen: Brownish above, whitish below with dark brown striations here.

One of the most commonly seen sunbirds in collections, the Scarlet-chested has been bred successfully on a number of occasions. Like other sunbirds, they are aggressive by nature, especially towards their own kind, whether of the same or other species, and it can even be difficult to house a pair together successfully without serious fighting. Close supervision is important, and it is a wise to supply several sources of nectar, since these birds tend to monopolise a food container and prevent their companion from feeding there. They may also eat a little finely diced fruit.

Once the hen starts to look around the aviary for nesting material, such as hair or feathers, it should be safe to leave the birds together, but they must still be watched closely for signs of aggression. A large aviary, well planted with thickly growing shrubs and climbing plants on trellis work to afford either bird with a refuge if it is persistently chased and persecuted by its mate, is recommended for these sunbirds. They have nested successfully in outdoor surroundings during the summer months, but they need to be housed in heated accommodation through the winter in northern climates.

One or two eggs form the typical clutch, with incubation lasting 13 days. Fruit flies, which can be bred quite easily using the commercial pastes now sold for this purpose, and other small soft-bodied live foods, such as aphids, should be freely available to the birds while they are rearing their offspring. Small spiders are also greedily taken. Fledging occurs after just over two weeks. Young birds resemble the adult hen at this stage but have blackish throats.

Scarlet-chested Sunbirds will be independent by the time they are about three weeks old, seeking nectar on their own and catching fruit flies in their quarters. At this stage, they should be transferred elsewhere, as their parents may then be keen to nest again and soon resent the presence of their previous offspring.

235 **White-bellied Sunbird** *Nectarinia talatala*

Origin: *east Africa*

Cock: 4in (10cm) *In breeding plumage, head, sides of the face and back are metallic green with a gold and blue sheen. Wings black; uppertail coverts predominantly blue; tail bluish-black, with metallic green edges and light tips. Neck metallic blue-green; chin dull black. Broad band of metallic violet across the chest, followed by a narrower band of black. Remainder of underparts white or white slightly suffused with yellow. Yellow tufts of feathers at sides of the chest, usually concealed by the wings. Iris dark brown; beak black; legs and feet blackish.*

Hen: Ashy-brown above, with blue-black tail, and metallic green edging both here and on the tail coverts. Underparts dusky white. It is possible to distinguish out-of-colour cocks by the presence of scattered metallic feathers on the head and mantle. The uppertail coverts and wing coverts also retain a metallic hue, and the tail is bluish-black. It can be harder to distinguish young birds, which more closely resemble the hen, but they tend to be olive-brown above, and more yellowish on their underparts.*

Feeding sunbirds can be a somewhat contentious area, since individual aviculturists favour their own home-made nectar recipes. These are traditionally made up from a teaspoonful of prepared human foods, such as Horlicks, with equal quantities of sweetened condensed milk and honey dissolved in ½–¾ pint (300–450ml) of warm water. Once a week, raw egg should be beaten up and added to the mixture.

If you opt for a mixture of this type, the proportions of the prepared food or milk should not be increased, nor the volume of water used reduced under any circumstances, as this is likely to be harmful. In addition, this nectar must be made fresh, and ideally, two feeds should be given, in the morning and later in the afternoon.

It is probably better to rely on one of the specially-formulated nectar substitutes, because these have been devised to meet the birds' requirements as closely as possible, usually after considerable research. In addition, they are also easier to use, with the required amount of powder or paste simply being dissolved in a specified volume of water. Such foods are also fortified with essential vitamins.

Mariqua Sunbird (Marico Sunbird) *Nectarinia mariquensis*
Origin: *east Africa*

Cock: 5in (13cm) Head, throat and whole of upperparts are metallic green with golden wash. Wings and tail black with blue-black gloss and some metallic green on the edge of the wings. Broad violet band across the chest followed by a band of maroon with metallic violet tips to the feathers. Underparts smoky-grey or blackish. Iris dark brown; beak black; legs and feet blackish.

Hen: Greenish-ash on the upperparts and darker on the cheeks. Throat dusky, with the remainder of the underparts yellow with dusky streaks. Tail black with a slight blue wash and whitish tips to all but the central pair of feathers, and whitish edges to the outer feathers.

Unlike many other species of sunbird, the Mariqua has no eclipse plumage.

In spite of their rather delicate appearance, the care of these and many African sunbirds is quite straightforward once they are established. They can prove surprisingly hardy, although this should not be tested unduly, and warm winter accommodation should always be provided. Mariqua Sunbirds can also be long lived, with a life expectancy of a decade or more.

Care needs to be taken when purchasing sunbirds, and their diet should not be altered at all if possible for the first few weeks, to minimise the risk of digestive disturbances, which could ultimately prove fatal. A sunbird which perches with its feathers ruffled, its head hunched on its shoulders and its tongue protruding beyond the tip of its beak is in poor health, and although the provision of a suitable heat lamp over its quarters may be of assistance, the prognosis is not good, even with the help of a good veterinarian. In recent years the use of probiotics, containing beneficial bacteria, has helped to reduce the likelihood of enteritis in these and other nectar-feeding birds.

Eastern Double-collared Sunbird *Nectarinia mediocris*
Origin: *east Africa*

Cock: 4in (10cm) Shining-green above, with the wings and tail dark grey. Rump blue. Underparts pale grey, with the upperpart of the breast bright red, separated from the green throat by a narrow band of dark metallic blue. Iris dark brown; beak black; legs and feet blackish.

331

Hen: Dusky olive-green.

All species with red in their plumage, including the Double-collared as well as the Scarlet-chested Sunbird, will tend to lose the brilliance of this colour over successive moults unless they are supplied with an adequate colour food. This should be used from just before the start of the moult until it is completed. The colouring agent is perhaps most easily supplied by means of a liquid preparation mixed in with the birds' nectar. Care must be taken to ensure that the stated dose is not exceeded, because this will lead to tarnished coloration. It is also likely to affect the birds' droppings and may suggest blood is being passed, although this phase lasts only while the colouring agent is being fed. The modification to coloration will remain until the next moult, however, and there will be nothing which can be done about it.

Yellow-backed Sunbird (Red Sunbird) *Aethopyga siparaja*

Origin: *Himalayas and west India across southeast Asia to Indonesia and the Philippines*

Cock: 5in (13cm) A small bird, with a long graduated tail. The top of the head metallic green, with the nape a duller shade of green. A band of blue runs from the beak to the sides of the neck; rest of head, upperparts of the back and breast scarlet; lower back golden. Tail green. Iris dark brown; beak black; legs and feet blackish.

Hen: Olive, with a shading of red on the throat.

Sunbirds are not confined to Africa, but they also range widely across Asia and Australasia. The Asiatic species are less well known in aviculture, possibly because they are usually more demanding in terms of care, since they are highly insectivorous.

The Yellow-backed Sunbird is one of the most colourful of the Asiatic sunbirds, but again, much of the brilliant red coloration will be lost unless a colour food is used. With each successive moult, the red areas of plumage tend to become more faded until it is eventually replaced by orange or even a dull, rather muddy shade of yellow.

Ideally, pairs should again be kept on their own, but if they are to be accommodated with other birds, small seedeaters make the best companions to minimise competition over food. It is possible to keep them with *Tangara* tanagers and similarly sized insectivorous birds, if the accommodation is spacious and plenty of natural cover is available to reduce the likelihood of any aggressive encounters.

If the aviary or flight is completely covered, the plants and shrubs should be frequently sprayed with water. Sunbirds are 'rain bathers', and will keep their plumage in good condition if they are able to bathe on the leaves of wet foliage. They can seldom be encouraged to descend to a shallow pan of water provided for bathing purposes at ground level. The Yellow-backed Sunbird is certainly not a hardy species, and it needs particular care when first acquired. These birds must be overwintered in heated surroundings.

Ruby Topaz Hummingbird *Chrysolampis mosquitus*

Origin: *northern South America, to north Bolivia and Brazil*

Cock: 4in (10cm) Scale-like feathers of the crown brilliant ruby-red; chin, throat and upper breast metallic gold; hindneck and mantle black. Remainder of upperparts olive-bronze. Tail bright chestnut edged with purple and bronze. Flight feathers dusky. Underparts warm brown with tufts of white feathers over the legs. Iris dark brown; beak black; legs and feet blackish.

Hen: Upperparts bronzy-green, becoming greyish on the forehead. Tail metallic green in the centre with dusky tips, and outer feathers chestnut tipped with white. Underparts pale brownish-grey with a dark stripe on the throat.

The hummingbird family includes the smallest of all birds, and when they are hovering in flight they often look like butterflies or large dragonflies. All species, of which there are more than 300, originate in tropical and sub-tropical areas of the Americas, where they feed on tiny insects and nectar which they sip from tropical flowers, using their long and often curved beaks for this purpose.

They seldom, if ever, come to the ground. Their minute legs and feet are suited only to perching on thin twigs and the stems of leaves. Much of their time is spent on the wing, hovering backwards and forwards around the flowering trees and shrubs where they feed.

Unfortunately, in spite of their small size, hummingbirds are highly territorial and aggressive. They require a large flight, for they will fight each other ferociously in a small enclosure. Preparing a suitable environment for these birds places considerable demands on the aviculturist. In addition, hummingbirds also require to be kept warm. Steady heat above 60°F (16°C), a daily spraying with tepid water or bathing facilities supplied by dampened leaves and the greatest cleanliness are absolutely essential.

There is considerable variation in the coloration of the Ruby Topaz Hummingbird, with some males appearing much more brightly coloured than others. Size can also be variable, as may be the length of the feathering on the head. It is usually possible to distinguish young cocks from adult females, however, by the presence of metallic orangish feathering on their throat.

At night, when the temperature falls, hummingbirds may enter a phase of torpidity. This results in a lowering of their body temperature and helps to retain their body heat. It is a normal state, although the birds themselves will appear inactive if they are disturbed at this time.

Glittering Emerald Hummingbird *Chlorostilbon aureoventris*

Origin: *widely distributed over the southern part of South America; not present in Chile*

Cock: 3in (7.5cm) Upperparts metallic green, with a coppery sheen. Underparts brilliant green. Tail dark with a bluish sheen. Iris dark brown; beak red with a black tip; legs and feet blackish.

Hen: Less brilliantly coloured on the back, with greyish underparts.

The race described as Pucheran's Emerald Hummingbird (*C.a. pucherani*) (Plates 237 and 238) has a long avicultural history. These hummingbirds are unusual in that they perch with their feathers fluffed up, which in this instance is not a sign of ill-health. They are cheerful by nature, with cocks singing readily for most of the year. In spite of their tiny size, they are highly aggressive by nature, both towards members of their own species and other hummingbirds. They are also very active and should only be accommodated in flights.

As with other species, these hummingbirds should be provided with a diet based mainly on nectar. Excellent proprietary brands of nectar are now available, either in the form of paste or powder, and these need only to be diluted with water before being fed to the birds. These foods do not contain milk in any form and therefore do not tend to turn sour, which is a particular advantage in warm climates. Even so, the mixture should be replaced with a freshly made solution every day.

If such foods are not available, the following mixture can be used for a morning feed. A teaspoonful (5ml) each of Mellins food or Horlicks, honey and condensed milk should be dissolved in a ¼ pint (150ml) of boiling water. This must be allowed to cool before being fed to the hummingbirds. Especially in warm weather, it will need to be removed around mid-day and replaced with a solution of honey, made using two teaspoonfuls (10ml) of honey to a quarter of a pint (150ml) of water again. A vitamin and mineral supplement should also be used regularly when a diet of this type rather than a specialist formulated nectar is being used.

In the wild, hummingbirds also consume quantities of tiny insects, and they must therefore be given a regular supply of fruit flies (*Drosophila*), which can be cultured quite easily using a proprietary medium or even banana skins.

A special nectar tube, with a red feeding spout is also needed, because hummingbirds find this colour especially appealing. The small, upturned tube will enable the birds to thrust their long beaks in to obtain the nectar, just as they would into the heart of a flower. If plants such as fuschias can be incorporated into their quarters, hummingbirds will also be able to obtain some nectar from these flowers.

Cock Glittering Emerald Hummingbirds will frequently display, but breeding successes are, perhaps not surprisingly, rather rare. They build a nest of spiders' webs, hair and similar fine material. This task, as well as those of incubation and rearing the chicks, is essentially the responsibility of the hen.

It is usually advisable to remove the cock bird once mating is thought to have occurred because he is liable to prove a disruptive influence once the hen starts nesting in earnest. Two eggs are likely to be laid, with the incubation period probably lasting about two weeks. Unlimited supplies of fruit flies must be available once the chicks hatch. Assuming all goes well, they are likely to leave the nest when they are just over three weeks old.

▶ Yellow-winged Sugarbird (Red-legged Honeycreeper)

Cyanerpes cyaneus

Origin: *parts of Central and South America, extending to Bolivia*

Cock: 5in (13cm) In breeding condition, the crown is a brilliant turquoise blue, with the feathers shining and scale-like. A black streak extends through the eyes and across the forehead, with a black mark from the sides of the neck extending down to the centre of the back. The remainder of the body is a bright purplish-blue with a brilliant sheen. Flight feathers black with the inner webs, which are concealed when the wing is closed, a bright canary yellow. Tail black. Iris dark brown; beak black; legs and feet bright red.

Hen: Upperparts olive-green, greyish on the head and with a dark eye stripe and whitish eyebrow mark. Flights and tail brownish, with the inner webs of the flights margined with pale yellow. The underparts, chin and throat greenish-white, blending into yellowish-white on the breast and abdomen, all being lightly striated with greenish-grey. Legs and feet pale pinkish-brown. It is possible to distinguish the cock bird, even when not in breeding plumage, because the red coloration of his legs is usually maintained. Otherwise, his body feathering at this stage resembles that of the hen.

Closely related to tanagers, these birds will thrive on a similar diet, although they require nectar on a daily basis as well. This should be placed in a drinker adjoining a perch, rather than on the ground. A standard tubular drinker is suitable for this purpose, although it must be cleaned thoroughly between feeds with a bottle brush and soapy water. It should be rinsed under a running tap to remove all trace of the detergent before being refilled.

A little fruit, laced with softbill food, should also be provided in a container that hooks near a perch, because these birds do not like to descend to the ground, although they will catch insects here. Aphids, spiders, small mealworms and waxmoth larvae can all be supplied when available, and live food is increasingly important once a pair start nesting if the chicks are to be reared successfully.

On this type of diet, Yellow-winged Sugarbirds will remain in excellent condition, and will pass through the moulting period, which occurs twice a year, with no difficulty or loss of colour. Breeding details are identical to those of the Purple Sugarbird.

241 Purple Sugarbird (Yellow-legged Honeycreeper)

243 *Cyanerpes caeruleus*

Origin: *northern South America*

Cock: 4in (10cm) *Upper- and underparts purplish-blue. Lores, wings, throat and tail black. Iris brown; beak black; legs and feet yellow with black claws.*

Hen: Rich green above; throat chestnut; underparts pale yellowish with dark green striations. A narrow pale violet-blue moustache mark is present on each side of the throat. Lores and feathers around the eyes chestnut-buff. Legs and feet greenish-brown.

The long, curved shape of the beak, the stumpy body and the short tail give this species a rather wren-like appearance. These sugarbirds are very similar in their requirements to the Yellow-winged Sugarbird, although cocks of this species remain in colour throughout the year. These birds are very suitable for a spacious flight cage or indoor aviary, although they can be kept quite successfully outside during the warm months of summer.

Bathing facilities must always be provided in indoor surroundings, because sugarbirds tend to bathe very regularly. Fresh, thin twigs should be provided as perches, but they must be replaced frequently so that there is no risk of them becoming sticky.

Successful breeding results have been recorded on a number of occasions, even in the confines of a cage. The nest is typically suspended in the fork of a tall bush and made from fine plant fibres and similar materials. The average clutch is of two eggs, and incubation lasts 12 days. The young sugarbirds fledge when they are just over two weeks old. In addition to their usual diet of nectar and soft fruit, quantities of small live insects, such as fruit flies and aphids, are required at this time if the young are to be reared successfully.

The chicks resemble adult hens at first, with cocks gaining odd purplish feathers, usually on the head. Several may be housed together if they are all cocks, but if hens are present, fighting is likely to result. A single pair may be safely associated with other small birds, however, but will need to be brought inside for the duration of the winter. These sugarbirds may live for 10 years or more.

Blue Dacnis (Black-throated Honeycreeper, or Turquoise Honeycreeper) *Dacnis cayana*

Origin: *Central America south to Argentina*

Cock: 5in (13cm) Head dark turquoise blue; lores, feathers around eyes, mantle, and a large throat patch black. Remainder of body plumage turquoise blue with greenish tinge. Wings and tail black; uppertail coverts and flights edged with blue. Iris yellow; beak dusky, lighter on the lower mandible; legs and feet pinkish-brown.

Hen: Head turquoise with dusky lores; chin and throat grey. Back brilliant green. Wings and tail dusky brown, with lesser coverts edged with turquoise. Underparts apple green shading into yellowish-green on the abdomen and indistinctly barred with grey on the flanks.

Slightly larger and with a shorter, more robust beak than the *Cyanerpes* honeycreepers, members of this genus are less common in aviculture. They also tend to be somewhat more belligerent, and need careful initial acclimatisation. A diet of nectar, diced fruit sprinkled with softbill food and berries when available should be provided for them, together with a daily supply of live food. The live food is especially important if a pair decides to nest. Breeding details are similar to those of the Purple Sugarbird. Blue Dacnis are not hardy, and they must have heated winter accommodation, even when they are well established.

Scarlet-thighed Dacnis (Scarlet-thighed Honeycreeper) *Dacnis venusta*

Origin: *Costa Rica and Panama south to Ecuador and Colombia*

Cock: 5in (13cm) Crown, sides of neck, nape, mantle, back and uppertail coverts brilliant greenish-turquoise; forehead, cheeks, throat, entire underparts and secondaries, flights and tail black. There is also a black bar on the shoulders. Thighs a brilliant crimson. Iris dark brown; beak black; legs and feet brownish.

Hen: Duller in coloration, with the areas of black plumage replaced by dark grey, and the blue by a dull greyish-blue. Demarcation between these areas is indistinct.

Although it is encountered in aviculture even less frequently than its blue relative, the Scarlet-thighed Dacnis requires similar care. The use of a colour food during the moulting period will help to ensure that the characteristic scarlet plumage on the thighs retains its brilliance over successive moults. Apart from this their diets and general care should be identical.

Although the Blue Dacnis was first bred in Britain in 1932, no success has yet been recorded with this species, almost certainly because of a shortage of available stock. Secluded surroundings, in the form of a well-planted flight would doubtless encourage a pair to commence nesting. They build their own nest with fine materials, including horsehair if available, with live food again assuming greater importance when there are chicks in the nest.

Black-headed Sugarbird (Black-crowned Honeycreeper, Green Honeycreeper) *Chlorophanes spiza*

Origin: *south Mexico south to Bolivia and Brazil*

Cock: 6in (15cm) Sharply defined head and cheeks black; remainder of plumage shining green, somewhat variable in shade and darker on the upperparts, flights and tail. Iris brownish; upper bill black, lower bill yellowish; legs and feet blackish.

Hen: Entirely green, lighter in tone than the cock, with the underparts being yellowish on the throat and apple green on the breast. Flights and tail dark brownish-green. Lower bill duller shade of yellow.

Variations in colour in this species result from individual races, which have evolved throughout its wide range. The most northerly subspecies, *C.s. guatemalensis* is a deep shade of green; birds from Colombia and western parts of Venezuela, on the other hand, which form the population *C.s. subtropicalis*, are bluish-green.

Black-headed Sugarbirds are relatively large and robust by nature, with quite a powerful beak. They can prove more disruptive than their smaller relatives in a mixed collection of small birds. Their diet should consist of nectar, fruit and berries, some softbill food and live food, and, as always, the nectar should be provided in a sealed vessel to prevent the birds from bathing in it.

In spite of their larger size, these sugarbirds cannot be considered hardy, and they must be brought inside for the winter months in temperate areas. A planted flight will offer the best likelihood of breeding success.

Violaceous Euphonia *Euphonia violacea*

Origin: *northern South America, from Venezuela south to Brazil and Paraguay*

Cock: 4in (10cm) Upperparts rich violet-black with an orange-yellow spot on the forehead. Underparts entirely orange-yellow. Iris brown; beak black; legs and feet black.

Hen: Entirely olive-green with paler underparts.

Young birds of both sexes resemble the hen, and it can even be difficult to distinguish between hens of different species of *Euphonia* because they are all of similar appearance.

They are lively birds by nature and should be kept in flights rather than cages. When they are first obtained, the birds must be carefully acclimatised, and the diet should not be changed if possible. Nectar can be particularly beneficial at this stage. A good selection of diced fruit, sprinkled with softbill food, and occasional live food should form their basic diet, and berries can also feature. Fresh bathing water must be provided every day.

The cock sings sweetly during the breeding season, but for the rest of the year a more plaintive call is heard. The song is not very varied, although sometimes they will imitate the call notes from the song of another bird.

Violaceous Euphonias build a domed-shaped nest with a side entrance, typically well-concealed in the vegetation of their flight. Incubation of the four or five eggs, which is carried out mainly by the hen, lasts about two weeks. Both parents feed their chicks, with fledging occurring about 21 days later. Two broods may be reared in succession.

It is usually better to keep these birds indoors in the winter, but they can be housed satisfactorily in a flight attached to a birdroom, where it is possible to shut them in when the weather is bad. Violaceous Euphonias are not normally aggressive birds, and they can be housed satisfactorily in the company of other softbills of similar size.

4 Superb Tanager *Tangara fastuosa*

Origin: *east Brazil*

Cock: 6in (15cm) *Head and neck shining emerald green, with the forehead being black. Upper back velvety black; lower back brilliant deep orange. Lesser wing coverts green; outer wing coverts purple; wings and tail black edged with purple. Chin black followed by a narrow band of green. Broad black crescent on upper breast. Breast and abdomen silvery-blue, deepening on belly and undertail coverts to deep ultramarine. Iris dark brown; beak black; legs and feet blackish.*

Hen: *Green of the head may have a bluish tone, with the feathers on the nape showing some black at the base. Lower back and rump less golden.*

Tanagers are widely distributed through the Americas, but some species, including this one, are very localised.

The Superb Tanager has now become an avicultural rarity, because it was not bred in any numbers when the species was available from Brazil, at a time when less was known about the breeding habits of these birds. More recently, breeding successes with tanagers have improved, partly because of the increased availability of commercially cultured live foods, which, supplemented with insects and spiders attracted to the aviary, can be used for rearing the chicks.

Superb Tanagers are generally considered to be peaceable, but they will sometimes squabble over roosting perches. They cannot be kept with other breeding birds, however, because they are likely to rob their nests. They are not great songsters, but their stunning coloration is adequate compensation.

246 **Emerald-spotted Tanager** *Tangara guttata*

Origin: *northern South America*

Cock: *5in (13cm) Upperparts bright green; feathers of the head, back and wing coverts spangled with black. Forehead and area around the eyes pale golden-yellow; lores black. Wings dusky, with the feathers edged with green. Tail blackish edged with green. Underparts greyish-white; flanks suffused with green; undertail coverts yellowish. Sides of the throat and upper breast conspicuously spotted with black. Iris brownish; beak black; legs and feet dark brown.*

Hen: *Similar in appearance.*

Six distinct races of these tanagers are recognised through their range, with some being more yellow on the sides of the head than others. They are not difficult to maintain, but will benefit from a supply of nectar when they are first acquired, while a selection of fruit should form the basis of their diet. The fruit should be supplemented with softbill food, which can be sprinkled over it, and with live food.

Although these tanagers can be housed in an outdoor aviary through the summer months, they will need to be brought indoors during the winter. Because of their active natures and rather messy feeding habits they should then be kept in a flight rather than in a cage. Particular attention must be paid to keeping the perches clean, because the birds may develop foot problems.

248 **Silver-throated Tanager** *Tangara icterocephala*

Origin: *Costa Rica and Panama south to Colombia and Ecuador*

Cock: *6in (15cm) Forehead and crown golden with faint greenish markings on the centre of the crown and greenish tone on the nape. Mantle, back and rump greenish-gold with black markings on the mantle. Wings and tail blackish with golden-green edges to the feathers. A black moustache mark runs from the gape below the eyes to the base of the nape. Throat silvery-grey. Entire underparts yellow, rather greenish on the sides of the breast and flanks. Iris brown; beak blackish-brown; legs and feet yellowish-brown.*

Hen: *Similar in appearance.*

All *Tangara* tanagers will thrive on a varied diet of fruit, and limited quantities of items such as well-washed soaked currants and raisins can be provided for variety. Fruits such as apple can be cut into large pieces or diced, so that the surfaces can be coated with softbill food.

One of the major difficulties in breeding tanagers has been recognising true pairs in the first instance. Nevertheless, a number of species have been bred successfully in aviary surroundings. They tend to become aggressive at this stage and should be housed on their own. Pairs can be transferred to an outside aviary about May, and need not be brought inside until October, with breeding taking place during the summer.

Hens will use moss, leaves and cobwebs to build a cup-shaped nest, which is likely to be well concealed among foliage. Two dull white eggs form the typical clutch, with the female incubating alone for two weeks. The pair share the task of feeding the youngsters, which fledge after a further two weeks.

Young Silver-throated Tanagers are duller than adults, with dusky shading most noticeable on the throat and upper breast. They should be removed from the aviary soon after they leave the nest, because the adult birds are likely to start nesting again without delay, and may resent the attentions of their older chicks.

Paradise Tanager *Tangara chilensis*

Origin: *Colombia, Venezuela, Guyana, Guyane, Brazil, Ecuador and Peru*

Cock: 6in (15cm) Nape, sides of the neck, back and shoulders velvety black; forehead and crown shining yellow-green, with the feathers resembling scales; throat cobalt blue. Lower part of back and rump orange-red running into golden-yellow; lower parts turquoise blue. Undertail coverts and tail black. Blue coloration apparent in the wings. Iris brown; beak black; legs and feet black.

Hen: Similar in appearance but may be slightly less colourful.

One of the most spectacularly coloured of all tanagers, the Paradise Tanager unfortunately proves to be a rather shy bird, even when it is well established in its quarters. As a result, it is not very conspicuous in a planted aviary, although it may be tempted out from cover by offers of live food.

In the wild, these tanagers are relatively social by nature, often being observed in groups of up to 10 birds. Purchasing several should help to ensure that you have at least one pair for breeding purposes, although the birds may need to be separated at this time.

Breeding details do not differ significantly from those of other members of the genus, and seclusion is particularly vital in this case. Young Paradise Tanagers resemble adults, but are typically rather paler in coloration, especially on the lower back and rump.

Black-eared Golden Tanager *Tangara arthus*

Origin: *northwest South America, ranging south to Peru and Bolivia*

Cock: 6in (15cm) Predominantly rich golden-yellow, with black markings. A small black triangle is present behind the eyes, with a larger black spot on the ear coverts. Back black with golden streaks. Wings and tail blackish with golden-yellow edging to both the wing coverts and inner flights. Underparts golden,

341

becoming golden-brown in some races. Iris brown; beak black; legs and feet dark grey.

Hen: *Similar in appearance.*

One of the most widely kept of the *Tangara* species, the Black-eared Golden Tanager usually proves keen to breed if a true pair can be acquired in the first instance. Nestboxes should be fixed up high, but if there are any dense bushes growing in the aviary, the tanagers will probably prefer to build in these. They use fine twigs and blades of grass for the outside of their cup-shaped nest, which is lined on the inside with finer grasses, moss and sometimes broad leaves. If possible, a piece of bowl-shaped wire gauze should be inserted under the spot where they are building to provide extra support.

Incubation and fledging periods do not differ from those of the Silver-throated Tanager. Live food usually assumes greater significance in the diet at this stage, and soft-bodied items, such as waxmoth larvae and tebos, which will be more digestible, particularly by the young tanagers, should be provided in preference to mealworms. As many as three broods of chicks may be reared successfully during the summer period once a pair are established in their quarters. The young birds should be removed as soon as they are independent.

247 Bay-headed Tanager *Tangara gyrola*

Origin: *Costa Rica and Panama south to Brazil, Ecuador and Peru*

Cock: *6in (15cm) Predominantly bright green with a golden wash on the upperparts and blue suffusion on the underparts. The head colour may vary from golden-brown to reddish-chestnut and, in most cases, this is divided on the nape from the green of the back by a golden collar. This may be narrow or even almost or completely inconspicuous. Flights blackish. Tail dark green on the outer edges of the feathers, becoming browner in the centre. Iris brown; beak blackish; legs and feet blackish.*

Hen: *Similar in appearance.*

Nine different races of this tanager are recognised, and they vary in the extent of the blue suffusion on the underparts, the golden band on the neck and the colour of the lesser wing coverts, which may be green through golden-yellow to cinnamon-rufous. For breeding purposes, therefore, it is wise to start with birds from the same source rather than purchasing odd individuals, which may belong to different races.

Recently imported birds should be kept in warm surroundings and provided with regular bathing facilities on the floor of their quarters. An earthenware pot is ideal for this purpose, and surrounding newspaper should be changed as it becomes soaked. Once established, the care of these tanagers is quite straightforward, and they may well live for 10 years or more.

Their diet should be based mainly on fruit, sprinkled with softbill food. Canned fruit is quite suitable for this purpose, although the juice should be drained off first. Grapes are often a favourite, while blackberries and other berries, which can be provided when in season, will contribute variety to the diet. Live food is also important.

45 Mrs Wilson's Tanager (Masked Tanager, Golden-masked Tanager) *Tangara nigrocincta*

Origin: *northern South America, south to Peru, Ecuador and Brazil*

Cock: 6in (15cm) Forehead and cheeks bright violet-purple, fading into turquoise. A narrow black line runs across the beak, through the eyes and on the chin. Crown, nape, sides of neck and throat shining golden-buff, with deep golden-buff at the centre of the throat. Mantle, scapulars, tail and breast velvety-black. Wing coverts shining turquoise; secondaries and flights black, edged with golden green and turquoise. Rump, uppertail coverts and flanks bright blue with cobalt and violet wash and some black flecking. Abdomen and undertail coverts pure white. Iris brown; beak black; legs and feet black.

Hen: Similar in appearance.

These tanagers have a reputation for becoming very aggressive during the breeding season. They may either build a nest in a fork of a branch, using a variety of materials for this purpose, or they may be persuaded to adopt a nestbox.

Breeding results with this species have been recorded on several occasions, with the earliest report from Tahiti, in 1938. More recently, a pair nested in Denmark, during 1964, with the hen laying the usual clutch of two eggs. These birds were especially ferocious to other birds sharing their quarters with blue coloration, and they killed a Blue Dacnis cock. Incubation was carried out by the hen alone, and lasted about 13 days. A single chick hatched and finally left the nest by 17 days old, it was brownish-green in colour. Adult plumage was obtained when the young tanager was nearly three months old.

Silver-beaked Tanager (Maroon Tanager) *Ramphocelus carbo*

Origin: *north South America, extending south to Bolivia, Brazil and Paraguay*

Cock: 7in (18cm) Overall dark wine red; the back almost black; breast red but becoming bluish-white towards the belly. Iris brown; beak silvery; legs and feet black.

Hen: Duller in coloration, being pinkish-brown overall with the rump and breast having a reddish glow. Wings and tail brownish-black; beak brown.

Cocks of this species are often more frequently available than hens, but pairs can be sexed visually. Although they are generally considered to be more robust than the smaller *Tangara* tanagers, members of this genus still require careful acclimatisation. In mild areas it may be possible to over-winter them outdoors without additional warmth, they should not be exposed to the worst of the winter's weather, and a birdroom where they can be shut in on cold or wet days is recommended.

Their diet should contain a mixture of fruit, softbill food and live food, although they will also eat a little seed, notably canary seed and millets.

For breeding purposes, pairs are best housed on their own. These tanagers typically build a fairly untidy nest, quite close to the ground and in a dense bush. Dead leaves are often used as a lining. When the nest is completed, the hen will usually lay a clutch of two eggs, which are bluish-green in colour, often with some darker markings. She incubates alone for about 12 days, with the young remaining in the nest for a similar period. At this stage, they resemble the hen in appearance. Three weeks later, the young tanagers will be independent, and they must be transferred to other quarters, before the adult birds start to nest again in earnest, or the earlier offspring will be persecuted ferociously or even be killed.

252 Scarlet-rumped Tanager *Ramphocelus passerinii*

Origin: *Central America from Mexico south*

Cock: 7in (18cm) *Overall velvety-black; rump and uppertail coverts brilliant scarlet. Iris brown; beak silvery-grey; legs and feet blackish.*

Hen: *Head and neck brownish-grey; otherwise brownish-olive, brighter in color-ation over the rump. Flight feathers and tail sooty.*

There is considerable variation in the plumage of individual birds of this species. Hens of the Costa Rican race (*R.p. costaricensis*) may have a fairly distinctive orange breast band, as well as a fairly bright orange rump, while the depth of red coloration on the rump of males is variable.

In the wild bananas are a popular food of these tanagers, but a wide range of suitable fruits and berries should be offered to aviary birds. Colour-feeding may also be recommended during the moult to retain the intensity of the coloration of the cock's rump. Breeding details are similar to those of related species, and Scarlet-rumped Tanagers also become highly insectivorous during the rearing period. After fledging, the chicks tend to be kept well hidden in vegetation by their parents for about three weeks until they are able to fly well and are fully independent.

There are two other very closely related tanagers, both of which occur further south in South America. These are the Flame-rumped Tanager (*Ramphocelus flammigerus*) and the Yellow-rumped Tanager (*Ramphocelus icteronotus*), which differ essentially in the coloration of their rump and uppertail coverts, as is indicated by their common names.

51 Scarlet Tanager (Brazilian Tanager) *Ramphocelus bresilius*

Origin: *Coastal areas of Brazil and Argentina.*

Cock: 7in (18cm) A vivid combination of black and scarlet, with black plumage on the wings and tail, while all the other feathering is a most intense shade of scarlet, darker across the back and becoming lighter and brighter on the lower back and rump. Iris brown; beak black with a silvery-grey patch on the lower bill near the base; legs and feet blackish.

Hen: Dull reddish-brown, darker and greyer above, notably on the wings and tail.

Largely as the result of a failure to coordinate breeding programmes, this striking species of tanager is now rarely seen in collections, and yet in the past breeding results were not uncommon, to the extent that hybrids between the Scarlet Tanager and the Maroon Tanager were also produced. Part of the difficulty was that cocks predominated in consignments, with hens being in short supply.

Once they are established, Scarlet Tanagers are easy to cater for, although their fiery coloration will fade over successive moults unless they are colour-fed for a short time before and throughout each moult. Adding grated carrot to their diet can also be of value, because this contains a natural colouring agent, but not all birds like carrots. Fruit, sprinkled with softbill food, and some live food should form the basis of their diet.

Hens usually build a relatively sturdy nest in a secluded part of the flight, where they will lay three eggs in a clutch. These should start to hatch about 12 days later, and while the chicks are in the nest, they are fed almost exclusively on live insects and spiders. A good range of food must be provided, and if necessary commercially available live foods such as waxmoth larvae can be augmented with insects swept up using a butterfly net from tall meadow grass on a warm summer's day. Insect traps of the kind used by entomologists to catch winged insects may also be valuable, especially if you have a large collection of softbills.

The young Scarlet Tanagers will leave the nest when they are about 12 days old, but they remain largely hidden as they cannot fly properly at this stage. Both sexes resemble the adult hen in coloration. It may take cock birds as long as a year to assume their stunning scarlet plumage. In the winter, additional heat may be needed.

249 **Black Tanager** (White-lined Tanager) *Tachyphonus rufus*

Origin: *Central America from Costa Rica and Panama south to Bolivia, Paraguay and Ecuador*

Cock: 7in (18cm) Overall glossy blue-black; wings and tail dull black; secondary wing coverts white. Iris brown; beak black with greyish-white area at the base of the beak; legs and feet black.

Hen: Rusty-brown with the underparts being more yellowish-brown. Wings dark brown with light margins.

A very varied menu is recommended for these tanagers, which should be offered a wide selection of fruits, some green food, softbill food, live food and even seeds, such as plain canary seed and groats. They also like chopped hard-boiled eggs and nectar. On a diet like this, Black Tanagers will thrive, and they have been known to live for 20 years or more. They will prove quite hardy as well, once they are properly acclimatised, being able to winter out of doors if a good shelter is available.

Obtaining a true pair is reasonably straightforward because of the clear distinction in plumage between the sexes. This was, in fact, the first species of tanager to be bred successfully in Britain in 1906. The nest is constructed from coarse grasses and leaves and is often lined with feathers. Although these birds usually prefer to build in a dense bush, they will sometimes use a nestbox or basket.

The two or three eggs are incubated solely by the hen, and they hatch after 12 days. The young leave the nest after a similar interval, while still largely unable to fly properly. During the rearing period, unlimited quantities of invertebrates should be supplied, and variety is important at this stage.

Immature Black Tanagers resemble the adult hen but tend to be paler in coloration. When the hen starts to show signs of nesting again, these earlier chicks must be removed without delay; otherwise they are liable to be persecuted and even killed.

Palm Tanager *Thraupis palmarum*

Origin: *Central America south to Peru, Paraguay, Bolivia and Brazil*

Cock: 7in (18cm) Pale olive-green above, and bluish-grey on the underparts. Wings brownish-black, as is the tail with olive-green margins. Iris brown; beak blackish; legs and feet greyish.

Hen: Similar in appearance.

Because it occurs over such a wide area, it is not surprising that there is some regional variation in appearance between individuals from different parts of their range. Sexing them on the basis of size or other visual characteristics is, therefore, rather hazardous; the most reliable guide is the song of the cock bird. Although their plumage may appear rather dull in subdued lighting, when seen in sunshine it has a rather distinctive violet tone. Palm Tanagers are rather aggressive by nature, and pairs should ideally be housed on their own in a well-planted flight for breeding purposes.

They have nested successfully on a number of occasions, and if a nestbox or deep basket is hung up high in a secluded, covered part of the aviary, a pair may well start to breed here. Grass, coconut fibres, roots of plants and mosses will all be used to form the nest. Incubation lasts for about 14 days, with the chicks fledging when they are approximately three weeks old. The parents share the task of feeding their offspring until they are independent. Insects are again very important during the rearing period.

Blue-grey Tanager *Thraupis virens*

Origin: *Central and South America into Bolivia*

Cock: 7in (18cm) Head pale ashy-blue, deeper on the back and more blue on the rump and breast. Wings and tail dark greyish-blue with a greenish sheen on the edges of the flights; upperwing coverts glittering pale blue. Iris brown; beak dark greyish-horn; legs and feet black.

Hen: Similar in appearance.

Requiring identical care to the Palm Tanager, this species is also quite hardy when it is acclimatised, and as long as the aviary has a frost-proof shelter, the birds may be safely kept outdoors throughout the year. Like all larger tanagers, Blue-grey Tanagers are inclined to be spiteful and should not be kept in the company of smaller birds. They are active by nature and should always be kept in a spacious flight or aviary surroundings.

A supply of fresh fruits, including diced apple and grapes mixed with softbill food, should form the basis of their diet. Live food should also be provided, particularly in the breeding season. Blue-grey Tanagers will live for many years on this type of fare. Like other tanagers, they are keen bathers, and they should be provided with an open pot of water for this purpose, especially if housed indoors during dry weather.

A third member of this genus, the Sayaca Tanager (*Thraupis sayaca*), which occurs in southeast South America, is sometimes seen in aviculture. It does not differ significantly in its requirements from related species. Where it overlaps with the Blue-grey Tanager, in south Peru, east Brazil and Bolivia, it can be distinguished by its blue-grey rather than white wing coverts.

254 Toco Toucan *Ramphastos toco*

Origin: *much of north South America, down to Paraguay and Argentina*

Cock: 22in (56cm) Upperparts velvety-black, except the rump which is pure white. Cheeks, throat and upper breast white, more or less tinged with reddish-orange at the edges. Undertail coverts crimson; remainder of the upperparts black. Naked orbital patch of skin orange, with a ring of rich cobalt encircling the eyes. Iris brown; beak predominantly orange, stained on the culmen and cutting edges with red; a broad black band across the base of both mandibles and a large, oblong black area at the tip of the upper bill; legs and feet bluish-grey.

Hen: Similar in appearance, but bill may be deeper and shorter in length.

This is the largest of the toucans, and it should be housed only in a large aviary where it can take plenty of exercise. It should not be kept with other birds. Although it can stand quite low temperatures when acclimatised, it dislikes damp, cold winter nights, and during the worst of the winter weather, it should be encouraged to roost in a well-protected, frost-proof shelter, where heat can be provided if necessary.

Although individual Toco Toucans can become delightfully tame and confiding, especially if hand reared, they are not suitable as household pets, in view of their large size, active nature and ungainly beak, which is about 9in (23cm) long. Their narrow, fringed tongue runs the entire length of the bill. In spite of its fearsome appearance, however, the beak itself is light and can be quite easily damaged, and perches in their quarters should be arranged so that the birds can land and turn round easily, without banging their beak on the aviary mesh.

Breeding has been achieved on an increasing number of occasions in recent years, but compatibility of adult Toco Toucans can be a problem. Cocks may turn savagely on their partners if they are not receptive to their advances, and pairs must be watched accordingly. A deep natural log is most likely to be adopted as a nest site.

Two or three eggs form the typical clutch, with incubation lasting just under three weeks. The chicks have small beaks at first and grow quite slowly. They are unlikely to fledge before they are two months old, at which stage they will be smaller than their parents and duller in appearance. Their feeding requirements do not differ from those of other related species.

253 Green-billed Toucan *Ramphastos dicolorus*

Origin: *northeast Argentina, southeast Brazil and Paraguay*

Cock: 20in (51cm) Upperparts entirely black. Cheeks, chin and throat yellow, becoming orange on the breast. Abdomen red. Area of red naked orbital skin encircling the eyes. Iris grey-green; beak green with red cutting edges and a black basal band; legs and feet grey.

Hen: Similar in coloration, but usually distinguishable by the shape of the beak, which is typically smaller in length and breadth.

Reliable sexing methods mean that it is no longer essential to rely on differences in the appearance of the beak to recognise a true pair, although compatibility is again important for breeding purposes. The calls of these and other *Ramphastos* toucans can be quite loud, especially when they are disturbed, but they also make a softer, purring sound. Hand-reared chicks are often quite tame and may even feed from the hand, but they must be kept in a spacious flight.

Toucans feed mainly on a mixture of fruit laced with softbill food. Their food should be diced into sufficiently small pieces to be swallowed whole if possible; large chunks are likely to be dropped and ignored. Grapes and cherries can be fed whole, and cherry stones will be regurgitated. Live food such as mealworms and locusts should be given regularly, along with 'pinkie' mice, which are available from herpetological suppliers. These and other toucans must never be kept in the company of smaller birds, because they are liable to kill and eat them.

6 Chestnut-billed Emerald Toucanet

Aulacorhynchus haematopygus

Origin: *Colombia, Ecuador and Venezuela*

Cock: 12in (30cm) Entirely green, except for a crimson rump. A golden sheen on the nape may be apparent. Underparts more apple-green and tend to become more bluish over successive moults. Wings a more dullish brownish-green. Tail bluish-green with chestnut tips to the central feathers. Naked orbital skin dark reddish-purple. Iris dark hazel; beak black, long, rather straight and tapering to a slightly hooked tip, with chestnut coloration running down the centre of each mandible. Broad white band at the base; legs and feet bluish-grey.

Hen: Very similar in appearance, but the beak tends to be shorter and broader when viewed from the side.

This species comes from a relatively high altitude in the Andes and is fairly hardy when acclimatised. However, it still needs some protection in the winter as it is subject to frost-bite. These toucanets are less pugnacious than the larger toucans, and a pair will usually live together in relative harmony. Even so, they should not be associated with species smaller than themselves because they will prey on small birds.

Chestnut-billed Emerald Toucanets require the same type of diet as recommended for the preceding species, although it should be of a rather smaller grade. Bathing facilities should also be provided, or these birds must be sprayed, especially when they are kept indoors. They are quite quiet, having a fairly persistent honking call, which is most likely to be heard if they are disturbed. A deep nesting box, preferably a hollow log, will be required for breeding purposes.

Other forms of Emerald Toucanet are also likely to be encountered occasionally in aviculture, and are distinguishable by their predominantly green coloration. All require similar care. The most widely distributed species is the Emerald Toucanet itself (*Aulacorhynchus prasinus*), which is found in the wild from Mexico as far south as Peru.

255 **Spot-billed Toucanet** *Selenidera maculirostris*

Origin: *Brazil*

Cock: 11in (28cm) Head, nape, throat and breast are glossy black, with a tuft of orange and yellow feathers on the cheeks and ear coverts. A half-collar of orange is present at the base of the hind neck. Remainder of upperparts glossy dark bottle-green, with the tail being tipped with chestnut. Abdomen greenish-brown; flanks golden-brown. Undertail coverts scarlet. Orbital skin bright greenish-blue. Iris orange; beak greenish-grey with black markings on both upper and lower mandibles, which shade into dull yellow at the tips; legs and feet bluish-grey.

Hen: Black areas of the cock are replaced by dark, warm brown feathering, with the tufts on the ear coverts being greenish-yellow. Collar at the back of the neck is dull, less conspicuous and sometimes entirely absent.

The 11 species of *Selenidera* toucanet are the smallest members of the toucan family, and they can usually be sexed without too much difficulty by the differences in the plumage between cock and hen. While the Spot-billed Toucanet itself is now quite scarce in collections, those occurring further north, notably the Guianan Toucanet (*Selenidera culik*) have been seen more often in recent years.

Both this group of toucanets and the various aracaris, which are slightly larger in size, require similar care to that described for the previous species. The *Selenidera* toucanets are less hardy, however, and they require additional heat in the winter, even when they are acclimatised.

The Spot-billed was first exhibited at Berlin Zoo in 1874, with the species arriving at London Zoo five years later. In Britain a chick hatched for the first time in 1913, and this appears to be the earliest recorded breeding of any toucan, although sadly in this case, the young toucanet failed to survive. Plenty of live food appears to be essential for rearing purposes.

Northern Mockingbird *Mimus polyglottus*

Origin: *USA, the Caribbean and Mexico*

Cock: 10in (25cm) Grey-brown on the upperparts, with these feathers having darker centres. Eyebrow streaks pale greyish-white, lores dusky. Wings very dark *brown with two white bars. Tail blackish with outer feathers white. Iris dark brown; beak black; legs and feet black.*

Hen: *Similar in appearance, but markings may be less prominent.*

Mockingbirds are widely distributed across the Americas, and although they are not colourful, their song is attractive. These active birds require plenty of space. When first imported, they require careful acclimatisation but once accustomed to an artificial diet and used to living outdoors, mockingbirds will prove hardy and can even winter in an aviary without artificial heating, although they should be encouraged to roost in the shelter.

Their diet should consist of a mixture of diced fruit and berries, as well as soaked mynah pellets and softbill food. Live food should also be offered regularly, especially during the rearing period when mockingbirds become largely insectivorous.

Pairs may well nest successfully in a planted aviary, but they can prove to be rather erratic when breeding. A careful watch should be kept on a pair at this stage, since the hen is often fiercely pursued by the cock. If she is allowed no rest, it may be necessary to catch the male and trim the flight feathers on one wing to slow him down. Alternatively, the pair may have to be separated, with the cock being reintroduced to the hen at a later stage.

Once the eggs have been laid, the incubation period usually proceeds without problems, but the cock must be watched for the first few days after the chicks have hatched, to ensure that he does not kill them. Sprinkling live food on the floor of the quarters should encourage him to hunt there, leaving the young unmolested. Once fledged, the young mockingbirds must be moved to separate quarters as soon as they are independent.

Mountain Bluebird *Sialia currucoides*

Origin: *west Canada and the USA, migrating south to the southwest USA and west Mexico*

Cock: *6in (15cm) Entirely light sky-blue, metallic on the upperparts, becoming paler on the throat and abdomen. Flight and tail feathers have an almost cobalt sheen. Undertail coverts white. Iris very dark brown; beak blackish; legs and feet blackish.*

Hen: *Upperparts dull brown, with only a wash of blue. Flight and tail feathers dull, deep blue. Underparts pale ash-brown. Beak and legs brownish-black.*

Immature birds of this species resemble the adult hen, but the breast is spotted with pearl-white feathering. There are actually two other species of American Bluebird. The cock Western Bluebird (*Sialia mexicana*) has a dark chestnut-brown marking across the shoulders and back. The remainder of the upperparts including the facial area, throat and tail are deep purplish-blue. The breast and flanks are rich chestnut, with the abdomen being dull blue and the undertail coverts white. The beak and legs are black. The Eastern Bluebird (*Sialia sialis*) differs in that the whole of the upperparts, including the face, are deep sky blue, while the underparts are chestnut-red.

The hens of all three species are similar in appearance to each other, but they may be distinguished by the shade of blue on the wings and tail, which corresponds to that of the cocks.

These bluebirds are comparatively hardy, although they are naturally migratory within North America, moving south for the winter months, and so they should be provided with adequate protection at this time of year. Unfortunately, they are quarrelsome by nature, and pairs are best kept in an aviary on their own.

Outside the breeding period it may be necessary to separate the sexes. A pair that have lived contentedly together during the summer may suddenly start to bicker when their nesting activities are over, and they may even fight viciously, with fatal results. The Mountain Bluebirds appear to be the most aggressive of all three species, and they need to be watched carefully throughout the year.

They can be maintained on a fine-grade insectivorous mixture combined with some live food. Fresh diced fruit should also be offered each day. In the wild, bluebirds eat berries quite readily. These birds will thrive in an outdoor aviary, and they will usually breed without too much difficulty, using any type of nestbox of suitable size that is concealed in a secluded position. They will build a cup-shaped nest of grasses and moss, lining it with finer, softer grass.

The eggs, which are pale blue and usually four in number, hatch after 14 days. Cock and hen share the task of rearing their offspring, which they feed entirely on live food, of which they require a constant and varied supply. They fledge at about 17 days old and will soon be independent. At this stage the young bluebirds should be removed from the aviary, as the adults are likely to want to nest again soon afterwards and are liable to attack them.

Yellow-headed Marshbird *Agelaius icterocephalus*

Origin: *northern South America*

Cock: 7in (18cm) Entirely glossy black, apart from the head and neck, which are bright yellow. Iris brown; beak black; legs and feet blackish.

Hen: Upperparts black, underparts yellowish, with the head being olive.

The vivid contrast in the cock's coloration is especially apparent in aviary surroundings. The song of these birds is insignificant, however, and includes some rather harsh notes. Little has been recorded about them as aviary occupants, although they are available from time to time. Certainly their care is straightforward. They will feed on a diet composed of seeds, such as plain canary seed, millets and groats, as well as softbill food, a little fruit and plenty of live food, such as mealworms; they will also eat berries. When offered mealworms regularly, they soon become quite tame. This species was first bred in 1955 at the Keston Foreign Bird Farm in England. Unfortunately, it can be difficult to acquire hens, since cocks predominate in the few consignments that are offered.

Red-winged Blackbird (Red-shouldered Marshbird) *Agelaius phoeniceus*

Origin: *Canada south to parts of Central America and the Caribbean*

Cock: 9in (23cm) Black with dull green sheen. Lesser upperwing coverts orange-red and vivid red. Iris dark brown; beak black; legs and feet black.

Hen: Usually smaller in size. Entirely dull brown, with heavy striations and lighter eyebrow stripes.

It can be difficult to obtain pairs of this species, and because hens are rarely available, breeding results tend to be seldom reported. The first success was achieved at London Zoo in 1911, and since then, a number of other pairs have reared young in aviary surroundings. Red-winged Blackbirds can be kept with other large birds, as long as these are unrelated. Because the cock is likely to become exceedingly aggressive during the breeding season, it is best to keep the pair in a separate aviary. The song is rather sharp and chirpy but certainly not disturbing.

As well as insectivorous food, Red-winged Blackbirds require a mixture of smaller cereal seeds, as recommended for the Yellow-headed Marshbird, and a daily supply of fruit and insects. A good selection of nesting material, such as grasses, small twigs and moss, should be provided to encourage breeding.

A pair will build a deep, cup-shaped nest, with the cock remaining close by, and singing loudly while the hen incubates on her own. He may drive her rather fiercely and should be watched closely. Young birds must be removed as soon as they are feeding on their own, and colour-feeding may be necessary to maintain the cock's red coloration. These birds can safely remain in an outside aviary that has a shelter throughout the year.

Yellow-headed Blackbird *Xanthocephalus xanthocephalus*

Origin: *southwest Canada, west USA and Mexico*

Cock: 10in (25cm) Head and neck orange-yellow; lores and remainder of body black. A white spot is evident on the wings. Yellow plumage (more extensive than in the Yellow-headed Marshbird) extends to the breast, mantle and shoulders. Iris brown; beak black; legs and feet black.

Hen: *Slightly smaller, greyish-brown overall with an eyebrow stripe and cheeks being yellowy-white. Side of the breast striped with white, upper breast yellow.*

Although it may be possible to keep these birds successfully with others of a similar size, they should not be mixed with related species or with each other. A lone cock housed in the company of a breeding pair, for example, may be killed as nesting time approaches. Yellow-headed Blackbirds will become very aggressive at this time, and a pair should be given an aviary on their own. The song of the cock is more likely to be audible at this stage, as he sings with creaking and cheeping noises mixed with metallic, fluting notes.

Yellow-headed Blackbirds can be kept outside throughout the year as long as they are provided with adequate shelter and they have been properly acclimatised. During the winter months, however, the yellow plumage on the cock's head is likely to be replaced by brown feathering.

These birds like sand baths and also bathe frequently when it rains. A diet based on softbill food, canary seed and millets, as well as live food and some fruit will suit them well. These birds often spend much of their time on the ground, hunting diligently for food and prodding at upturned turves for worms and other live foods. They will build their nest in a rather slovenly fashion, in a pine tree or nestbox, using grasses, coconut fibres, moss and similar material.

Shiny Cowbird *Molothrus bonariensis*

Origin: *most of South America*

Cock: 7in (18cm) *Glossy purplish-black, with the wings and tail being suffused with greenish-blue. Shades of purplish gloss most prominent on the head, neck and breast. Iris brown; beak black; legs and feet black.*

Hen: *Greyish overall, sometimes of a brown shade, and palest on the underparts. White streaks may also be apparent behind the eyes.*

Occurring over a vast area, there is often a distinctive variation in the size of these birds, with the Colombian race being the largest, while the sub-species from Guyana is smaller than those from elsewhere. Never popular avicultural subjects, possibly because of their coloration, these and other cowbirds are not difficult to maintain, however, and cocks have a not unattractive song. A varied diet, composed of canary seed, millets, softbill food, live food, some greenstuff and fruit, will help to keep them in good condition.

Breeding presents more of a challenge because cowbirds are parasitic when nesting. Hens have no particular host species but will lay their eggs in a range of passerine birds' nests. The Screaming Cowbird (*Molothrus rufoaxillaris*) is tied in its breeding habits to the Bay-winged Cowbird

(*Molothrus badius*) because of their natural range, and the latter species is the only non-parasitic member of the genus, usually building a cup-shaped nest, but sometimes opting for a domed structure. Incubation is believed to last about 12 days.

Military Starling (Red-breasted Blackbird) *Sturnella militaris*

Origin: *north South America to Bolivia; also present in Costa Rica and Panama*

Cock: 10in (25cm) Brown, heavily striated with buff eyebrow stripes and an area of red in front of the eyes. Chest and abdomen red. Iris brown; beak dark horn-colour; legs and feet grey.

Hen: Less red on the breast, and tail feathers barred with brown.

In spite of its name, this is another member of the icterid family, and it is not a starling. This species is not regularly obtainable, but it is easy to keep, attractively coloured and, because of its inquisitive nature, quite easily tamed. It also sings pleasantly, although the voice is not especially powerful.

Military Starlings will often spend much of their time on the ground searching for food. A mixture of seeds, such as canary seed, paddy rice, millets and groats, should be offered to them, along with softbill food, diced fruit, greenstuff and assorted insects. Colour-feeding is necessary to retain the depth of red coloration in the plumage.

They must be kept separately or with other large birds in spacious surroundings as they are inclined to be aggressive. Their sharp beaks may easily cause serious injury to smaller birds less able to defend themselves. Military Starlings often like to sleep on the floor of their quarters. This need not be a cause for concern, and in a planted aviary they may choose to hide beneath tussocks of grass.

In the winter, these icterids need to be brought indoors, and a flight connected to a birdroom is ideal. They can then be allowed into the flight on sunny days and kept inside when the weather is bad. Breeding results have not yet been recorded, certainly in Britain.

Common Hangnest (Troupial, Brazilian Hangnest, Buglebird)
Icterus icterus

Origin: *north South America*

Cock: 9in (23cm) Head, throat, nape and tail feathers are black. Wing coverts orange and black with white bar on the flights. Underneath the breast is orange merging into yellow. Nape feathers long and rather loose. Naked blue area of orbital skin. Iris yellow; beak blackish, becoming silvery towards the base of the lower bill; legs and feet greyish.

Hen: Similar in appearance.

The distinctive colour of the iris enables this species to be distinguished easily from other orioles. There is some variation in the appearance of their plumage however, with the amount of black feathering reduced in some races. This is not a sexual distinction. Common Hangnests are highly active and inquisitive by nature, but they will also prove aggressive. A diet as suggested for the Military Starling suits them well. The alternative name Buglebird is derived from their calls, which are quite pleasant and may also sometimes resemble the notes of a flute.

Although they are easy to cater for, there appears to be no breeding record for this species. Pairs should be housed on their own in a planted flight, and provided with twigs and grasses, which may help to persuade them to construct a nest. Insects would doubtless become more significant in the diet if chicks were hatched successfully. Some winter protection should be provided in due course, although these hangnests are reasonably hardy once they are acclimatised.

259 Baltimore Hangnest (Baltimore Oriole) *Icterus galbula*

Origin: *from Canada through Central America to Colombia*

Cock: 7in (18cm) *Orange-yellow in colour; black head, throat and back. Tail and wings black, with white markings evident on the wings. Iris greyish; beak black; legs and feet black.*

Hen: Brownish above, being greyest on the back. Wings show two rather than one white wing bar; underparts a paler shade of yellowish-orange.

All hangnests are a typical combination of yellow, black and white in colour, so it is not always easy to identify the different species correctly; reference to a field guide should resolve any confusion. The Baltimore Hangnest is one of the more commonly seen members of the group, and it will build beautiful nests in aviary surroundings. Occasional breeding successes have also occurred in these long, hanging nests, which are typically located off branches or even directly suspended from the roof of the aviary.

It may be possible to accommodate more than one pair in a spacious aviary, and this may encourage breeding activity since they are social birds by nature. Care must be taken under these circumstances to ensure that fighting does not occur, because their bickering can lead to more serious outbreaks of aggression.

A diet as recommended for other icterids suits them well. Their song is varied and pleasant. Active by nature, Baltimore Hangnests should be housed either in flights or aviaries, with the perches arranged so that they can jump easily from branch to branch. These birds are seldom seen on the ground, but they are fond of bathing, especially in showers of rain.

INDEX OF COMMON NAMES

INDEX OF LATIN NAMES